MICHAEL COLLINS

AND THE ANGLO-IRISH WAR

RELATED POTOMAC TITLES

Flawed Patriot: The Rise and Fall of CIA Legend Bill Harvey
by Bayard Stockton

*Ireland's Most Wanted™: The Top 10 Book of Celtic Pride,
Fantastic Folklore, and Oddities of the Emerald Isle*
by Brian M. Thomsen

BRITAIN'S
COUNTERINSURGENCY
FAILURE

MICHAEL COLLINS
AND THE ANGLO-IRISH WAR

J. B. E. HITTLE

Potomac Books
Washington, D.C.

Library of Congress Cataloging-in-Publication Data
Hittle, J. B. E.
  Michael Collins and the Anglo-Irish War : Britain's counterinsurgency failure / J.B.E. Hittle. — 1st ed.
      p. cm.
  Includes bibliographical references and index.
  ISBN 978-1-59797-535-3 (hardcover)
  ISBN 978-1-61234-128-6 (electronic edition)
  1. Collins, Michael, 1890–1922—Military leadership. 2. Revolutionaries—Ireland—Biography. 3. Ireland—History—War of Independence, 1919–1921. 4. Irish Republican Army—History. 5. Insurgency—Ireland—History—20th century. 6. Great Britain. Army—History—20th century. 7. Counterinsurgency—Ireland—History—20th century. I. Title.
  DA965.C6H58 2011
  941.5082'1—dc23

                                                    2011019988

Potomac Books
22841 Quicksilver Drive
Dulles, Virginia 20166

First Edition

10 9 8 7 6 5 4 3 2 1

To my parents

CONTENTS

FOREWORD

In 2005, when I was serving as head of U.S. counterintelligence, I traveled to London for my first meeting with the director of the British Secret Service (MI5). She received me at her formal office, a well-appointed room with one white orchid on her desk, that provided the perfect backdrop for intimate conversations. There was much to talk about. The U.S. Department of Homeland Security was barely two years old, and already Congress was deliberating yet another major governmental reorganization: the creation of a new director of national intelligence. What would all of this mean for American intelligence and counterintelligence?

As we were saying our good-byes, she handed me the following passage:

> We trained hard but it seemed that every time we were beginning
> to form up in teams we would be reorganised. I was to learn later
> in life that we tend to meet any new situation by reorganising, and
> a wonderful method it can be for creating the illusion of progress
> while producing confusion, inefficiency and demoralisation.[1]

Her Service had come by those lessons the hard way.

"The Troubles" marked a pivotal point in the history of MI5 and Special Branch, and a time when Britain paid the price for its flirtation with an umbrella homeland security office. In the United States, we are still reaching for better answers to protect against threats to our homeland and to provide the intelligence insights essential to the nation's security and the advancement of freedom, prosperity, and peace. Well-intentioned proponents of reforming U.S. domestic intelligence along the lines of "the British model," which owes so much to the distinctive experiences of the Anglo-Irish War, would do well first to understand what in fact that means.

Even today, nine years after its creation, the U.S. Department of Homeland Security and its intelligence-related responsibilities remain something presumed ("of course the Homeland Security Department has an intelligence mission!") rather than defined, i.e., what is the department supposed to do by way of collecting, analyzing, and disseminating domestic intelligence and threat information? Ask the congressional oversight committees, the director of national intelligence, the secretary of the Homeland Department, CIA, and the FBI, and you are likely to get as many different answers as there are voices to be heard.

Indeed, the history of Great Britain's security services in the post–World War I years and contemporary American experience in the twenty-first century share at least one central lesson in common: new organizations are no substitute for clarity of thought on what needs to be done and how to do it. Read through the current organizational documents and directives of the director of national intelligence, and you will unearth a labyrinth of reporting responsibilities and overlapping jurisdictions that leave even the most careful student wondering, "Who's on first?" On that point, one might cite yet another insightful organizational theorist who cautioned, "If you don't know where you're going, you're likely to wind up somewhere else."[2]

As J. B. E. Hittle makes abundantly clear, Michael Collins never had that problem. Not only did he know where he was going, but that knowledge was the key to his charismatic leadership as well as his accomplishments as an intelligence strategist. What happened next is an engrossing case study of an intelligence/counterintelligence war.

Counterintelligence is a contingent discipline, meaning that in order to understand and evaluate counterintelligence activities, one must start with an understanding and evaluation of the intelligence activities that are meant to be countered. In other words, one needs to understand British intelligence and security in order to understand the Irish counterintelligence successes, and vice versa. Hittle brings to that task the critical judgment of a professional assessing the tradecraft, strategy, and tactics of fellow professionals.

Of course, as the author writes, a complete picture of the secret service's activities against Collins and the Irish Republican Army (IRA) may never be fully revealed. But for the student of the intelligence disciplines, this book is an excellent place to start.

An intelligence service suffering from confusion, inefficiency, and demoralization is a ripe target for the adversary to penetrate, defeat, and exploit. That is why a strategically coherent counterintelligence capability is never more important than in times of turmoil and change. We see this in the story of Ireland that follows, and yes, we see this dynamic at work in the United States today.

Michelle Van Cleave
Washington, D.C.

PREFACE

This book presents an analysis of Britain's intelligence and counterinsurgency efforts in Ireland from 1919 to 1921, the period known as the Anglo-Irish War. It is not a history of the life and times of Michael Collins per se, nor is it a comprehensive history of the Anglo-Irish War. Virtually every aspect of the conflict and of Collins's life has been studied, dissected, debated, and scrutinized by historians, journalists, novelists, playwrights, poets, and filmmakers over the past nine decades. Rather, this book examines the Anglo-Irish War as a case study of intelligence management under conditions of low-intensity conflict.

The study tracks the key events of Michael Collins's career and the Anglo-Irish War, a major national security crisis for Britain from 1918 to 1922. It examines Britain's national-level and colonial intelligence systems as instruments of colonial security policy prior to the conflict, and reviews key weaknesses, vulnerabilities, and intelligence management errors within those systems that resulted in Ireland becoming a major intelligence failure. Further, the book reviews the ineffective system of parallel and competing civilian and military intelligence management at both the strategic and theater levels and explores how British security officials struggled to create an ad hoc intelligence collection system to meet conditions of guerrilla warfare. Finally, it attempts to contrast these efforts with the intelligence performance of the Irish Republican Army.

This analysis relies primarily upon contemporary memoirs and standard histories of the period, so a word of caution about the historiography of the Anglo-Irish War is necessary. Until fairly recently, a great deal of this history has been presented from a decidedly pro-Irish point of view. Consequently, Collins's achievements as a revolutionary soldier, intelligence chief, statesman, and leader of men have assumed a larger-than-life quality. Beginning with Frank O'Connor's 1937 biography, *The Big Fellow,* the historical literature of the period 1916–1923, known as "the Troubles," is rich with colorful portrayals of Collins's daring exploits. They describe a daredevil genius outsmarting Dublin Castle, the British Secret Service, and Lloyd George himself at every turn—all with a spring in his step, a smile on his face, a song in his heart, and a wisecrack on his lips.

Such romanticized nationalism stems in part from the fact that the Anglo-Irish War—often called the Irish War of Independence—did not achieve independence, but rather Dominion status for an "Irish Free State" that left the country partitioned and firmly under Crown authority. This fell far short of the objective that thousands of IRA veterans had risked their lives for during the previous three years, and it led to Ireland's tragic civil war from 1922 to 1923. In the wake of the civil war, and for many years thereafter, a substantial portion of the Irish people experienced profound disillusionment, alienation, and uncertainty. Unsure of their fate and that of their nation, they could only hope for a brighter and happier future where the country might be united and free from the political and economic chains that still bound them to the English Crown.

Thus the civil war affected the historiography of the rebellion. The split between pro-Treaty and anti-Treaty IRA factions led not only to Collins's own death but to entire families being pitted against each other. This desperate internal struggle was more violent and cost more lives than the struggle with Britain had. And it resulted in decades of lingering feuds, ostracism, suspicion, gossip, intimidation, and revenge. The bitterness was sustained by sporadic but ineffectual IRA violence campaigns in Britain and its Northern Ireland colony through the 1930s, 1940s, and 1950s, and by ongoing sectarian violence in the north, where the rule of the gunman continued to be a fact of life for eighty years. Whether any author was ever subjected to physical violence by Irish extremists is doubtful. Yet the vitriolic atmosphere has been a strong incentive to discourage Irishmen from writing history that may reflect poorly on national heroes, or from advancing an alternative analysis that may run cross-wise to the opinions of dangerous people with different agendas.

Every culture seeks its heroes, and Ireland has a long tradition of he-roes. The Irish especially sought them in the 1920s, 1930s, and 1940s so that future generations would keep national aspirations alive. But in the process of honoring a genuine hero, some of Collins's biographers created a myth.

Culture and religion also affected the way in which the Irish Revolu-tion has been portrayed. The pervasive influence of the Roman Catholic Church, and a correspondingly keen desire to portray Irish morals, val-ues, and ideals as somehow fundamentally more decent and noble than English morals, values, and ideals, discouraged realism for many years. The ugly realities of war, particularly a brutal civil war, and the sheer ter-ror that is the result of assassination on a mass scale, are very hard indeed to reconcile with such morals, values, and ideals.

In fairness to the early Collins biographers, the fact that the British burned or sealed most of the intelligence files when they evacuated Dub-lin Castle in 1922 compelled early writers to rely primarily upon the oral histories and memoirs on the Irish side. This made it very difficult to get at a clear and objective understanding of events. While significant infor-mation has been released to the British Public Records Office in the past ten years, virtually everything that is known today about the secret Irish Republican Brotherhood (IRB) and the IRA intelligence service is from personal memoirs—some reliable, some exaggerated, and others quite unreliable.

Beginning in the 1990s, the historiographic pendulum began to swing in the opposite direction. At the forefront of this movement was the late Canadian historian Peter Hart, whose three important works—*The IRA and Its Enemies* (1998); *The IRA at War, 1916–1923* (2003); and *Mick: The Real Michael Collins* (2006)—have challenged conventional thinking about the years 1916–1923. Hart advocated the "re-conceptualization of Irish revolutionary history," and called for "interrogation of standard narra-tives" on the subject. Using demographics and statistics Hart challenged some long-held beliefs about the IRA and the Republican movement, and painted a much darker image of the Anglo-Irish War. This was a welcome move toward more objective analysis and was not only groundbreaking but a breath of fresh air.

Predictably, Hart quickly came under fire, first from the romantic na-tionalists and later from some fellow academics. Ultra-nationalists found it hard to accept the argument that Collins's ascent to leadership may be attributed as much to pure political ambition, relentless maneuvering, and leadership vacuums as it was to any keen, calculating genius or overarching revolutionary strategy. Likewise, they have great discomfort with the fact that much of the IRA's war strategy was driven by dangerous local warlords with little regard for the wishes of either Collins, IRA headquarters, or the Dail Eireann (Assembly of Ireland)—a fact recognized by other historians before Hart. Nor do traditionalists wish to read that Collins himself was ineffectual in opposing these gunmen, so he rubberstamped and encouraged their independent actions in order to preserve unity in the movement and keep it focused on the broader political-military objective. Yet another myth about the IRA flew out the window when Hart demonstrated with statistical evidence that the largest number of the IRA rank and file were urban dwellers: shop attendants, factory workers, service employees, and students, not the more romantic image of noble devil-may-care farm lads and sheepherders just out to have a go at the Brits.

Hart quickly became a polarizing figure in the Irish historical community, and the more he was challenged by old-school traditionalists, the more pointed the exchanges became. So bitter had the dialogue become by 2008 that traditionalists wrote Hart off as a revisionist, while Hart dismissed the traditionalists as "amateurs" and "apologists." It seemed as if romantic nationalism had run head-on into academic hubris.

And then the arguing took an even more serious turn when fellow academics joined in questioning some of Hart's more controversial assertions. These include Hart's contentions that the IRA committed atrocities in carrying out hundreds of indiscriminant killings of innocent civilians and that the IRA in Cork pursued a sectarian murder policy against Protestant loyalists. Focusing not on Hart's statistical findings but rather on some of his other evidence, they raised serious questions about Hart's historical method. After closely scrutinizing his sources, which included interviews with anonymous IRA veterans and alleged classified reports from anonymous sources, these professionals assert that many of Hart's sweeping conclusions about Collins and the IRA's conduct of the war are based on thin or nonexistent evidence.[1]

This bitter dialogue has subjected students of the Troubles to a second "Irish Civil War" for the past few years. Brian P. Murphy and Niall Meehan perhaps put it best in 2008 when they labeled the current state of Irish historiography as "Troubled History."[2]

Underlying this debate is the ubiquitous struggle between empiricism and relativism that plagues so much of history today. At one extreme are scholars relying upon documentary evidence and statistics; at the other end are those of limited scholarship whose comfort zone lies exclusively in oral tradition. Illustrations include some contemporary biographies of IRA leaders that not only dismiss the empirical method but openly mock academics in general, declaring rather unwisely that personal memoirs and "legends" present a more reliable picture of events than documentary evidence. Such relativists appear to confuse hearsay with fact and myth with legend to such an extent that these biographies read more like nominations for canonization than solid history. Without doubt, Daniel Breen and Sean Treacy were legendary IRA fighters. Neither was a saint.

Regarding the record of British intelligence in Ireland, there has been much new scholarship in the past few years. Since much of the British records remain sealed, Christopher Andrew's long-awaited *The Defence of the Realm* (2009)—based on the author's exclusive seven-year-long access to MI5's historical files—was anxiously anticipated. Andrew offers an interesting account of collaboration between the Admiralty's Naval Intelligence Division (NID), MI5, and Special Branch to uncover the plans for the 1916 Easter Rebellion on the eve of the Rising. Likewise, his discussion of the power struggle between Special Branch and MI5 sheds new light on the bureaucratic rivalry that so weakened the capabilities of British clandestine intelligence collection at that critical period. He also provides a most colorful narrative of Special Branch's flamboyant, ambitious, and self-serving Basil Thomson, who was one of the principal culprits in the intelligence failure that was Ireland. And the British intelligence response in Ireland between 1919 and 1921 *was* an embarrassing failure, even though the terms of the Anglo-Irish Peace Treaty are generally regarded as a strategic political success for London.

Andrew makes clear that Special Branch had been, by tradition, the lead agency in Ireland and notes that MI5 had no clearly defined role during the Anglo-Irish War. Paul McMahon, one of Andrew's protégés, fills in the picture in his comprehensive *British Spies & Irish Rebels* (2008). Even without McMahon's important contribution, however, it is easy to discern from alternative sources that MI5—sidelined in 1919 after an ill-advised national intelligence reshuffle—had very limited resources to commit to Ireland. Its principal contribution lay in advice, training, and administrative support to army case officers from the Department of Military Intelligence (DMI), upon whose shoulders much of the burden of intelligence core collection and covert action in Ireland fell. This support to army intelligence, and the service of some MI5 alumni who went to Ireland for Special Branch, were the chief contributions of the Imperial Security Service in the war against Michael Collins.

Compounding the distractions of historiographical chaos is the fact that, while most histories recognize that the Anglo-Irish War was largely an intelligence war, few, if indeed any, of the authors has had any professional intelligence experience. The history may be solid, but critical analysis of the intelligence modus operandi is simply missing. The story of Collins's intelligence struggle with the British Secret Service is usually presented in an analytical vacuum, bereft of any fundamental understanding of the craft of intelligence, much less specific analytical or operational tradecraft.

I believe this is, to a great extent, the result of a fundamental culture gap between academics, journalists, and intelligence professionals, all of whom see the world through different lenses. It is easy for academics and journalists to criticize those engaged in the profession of espionage, particularly when the spies are prohibited under oath from discussing or defending their methods, goals, or actions. Having had a good taste of both academia and the world of clandestine intelligence operations, I can attest to the fact that the motives, dynamics, challenges, and outlooks of these professions are light-years apart.

Moreover, in the restricted world of national security, where successes are never acknowledged yet failures are often gleefully leaked and trumpeted to advance a political cause, or to sell books and newspapers, the public (including academia and the media) invariably receives a very limited, biased, and lopsided view of "intelligence." And in the not infrequent cases where academic critiques or media accounts of alleged intelligence failures are subsequently shown to be in error, rarely does an acknowledgment of error by the offending authors appear. Nor do we often see any effort by critics to publish a correction. That is reason enough to be skeptical about the objectivity of contemporary histories of the Anglo-Irish War, many of which were authored by journalists and university professors.

In addition, while almost all of the new empirical history provides some important fresh information about Britain's *tactical* theater intelligence failures, it largely ignores the *strategic* failure of the British national intelligence community between 1919 and 1921. These histories ignore the political and institutional handicaps confronting British intelligence officers of the period. Thus, there has been no baseline upon which to measure the success of IRA intelligence. The weakness of this methodology has resulted in analysis of an intelligence war that remains essentially invalid from a national security point of view. That Collins developed a superior intelligence apparatus that outperformed the British services is undeniable, and this *is* apparent in the historical writings of the period in spite of the shortcomings in much of that literature. That the British national intelligence community was severely handicapped by bureaucratic infighting, organizational problems, competing and overlapping responsibilities, political interference, budget cuts, cover constraints, and external events beyond its control, *is not* so apparent.

When viewed within that overall strategic national context, therefore, Collins's achievements appear more realistically as tactical victories. This perspective suggests that Collins was *not* ten feet tall, that the IRA *was* vulnerable to a series of clever British double-agent and surveillance operations, and that, by the time of the July 1921 truce, Collins's intelligence service held only marginal advantage over the British service. It also strongly suggests that had the truce not been called when it was, the British would likely have succeeded in locating Collins within a few months, if not weeks. Whether that would have ended the conflict more to Britain's advantage is a matter of debate, but all agree that Collins, as director of intelligence, director of organization, and minister of finance, was the driving force in sustaining the guerrilla campaign, and his elimination may very well have been the coup de grâce ending the rebellion. Finally, the outcome of treaty talks in London only underscores the position that, while Britain lost the tactical intelligence war, it scored a strategic intelligence success in assessing Collins and the Dail leadership, and in maneuvering the Irish delegation to a Home Rule–type solution that Britain had been prepared to grant in 1914 without firing a shot. It was not until the Second World War, when Eamon de Valera declared the Dominion of

Ireland neutral, that the British finally began to acknowledge full independence for southern Ireland.

Given these challenges, the way ahead seems to lie in examining the evolution of the modern British intelligence community and using that as the baseline upon which to gauge events in Ireland during the period. Perhaps an accurate analysis of Britain's counterinsurgency performance can best be discerned through analysis of known events measured within the context of professional intelligence standards. When examined in that context, hopefully the polarizing debates can be avoided. But such a methodology requires a thorough grasp of intelligence and counterintelligence modus operandi and tradecraft.

ACKNOWLEDGMENTS

The author acknowledges several people who assisted in the production of this book. Foremost among them is London publisher Bill Dee, a keen student and experienced analyst of Collins and the Anglo-Irish War. Bill generously reviewed most of the text, freely shared his valuable insight into the career of David Neligan, and offered numerous helpful suggestions. Thanks also to Elizabeth Demers, senior editor at Potomac, for her patient guidance of this project, and Kathryn Owens, senior production editor at Potomac, for her expert and professional supervision of the text-editing process. My thanks also to Glenn Dunne of the National Library of Ireland and to Commandant Victor Laing and Hugh Beckett of the Irish Military Archive for their invaluable assistance. Much credit is also due to my wife, Barbara, who kept home and hearth together during my thirty years on the night watch, and who was cheerful and supportive during the writing of this book.

INTRODUCTION

The Irishman, without any insult being intended, somewhat resembles a dog, and understands firm treatment, but, like the dog, he cannot understand being cajoled with a piece of sugar in one hand, whilst he receives a beating from a stick in the other.

—Ormonde Winter, Chief of British Intelligence in Ireland, 1920–1921

On the morning of November 21, 1920, fourteen British officers were dragged from their beds in flats and hotel rooms across central Dublin and summarily shot by operatives of the Irish Republican Army. That same morning a British informer was also executed. At least ten of the executed or seriously wounded men were intelligence officers; another eight or so suspected British spies were on the IRA's assassination list that morning but managed to evade attackers. In the days that followed, Whitehall ordered the hasty withdrawal of many of their clandestine operatives from Ireland for fear they too would be hunted down and killed.

In retaliation, that same Sunday afternoon, British mercenary police—the Auxiliaries—burst into a Gaelic football match in Dublin and opened fire on the crowd, killing sixteen unarmed civilians and wounding scores more. These events, known ever after in Irish history as "Bloody Sunday," not only marked a new level of brutality in the struggle but also the greatest loss of intelligence officers in the history of the British Secret Service.

Many consider Bloody Sunday a turning point in the Anglo-Irish War, marking the high point of violence in an intelligence war that formed the nexus of a wider insurgency/counterinsurgency struggle. How could the world's most experienced secret service suffer such an embarrassing failure?

The answer lies in the political miscalculations of the British government and resulting disarray of Whitehall's intelligence efforts, as well as institutional handicaps, internal turf wars, and cover disadvantages. It also lies in the genius of a thirty-one-year-old ex–bank clerk named Michael Collins.

An organizational genius with a natural gift for espionage and a revolutionary visionary, Collins established an intelligence department within the IRA designed from the beginning to "put out the eyes" of the British in Ireland. That he succeeded so effectively is quite remarkable, considering the size and determination of the British forces arrayed against him. Moreover, Collins deserves the title of revolutionary visionary if only because he alone among the senior-most rebel leadership possessed the will to be ruthless.

This book analyzes the Anglo-Irish War based on the standard historiography of the period, measuring the key events of that period using professional intelligence standards. It examines the events leading up to Bloody Sunday and the aftermath of that episode. It further examines the impact of the Irish Republican Brotherhood on early-twentieth-century Irish nationalism and the importance of that secret society to Irish intelligence successes in the final struggle against the British. It traces the development of Michael Collins from early ardent separatist to IRB chief to Director of IRA Intelligence, Director of IRA Organization, and Minister of Finance in the revolutionary cabinet. It explores the final months of the Anglo-Irish intelligence struggle, the events surrounding the truce and the outbreak of the subsequent Irish Civil War. Finally, it provides an assessment of the disastrous British security policy toward Ireland, its failure to contain the Irish nationalist movement under the direction of a national Director of Home Intelligence, and a discussion of lessons learned.

This study aims to measure the Anglo-Irish war from the perspective of professional intelligence standards. It does not seek to downplay the remarkable achievements of Michael Collins and his intelligence staff but rather attempts to place those activities into a broader strategic context by exploring in greater depth the British intelligence forces arrayed against Collins, their strengths, weaknesses, successes, handicaps, and vulnerabilities. Thus, while this is the story of the remarkable revolutionary Michael Collins, in a broader sense it is really a case study of Britain's failed experiment in prosecuting a counterinsurgency under the direction of a national intelligence director.

1

ENGLAND'S TROUBLED COLONY

It is a proverb of old date, that the pride of France, the treason of England and the war of Ireland shall never have end. Which proverb, touching the war of Ireland, is like always to continue, without God sets it in men's breasts to find some new remedy that never was found before.

—*English civil servant, sixteenth century*

Ireland at the dawn of the twentieth century was approaching one hundred years of official political affiliation with Great Britain under terms of the Act of Union of 1801. That act created the United Kingdom of Great Britain and Ireland; established a unified parliamentary system; cemented political, economic, and religious ties between the two countries; and thereby ensured complete English legal, political, economic, and religious domination of Ireland.

Prior to the Act of Union, Ireland had been governed for five hundred years by an independent Irish Parliament that nonetheless met at the command of an English king. It comprised mostly members of the old Anglo-Irish aristocracy—the landed gentry and wealthy manufacturers. Given its makeup, the Irish Parliament evolved over time into a virtual mirror image of the English Parliament, taking care to protect the interests of the predominantly Protestant Anglo-Irish landlords at the expense of the overwhelmingly Catholic native Irish. This arrangement of lords and peasants extended well beyond the demise of feudalism elsewhere in Western Europe. Nevertheless, for all of it deficiencies, the Irish Parliament had been a symbolic representation of Irish independence in the community of nations for five centuries.[1]

OF NORSEMEN AND NORMANS

Before the Irish Parliament, Norman kings had dominated Ireland for nearly two centuries; prior to that, Norse Vikings had twice invaded the island between A.D. 800 and 970. The Norman Conquest, which occurred between 1166 and 1171, is one of the great ironies of history, for it was brought on by the rivalry of two independent Irish kings, Diarmait MacMurrough and Rory O'Connor. When O'Connor deposed MacMurrough and became high king of Ireland, MacMurrough sought relief from Henry II, the Norman king of England. In a further irony, the English pope, Adrian IV, issued a Papal Bull encouraging Henry to place Ireland under his protection and to redress ecclesiastical corruption there. Henry dispatched one of his knights, Richard fitzGilbert de Clare, the Earl of Pembroke—commonly known as Strongbow—to the island with a limited charter to establish peace between the Irish warlords. When Strongbow subsequently declared himself King of Ireland, however, Henry was so incensed that he launched a full-scale invasion of the island. When word reached Strongbow that Henry was en route, he wisely intercepted the King, apologized for his transgression, and fell back in line. Henry and his Anglo-French allies then proceeded to place the larger towns and trading centers under their control, leaving much of the outlying rural districts in the control of native Irish family dynasties. Ireland may have been conquered by the Normans, but the Irish were far from subdued. Not all of the Irish kings were deposed by the Normans; a number of them courted favor or struck alliances with Henry's royal descendants and thus retained a degree of local autonomy for the next three hundred years.[2]

THE REFORMATION AND CROMWELL

The Reformation of the sixteenth century led to enforced colonization— the Protestant Plantations. The Church of England and its sister institution, the Church of Ireland, became state religions, while the traditional

Catholicism of the majority was suppressed. The native Irish, as well as the barons and lawyers who had descended from the Norman settlers—known as the Old English—stridently resisted the English Church of Henry VIII and Elizabeth I. Inspired by the Counter-Reformation movement on the continent, the Old English sent their sons to French universities rather than to Protestant colleges in England and Ireland.

The repression of the native Irish and Old English Catholics was intensified during the subsequent English Civil War. An insurrection by Ulster Catholic landowners in 1641, which aimed to restore their former baron status and safeguard their lands from further Protestant colonization, soon spread across the country. From 1641 to 1649, some two thousand Protestant colonists were murdered while tens of thousands more were stripped of their possessions and driven from their settlements. While not quite the pogrom portrayed in exaggerated reports to London, it was brutal, and almost every Catholic landowner in Ireland had participated to one degree or another. These events coincided with the outbreak of civil war, which delayed the Crown's response to the insurrection until 1649. In that year, Oliver Cromwell led a large disciplined English army to Ireland to avenge the deaths of the Protestants and impose a Protestant mandate. At this time a series of parliamentary acts, the Penal Laws, were introduced that systematically abolished the legal and human rights of the Catholic majority. Over time, Catholic lawyers were disbarred, the Catholic clergy was banished or murdered, Church lands were confiscated, and the franchise was withdrawn from Catholics. The Irish responded with clandestine organizations that secretly harbored Catholic priests and stood guard against Crown forces while they celebrated Mass. Meanwhile, the Crown expanded colonization by paying off its soldiers and mercenaries with Irish land grants. The eviction of the native Irish from their traditional lands intensified a desire for nationhood and ignited a revolutionary flame that burned in the hearts of Irish nationalists for the next five hundred years.

Succeeding English kings periodically convened the Irish Parliament to take up administrative and legal issues in advancement of their agendas until, inevitably, a regularized dual parliamentary system became established. The concept of unifying the two bodies grew into a formal Unionist movement that increasingly demanded attention at Westminster throughout the latter half of the eighteenth century.[3]

UNION AND DISILLUSION

Compared with previous Crown schemes of governance in Ireland, the Act of Union seemed an enlightened approach. The legislation transferred the Irish Parliament's 132 delegates to Westminster: 32 in the House of Lords appointed for life, and 100 elected members in the House of Commons representing towns, cities, counties, and boroughs. But while Unionism granted the illusion of democratic representation, the majority of the Irish delegates were from the Protestant aristocracy. They were inclined to maintain the status quo at home while working primarily to improve the economic fortunes of the privileged class—landlords, manufacturers, and commercial shopkeepers. Not surprisingly, they focused their legislative efforts on trade bills, customs arrangements, excise taxes, and the like.

Further, the transfer of Ireland's parliamentary delegation to Westminster had the effect of destroying all sense of national cohesion, as the delegates never focused on uniquely Irish issues. Consequently, Ireland had no true national voice in Parliament and for millions of native Irish and Old English Catholic stock, Unionism represented a mere illusion of equality. Freedom of religion remained a lingering grievance since Cromwell's bloody campaign, and, Union notwithstanding, it took three decades before Daniel O'Connell wrestled a Catholic Emancipation bill from Parliament in 1829. Still, Irish subjects enjoyed no freedom of self-determination. British administration remained colonial in nature, marked variously by arrogance, condescension, or indifference toward the native Irish. It was not until 1870 that Isaac Butt proposed an Irish Home Government Association. From this modest beginning, a Home Rule movement—strengthened by an Irish literary and cultural renaissance—took hold, leading to an all-out bid for Irish independence by the turn of the twentieth century. The new intellectual movement that blossomed in this period established a totally new way of viewing the relationship between England and Ireland, but to the average Irishman, the issue remained simply one of hatred for England—pure and simple nationalism.[4]

Meanwhile, a cabinet-appointed lord lieutenant, or viceroy, served as the ceremonial leader of Ireland from his Viceregal Lodge in Dublin's Phoenix Park, while a cabinet-appointed permanent secretary and one or more undersecretaries handled the day-to-day management of the country in colonial fashion from the administrative seat at His Majesty's Royal Castle in Dublin. English customs, currency, and religious practices were the law of the land, while Irish customs, language, music, dance, literature, and athletics were discouraged or suppressed. Teachers were forbidden to teach Irish cultural ideals or native history; only a London-approved curriculum could be taught.

To leading English politicians of the eighteenth and nineteenth centuries, Ireland was an indispensable part of the empire because it formed a natural defensive barrier to the Atlantic approach to England. Beyond that, however, Ireland was an economic jewel in the Royal Crown, and it assumed greater luster with the arrival of the Industrial Revolution and the expansion of the empire. It afforded shipyards and coaling stations that were critical to England's dominant naval and merchant fleets. Ulster textile mills were essential to render native wool and imported American cotton into consumer goods for London shops. The native working class provided a steady supply of cheap labor to run England's factories, build its roads, and fight its wars. Moreover, the island provided convenient bases for England's army and navy. The Crown quartered army regiments throughout the island and the Royal Navy occupied every port.

Despite Ireland's place at Westminster, the Anglo-Irish aristocracy that controlled Ireland's resources ensured that the country was governed in colonial fashion. The permanent secretary administered the island on his own initiative, making Dublin Castle a sleepy backwater for English civil servants. Ireland was a popular destination for middle- and upper-class English tourists—an adventure in a backward little colony occupied by people with strange if quaint customs, and speaking a colorful form of English marked with a distinctive brogue. The reality of Unionism, therefore, was not equality but a complete stranglehold on Ireland's native people, their natural resources, and their means of production.

THE STRUGGLE FOR NATIONAL IDENTITY

Beyond the fact that generations of Irishmen had served with distinction in the British Army and Royal Navy—and the strategic advantage of convenient military and naval bases to help guard English shores—there was another important reason to maintain military garrisons in Ireland, namely, a perennially hostile undercurrent within the native population. Irish tribal kings had contested the invading Norse Vikings in Celtic times and they had resisted the Norman invasion. The native Irish had contested the Protestant Plantation and had stridently resisted the Penal Laws from the time of Cromwell. From the seventeenth century onward, insurgents of one stripe or another—Catholic and Protestant—had rebelled against the Crown in almost each generation. The uprising so brutally suppressed by Cromwell was followed by others in 1798, 1803, 1848, and again in 1867. All were failures, thanks to a combination of poor timing, bad luck, weapons shortages, and poor security.[5]

The conspiracy of the United Irishmen party during the 1790s illustrates how effective Britain's system of informers was. Inspired in part by the French Revolution, Ulsterman Theobald Wolfe Tone was convinced that a united, nonsectarian separatist movement could succeed in overthrowing English rule, and he led a conspiracy of nationalists drawn from all economic classes and religious creeds. With the prospect of war between England and France growing, Tone and his agents met with French officials over three years, resulting in the dispatch of a French fleet with embarked troops to Ireland. Reaching Bantry Bay in 1796, the French were prevented from landing by weather and compelled to abandon the expedition. Meanwhile, Dublin Castle's alert network of spies had infiltrated Tone's conspiracy, and in 1798 it collapsed. It was the first effective employment of British intelligence against Irish rebels in the modern post-Reformation era.[6]

British informers penetrated all levels of Irish society and these spies promptly alerted authorities to every subsequent conspiracy. The British system of spies and informers was so well organized and institutionalized in Ireland that Dublin Castle at one time maintained a retirement home where they could live out their last years in comfort under Crown protection.[7]

Tone's United Irish movement was soon resurrected by university students, and in 1803 Robert Emmett, a young Irish aristocrat, attempted another rebellion. An accidental explosion in one of Emmett's secret bomb factories betrayed the conspiracy, and the whole affair ended with a scuffle in the street.[8] The twenty-five-year-old Emmett was hanged for treason, his corpse drawn and quartered.

The Young Ireland Party that fomented the 1848 uprising was a key development in Irish nationalist history because it represents the birth of modern physical-force separatism. Young Ireland had come to prominence as political allies of Daniel O'Connell in his second great cause—the parliamentary struggle for repeal of the Union. But O'Connell rejected Young Ireland's extremist views and he threw them out of his parliamentary coalition. The most radical of the Young Irelanders—John Blake Dillon, Thomas Smith-O'Brien, James Stephens, Thomas Francis Meagher—kept the movement alive. Cut off from its parliamentary base, Young Ireland morphed into a secret revolutionary organization. Its rebellion was aimed at dissolving the Union and was inspired by revolts across continental Europe in 1848, themselves spurred on by the writings of Karl Marx, who challenged the economic exploitation of the masses and called upon them to revolt. Yet Young Ireland had a more immediate grievance, namely the Crown's mishandling of a devastating famine arising from several successive years of potato crop blight that led to the death and displacement of millions of Irish from 1845 to 1849.

As J. C. Beckett notes, the Great Famine is the watershed event in modern Irish history. Although as early as 1845 the Peel government recognized the potato blight as a looming major catastrophe and made a sincere attempt to meet the crisis, local relief administrators botched the effort. The expenditure of famine relief funds from the Exchequer was delayed by indignant opposition party members who believed in the new economic principle of laissez faire, and who expected the Anglo-Irish gentry to solve the problem themselves. While Westminster dithered, the government busied itself with feckless public works schemes to employ hungry and destitute Irish peasants. Millions of peasants starved to death, and millions more were displaced from their cottages and compelled to emigrate. During this debacle, imported American grain rotted in the holds of ships anchored in English ports awaiting customs clearance as required by England's protectionist grain tariffs, the Corn Laws.[9]

Witnesses to widespread misery and starvation among the Irish peasantry, Young Ireland was moved to action. Their "Rising" in August 1848 was a small affair that ended in a shoot-out with the police. Crown forces rounded up the ringleaders and charged them with high treason. Loath to make martyrs out of them as Wolfe Tone and Robert Emmett had become, the Crown commuted the sentences to deportation for life. The prisoners were transported to Australia but several escaped and found their way to America, where their revolutionary spirit and determination only grew stronger.[10]

THE RISE OF FENIANISM

The scattered survivors of 1848 regrouped to form the Fenian or Irish Republican Brotherhood in New York in 1858. The Fenians plotted to liberate Ireland by force and attempted to foster revolt in Irish-manned British Army regiments in 1866. They launched additional plots the following year, including an abortive rising in Ireland and an ill-advised, somewhat comical "invasion" of English Canada launched from upstate New York.[11]

These treasonous acts, although quickly suppressed by Crown forces (with significant intelligence forewarning), attracted the attention of no less a commentator than Karl Marx. Disillusioned over the failure of revolutions in continental Europe and unable to sell writings that the cherished proletariat could scarcely comprehend, Marx nevertheless took an active interest in Irish events. Commenting on the Fenians from his comfortable armchair in the reading room at the British Museum, he made a prophetic observation:

> Here is what baffles the English: they find the present regime mild compared with England's former oppression of Ireland. So why this most determined and irreconcilable form of opposition now? What I want to show—and what even Englishmen who side with the Irish, who concede them the right to secession, do not see— is that the regime since 1846, though less Barbarian in form, is in effect destructive, leaving no alternative but Ireland's voluntary emancipation by England or life and death struggle.[12]

Fenian revolutionary activities continued with funding and moral support from New York, Boston, and Chicago. A terrorist bombing campaign in English cities in the early 1880s shook the government and posed a serious new challenge for the detectives of the London Metropolitan Police.[13]

THE PROMISE OF HOME RULE

By the late 1870s, the Fenian movement was already overshadowed by political initiatives at Westminster, as the cause of Irish independence proceeded on a parliamentary path for the next thirty years. Under the leadership of the dynamic Charles Stewart Parnell, a new Irish Parliamentary Party (IPP) emerged as a force to be reckoned with at Westminster. Parnell's successor, James Redmond, brought new momentum to the Home

Rule debate, and Irish nationalists succeeded in getting a bill introduced at Westminster by 1912. This sparked a crisis that caught the government of Prime Minister Herbert Asquith off guard. Sir Edward Carson, a fiery conservative MP (and Dublin native), led Ulster's vigorous opposition to Home Rule on political, economic, and religious grounds. Carson's predominantly Protestant followers controlled most of the business and industrial sectors of northern Ireland and sought to remain part of Great Britain, even if that meant they would have to use extralegal measures to achieve their aims.

Carson's inflammatory rhetoric helped him recruit a paramilitary force of 100,000 men in 1911 — the Ulster Volunteers — who vowed to resist Home Rule by force. In response, 70,000 southern Nationalist Volunteers, encouraged by a strong nationalist cultural and literary revival at the turn of the century, organized in Dublin in November 1913, vowing to defend Home Rule by force. When the bill finally passed in May 1914, Carson and his Unionists threatened civil war. Asquith ordered the British Army north from their base at the Curragh Camp to disarm the Ulster Volunteers and restore calm, but the troops mutinied and refused to mobilize. The *London Daily News* condemned the mutineers, noting, "The Country is faced with the gravest issue that has arisen in our time. It is whether we are to be governed by Parliament or the Army."[14]

It was in this atmosphere that Britain entered the First World War in August 1914. The government promptly suspended the Irish Bill for the duration, once again frustrating nationalist aspirations. Thousands of Irishmen — including both Ulster Volunteers and National Volunteers — responded to James Redmond's call to join the British Army, and marched off to France. Of 180,000 National Volunteers at the outbreak of the war, only 11,000 refused to join the British. But these men, now renamed the Irish Volunteers, would form the nucleus of another armed insurrection.[15]

The old Irish separatist saying, "England's trouble is Ireland's opportunity," never seemed more apropos than in 1914. As Britain was preoccupied on the Western Front, the Irish physical-force nationalists envisioned an opportunity to gain independence through armed insurrection, and they began to organize a plan. Fearing that the war with Germany might end before they could strike their blow, the nationalists at last made ready for an armed uprising to take place in 1916.

2

COLONIAL SECURITY POLICY

Just as the Vatican has given its name to the pope's government, and the Sublime Porte to the sultan's, so Dublin Castle has come to signify England's rule of Ireland: always a vile, corrupt government, too brutal in the seventeenth century, too flaccid, too weak and too sentimental in the twentieth.

—*Major Hervey De Montmorency,*
British intelligence officer during the Anglo-Irish War, 1936

Britain based its security policy in Ireland in 1916 on longstanding colonial administrative procedures in effect since the 1801 Act of Union. Whitehall relied on its local colonial administrations and colonial police special branches to keep tabs on revolutionaries and dissidents. In Ireland, this translated into a British administrative seat at Dublin Castle and local Irish police services, namely the Crimes Special Branch of the Royal Irish Constabulary (RIC), and the Special Intelligence Division (G Division) of the Dublin Metropolitan Police (DMP).

Although the armed rebellion of Easter 1916 should have telegraphed a stark warning to London of troubled waters ahead, Crown security policy in Ireland did not change. Britain continued to focus its national intelligence resources primarily on defeating Germany and combating Bolshevism in the immediate postwar period.

This was an intelligence failure in the making. It happened because Prime Minister Lloyd George and the cabinet were preoccupied with other threats, and because they had a false sense of security. After all, history had shown that the colonial security system had always been adequate in dealing with subversives, and nowhere was this truer than Ireland. Irish secret societies had fomented armed rebellions in almost every generation since the sixteenth century, but Britain's local political police had effectively penetrated the insurgent organizations and the British Army had easily squashed their rebellions. Moreover, heavy-handed British magistrates had dealt decisively with the survivors.

The RIC, a uniquely Irish force of paramilitary police, and G Division of the DMP, had traditionally handled all security and intelligence matters in Ireland, and they would be at the forefront of the struggle with the IRA during the early stages of the Anglo-Irish War. London had full confidence in them.[1] Meanwhile, some twenty thousand British occupation troops were garrisoned in Ireland to handle any serious contingencies.

It was a security structure based on a familiar but outdated British model that had been used for hundreds of years. What neither Whitehall nor Dublin Castle envisioned after 1916 was the emergence of a popular local insurgency supported by a first-rate intelligence service. From 1917 through 1921, Michael Collins developed such a service. His espionage and counterintelligence apparatus was designed to blind British intelligence and security forces by attacking them directly, wearing them down, and demoralizing them, thus enabling a separatist political movement to take hold and flourish. The objective of Irish Republicans never was to defeat England militarily; rather, it was to gain British recognition of Irish sovereignty, force a political settlement, and win independence.

To appreciate the magnitude of Britain's intelligence failure in Ireland between 1919 and 1921, it is worthwhile to examine the evolution of Britain's strategic national intelligence community in the years preceding the conflict.

THE BRITISH INTELLIGENCE COMMUNITY

As previously illustrated, British sovereigns had conducted intelligence activities for centuries with good results domestically and in its closest colony, Ireland. The RIC and its Crimes Special Branch had served as London's primary intelligence service in Ireland for decades, and indeed the

RIC would remain the principal British intelligence service on the island until the end of 1919—fully three years after the Easter Rising.[2]

Nevertheless, while the RIC had forewarned Dublin Castle of an armed conspiracy before the Rising, it was already in a state of decline as an intelligence service by then. Indeed, by the turn of the century, London began to view the large and expensive RIC as a costly liability and Chief Secretary Augustine Birrel enforced demoralizing budget and manpower cuts on the service beginning in 1907.[3] Birrel's successor, H. E. Duke, attempted to reform the local intelligence apparatus, but the work was never completed. Thus, the decline of the RIC continued right up until 1919, when—incredibly—the government decided to cut the special subsidies to the RIC Crimes Special Branch that funded intelligence work, an extremely ill-advised decision at the very outset of the Anglo-Irish War.[4]

The deterioration of local intelligence-gathering in Ireland from the beginning of the twentieth century may also reflect London's shift of attention to strategic, global intelligence issues that began in the latter half of the nineteenth century. As the empire extended its reach and became embroiled in a succession of foreign confrontations, strategic intelligence became much more important. Development of national intelligence resources was a slow process, however, and in the modern era the Crown had a long and dismal track record of improvising strategic-level intelligence resources to meet various wartime crises both outside and inside the empire. Beginning with the Crimean War, and later during the Indian revolt, the Afghan Wars, and in South Africa, the government always seemed to start from scratch to improvise an intelligence collection system, with very unsatisfactory results. Churchill's own experience as an intelligence officer in South Africa in 1897 convinced him that British intelligence lacked flexibility.[5]

Compounding this problem was the fact that there was no national-level system of clandestine core collection—what the British generically termed "secret service." The Criminal Investigation Department (CID), of the London Metropolitan Police—Scotland Yard—had served as an intelligence and security service for the Home Office since its establishment in the nineteenth century. In one famous example, the Home Office had employed barrister Sir Robert Anderson to run espionage operations abroad, including those carried out by the brilliant British spy Thomas Beach—better known by his operational alias, Henri Le Caron. An adventurer and soldier of fortune, Beach/Le Caron had met expatriate Irish Republican—or Fenian—Brotherhood conspirators while serving as an officer in the American Union Army during the Civil War. He thoroughly penetrated the organization in the United States and faithfully provided timely reports on various Irish plots to Sir Robert, which in turn were passed to G Division and the RIC's Crimes Special Branch in Dublin. Through these efforts, the Home Office was able to identify and monitor all the key American Fenian leaders, and to round up Fenian agents in Ireland.[6]

By 1883, a small "Special Irish Branch" (SIB) had been set up at CID in collaboration with the RIC to contend with a virulent Fenian dynamiting campaign across England. In the 1890s, this counterterrorism function was expanded to cover all foreign radicals, syndicalists, and anarchists, and SIB became simply "Special Branch," retaining its critically important cadre of native former RIC constables who possessed unique knowledge of Ireland.[7]

While it was an overt, publicly acknowledged, and publicly funded investigative and law enforcement arm of the police, Special Branch had established a reputation as a formidable countersubversive organization by 1900. Under the direction of Chief Inspector William Melville—a Kerry native—Special Branch detectives monitored immigrants and exiles in Britain, foiled anarchist plots, developed informants, and gathered information on foreign political and military matters. Special Branch inspectors served in liaison roles abroad, and their agents reported from numerous foreign capitals. Meanwhile, Special Branch detectives also served as "spotters" of potential agents from among the émigré community in the United Kingdom. Indeed, Melville would later become the first British handler of a Polish émigré and czarist *Okhrana* (secret police) informer named Sigmund Georgievich Rosenblum—who would later emerge as the notorious suspected murderer, international arms dealer, freelance espionage agent, and Imperial Secret Intelligence Service (SIS) case officer Sidney Reilly.[8]

By the turn of the century, therefore, Special Branch was Britain's principal human source intelligence service. It was neither a true clandestine service, nor did its authority extend to military matters. It operated as an openly acknowledged overt arm of the British government; its foreign expertise hinged primarily upon close official liaison cooperation with foreign police services and only secondarily upon foreign unilateral capability.

For most of the period between 1887 and 1904, intelligence at the War Office was relegated to a subfunction of the army's Military Operations Branch (MOB). MOB cooperated with the Admiralty's Naval Intelligence Division (NID) to compile the orders-of-battle of perceived enemies, to keep track of Japanese and czarist operatives in the run-up to the Russo-Japanese War, and to monitor exile Bolshevik organizations in England and continental Europe. By tradition, the Admiralty was responsible within the defense community for home intelligence (including Ireland and the colonies), and it was in the NID where Britain's first code breakers took residence prior to the First World War. The Government Codes & Ciphers School (GC&CS, also known as Room 40), became the signals intelligence (SIGINT) center of Great Britain and arguably the most important British national intelligence resource during the war. "Secret service," or clandestine human source core collection activity, was still handled almost as an afterthought, however. Because no one agency had a sufficient intelligence budget, human agents were employed variously by the Admiralty, Foreign Office, War Office, and Colonial Office. A system of freelance spies—which included newspaper reporters, adventurers, businessmen, explorers, smugglers, and other assorted nefarious characters—looked after human source intelligence (HUMINT) collection abroad.

Despite the ad hoc nature of this system, Britain did have its successes. Sidney Reilly appears to have been employed simultaneously for both the British and the Japanese in the Far East in 1898. After studying chemistry at a German university (time well spent learning the fundamentals of ink making, document forging, and explosive ordnance composition), the handsome young émigré graduated from Special Branch street informer to freelance double agent selling information to the highest bidder. Reilly went to Port Arthur, Manchuria—then Russia's most important Pacific naval base—under the guise of a commercial shipping agent. This gave him perfect cover-for-action to meet Russian military and political officials and to gather key intelligence on the Russian fleet and port defenses, which he promptly sold for a handsome price to the Japanese, while apparently also keeping Whitehall informed.[9]

Thanks to Reilly's mission to Port Arthur, the British scored a strategic intelligence coup in obtaining foreknowledge of the Russo-Japanese War, but such unilateral foreign espionage operations were the exception, not the rule. Absent a dedicated secret service budget (which British politicians were reluctant to approve) and a single dedicated command-and-control mechanism, the government found such operations difficult to sustain.

War Office management of military intelligence had proceeded haphazardly. While a formal intelligence staff functioned at Whitehall, theater-level resources were dysfunctional. Most division, regimental, and brigade commanders had a foggy concept of what was required for gathering tactical intelligence; worse still, officers assigned to intelligence officer (IO) billets tended to regard their assignments as a lark. Intelligence billets in the army were considered a special club, attainable often through patronage and influence. There was some prestige in being selected, screened, and appointed to a select group of officers engaged in classified work, but brains and skill were not always the principal criteria for selection. Moreover, many young IOs looked upon "secret service" much like membership in a college fraternity and viewed its duties as a game. Brigadier General Sir William Robertson's experience as a young newly selected IO in India in 1892 is revealing:

> Early in 1892 the Intelligence Branch at army headquarters was about to be strengthened by an increased number of officers. The intention was to take these officers partly from native and partly from British regiments, and after they had served a period of probation as "attaches" to select from amongst them for permanent employment such as it was considered desirable to retain. It was necessary, of course, that they should possess the linguistic attainments required by the nature of the work they had to do, and as I had five languages to my credit I was one of those chosen from British regiments, and was ordered to proceed to Simla forthwith. . . . Apart from the faulty organisation of headquarters as a whole, the Intelligence Branch had suffered because of the inadequacy— and perhaps of the inferior quality of its personnel. Although much had been done by the Commander-in-Chief, Lord Roberts, to ensure that priority for staff employment should be governed by professional capacity, favouritism and social influence were not yet deemed by the outsider to be extinct. It was alleged that staff

officers were still too often selected from amongst those who were likely to be successful performers in amateur theatricals, or be useful in some other way at the various entertainments provided for the amusement of Simla society. I was frequently asked on first arrival at this smart hill-station what my special accomplishment was—acting, singing, or whistling—and what my contribution to the amenities of the season was to be. It was taken for granted that I could do something of this nature, and do it well, and my interrogators were surprised to learn that I could contribute nothing.[10]

With the outbreak of the Boer War, the inadequacy of Britain's military intelligence infrastructure was quickly exposed. War Office IOs attached to field units were once again a collection of amateur stock players with little understanding of clandestine service. They collated and analyzed whatever news came their way courtesy of volunteer informers, journalists, native scouts, or from interrogation reports and captured documents. They had no expertise as clandestine core collectors and little knowledge of the process of vetting sources or mounting offensive counterintelligence operations. Moreover, there were too few IOs in the field.

The results were disastrous: British forces were scarcely able to suppress the Boer insurgency. By war's end, it was painfully clear to the government that any large military confrontation with a major European power would clearly find British Armed Forces ill prepared in intelligence matters. Whitehall began to consider reforms.[11]

Special Branch had developed superb and extensive intelligence liaison contacts with police services abroad and its reports became valuable commodities at the Foreign, Home, and War ministries. Yet Special Branch was a civilian organization and not sensitive enough to the army's unique intelligence requirements. Nor was it capable of mounting sustained unilateral espionage and counterespionage operations. That is what the military and the War Cabinet needed most.

TOWARD CLANDESTINE SERVICE

Faced with this state of affairs, when Chief Inspector Melville retired from the CID in 1903, the War Office Intelligence Division secretly tapped him to set up a small espionage chamber of his own. Reporting to Brigadier General George Cockerill, a veteran IO with experience during the Boer

War, Melville's new unit was officially, and euphemistically, known on the manning charts as the War Office Special Section and designated MO3. Two years later it was redesignated MO5g under the Department of Military Intelligence, or DMI. The organization that Melville set up was a significant refinement of the foreign liaison modus operandi he had himself perfected while at Scotland Yard. As Deputy Director of DMI, the enlightened Cockerill was a driving force for modernization. He envisioned a truly clandestine service with officers operating under official and nonofficial cover and undeclared to foreign governments. Melville ran MO5g pretty much out of his hip pocket, himself operating in alias persona and under commercial cover from an innocuous office building in London. From this humble beginning, the War Office now had its own organic capability to mount offensive foreign intelligence collection and defensive counterintelligence operations. MO5g also undertook special assignments on behalf of the Admiralty. Melville's small organization was Britain's first truly clandestine HUMINT collection organization between 1903 and 1909. In 1907, as Melville's foreign spy apparat began to grow and produce good results, Major James Edwards was brought in as senior military officer in charge of MO5g; Edwards was succeeded in 1909 by Colonel George Macdonagh. Both wisely retained Melville on staff as the senior-most civilian officer.[12]

Although Melville's sub-rosa organization enjoyed the full confidence of the War Office and the gratitude of the Admiralty, its establishment outside the realm of civilian control planted the seed of jealousy with Special Branch that would continue for the next quarter century. This rivalry, combined with the attitudes of naive politicians, fickle prime ministers, and mistrusting cabinets, would reach its zenith at the outbreak of the Anglo-Irish War.

This assembly of agencies constituted Britain's national strategic intelligence community until 1909. In that year, with key advocacy from War Secretary Richard Burdon Haldane and Winston Churchill, former Colonial Office Undersecretary of State and Liberal Party MP, Britain formally established a new Secret Service Bureau at the War Office under DMI. The new service would be clandestine, neither acknowledged nor publicized by the government. It would build upon the achievements of Melville's organization, but it would combine the resources and functions of the War Office and Admiralty (with the exception of the Admiralty's

SIGINT role) under one roof. MO5g's domain was subdivided into two departments under new leadership. Army Major (later Brigadier General) Vernon Kell of the South Staffordshire Regiment, would lead the home section, focusing on domestic and colonial counterintelligence matters, while Navy Commander (later Admiral) Mansfield Cumming took charge of the foreign section.

Within a short time, it was apparent that the two sections would seek their own separate identities and budgets. Each branch had its own sensitive assets, and sharing office space impeded the necessary compartmentalizing of clandestine operations. In addition, for his part, naval officer Cumming was quite depressed to learn that the War Office considered him Kell's subordinate—a point driven home when Kell personally handed him his first paycheck.[13] In 1910, therefore, the Secret Service Bureau was further reorganized into two departments: the Imperial Secret (or Special) Intelligence Service (SIS, which acquired the military staff designation MI1c after 1915) under Cumming for foreign espionage, and the domestic Imperial British Security Service (BSS, which retained the designator MO5g) for domestic and colonial counterespionage, under Kell. Officially, none of this impacted Special Branch, which—unlike MO5g and MI1c—was not a clandestine service and which remained under civilian control. But Special Branch had lost a good measure of authority and independence in counterespionage matters. With the prospect of a European war growing by the day, Whitehall placed its emphasis and its money on improving the military intelligence infrastructure. For the foreseeable future, therefore, Special Branch would work largely at the direction of Kell's department.

What sort of personnel could be found in this new government department known collectively as the secret service? Unlike Special Branch, MO5g was an undeclared service employing completely sub-rosa methods. It drew most of its personnel from the commissioned corps of the regular army as well as from the ranks of the Indian Colonial Police (ICP), with a few additional ex–Special Branch detectives thrown in for seasoning. Redesignated MI5 in July 1916, the service continued this manning tradition until 1940, when Kell was sacked by Churchill, and new blood was brought aboard to face the challenges of Nazi Germany

Like Kell's department, Cumming's foreign section recruited heavily from the regular army and the ICP ranks. But Cumming also recruited an odd and interesting assortment of adventurers, foreign correspondents, and expatriates to serve as operations officers abroad—including none other than former Special Branch informer and freelance spy, Sidney Reilly, who was formally sworn in as an SIS case officer in 1918 to work on anti-Bolshevik operations in Germany and Russia. In the late 1930s, MI1c would be re-designated MI6 as a temporary wartime convenience, but that term stuck and has remained in colloquial references to the SIS ever since.[14]

These two departments constituted Britain's only truly clandestine espionage services in 1918. They were staffed by an interesting assortment of officers with foreign knowledge and experience in undercover work against radicals, and a smattering of former Special Branch investigators with knowledge of legal procedures who could convey guidance to police and magistrates in prosecutions of spies, saboteurs, and subversives. Significantly, bright young intellectual Cambridge and Oxford graduates who habitually found career appointments in the Foreign Office or other branches of civil service would not make an appearance in either the domestic or foreign intelligence sections of the British Secret Service for two more decades. Kell personally did the hiring at MI5 and he rated candidates on their family connections, interests, and hobbies. Foreign language ability was also important to Kell, who himself spoke Chinese, French, German, and Russian. Equally important was a fair amount of cross-fertilization between the two departments, and it was not uncommon for intelligence officers to move from one service to the other, and back again to meet the shifting demands of the War and Foreign Offices.[15]

Curiously, no special security vetting of MI5 applicants occurred, aside from an examination of their military or police service record and their family's social status and connections. Indeed, Kell's budget was so small that he could not afford to pay his officers a regular salary. His remedy was to hire well-heeled young men who had independent sources of income. He also sought and won exemption from paying income taxes as a highly desirable perquisite for his staff. Thus, Kell surrounded himself with a coterie of well-rounded and solidly middle-class military officers on detached assignment, several ex-CID detectives, upper-class men of leisure, and a good number of former ICP detectives. It was Kell's firm but faulty contention that members of the British upper-classes were naturally more discreet and security conscious.

In appointing such men, Kell certainly obtained the personal loyalty of his staff, but he largely ignored their professional qualifications, if any, for clandestine work. What Kell and the War Office clearly understood was that uniformed IOs serving at the battalion and brigade level—while essential for collating and analyzing various information and providing it to their chain of command—were not suitably positioned to carry out clandestine, or "secret service," operations. At this stage Kell and MI5 had no established model to follow, at any rate; clandestine tradecraft was still a work in progress, but the key point was that MI5 had Melville on staff to provide guidance and its activities were clandestine—so clandestine that the British public remained ignorant of the very existence of the Secret Service Bureau.[16]

As for Special Branch, it was a civilian-controlled service staffed by detectives who had worked their way up through the ranks. Not a few of its members had extensive foreign area experience, having served in the colonies or worked in liaison capacity with foreign police agencies as well as serving on executive protection assignments with the Royal Family or on behalf of visiting heads of state. But Special Branch was not a clandestine service, and with few exceptions its officers were fairly conventional-thinking cops who thrived more on the chase and the arrest of suspects than on the slow methodical process of researching, gathering evidence, building dossiers, recruiting and running clandestine agents, and mounting discreet surveillance. And it was these latter functions that would become the keys to MI5's methodology.

HUSH-HUSH MEN

When war with Germany came in August 1914, the MI5–Special Branch relationship proved to be a winning combination. It was an effective fusion of clandestine investigations backed up by national-level law enforcement. Kell's department, with street muscle and prosecutorial assistance from Special Branch, was fully engaged in tracking and trapping German spies. The two services combined to amass an impressive record. From the beginning, MI5 relied upon an exhaustive records system of individual file cards compiled by a small army of female file clerks. This secret central registry of 30,000 domestic subversives, syndicalists, labor leaders, communists, socialists, and alien residents permitted MI5 to identify targets, recruit and handle penetration agents, surreptitiously open and examine mail, and build evidence. MI5 in turn guided Special Branch in surveillance and arrests of German agents, saboteurs, and subversives, generally neutralizing threats at home and in the colonies.[17] Under the direction of former British diplomat and prison governor Basil Thomson, who had joined CID in 1913, Special Branch soon garnered sensational newspaper headlines for raids conducted upon MI5's behind-the-scenes direction. By the summer of 1916, when MO5g was renamed MI5, the service had grown to 844 officers (84 officers, 281 female clerks and secretaries, 15 male clerks, 77 support staff, and 23 police officers served at London headquarters).[18]

Further, upon the outbreak of hostilities, Brigadier General Cockerill, who had conceptualized Melville's War Office Special Section a dozen years earlier and who oversaw its development into a full clandestine service under Kell, assumed command of a new clandestine branch, MO9, which was responsible for censorship and propaganda. In 1915, this branch achieved separate identity as MI9. Cockerill employed a staff of 170 engaged in censorship of the mail and the formulation of very effective propaganda campaigns.[19]

Kell was growing adept at internal politics. Although his department, like MI1c, was under the War Office, Sir Vernon had managed to achieve significant bureaucratic independence for his service, and he enjoyed access to both the Home Secretary and the Prime Minister. Because MI5's mission was supposed to be dedicated to domestic homeland security, schemes were afoot as early as 1912 to rein in Kell's department by resubordinating it from the War Office to the Home Office and placing it under civilian leadership. Kell managed to fend off these moves for six years, no doubt because of MI5's importance to the defense community during the Great War. However, the issue resurfaced following the armistice with Germany, and Kell's quiet, retiring manner would soon be overshadowed by more ambitious personalities with greater influence at Whitehall.[20]

While the MI5–Special Branch combination had not prevented every act of German sabotage, it had proven to be an extremely formidable homeland security formula. At war's end, MI5's esprit was soaring. Kell and his staff were proud of their successes in the clandestine war against Germany, and MI5 war veterans reveled in their unofficial nickname, the Hush-Hush Men. Kell was knighted. For his part, Basil Thomson reveled in the spotlight of national media coverage. To the British public, which had no knowledge of the existence of either MI5 or MI1c, Special Branch *was* the British "Secret Service." MI5 officers bristled at Thomson's headline grabbing, knowing that true expertise in counterespionage matters lay within MI5, not Special Branch. Writing to the NID's Admiral Reginald "Blinker" Hall after the war, Reginald Drake, Kell's counterintelligence chief, commented on Thomson's tactics: "As you know, B.T. did not know of the existence, name or activity of any convicted spy until I told him, but being the dirty dog he was, he twisted the facts to claim that he alone did it."[21]

In his memoirs, Basil Thomson described Special Branch during the war as "Servants of the Admiralty and War Office," but he also goes on to describe myriad meetings throughout the war with his agents from Holland, Norway, Africa, and the United States. From this it is fairly clear that Special Branch did not relinquish its valuable foreign agents to either Mansfield Cumming or Vernon Kell when Special Branch was seconded to the Secret Service Bureau in 1914. Given the extent of Thomson's own unilateral foreign spy network, his postwar bid to become supreme director of all British intelligence is not surprising.[22]

Special Branch was not the only agency pursuing foreign intrigues outside of the authority of the Secret Service Bureau, however. While MI1c and MI5 formed the nucleus of a national espionage and counterespionage community, their focus was strategic, not tactical, and there was still a gaping hole in British collection efforts at the theater level. Upon the outbreak of hostilities in France, therefore, the War Office had created the Army Field Intelligence Corps under DMI to support tactical requirements. Not surprisingly, the need for a corps of IOs to support theater-level military operations had been discussed in DMI for years, but it was not acted upon until there was a real imperative. As Christopher Andrew documents, a good many Army Field Intelligence Corps collection initiatives crossed paths with those already under way in MI1c, much to Cumming's annoyance, and steps had to be taken to deconflict operations and delineate operational boundaries between the Intelligence Corps and MI1c all along the Western Front from the Holland-Belgian frontier to the Swiss border. Nevertheless, a good many IOs serving with the Intelligence Corps over the next few years would gather valuable experience that would later be put to good use against the IRA.[23]

WARTIME INTELLIGENCE IN IRELAND

Concerned with the security of British army and navy bases in Ireland, and anticipating the potential for Irish nationalists to collaborate with

German spies and saboteurs, the War Office appointed a central chief of intelligence for Ireland upon the outbreak of hostilities in France. In 1914, Senior RIC Inspector Ivor H. Price was seconded to the army with the rank of Temporary Major, to set up the "Special Intelligence Section" in the Castle.[24]

This too was an improvised effort—really just a microcosm of the confusing British intelligence system as a whole. Although working under War Office authority, Price nevertheless reported directly to a civilian, the permanent undersecretary. It was his job to collect and analyze information on subversive activity in Ireland, including that collected by the RIC Crimes Special Branch and G Division of the DMP—and whatever information Admiralty NID listening stations could supply—and provide it to the army's Irish Command and the Castle. Price also cooperated with the Ministry of Munitions Intelligence Branch and the Irish Post & Telegraph Department. With a staff of fewer than a dozen men, he concentrated his own collection efforts on mail censorship, through which his team gleaned substantial information on suspected subversives. He kept both MI5 and Special Branch informed of significant developments.

For his part, Kell was interested primarily in detecting German espionage and sabotage activity in Ireland, not with Irish nationalists, which he left for Special Branch and NID to sort out. On the whole he was pleased with Price's work, noting in 1916 that of the various sources of intelligence in Ireland, the information provided by RIC District Inspectors and Price's office were the most reliable. Price's collection network was good but his analysis and assessments left much to be desired. He was aware, for example, that Fenian conspirators were in contact with the German government after 1914, but he did not assess this to be a grave threat even as late as the spring of 1916. When the indicators of an uprising grew stronger, Price passed these on at the theater level through his military intelligence summaries, only to learn later that Castle officials had not bothered to read them. Price later compared himself to "John the Baptist, preaching in the wilderness." Once the rebellion started, however, Price provided good service in keeping the local army commander, the Castle, and Special Branch informed of developments.[25]

The establishment of Price's office was no doubt considered a successful and prudent step by the War Office and the army's Irish Command, but civilian policymakers were dissatisfied. H. E. Duke, the Irish Undersecretary, was highly critical of the hydra-headed intelligence presence and obviously dissatisfied with Price's inability—or lack of authority—to speak for the British intelligence community as a whole. Policymakers and administrators rarely have the time or patience to sit through several briefings from multiple agencies to get the big picture. In Duke's case it meant having to meet with Price, representing the Army Special Intelligence Section; with the local MI5 Center, or head of station; as well as with the local Special Branch liaison officer, the Superintendent of G Division, the Inspector-General of the RIC, and the local Admiralty/NID representative. Such a schedule would consume almost a full calendar week. Worse yet, while all five local offices might have their own spin on what their respective sources were reporting, no one synthesized it into a bottom-line assessment. Duke had to do his own analysis.

By 1916, Duke was so concerned that he issued a recommendation that all five departments be consolidated under a single unified Irish intelligence command. The memorandum merely gathered dust in London, and when Duke left office in May 1918, the initiative died.[26] Major Price might have been a candidate to assume command of an improved consolidated intelligence service in Ireland, but at war's end a shortsighted British administration decided that Price's Special Intelligence Section had served its purpose. In January 1919, Major Price reverted to Inspector Price and returned to his former RIC duties—just as Irish nationalists were going on the offensive. Not only would there be no unified command, but the Special Intelligence Section would never be resurrected, although the army advocated it after Irish rebels again declared independence in 1919. It would take nearly eighteen months before the British realized a replacement organization was essential, but what they eventually set up at Dublin Castle in May 1920 would not measure up to expectations.[27]

A HOMELAND SECURITY CZAR

At war's end, the government was looking for ways to economize and streamline the management of national intelligence. Churchill, who had been instrumental in establishing the Secret Service Bureau in 1909, was also cognizant of Special Branch's traditional HUMINT role. Moreover, he had become well acquainted with Basil Thomson; three months before Churchill was appointed Munitions Minister, Thomson had been given exclusive responsibility for investigating British labor radicals. It was to Thomson, not Kell, that the War Cabinet turned for briefings on domestic subversive activities. While MI5 worked silently in the background building cases against German spies and domestic subversives, it was the tough, no-nonsense detectives of Special Branch who swept the Kaiser's agents off the streets and jailed perceived disloyal subjects during the war. The overlap of duties between MI5 and Special Branch on domestic subversives planted the seed of a rivalry between Thomson and Kell. In the final analysis, however, it was the hardball, door-kicking raids and arrests and the vigorous prosecutions by Thomson's overt Special Branch that grabbed newspaper headlines, resulting in Thomson's knighthood in 1918.[28]

Undoubtedly emboldened by this recognition, Sir Basil sought to regain Special Branch's former primacy in home security matters. Collaborating with his close friend, Admiral Reginald "Blinker" Hall, the Director of Naval Intelligence at the Admiralty, Thomson began to warn the cabinet about the presence of Bolsheviks under every rock. This proved to be an ill-fated alliance. Thomson was a flamboyant war hero with further career ambitions. Hall was a bombastic reactionary whose shoot-from-the-hip style habitually moved him to read more into raw bits of intelligence and to draw analytical conclusions that were questionable, misleading, or wrong.

Moreover, Hall committed the cardinal sin of an intelligence officer in trying to direct government policy, and toward that end he was not above inflating—or even withholding—key intelligence information from the cabinet. While Major Price reported the impending Easter rebellion to Dublin Castle, for example, Blinker Hall was the only person within the British national intelligence community who had corroborating HUMINT and SIGINT evidence of the rebellion, yet he withheld that key information from the cabinet, hoping the revolt would proceed and that British forces would crush the conspirators, putting an end to radical nationalism in Ireland once and for all.[29]

By promoting the notion of a "Red Menace," Hall and Thomson lobbied and won support from Churchill—now Secretary of State for War—and other members of the Government Intelligence Committee for the creation of a new civilian-managed home intelligence service independent of both the War Office and the Admiralty. To make matters worse, some British politicians began to question the continuing need for MI5 in the postwar period. It was against that backdrop in February 1919 that the Government Intelligence Committee abruptly appointed Basil Thomson to be "Director of Civil Intelligence" and also to lead a new Home Office Directorate of Intelligence, with headquarters at Scotland House, London. Sir Basil's official charter included responsibility for labor unrest, aliens, counterespionage, and revolutionary matters. Thomson acquired supreme authority over all domestic counterintelligence and counter-subversion matters—at least for the next two years. Thus, Thomson became both Britain's homeland security czar and its National Intelligence Director with a mere pen stroke.[30]

Not bound by the same restrictions imposed by MI5's secrecy oath, Thomson knew that Kell could not publicly acknowledge even the existence of the Security Service, much less speak out to defend his department from this bureaucratic coup d'état. The Secret Service Bureau had been created in complete secrecy in 1909 and the government never announced or acknowledged its existence. "Secret service" was considered so sensitive that members of Parliament were supposedly prohibited from discussing it in public. Even cabinet members rarely discussed sources or methods among themselves.

To solidify his new position, Thomson began giving press interviews touting the new "secret service" he had been appointed to lead. The conservative *London Morning Post* quoted Thomson saying that his new Special Branch would operate "on the lines of Continental Secret Services and will ultimately have agents throughout the United Kingdom, in the colonies, and in many parts of the world outside the British Empire."[31]

Thomson had not yet moved his staff to the directorate's new digs in Scotland House before he was already making headlines.[32] And this in turn made it difficult for the government to conceal secret service affairs. When opposition MP Patrick D. Malone pressed the Home Secretary on the subject of Basil Thomson and secret service matters during question time in the Commons in March 1920, John Baird, undersecretary of state for the Home Office was less than candid. Malone wanted to know, "What is the organization of which Sir Basil Thomson is in charge; and whether there is now in existence in this country a secret police force on lines similar to those which have existed in many countries on the Continent?" Baird responded half-truthfully:

Sir Basil Thomson is in charge of the Special Branch of the Metropolitan Police, which has existed in its present form for more than 40 years. The only changes are that he has given up the charge of the Criminal Investigation Department in order to give his full time to the Special Branch, and that his staff has been slightly increased in order to deal with the increase of work necessarily arising under present conditions. The answer to the last part of the question is in the negative.[33]

Thomson's high profile was a questionable tactic for a service chief who was charged with managing some of the government's most sensitive clandestine activities.

While Irish dissidents certainly knew that the British police and army operated an international network of secret service operatives, it is probable that they did not know of the existence of either MI5 or MI1c per se at that stage. When the irrepressible Thomson publicly declared that Special Branch was Britain's "secret service," however, Fenian subversives could not have failed to notice. Counterespionage, countersubversion, and counterterrorism were now Thomson's exclusive—and very public— domain. There was nothing clandestine about his Special Branch or its intentions. Since Special Branch had historically handled all matters of subversion in Ireland, the way was clear for Thomson's agency to assume the lead against Irish insurrectionists as well. It would soon become one of Thomson's biggest headaches.

As for Kell, his budget was slashed from £100,000 in 1918 to just £35,000 in 1919, accompanied by a corresponding reduction in MI5 manpower from 150 to 35. By 1921 his budget would be further reduced to just £10,000. While MI5 was not subordinated to Thomson per se, Kell's mission was limited to counterespionage and countersubversion within the armed forces. With a drastically reduced budget and staff, Kell would be hard-pressed to monitor Bolshevik activity within the forces over the next few years, let alone undertake broader home or colonial security assignments. To add insult to injury, some of Kell's cashiered case officers went over to Scotland Yard. While an embittered Kell considered the new Director of Home Intelligence an interloper, that did not change the fact that MI5 had essentially been relegated to an obscure office on the sidelines.[34]

Andrew has recovered an MI5 memorandum from 1920 attributed to Kell's number two, Major Eric Holt-Wilson. Holt-Wilson noted that Special Branch was not qualified to undertake MI5's clandestine work and that those MI5 officers who had defected to Thomson's Directorate of Intelligence were far from the cream of the crop:

> Despite statements to the contrary in the press and elsewhere, Sir Basil Thomson's organization has never actually detected a case of espionage, but has merely arrested and questioned spies at the request of MI5, when the latter organization, which had detected them, considered that the time for their arrest had arrived. The Army Council are in favour of entrusting the work to an experienced, tried and successful organization rather than to one which has yet to win its spurs. Sir Basil Thomson's existing higher staff consists mainly of ex-officers of MI5 not considered sufficiently able for retention by that Department. The Army Council are not satisfied with their ability to perform the necessary duties under Sir Basil Thomson's direction, and they are satisfied that detective officers alone, without direction from above, are unfitted for the work.[35]

Such bitterness is understandable, under the circumstances. Nevertheless, when Holt-Wilson was sacked by Churchill in 1940 along with Kell, he admitted that MI5 did not manage operations as much as it supervised a large bureaucracy consisting of military, civil, and police services, and managed its vast Central File Bureau and Register "for the whole Empire."[36]

Regardless, Churchill and the Government Intelligence Committee were confident that the same effective capabilities that Thomson and Special Branch had displayed against German spies, labor leaders, and radicals could be brought to bear with good effect on Irish dissidents. It would not prove that simple, or easy.[37]

THE ARMY IMPROVISES

Basil Thomson was sworn in as supreme intelligence chief at Scotland House in May 1919, and after just four months on the job, there was concern in the military that his home intelligence scheme was not going to fill the army's secret service requirements. Having recognized this, Churchill, as War Secretary, quietly authorized the creation of another clandestine unit to fill the military intelligence gap.

Referred to by planners as the "Silent Section," this new undercover department of DMI was founded in September 1919, designated MO4x, and placed under the command of Major General C. F. Romer. MO4x's mission was to provide a clandestine tactical intelligence collection capability expressly to support local British theater-level commanders in chief (CINCs). It drew its staff from the ranks of current and former uniformed IOs of the Army Field Intelligence Corps with experience all over the empire. Ex-officers with combat experience were also recruited, given temporary commissions, and placed on the army's General List before silently joining MO4x. The men of MO4x would serve in both the colonies and foreign posts, wherever the British ground forces maintained a presence or had an expeditionary mission. By 1919, and in the next few years, the British Army was committed in several foreign theaters. Part of it remained on occupation duty in Germany. Several regiments were deployed to north and south Russia and to Siberia to fight alongside a Russian White Army struggling to destabilize and topple the Communist regime that had seized power two years earlier. The army was also in the Balkans and Turkey, assisting nationalist Kemal Atatürk's forces in suppressing Turkish rebels and establishing a military cordon to prevent the Russians from threatening Persia and India. It was in Egypt and Palestine and it had entire infantry and logistics corps returning to Shanghai, Singapore, and India from France. In addition, two infantry divisions were in the process of returning from France to their traditional garrisons in Ireland. Once there, the veterans were to be demobilized, and the Fifth and Sixth Divisions would be rebuilt into a seven-brigade security force with an influx of new recruits.[38]

Having grown accustomed to a robust manning level and support from MI5 and MI1c during the Great War, DMI was unprepared to field its own clandestine collectors in 1919. Due to demobilization, DMI strength had been reduced from 5,969 on November 1, 1918, to just 969 personnel by July 1, 1919. Romer was therefore faced with the task of building up this secret service almost from scratch. There was no question in the general staff that such a service was needed, however, for in addition to a role for army case officers abroad, they perceived a new threat at home from

Figure 1. Structure of British National Intelligence 1909–1921

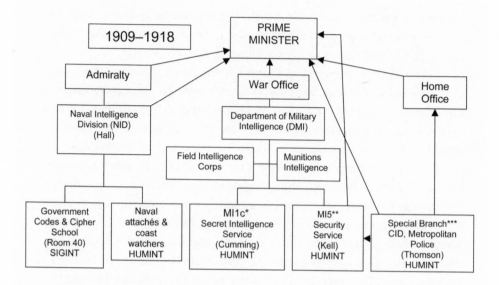

* Foreign espionage
** Domestic and colonial counterespionage and countersubversion
*** Support to MI5 in counterespionage, and lead agency on Ireland

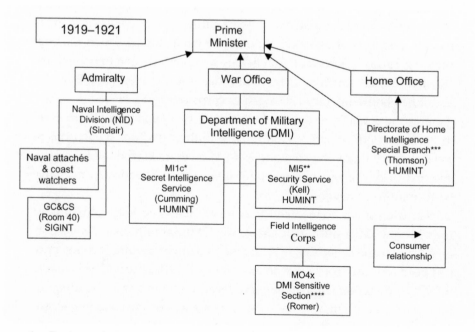

* Foreign espionage
** Counterespionage in the armed forces
*** Civil counterespionage and countersubversion
**** Army theater-level clandestine operations

leftist elements in Britain who were suspected of sowing disloyalty in the army. Up to the fall of 1919, such reports had been investigated by general staff sections. One of these, A2, had infiltrated the Soldiers', Sailors' and Airmen's Union (SSAU) quickly enough, but this clandestine effort was shut down in February 1919, leaving a gap. MO4x was officially assigned to investigate internal disloyalty in the army and picked up the investigation of SSAU where A2 had left off seven months earlier. It recruited informers within the ranks to gauge the loyalty of soldiers and monitor potential radical activities.

Over time, Romer began to deploy MO4x officers in support of British expeditionary forces around the globe. Essentially then, MO4x combined the functions of criminal investigation and clandestine intelligence operations. This would be akin to combining the U.S. Army's Criminal Investigation Department (CID) and its Military Intelligence (MI) Branch into one comprehensive department. The officers appointed to MO4x would not only have law enforcement and intelligence-gathering authority, similar to those enjoyed by Basil Thomson's Special Branch on the civilian side, but also executive authority to carry out lethal action against targets, if necessary or as directed.[39]

Thus, with the virtual demobilization of MI5 at the end of the war, the British Army was thrust back into precisely the same situation that had existed when Churchill was a young adventure seeker in South Africa. That scenario, namely the need to improvise professional clandestine intelligence collection keyed to the army's unique requirements, had plagued army efficiency in the Crimea, India, Afghanistan, and during the Boer War. Instead of representing a bold new initiative, therefore, MO4x represented another stopgap measure, and one that would lead it into conflict with competing civilian intelligence agencies in the next few years. This would have dire consequences in Ireland.

The effective MI5–Special Branch partnership that had so admirably served homeland defense during the First World War—with its important cross-pollination of military and civilian resources—was abandoned by Whitehall just as Irish Republicans were preparing to go on the offensive. As events would show, the coming insurrection in Ireland would target all instruments of government—civilian institutions, the constabulary, and the British Army. The establishment of Thomson as homeland security czar established a bureaucratic roadblock that would hinder the coordination of resources and information between the police and military and become one of the critical handicaps of Crown intelligence activities against the IRA. It was a lapse in national security policy driven by political favoritism and budgetary shortsightedness.

This bureaucratic reshuffle and concurrent evisceration of MI5 just as the Irish crisis unfolded constituted a major miscalculation. Compounding this blunder was the stand-down of Ivor Price's Special Intelligence Section at Dublin Castle in January 1919. London would pay dearly for these errors. By the time Michael Collins had destroyed the colonial police intelligence system of G Division and the RIC, the British Army was left to jury-rig a clandestine service with inadequate support from the War Office and Special Branch. Basil Thomson would launch some clever operations to get Collins, but Collins had the advantage of knowing in advance what he faced because of Thomson's high profile. Moreover, as Home Intelligence Director, Thomson would prove ineffectual as a strategic homeland security advisor. The elevation of civil, or police, intelligence over military intelligence would become a key factor hampering Crown efforts to restore order in Ireland, and it would force London to abandon its security policy there by mid-1920. An entire new regime would take over in that year, complete with a promising new theater intelligence commander. However, that, too, would be a confusing, improvised effort directed by an amateur sleuth.

And there was another fundamental problem on the British side: no one anticipated the emergence of an organized and pervasive rebel intelligence network or, indeed, knew much about its mysterious leader, Michael Collins, or where to find him. Worse yet, the British did not possess even a single photograph of him.

3

THE IRISH NATIONALIST

He comes from a brainy Cork Family.
— *Secret Police report on Michael Collins, 1918*

It is impossible to recount the events of the Anglo-Irish War without examining the background, education, motivation, and character of the man who did the most to bring it on. Michael Collins has been called the first urban terrorist, and he was the architect of modern guerrilla warfare.

History shows that successful guerrilla insurgencies have ignored compassion. The successful revolutionary must be absolutely ruthless in the pursuit and elimination of enemies. Collins stands out among his peers for never wavering when events called for such ruthlessness. Many of his contemporaries disagreed with his violent tactics and still others who agreed with Collins faltered. However, Collins possessed a tremendous inner strength and courage, and that was an important reason for his success. While the so-called Irish War of Independence failed to win full independence, that failure was certainly not from lack of resolve. The war did succeed in compelling Britain to relinquish control of most of their prize colony, opening the door to eventual independence.

Moral qualms—including the serious dilemma of taking human life within the confines of an overwhelmingly Catholic society—certainly haunted Michael Collins, for his closest colleagues in the Republican movement later testified to the somber mood that always came over him when ordering assassination. Such qualms never stopped him from doing his duty, however, and making war on the British colonial system *was* his duty.[1]

As chief of the Irish Republican Brotherhood, Adjutant General of the Irish Republican Army, Minister of Finance and Director of Intelligence for the revolutionary Irish Parliament, Collins had all of the power at his fingertips to launch an intelligence-driven guerrilla war that would tax the resources of the British government to the limit. Admired or hated as he was, Collins nevertheless was the first Irish nationalist to recognize that the British government could be defeated by refusing to recognize the authority of the Crown. While Irish political leader Eamon de Valera first conceived the strategy of ostracizing local British officials, it was Collins who upped the ante by putting the conflict in motion with direct attacks against the government police and intelligence network, thereby neutralizing Britain's system of informers. He was well aware that these acts would bring a terrible retaliation from England, but this, too, he calculated, would help to galvanize total resistance. He also hoped it would bring international condemnation upon Great Britain and force a political settlement.

Collins was a naturally gifted leader who possessed many of the qualities of an effective intelligence officer. He had a forceful, charismatic personality anchored by an unwavering determination to get the British out of Ireland. He could be compassionate to a fault and ruthless when necessary. He had physical energy well beyond that of any member of his staff, and he had an extraordinary ability to spot and assess others as friends or foes. Moreover, he was a supremely gifted speaker and actor.

Collins could make very difficult decisions—often with life-or-death consequences—with a clear mind on a moment's notice and under tremendous strain. This was no small feat for a man living on the run and operating an underground intelligence service. He never asked his staff to undertake any work that he himself would not do. He hated bureaucracy of all kinds and was impatient and intemperate with anything and anyone that diverted him from his goals. Simply put, Collins knew in his gut what needed to be done to throw the British out and he did not suffer fools easily. He certainly did not like decision by committee, and he frequently bristled and fumed when dithering Irish politicians enforced restrictions on him. Consequently, he often took matters into his own hands. In so doing, Collins set down his markers: either you loved him and were totally dedicated to him, or you despised him. There was not much middle ground, and Collins had many enemies inside the Republican movement. All that said, Collins was a uniquely gifted individual, and he was likely the greatest patriot that Ireland has ever produced.

As morally reprehensible as violence may seem and as outrageously violent as war itself is, Collins nevertheless knew that violence was necessary. Moreover, he was the most well placed revolutionary of his generation to prosecute a ruthless campaign of violence. To be sure, a good many other strong-willed, courageous, and ruthlessly efficient men could be found among the IRA leadership as well as in the IRA rank and file of 1917–1921. However, few outperformed Michael Collins, who seemed to be everywhere at once. Working as many as twenty hours a day, he might be found speaking at a Sinn Fein rally, training a flying column, meeting his clandestine agents, laundering the secret movement's funds in order to hide them, or organizing a jail break or gun-running scheme.

Collins commanded as much respect as some of the IRA's most famous fighting leaders—Sean Treacy, Daniel Breen, Tom Barry, Sean Hales, Matt Brennan, Tom Kelleher, Jimmy Conroy, Tomas Malone—and more than most, even from those who disliked or utterly despised him for his tactics. And he continued to command this respect from erstwhile colleagues who later turned against him in the bitter civil war that followed the Anglo-Irish War. If most revolutionaries have a Type A personality, then Michael Collins was Type AAA. He was a driven man. In addition, while many questioned his tactics, his financial management, or his military authority, no one outworked him, and no one ever questioned his dedication.[2]

COLLINS AS MYTH AND REALITY

Michael Collins has emerged as a revolutionary figure of mythic proportions in Irish nationalist history. More than a popular hero, Collins achieved an almost supernatural reputation, even in his own lifetime. Although he remains a national hero to every Irish schoolchild, he is too often remembered for masterminding bold prison breakouts, daring raids on police stations, and other hair-raising escapades. He also liked sports, drank a lot, and chain-smoked cigarettes until 1920, when he quit both alcohol and tobacco cold turkey. He was one of those busy personalities who could not sit still, and in private with friends, he enjoyed rough-housing and wrestling. To blow off steam, he was apt to suddenly tackle whomever happened to be visiting with him, pin him to the floor, and bite the victim's ear to underscore victory. While all of this is a matter of re-cord, the sensationalist popular image (aided not a little by Collins's own ego) overshadows the true nature of his intelligence organization and its work. The reality of Michael Collins is a career of underground revolu-tionary planning and secret intelligence work: walk-ins, recruitments, as-set validation, false-flag operations, penetrations, double agents, dangles, propaganda, dirty tricks, safe house meetings — and lethal covert action.

In spite of his humble origins and simple upbringing, Collins had a complex personality. Contemporaries have described him variously as crude, brash, boisterous, arrogant, urbane, ferocious, ruthless, shy, generous, sensitive, emotional, and charming. To the average person this complex psyche is difficult to appreciate, yet it is not that unusual for intelligence officers and others leading a clandestine life. A well-documented incident that occurred at the height of his war against the British may illustrate mood swings or it may simply reveal the wisdom of a skilled intelligence manager. Collins liked to meet some of his staff in the restaurant of Dub-lin's Wicklow Hotel where the waiter was a solid Sinn Feiner who could be relied upon to protect the identities of Collins and his men. That same trust was placed in the hall porter — forty-five-year-old William "Willie" Doran. However, when Collins discovered that Doran had given informa-tion to the authorities about these frequent dinner guests, Collins did not hesitate to order Doran executed. Doran's wife assumed that her husband worked with Collins, so she applied to Sinn Fein for a widow's pension. Collins granted the pension, but he ordered that no mention of Doran's treachery or the circumstances of his death be revealed to the family, who assumed Willie had been assassinated by British agents and had died in the cause of Irish freedom.[3]

The episode is often used by Collins biographers to illustrate the sen-sitive side of his personality — a noble gesture that would save the Doran family from embarrassment and stigma. For an intelligence chief man-aging clandestine offensive operations against a cunning, numerically superior, and extremely dangerous adversary, however, Collins's action was simply good tradecraft—manipulation. Doran's widow, after all, had already falsely concluded that her husband had died a hero; better to let her go on believing that and to provide her with sufficient funds to support her and her family for the rest of their lives. This would cement her loyalty to the organization, secure her silence, and thereby avoid a troublesome public inquiry into an ugly matter that might expose Collins's intelligence apparatus, jeopardize any number of other clandestine operations, or compromise and endanger his case officers or their assets. Similar decisions are routinely made every day in the world of intelligence operations. Such cases must be treated delicately and tactfully; no matter what empathy the service may have for a fallen operative's next-of-kin, it is the preservation of operational security that is always the primary consideration.

Regardless of this complicated personality, all of his biographers agree that Collins had a quick wit, an engaging smile, and a brilliant mind, and therein lay Collins's genius for intelligence work. He was a natural actor and quick-thinking role player—important characteristics for any successful case officer. Beneath his broad West Cork accent and somewhat awkward country boy strut was a brilliant and calculating intellect. The easy country manners and broad smile won friends instantly. It was easy for him to walk up to complete strangers from all walks of life and engage them in conversation. Often this irrepressible charm enabled him to bluff his way out of police raids and through army checkpoints. With a hefty price on his head—dead or alive—these refined skills saved him on more than one occasion. Furthermore, Collins possessed an uncanny sixth sense that allowed him to size up a person quickly and decide whether that person was trustworthy or had potential access or skills of importance to him. When he decided someone was suited to help his cause, he wasted no time in recruiting that individual. Collins was burned on a few occasions by penetrations and agents provocateurs, but on the whole his senses were right and his methods highly successful, although some might argue that his ferocious personality and imposing physical presence were sufficient to intimidate most men. And this presence helped Collins underscore to all those working for him that disloyalty or treachery would cost them their lives. A brief look at Collins's formative years provides interesting insight to his character and political motivations.

REVOLUTIONARY EDUCATION

Born at Woodfield, a small holding near Sam's Cross in County Cork in 1890, Michael "Mick" Collins was the youngest of five children. His father, John Collins, had been a member of the IRB, or Fenian movement, in the nineteenth century, as had been Collins's elementary school teacher, Denis Lyons. Lyons taught the "illegal" nationalist history of Ireland rather than the approved government version, and thus indoctrinated his pupils with accounts of bold revolutionary acts and the long-held nationalist dream of an independent Irish republic. The Fenian spirit and tradition took hold in the young boy as in so many young Irishmen before him.[4]

In 1906, at age fifteen, Collins passed the civil service exam and moved to London to work in the Post Office Savings Bank at West Kensington Branch. Nancy O'Brien, his cousin from County Cork, was employed at the same bank, and this undoubtedly eased Collins's adjustment to the busy pace of London life. Another fellow Irishman working there was Sam Maguire, who took Collins under his wing and mentored him. In 1910, he left the bank to join Horne & Company, the London stockbrokers, and remained there until August 1914 when he again rejoined the civil service, becoming an accountant at the Board of Trade in Whitehall. By 1915, Collins was contemplating immigration to the United States and, apparently in anticipation of his move to America, he left the Board of Trade and secured an accounting job with the London office of an American firm, Guaranty Trust Company.[5]

Collins continued his education during his London residency, reading history and economics and joining the various Irish nationalist organizations, including the Gaelic Athletic Association (GAA) and Sinn Fein (usually translated as "Ourselves," or "We Alone"). Founded by Irish journalist Arthur Griffith in 1905, Sinn Fein was an Irish nationalist debating society that advocated nonviolent means. Griffith believed that a restoration of the old Irish Parliament and a dual monarchy based on the Austro-Hungarian Empire model was the best path toward restoring Irish nationhood. Collins read voraciously. He took a keen interest in studying Christian de Wet's tactics against the British Army during the Boer War—a war marked by disastrous British miscalculations attributable in part to poor intelligence.[6] It was while attending GAA and Sinn Fein functions in London that Collins met Harry Boland, a dynamic Irish athlete, GAA official, and—secretly—a senior member of the Irish Republican Brotherhood. This association would change Collins's life and alter the course of Irish history.

THE ORGANIZATION

As noted in the introductory chapter, the IRB was founded in 1858 in America by survivors of the 1848 Young Ireland revolt. It was a revolutionary organization binding its members by an oath of secrecy, and its unrelenting purpose was the establishment of an independent Irish republic by force of arms. With its network of informers, Dublin Castle's secret police and Scotland Yard kept the IRB in check throughout the last half of the nineteenth century, although a virulent IRB bombing campaign shook Britain during the 1880s, prompting the establishment of Scotland Yard's Special Irish Branch.[7] By 1900, most IRB operatives had been jailed, hanged, or deported and Fenianism was virtually nonexistent in Ireland at the turn of the century. Only in the United States, where the IRB was known as Clan na Gael, was the aging leadership still actively raising money, recruiting members, and plotting revolt.[8] In 1907, American Fenian leaders met in New York with the recently paroled IRB dynamiter Thomas Clarke. The clan gave Clarke money and asked him to return home to rebuild the organization preparatory to an armed insurrection. Clarke did his job well, recruiting younger members involved in Irish political, literary, and athletic circles, as well as operatives at all levels of civil service throughout the British Isles.[9]

A tightly compartmentalized organization, the reconstituted IRB was headed by a supreme council that set policy, while rank-and-file members belonged to compartmentalized cells, called circles. Each circle was led by a center; only the centers knew all the members of the circle and the identity of their fellow centers. Thus, the revitalized IRB, with its near-paranoid emphasis on secrecy, sobriety, and counterintelligence, formed the natural foundation for Collins's future IRA intelligence service. Significantly for the subsequent revolution, members took an oath pledging fealty to the IRB and recognizing the chief of the IRB supreme council as the president of a free Irish republic. As an eighteen-year-old apprentice banker and civil servant with strong nationalist leanings and an engaging personality, Collins was an ideal candidate for the IRB. In 1909 Harry Boland and Sam Maguire—Collins's mentor at the Post Office Savings

Bank and, secretly, IRB London Center—recruited Collins into the Organization.[10]

Another recruit to the IRB at the time was a middle-aged college math instructor named Eamon de Valera. Born George de Valero in New York in 1882, he was the son of a Spanish father and an illegal alien Irish mother. Although entitled to claim American citizenship, de Valera never did. His father died of tuberculosis while he was an infant and de Valera was taken back to Ireland by an uncle and raised by relatives in Limerick. De Valera grew to become a committed nationalist, although he was never a proactive IRB man. As commander of the last Volunteer unit to surrender during Easter 1916, de Valera was emerging as a national hero and would soon become the preeminent political figure and eventual leader of both Sinn Fein and the Irish Volunteers. His path and Collins's path would remain closely intertwined in the next few years.

De Valera had resisted joining the IRB because he detested its obsessive secrecy and the de facto dual chain of command that the Organization's penetration of the Volunteers had created. After taking command of the Irish Volunteers' Third Battalion before Easter Week, however, de Valera found that subordinate IRB staff officers were receiving intelligence reports that were denied him. De Valera reluctantly joined the IRB simply to get access to the same information. He was sworn in by senior IRB man Sean MacDiarmada (McDermott)—one of the inner circle plotting the revolt. However, de Valera told MacDiarmada that he would attend no secret IRB meetings—and he never did.[11]

By 1914, with war clouds on the horizon and the Home Rule debate raging in Parliament and in Ireland between southern nationalists and Ulster Unionist opponents, Collins enrolled in Number 1 Company of the Irish Volunteers and drilled secretly with them at the German Gymnasium, near St. Pancras–King's Cross Station. The IRB quickly infiltrated the Volunteers, and it was therefore no surprise that Collins quickly advanced to the grade of Staff Captain.[12]

Yet the inner circle of conspirators was in Ireland, not England. The principal IRB ringleaders were Tom Clarke, Sean MacDiarmada, Eamon Ceannt (Kent), Thomas MacDonagh, Joseph Plunkett, and Padraig Pearse. Pearse, who would become the overall commandant in the coming rebellion, was an essayist and schoolteacher who had come to prominence for his mystical nationalist writings, including his book, *From a Hermitage*.[13]

SOCIALISM AND NATIONALISM

Eventually the IRB conspirators were joined by James Connolly of the Irish Transport & General Workers Union (ITGWU). One of the most interesting of the rebel conspirators, Connolly was born in Scotland and was a printer's assistant and tile setter by trade. In his twenties he deserted the British Army while stationed in Ireland and fled to Edinburgh with an Irish bride. After several years of activity in the Scottish Socialist Federation (SSF) and the British Independent Labour Party (ILP), Connolly emerged a militant Marxist. Determined to make politics his life's work, he returned to Ireland in 1896 to found the Irish Socialist Republican Party (ISRP), which promoted a platform upholding socialist labor principles but incorporating radical anticolonial, pro-Irish sentiment. After seven years of hard work, Connolly failed to attract much of a following and he had lost several electoral bids; he and his growing family were in dire poverty. In 1903, he accepted an offer to make a paid speaking tour in the United States and at its conclusion he decided to remain in New York. He first joined the militant Socialist Labour Party (SLP) of Eugene De Leon and later became an organizer for the International Workers of the World (IWW, or "Wobblies").

Bitter doctrinal disagreements with De Leon and disgust with moderate mainstream American labor organizations led to Connolly's disillusionment. In 1910, he returned to Ireland to become an officer in the newly formed ITGWU, led by James "Big Jim" Larkin, a fiery orator and two-fisted brawler. Connolly and Larkin led the union through an ugly transport strike and a six-month-long management lockout in 1913 that paralyzed Dublin commerce but almost destroyed the union. Connolly based his opposition to England on English economic exploitation of the Irish working class and soon had an enthusiastic following of working men. When the First World War erupted, he had confidently predicted that international labor solidarity would prevent workers in the hostile countries from taking up arms against one another. When millions of working men left their jobs to enlist in the British, French, German, Austrian, and Russian armed forces in August 1914, however, Connolly witnessed the triumph of nationalism over the international unionism that had been his life's work. From this point onward, Connolly's internationalist sentiments took a backseat to pure and simple Irish nationalism. He had been impressed by Pearse's *From a Hermitage*, and when the first rumblings of conscription were heard from London in 1914, Connolly committed the ITGWU against it. Connolly had been itching for a class war since the ITGWU's bitter defeat in the 1913 transport strike and lockout. Now he hung a banner on union headquarters proclaiming, "We Serve Neither King Nor Kaiser, But Ireland."[14]

Connolly now threatened his own war on England; toward this end he recruited four hundred union men into a paramilitary force, the Irish Citizen Army (ICA). Smaller by far than the Irish Volunteers, the ICA was nevertheless better disciplined and trained under the stewardship of ex-captain Jack White, a highly decorated combat veteran of the British Army (and Ulster Protestant). As the war in France stretched on, Connolly, ignorant of the IRB's plans, appeared to be goading the Irish Volunteers to take action. He prepared the ICA for armed rebellion and his public speeches grew more inflammatory. Fearful that Connolly might move before the Volunteers were ready, the IRB finally came calling—apparently with revolvers—in January 1916. Connolly disappeared for three days while the Fenians revealed their plans to him and sought his cooperation. By the time Connolly reappeared at union headquarters, he had entered into a political alliance with the same Irish bourgeoisie he had publicly maligned as decadent capitalists for more than twenty years. In exchange for his alliance, the IRB leadership gave him a senior command in the coming rising; from that point on, the Citizen Army was committed to join the Irish Volunteers in the rising. The stage was now set for imminent armed revolt.[15]

When Michael Collins learned through the Organization that the rising was set for Easter Week, 1916, he cancelled his immigration plans, resigned his accounting job, and returned to Dublin.

THE RISING

The 1916 Easter Rising was programmed to fail. Following a frenetic weekend of confusing orders and counterorders, a mere 1,200 Irish Volunteers assembled and calmly marched to government buildings and industrial sites in Dublin and barricaded themselves inside on Easter Monday morning. A proclamation declaring the establishment of a Free Irish Republic was read aloud from the steps of Dublin's General Post Office (GPO) to a sparse crowd of curious and bemused onlookers, and the insurgents settled back to await the arrival of the British Army. The Volunteer leadership made the critical mistake of challenging the British to an open confrontation by bottling themselves up in fixed defensive positions and awaiting the inevitable onslaught. Dressed in their smart uniforms, the Volunteers were armed with a variety of pistols, rifles, a few homemade bombs, and even a medieval pike or two, but they possessed no automatic weapons or artillery of any kind. British regulars—including some veterans of the Western Front—used machine guns and artillery to suppress the poorly trained Volunteers in a week. They also bombarded rebel strongholds with incendiary shells from a Royal Navy gunboat anchored on the Liffey River. Collins was with the Volunteers barricaded inside the GPO and he acquitted himself well during the weeklong fighting.[16]

Collins was impressed with most of the Volunteer leaders surrounding him—the dashing young MacDiarmada, the tough old IRB dynamiter Thomas Clarke, and the fiery James Connolly. He was equally unimpressed with Padraig Pearse. Pearse was no soldier; he was an academic, awkward in mixed company, yet a brilliant thinker who had emerged as the leading revolutionary poet-philosopher of his generation. Obsessed with blood sacrifice, he held the conviction that every generation of Irishmen was obliged to resist the British government by force, even if it amounted to a hopeless cause. To Pearse, it was the symbolism of the sacrifice that mattered. When fighting intensified at the GPO, the delicate Pearse sat down amid the smoke, blood, and gore, took out his notebook, and penned a poem dedicated to his mother.[17]

For all his fervent nationalism, Pearse was, as T. Ryle Dwyer has observed, "an impractical dreamer," and it was no accident that Easter Week was selected for the rising. Just as Jesus was the sacrificial lamb for the sins of humanity, Pearse reasoned the Volunteers might become sacrificial lambs in the cause of Irish nationhood. On the practical side, Pearse had no military experience and, as Dwyer aptly notes, his bearing was less that of a military officer and more that of a Boy Scout leader.[18] And he was someone, it seems, whom most scouts would follow only out of curiosity. As Collins later summed it up:

> On the whole, I think the Rising was bungled terribly costing many a good life. It seemed at first to be well organized, but afterwards became subjected to panic decisions and a great lack of very essential organization and cooperation. . . . Connolly was a realist,

Pearse the direct opposite. There was an air of earthy directness about Connolly. That impressed me. I would have followed him through hell had such action been necessary. But I honestly doubt I could have followed Pearse, not without some thought anyway.[19]

After a week of heavy fighting, the Irish Volunteers found themselves completely surrounded, low on food and ammunition, in need of medical assistance, and no longer able to withstand the withering gunfire and artillery of veteran British troops or the choking smoke and dust emanating from the collapsed and burning buildings of central Dublin. When Pearse finally ordered a white flag to be shown from a GPO window at week's end, Collins was arrested with the others. The Rising was over.

Within a month of the Volunteers' capitulation, the ringleaders—MacDiarmada, Clarke, Ceannt, Plunkett, MacDonagh, Pearse, and Connolly were tried by military courts-martial and executed by firing squad. Although a captain in the Volunteers, Collins had spent the previous ten years in England and was therefore unknown to the sharp-eyed detectives of G Division of the Dublin Metropolitan Police. As they moved among the prisoners identifying the ringleaders, they passed Michael Collins by. Along with the large majority of captured Volunteers, he was shipped immediately and without trial to an English prison.

De Valera's battalion had defended a mill situated along a strategic route on the outskirts of the city. His command had distinguished itself by inflicting the heaviest casualties on the British forces and by being the last to surrender.[20] The authorities jailed de Valera separately from the other ringleaders, apparently by sheer coincidence, and this was likely the foremost reason he was not executed. Moreover, de Valera had not signed the treasonous independence proclamation and there was thus no written documentation on which to base a credible legal conviction for treason as there had been with the other ringleaders. In addition, when de Valera's family revealed to members of the clergy that he had been born in New York City, the authorities were confused about de Valera's citizenship. Desperate to bring the United States into the war against Germany, Downing Street did not want to make the mistake of alienating Washington and millions of Irish Americans by executing a U.S. citizen. De Valera, along with prominent IRB men Thomas Ashe and Harry Boland, remained locked up in Dartmoor Prison or Lewes Jail. The remainder, including Staff Captain Collins, were transferred to a hastily organized internment camp at a filthy former distillery in Frongach, Wales. Seeking to identify other key members of the conspiracy, the British did bring Collins and several other prisoners to London for questioning. But Collins was deemed unimportant, and they returned him to Frongach.[21]

REPUBLICAN UNIVERSITY

It was during his confinement at Frongach that Collins emerged as a dynamic, if overbearing, leader. He established an IRB circle at Frongach to galvanize resistance and, not surprisingly, was elected its center. All of this was at Collins's initiative, without authorization from surviving members of the IRB Supreme Council. His recruiting efforts at Frongach did not meet the strict vetting standards demanded by the Organization. Moreover, his rough, bullying tactics with fellow prisoners would later come back to haunt him when he returned to Ireland and recontacted the IRB Supreme Council in 1917. For the time being, however, these measures seemed to Collins to be the best means of mounting unified resistance at the prison camp. Thus it was that he emerged as spokesman and leader of the Frongach internees.[22]

Many Volunteer veterans referred to Frongach as "Republican University." This was in large part because of Collins's efforts there. His leadership united the prisoners in their resistance to British authority and enforced Republican sentiment. Collins's aggressive tactics annoyed many, including the prison warders and some of the internees. He was a troublemaker, demanding political recognition here, challenging camp regulations there, and above all ensuring discipline among the internees. He organized Irish language classes and lectures, and enforced passive resistance to regulations. The camp consisted of two compounds separated by wire; he helped set up a code system enabling prisoners in the two compounds to communicate. In November he promoted a hunger strike and smuggled out several notes with detailed reports of camp conditions to sympathetic contacts. He did all within his power to enforce IRB control over the internees and, along with other members of the IRB cadre, he kept the Organization alive and maintained the internees' status as political prisoners. It was the first step in reorganizing a movement that would become a revolution. The internees expected and feared being drafted into the British Army. When camp warders began to compile a list of internees' names and addresses, Collins defied them by stepping forward and ordering his fellow prisoners to "shut up and sit down." He then convinced the authorities that the prisoners themselves should prepare the required list, then handed in a roster filled with aliases and false addresses. Not all of the internees appreciated Collins's tactics. It was at prison camp that he would receive the nickname "the Big Fella," and it was not a reference to his height but rather to his ego.[23]

The notes and letters Collins smuggled out reached British and Irish newspapers, resulting in an exposé that caused uproar in the United States and the House of Commons. This in turn contributed to the Crown's decision to grant a general Christmas amnesty to the prisoners in December 1916. Not surprisingly, troublemaker Michael Collins was among the last of the internees to be paroled.[24]

In 1916 the British government convened a commission to investigate the Easter Rising, and in September issued its report, which included a very frank assessment of the government's intelligence shortcomings by Basil Thomson, Chief of Special Branch:

> Intelligence in Ireland is obtained by no less than five public bodies, viz—The Admiralty, War Office (MI5), Irish Command, Royal Irish Constabulary and Dublin Metropolitan Police, and in America by the Home Office, Foreign Office and Royal Irish Constabulary, and . . . although all the material reports may reach the Irish Executive, there is certainly a danger that from lack of co-ordination the Irish Government may be the last Department to receive information of grave moment to the peace of Ireland.[25]

Thomson was certainly in a position to know how poorly the indications and warning intelligence had been handled in Ireland. He and Major Frank Hall of MI5 had sat in on Admiral Blinker Hall's interrogation of Sir Roger Casement in April 1916 when Casement revealed plans for the Rising; yet there is no evidence that Admiral Hall, Thomson, or Major Hall raised any alarm with that "information of grave moment." Thomson's postmortem assessment seems disingenuous at best, and perhaps calculated to promote his own career as he laid plans to nudge MI5 to the sidelines and take over all postwar domestic counterintelligence and countersubversive operations. There is no question that the problems he noted were real. They would soon be his to solve.

4

THE PHOENIX

What a little detail causes a disaster—often it's the details that do it.
—*Michael Collins*

Like the mythical phoenix, the IRB rose from the ashes of Easter Week to become the vanguard and driving force of a renewed physical struggle as the Volunteers reorganized during 1917. With recently released Irish parolees now making their way back to Ireland, British authorities had made a critical mistake in assuming that the IRB was a broken organization and in releasing such desperate physical force separatists such as Cathal Brugha, Thomas Ashe, Richard Mulcahy, Harry Boland, and Eamon de Valera. They also miscalculated in their release of one particularly clever IRB officer named Collins who would soon turn the tables on them, making them the prey not the hunters. All of these men were of like mind; they would renew the fight for independence, and they would not make the same mistakes as the 1916 leaders had; they would not play the game by the traditional rules of war.

Sinn Fein, meanwhile, would coalesce into a revolutionary political party under the leadership of Eamon de Valera to provide a new nationalist political infrastructure. The party would serve the goals of the revolution by promoting dissent, passive resistance, strikes, demonstrations, and a general rejection of the British legal and tax systems. Most important, however, Sinn Fein would become a mechanism for contesting elections—thereby lending political legitimacy to the Republican movement.

Meanwhile, as he gained influence within the IRB, Collins would commence rearming the Irish Volunteers and creating an intelligence service from the ranks of the Organization to support these activities.

NURTURING REVOLUTION

By the time Collins and the majority of Volunteers returned to Ireland in December 1916, the popular mood had changed.[1] The executions of the Volunteer leadership had made heroes of them (as Pearse had envisioned). The Irish public (as well as a significant portion of the British public) was shocked, and angered. Even nonviolent moderates were growing disillusioned with the delays in Home Rule. But voicing discontent or criticizing the Crown was now a much riskier proposition than before Easter 1916. The heavy-handed RIC and the political police of Dublin's G Division had informers everywhere, and those suspected of disloyalty were subject to arrest and imprisonment. Dublin and outlying cities and towns were steadily transformed into occupied camps where the people moved in fear of, rather than in support of, Crown authority.

Collins's first tasks upon winning his freedom were to rejoin the Volunteers and recontact the IRB leadership. The first posed no real problem, but Collins had ruffled feathers in the Organization with his establishment of the Frongach Circle. In addition, although he had fought at the GPO on Easter week, Collins had spent most of the previous ten years in London, and he was still an outsider and an unknown entity to the IRB leadership in Ireland. It took some maneuvering by Collins and careful deliberation by the surviving IRB leadership before they consented to giving Collins a place on the Supreme Council.[2]

REBUILDING THE VOLUNTEERS

Thomas Ashe was a dashing, young high school teacher and IRB officer, whose Volunteer company had performed very effectively in North County Dublin during Easter week. Although he was originally sentenced to death, the British commuted his sentence, and upon his release in the summer of 1917 he ascended to the IRB presidency. Ashe and Collins became allies through their mutual friend Harry Boland; Collins was still relatively unknown in Dublin, and his friendship with Ashe helped to boost his influence. These three realized that if they moved quickly they could exploit growing popular discontent with the government. Having inherited the IRB network of operatives, they set about secretly rearming and reorganizing a revitalized Irish Volunteer Army.[3]

Similar reorganization occurred in the outlying counties, independent of efforts in Dublin. Rapid reorganization and election of officers had begun in earnest in 1917 and continued into 1918. In March 1917, Richard Mulcahy and Collins selected young medical student and IRB member Ernest O'Malley from the Dublin Brigade to undertake a formal program of organizing Volunteer companies and training IRA officers in the outlying provinces. Reporting directly to Collins, O'Malley set up secret officer instruction camps in counties Tyrone, Leix, Offaly, Roscommon, Donegal, Clare, Monaghan, Limerick, and Tipperary over the next eighteen months. He soon learned that levels of enthusiasm, skill, and leadership were uneven among country Volunteer officer cadre. Some gladly accepted his assistance; others merely tolerated his presence. This type of attitude would later result in serious policy disagreements between provincial Volunteer leadership and IRA General Headquarters (GHQ). When war finally came, GHQ had little actual influence over IRA leaders in the outlying counties who were reluctant to follow the direction of outsiders who did not understand local conditions. As historian Michael Hopkinson points out, while the leading Cork IRA leaders eventually aligned their operations to comply with GHQ's wishes, some units in County Tipperary never did.[4]

Collins was firm in his determination that the new Volunteers understand the concept of guerrilla warfare: stage unconventional hit-and-run attacks to inflict as many casualties as possible and then disappear into the countryside, thus keeping the enemy off guard and demoralized. Not every Volunteer leader accepted this strategy; some believed that ambushes were a cowardly—even immoral—form of warfare. Some, like 1916 heroes Eamon de Valera and Cathal Brugha, would ascend to senior political rank in the revolutionary government and their disagreement with Collins's unconventional strategy would lead to bitter confrontations in the years to come.

The IRB Supreme Council approved a revised constitution in Dublin shortly after the last prisoners were released from detention in June 1917. The document stated that the organization would not subordinate itself to any other nationalist organization. The leadership also formed a permanent military council for the reconstituted Irish Volunteers—something lacking in 1916—and placed it firmly under IRB control.[5] This set the stage for a series of political intrigues as the IRB once again began to infiltrate and take over moderate Irish nationalist elements. When the first Irish Parliament, Dail Eireann, was established two years later, the IRB would have to modify its constitution yet again to accommodate the political wing of the revolution. But in the minds of all IRB members, the president of the IRB would always be the true representative of the Irish Republic.

Thomas Ashe was arrested by the RIC for seditious activity in the fall of 1917. During a subsequent hunger strike, he died after prison warders botched an attempt to force-feed him. This resulted in an IRB-inspired national uproar, accompanied by a mass street demonstration during Ashe's funeral in Dublin. Sean McGarry briefly assumed the IRB leadership until he too was caught in a police raid. The leadership of the IRB physical-force element thus devolved upon Harry Boland and Michael Collins. Boland and Collins had become the best of friends and worked well together. They quickly agreed to a division of labor: Boland taking the lead in the IRB's political work and Collins taking the lead in reorganizing the Volunteers.[6]

WE ALONE

De Valera also returned to Ireland following the amnesty, equally determined to have a leading role in renewing the struggle. Unlike Collins and other physical-force separatists, however, de Valera dropped out of the IRB and began to concentrate on creating a political infrastructure to challenge the old Irish Parliamentary Party at Westminster and seize the political initiative against Britain. This infrastructure centered on Sinn Fein. But whereas founder Arthur Griffith had espoused a nonviolent transition from Unionism to a dual monarchy for England and Ireland, de Valera, Collins, and other veterans of 1916 would transform Sinn Fein into a revolutionary party.

Although de Valera had resigned from the IRB, and was focusing his efforts on developing political opposition to British rule, these activities made him no less a rebel. He was still an Irish Volunteer, and he acknowledged the importance of armed force to the Irish revolutionary tradition.

He was in agreement with other separatists on the need to challenge British authority, including military authority, but he also pinned his hopes on world opinion and recognition of an independent Ireland by the victorious Allies. Moreover, he tended to think in conventional military terms. No one knew better than de Valera the folly of trying to defeat the British Army in a stand-up battle. His memories of challenging British machine guns with unreliable Ross rifles and secondhand German Mausers during Easter Week may have convinced him that the IRB's strategy of 1916 was no longer valid. But if a conventional military confrontation with the British was unrealistic, how should Irish separatists proceed? And would the political movement take precedence over a military strategy?

It is possible that de Valera may not have discerned the potential effectiveness of a guerrilla campaign in the same way that Collins envisioned it. Or perhaps he understood all too well what an underground guerrilla conflict would mean and hoped to distance himself from it. In any event, de Valera mistrusted the obsessive secrecy of the IRB and found the concept of political assassination abhorrent. He was therefore inclined to build up and maintain the Volunteers as a show of national determination, but to avoid actual armed conflict as much as possible—and to engage the British in open skirmishes only when the odds were overwhelmingly in the Volunteers' favor, while fomenting a political revolution. Toward that end, de Valera idealistically hoped that Woodrow Wilson's celebrated advocacy of self-determination for small countries would be applied to Ireland in the postwar world.[7]

It was therefore critically important to de Valera that a new nationalist revolutionary party be formed as soon as possible to challenge the old Irish Parliamentary Party and become the standard-bearer of the revolution. Sinn Fein would become that party, the legal representative of political dissent, and, ultimately, the official voice of rebellion. Collins had joined Sinn Fein as a young clerk in London and was practically a charter member. Just as MacDiarmada, Clarke, and the leaders of the Rising had ensured that the Volunteers were dominated by the IRB before 1916, Collins, Ashe, and Boland wanted to ensure that Sinn Fein would be controlled by the IRB and linked to the armed struggle for the remainder of the conflict. It would not be so simple.

Their efforts to orchestrate an IRB takeover of Sinn Fein during its October 1917 convention failed miserably. Griffith stepped aside in favor of de Valera as president of the party, but only three IRB men—Collins, Boland, and Diarmud (Jeremiah) Lynch—succeeded in manipulating their own election to the twenty-four-member Executive Council.[8] While their intended coup d'état did not materialize, their elevation to the party executive level nevertheless ensured that de Valera and the political faction could not ignore them. De Valera would thus emerge as the principal moderate of the revolution; Collins would represent the physical-force element. This radicalization and reshaping of Sinn Fein was a marriage of convenience—but just barely so.

Two days later, a Volunteer convention met to select new leadership and to decide how to proceed in the event the government should introduce conscription in Ireland. An Executive Council was formed and de Valera was elected president. Collins angled for chief of staff—effectively the overall commander—but again his ambition was foiled by backroom maneuvering. Reports from Frongach veterans included his enrollment of dozens of new members into the IRB without having conducted proper vetting. Collins's pushy, ambitious reputation, as well as his frequent use of foul language, apparently also preceded him to the convention. Veteran Volunteer officers Dick McKee and Richard Mulcahy had agreed beforehand that Mulcahy should be elected to the top post, and that is what happened. Collins had to settle for two relatively minor posts: Adjutant General and Director of Organization. As Mulcahy recalled,

> McKee, as he came away from the meeting with me expressed satisfaction and relief that Collins was not being recommended. The main reason for this was that in the light of what he knew of Collins's temperament, and the short period and the circumstances in which my information about him had been outlined, McKee—like the others—was a little bit wary of entrusting him with anything like complete control. In fact he did want time to disclose himself and his qualities.[9]

A prime purpose for calling this meeting was to empower the Volunteer Executive to declare war, should the British introduce conscription. The Volunteers began to organize into regionally based divisions and brigades. Pax O Faolain (Whelan) of Dungarven, County Waterford, had joined the Volunteers in 1913 and was second in command of an IRA

flying column throughout the Anglo-Irish War. He recalled this rebuild-
ing phase of 1917–1918:

> As soon as the release took place after the Rising, re-organization
> recommenced. Groups became companies, companies became bat-
> talions and battalions became brigades. They were all subject to
> control from Dublin. Every one of us was subscribing to buy a rifle.
> In 1917 I was arrested for taking a rifle from a soldier. I walked into
> his house and removed it. At that time they were allowed to take
> them home, but with the increasing tension in the country, that
> soon ended.
>
> Anyway myself and another chap were remanded to the jail in
> Waterford. . . . Eventually we were released as they were unable to
> prove anything against us.[10]

Meanwhile, despite holding the top executive positions in Sinn Fein
and the Volunteers, de Valera's primary strategy remained that of gaining
recognition by the Allies for Ireland at the end of hostilities on the Western Front. He was clearly concerned that a preemptive military operation
by the Volunteers could destroy this initiative and, with support from
other moderates, he managed to keep the IRB in check for the time being.
Collins—still relatively unknown—participated in a delegation to London
in an effort to get an audience with President Wilson in December 1918, but
the American president refused to meet with them (see appendix A).[11]

While Collins was passed over for Chief of Staff, his appointment as
Adjutant General and Director of Organization placed him in charge of
training and rearming the Volunteers—functions that he exploited to his
advantage. Animosity began to fester between Collins and Brugha, who
grew to distrust the IRB and was uncertain about guerrilla tactics. The
tension between the two would escalate over the next few years as Brugha
was destined to become Minister of Defence in the revolutionary government.

Despite these tensions, de Valera and Brugha recognized that Collins's powerful position in the IRB made him the only real choice to take
charge of intelligence matters. No one objected when Collins, as Director
of Organization, began to organize a formal intelligence section within
the Volunteer Headquarters Staff. Attorney Eamon Duggan had been the

Volunteers' first head of intelligence, but he brought no energy to the post and had only one officer working for him. Collins took up the post with characteristic élan.[12] In 1919, this portfolio would be formalized when de Valera appointed Collins Director of Information in the Dail Eireann cabinet.

With the death of Ashe and jailing of McGarry, Boland assumed leadership of the IRB Supreme Council and he and Collins began to take matters into their own hands. Boland concentrated on political affairs, and Collins tackled military and intelligence matters. That division notwithstanding, Collins was among the most active speakers on behalf of Sinn Fein at rallies and meetings across the country. Collins was beginning to prove his revolutionary bona fides to doubting members of the Volunteer Executive. At the same time, however, he was raising his profile to a dangerous level, particularly for the new head of Volunteer intelligence. Collins had not yet gone on the run, but it was only a matter of time before he would be compelled to adopt a clandestine life.

As Mackay has noted, de Valera emerged with supreme power over the party and the army by the close of 1917, and the battle lines had been drawn.[13]

CREATING AN INTELLIGENCE SERVICE

As an increasingly powerful member of the IRB Supreme Council, Collins had that organization's network of cooperative contacts and informers at his fingertips. He could count on shopkeepers, locomotive engineers, brewers, dairymen, seamen, streetcar conductors, farmers, fishermen, hotel clerks, and maids to report to him. Even the Fianna—the Irish Boy Scouts —served as IRB couriers, as did the Cumann-na-mBan, or Irish Volunteer Women's League, a paramilitary Volunteer auxilliary corps.[14] Collins spent the balance of 1917 developing this network and crafting an improved intelligence-gathering organization.

Collins knew that simply relying on a passive network of informers, no matter how widespread, would be insufficient to support the proactive guerrilla campaign he envisioned. During the nineteenth century, IRB plans had been repeatedly compromised almost single-handedly by a single British agent, Henri Le Caron, and Collins realized how much damage just one British penetration could do to the movement. Now that Sinn Fein was galvanizing nationalist resolve, opening the possibility for a popularly supported insurgency campaign, there was too much at stake to depend solely on the old IRB network. He envisioned a new intelligence organization that would bring a centralized structure and professional discipline to the business of intelligence.[15]

Collins set up a full-time intelligence section within the Volunteer staff and manned it with trusted IRB members. Liam Tobin became Deputy Director of GHQ Intelligence Staff and established an underground office above a bookstore on Dublin's Crow Street. Later a second office was established at Number 5, Mespil Road. Volunteers Frank Thornton and Tom Cullen were Tobin's deputies. Other members of GHQ intelligence staff included Charlie Dalton, Joe Dolan, Dan McDonnell, and Joe Guilfoy. Joe O'Reilly, a fellow Corkman who had worked with Collins in the civil service, fought in 1916, and was interned at Frongach, became Collins's bodyguard, courier, counselor, and general guardian angel. Sinead Mason, a devoted and sensible woman, served as Collins's correspondence secretary and reportedly worked twelve-hour days throughout the war.[16]

David Neligan, who would become one of Collins's most important agents, described Liam Tobin, Collins's deputy:

> Tall, gaunt, cynical, with tragic eyes, he looked a man who had seen the inside of hell. He walked without moving his arms and seemed emptied of energy. Yet this man was, after Collins, the Castle's most dangerous enemy. Like all of us, a poor man, an ex-shop assistant, he had a great flair for intelligence work and was Collins' chief assistant. He ran a secret intelligence office within a stone's throw of the Castle. It was never discovered by the British. Untrained or self-trained as he was, he was an efficient counter-espionage agent and I believe would have been worth his place in any intelligence bureau.[17]

With expansion of his staff organization, Collins increased the number of safe houses, hotels, and pubs available for operational work in metropolitan Dublin and elsewhere. He referred to these venues collectively as his "joints," and each was numbered. The only person who always knew Collins's whereabouts was his private assistant, Joe O'Reilly; consequently, whenever Collins was off visiting one of his "joints," only O'Reilly could be relied upon to reach him. With the assistance of his close friend,

IRB man and master builder Batt O'Connor, Collins ordered custom-built concealment cavities installed in some of the safe houses. O'Connor also built a vault concealed beneath the floor of his own Dublin residence to hide operating funds, and also built several concealment cavities at Sinn Fein headquarters in Harcourt Street.[18]

It is noteworthy that many historians have seen IRA GHQ intelligence staff primarily as a counterintelligence effort, and initially this was so. The organization that evolved, however, was considerably broader in scope.

COVER AND TRADECRAFT

For three years, Collins and his staff used both aliases and pseudonyms to carry out their work from safe houses across central Dublin and the suburbs under the noses of the police and British intelligence. Recruited assets were assigned both number codes and codewords. Dressed in a neat pinstripe suit, Collins roamed daily throughout Dublin on a bicycle, masquerading as a respectable businessman. He employed aliases and used a pseudonym in written communications. Similar pseudonyms were created for key members of Sinn Fein and the Volunteers.[19] Following the establishment of the revolutionary cabinet under de Valera in 1919, Collins eventually maintained three separate offices, one for each of the portfolios he would hold: Minister of Finance; Adjutant General and Director of Organization of the Irish Volunteers (later called the IRA); and Director of Information (Intelligence). He used pubs, hotel rooms, and safe houses to conduct most of his business and never visited Tobin's intelligence office on Crow Street. Collins often traveled armed, and with incriminating papers on his person. Although police and army roadblocks stopped him more than once, he had some remarkable escapes, always relying on his quick wit and winning smile to talk his way through.

When the British later offered a £10,000 reward for the perpetrators of IRA attacks on the police, Collins discovered that no one in the police or intelligence services had a good photograph of him or even a clue where to look for him. His ordinary businesslike appearance in the crowded streets of Dublin enabled him to remain anonymous and operate within the shadow of Dublin Castle with relative impunity, at least in the early years.

To cover his activities Collins adopted the alias persona "John Grace" and secured a job as secretary of the Irish Volunteer National Aid Fund —

Figure 2. Structure of IRA Intelligence 1919–1921

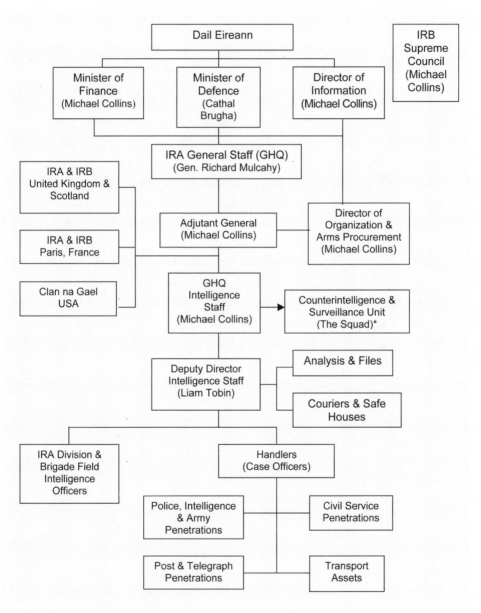

* Detached from Dublin Brigade

a legal pension organization that looked after the welfare of Irish Volunteers killed or incarcerated after the 1916 Easter Rising. Collins moved throughout the country with relative ease, secretly reorganizing, arming, and training Volunteer units, speaking at Sinn Fein rallies, and extending his intelligence network. An officer in each company was notionally responsible for intelligence, but coverage was uneven. Some of the more important of these regional intelligence officers included Florrence O'Donoghue and Sean Culhane in Cork, Frank Saurin in County Dublin, Sean Treacy and Dan Breen in County Tipperary, Gus Colgan in County Wicklow, and Seamus O'Maoileoin in Limerick. O'Donoghue ran the most organized intelligence section outside of Dublin. He had proceeded independently to set up an intelligence apparatus within the Cork No. 1 Brigade by 1919 and began close collaboration with Collins's Dublin organization by the spring of 1920.[20]

In London, IRB leader Sam Maguire served as Collins's overall intelligence chief for England, while Steve Lanigan was the IRB Center in Liverpool. The IRB had units in all British and Scottish cities, in Belfast, and in Paris and some other continental locations. As Volunteer training resumed with intensity throughout 1917, Collins also sent agents to the continent to set up arms-smuggling networks.[21]

GUN RUNNERS

Liam Mellowes and Sean MacBride were two IRB officers who served Collins extremely well. Mellowes was a longtime IRB member and veteran Volunteer who had escaped to the United States after taking part in the Easter Rising. There, he worked tirelessly to organize funds and procure weapons for the Volunteers until he was arrested and jailed without trial in 1917 for communicating with the German government—seditious activity in the view of the U.S. Bureau of Investigation, the FBI's forerunner. Following his release from New York City's infamous Tombs jail in 1918, Mellowes returned to Dublin and threw himself into reorganizing work. With his international experience and contacts, Mellowes was the natural choice to become "director of supplies"—a euphemistic title for an intense IRA covert arms acquisition program, a high-risk intelligence specialty that requires considerable long-term planning, attention to detail, financial savvy, and vigilance against myriad counterintelligence threats.

MacBride was a sixteen-year-old Volunteer whose father had been executed for his role in the Easter Rising. Raised and educated in Paris, the younger MacBride spoke fluent French and his English was tinged with a decidedly French accent. This made him an attractive candidate for intelligence work and he eventually became a staff captain on Collins's staff. He was very close to Collins throughout the war and was frequently present at intelligence meetings. MacBride was one of Collins's valued jacks-of-all-trades, engaged in training Volunteers here, leading an ambush there, and handling highly sensitive courier assignments seemingly everywhere. Eventually Collins asked MacBride to assist Mellowes in arms acquisition operations and they made a solid team. MacBride could easily pass as a French citizen, giving him international mobility that other IRA operatives lacked. Together with Mellowes's chutzpah, the two succeeded in acquiring large quantities of weapons and ordnance from Germany. MacBride later claimed to have covertly delivered four arms shipments to the IRA by the end of hostilities, concealing the cargoes in the holds of freighters and fishing trawlers. Shortages continued to plague the IRA's efforts right up to the cease-fire, however.[22]

By 1918, Collins had already significantly expanded the Volunteer intelligence service. Before long it would prove critical to the survival of the movement.

5

REVOLUTION IN EARNEST

The right place for the bullet from an Irish rifle is in the
heart of an Englishman.

*— Father Gaynor, parish priest, at a Sinn Fein
Anti-Conscription Rally in Tipperary, 1918*

In all revolutions there is invariably some event or series of events that
serves as a catalyst to move people from ideas to action. In America, it
was enactment of an unpopular colonial tax policy that led to armed confrontation. In France, the simple scarcity of bread sparked the riot that
led to the storming of the Bastille. The agitation of Marx and the Communist League is seen as a catalyst for widespread revolutionary movements
across Europe in 1848. In Ireland, the chain of events was dramatic and no
less profound. They were Lloyd George's proposal in the spring of 1918
to introduce military conscription into Ireland, followed shortly thereafter by a misguided and alarmist British intelligence assessment known
as the German Plot that led to direct government suppression of Sinn
Fein.

RESISTING THE DRAFT

When Germany launched its final great offensive on the Western Front in
the spring of 1918, Britain's military manpower was stretched to the limit.
The government therefore proposed to introduce an army Conscription

Act for Ireland. While some 300,000 Irishmen had volunteered to join British regiments to fight the Germans since 1914 (including many Irish Volunteers), the notion that the Crown could establish a draft in Ireland was unacceptable to most Irish citizens. Popular resistance to British rule stiffened overnight. Sinn Fein launched protest demonstrations across the country. In the ensuing months, anti-British sentiment reached a boiling point, and the government tabled the suggestion for the time being.

Collins was arrested after a visit to County Longford in early March of 1918. He had been the featured speaker at a Sinn Fein rally of about three hundred people in the village of Legga. He addressed the crowd for perhaps ten minutes, concluding his remarks with a sarcastic, veiled threat that Irishmen would resist conscription by force if necessary:

> The British government is at its wits [*sic*] end now about the man-power question of the Empire. Ireland too is thinking about her manpower. Emigration has ceased for the past few years and it has increased considerably. The Irish Party [in Westminster] claims to have defeated conscription but I claim it was the men of Easter Week who defeated it. The cabinet might attempt to do it again but it will take five soldiers to take one man and 50,000 with fixed bayonets to enforce it on Ireland. I will say to the Irish Volunteers if such is attempted, stand together and remember Thomas Ashe.[1]

Following these remarks, Collins read out a general order to the local Volunteers prohibiting the raiding of private homes for arms and the harassment of local cattle owners. Then Collins remarked, "When Volunteers do raid for arms, they will go where they will find ones that will be of some use to them." He concluded the rally by reviewing the eighty-eight Volunteers assembled. He thought no more about the day's events, but local RIC constables had taken copious notes.

On April 2, Collins had an opportunity to get acquainted with a few members of the Castle's secret police when he was arrested by two G Division detectives outside the National Aid Fund offices in Dublin. Charged under provisions of the Defence of the Realm Act (DORA) for inciting citizens to raid for arms, he was incarcerated in Dublin, then remanded back to Longford to face a magistrate. Addressing the court, Collins first took the standard Republican position of denying the authority of a British court to judge him. In response to his charge, he read out the general order he had read at Legga but did not mention his added remarks afterward, which were the basis of the charge against him. The judge set trial for July and Collins was offered release on £40 bail. Collins refused, again challenging the authority of the court, declaring, "I don't enter into bail with blackguards and tyrants."[2]

Peter Hart has pointed out that it was a minor criminal charge and he derides Collins's courtroom defiance as rather theatrical under the circumstances. Yet, here was the old troublemaker of Frongach days. While one could criticize Collins for his egotistical heroics, he at least was consistent in his purpose, and this is one factor that propelled him to leadership. At the end of this day, however, his heroic stand had landed him in jail for another week, after which he was summarily ordered to leave on bail. After spending several miserable days in a cramped, dank cell, his enthusiasm ebbed. Collins was a man who could not tolerate confinement like this. At least in Frongach the prisoners were allowed to move around a large compound. Here, Collins sat alone, mostly incommunicado, no surrounding audience to entertain with ribald humor, no malleable warders to bribe or mock, no one to wrestle or browbeat. Besides, with important work to do on the outside, Collins wanted to get on with his revolution. He quietly relented to the court order and was released on bail. Now at least he could say that he had twice been jailed for Ireland. He skipped the trial in Longford and went on the run. He would remain underground for more than three years, but he never behaved like a man on the run.[3]

In April 1918, Eamon de Valera organized an all-Irish conference of nationalist organizations to condemn the draft bill and formulate a response to the prime minister. The document issued from the conference contained strong separatist language and condemned the British government.[4] At last, Downing Street realized the situation in Ireland was spinning out of control; the Conscription Act could not be implemented so long as de Valera and Sinn Fein kept things in an uproar. Then, a misguided intelligence assessment launched by NID's Blinker Hall, accusing Sinn Fein of being a German front, was delivered to Downing Street. While Hall may have believed that his intelligence added up to a conspiracy, his assessment was typical shoot-from-the hip work, and it is likely that Hall hoped once again to influence policy by inducing the government to act against

Irish nationalists. The cabinet would use Hall's alleged German Plot as its pretext for rounding up the Sinn Fein leadership.[5]

WALK-INS

Against this backdrop, Collins had a remarkable stroke of luck. Sergeant Eamon "Ned" Broy, a young detective from G Division, had been sending notes to the separatists through a Sinn Fein cutout since 1916 and had been trying to make contact with the mysterious Michael Collins for months.[6] Broy's approach was understandably met with skepticism, but when the detective learned of the German Plot and impending arrest of the Sinn Fein leadership, he passed on a note with the details that in turn was delivered to Collins on May 15th.[7]

Collins then got another opening. Unbeknownst to Broy, for the previous two years sixty-year-old Detective Sergeant Joe Kavanagh, also of G Division, had been trying without success to contact the IRB to share confidential police information. GHQ intelligence staff had made note of Kavanagh's apparent sympathy for Sinn Fein; the detective had been present when authorities rounded up the Easter insurgents in 1916, and had moved among them whispering encouragement and offering to relay messages to their families. Despite this, Kavanagh was not trusted.

Collins moved cautiously with Broy and Kavanagh for good reason. G Division was the principal spy service for the Castle in metro Dublin. Operating from their headquarters in Great Brunswick Street, the plainclothes detectives were armed and known as G men, a phrase coined in Ireland long before the American gangster George "Machine Gun" Kelly applied that moniker to special agents of the FBI. According to David Neligan, an IRA-controlled double agent inside G Division, it was organized into two branches: the first investigated major nonpolitical crime such as murder and robbery. The other branch investigated political crime, and kept tabs on subversives and revolutionaries, functioning, in Neligan's words, as a "secret police."[8]

Smaller than Scotland Yard's Special Branch, G Division was a dozen years older than the British service, having been formed to disrupt the activities of the Fenian Brotherhood at the time of Sir Robert Anderson's investigations in the 1860s. G Division had a normal complement of about forty detectives between its two branches, but according to Neligan only a handful of these were actually engaged in political work. Following the successful roundup of the 1916 Easter Rising ringleaders, the Castle admin-istration apparently believed it had eliminated the threat, and dozens of G men were reassigned. Later, when Collins's counterintelligence squad commenced direct attacks against G Division, the unit was reinforced by about a dozen new detectives promoted from the uniformed ranks.[9]

G men conducted surveillance of rail stations, hotels, and the port areas, handled street informers, and apprehended and interrogated those involved in subversive or illegal political activity. Although not trained in clandestine penetration operations per se, G Division detectives were smart, experienced, resourceful, tough, and brave, with impeccable knowl-edge of local conditions and terrain—and a superb track record against internal subversives dating back more than sixty years. Although native Irishmen, members of G Division were carefully vetted and were pre-dominantly Protestant. All members were required to swear an oath stating they belonged to no secret societies—freemasonry being the only exception.[10]

Collins recognized the threat posed by G Division but he also assessed its vulnerabilities. Some of its cops were certain to be sympathetic to Sinn Fein, and others vulnerable to intimidation. He recognized that they were poorly paid and also that a certain percentage of all civil servants were liable to be lazy, bureaucratic, or corrupt. At this stage, he could only hope that threats might convince most of them to resign or stall their investiga-tions of Sinn Fein. But he certainly knew that most would not lie down on the job and these would have to be dealt with.[11]

In April 1918, Kavanagh also learned of the German Plot and had tried repeatedly to warn Collins. Though mistrusted as an agent provoca-teur for the Castle, Kavanagh persisted and at last was directed to Thomas Gay, manager of Dublin's Capel Street public library. From outward ap-pearance, Gay was a mild-mannered and innocuous bookworm; in fact, he was a veteran Volunteer who had fought in 1916, had been interned at Frongach, and was a key IRB operative. He also served as an IRB courier, and Collins used his home as a safe house.[12]

With a police pension on the line, not to mention the welfare of his wife and children, Kavanagh was taking an extraordinary risk. Events moved cautiously. When Gay relayed Kavanagh's German Plot informa-tion, Collins's staff remained skeptical. Collins sent a £5 note to Kavanagh, only to have Gay return the funds the same evening, explaining that the detective had refused to accept it. Hearing this, Collins overruled his staff and decided to meet personally with the G man. Gay arranged the rendezvous at his home. After meeting with Kavanagh, Collins recruited his first significant penetration of the British intelligence system. On May 18, Kavanagh reported that the raids were set to take place that night.[13]

Within days two secret police walk-ins had independently provided Collins with the same list and date for the raids. With this corroborating intelligence in hand, Collins informed the Volunteer Executive at an emergency meeting. De Valera was still heavily engaged in the anticonscription fight, however, and was reluctant to go underground in spite of the clear intelligence. Consequently, Crown forces had no difficulty locating them and rounding them up in the subsequent raid. Both Collins and Boland were on the police list; they took evasive action and escaped the dragnet. For his part, double agent Broy was furious that he had risked his life to pass on the arrest list but had not been trusted:

> I had a list of suspects who were to have been arrested. Forty-eight hours before the correct date I handed on the list. . . . I was brought to the Castle and put on the phone. I listened to an account of the arrests that were being made. I was cursing, for none of them seemed to have got out of the ring. . . . "They are cods, these Sinn Feiners," I said. "They don't mean anything, they won't trust a source."[14]

Sergeant Broy, as confidential clerk for G Division, was in a particularly sensitive position. It was his job to review and type up all G Division reports. IRA intelligence apparently vetted Broy for a considerable length of time, for as Dwyer notes, Collins did not meet the detective face to face until early January 1919. Coogan quotes a contemporary observer's description of Broy:

> A strongly built, broad-shouldered and stiff backed man entered the room. . . . I found it difficult to believe that this gauche, ill-at-ease, obsequious person was Ned Broy, the famous "G" man who had turned traitor and wilily [sic] double-crossed his British masters, But not for long: soon I was convinced that his hard, cruel green eyes were indicative of his character.[15]

Eventually Collins agreed to meet Broy. During their initial encounter, the plucky detective took one look at Collins and pointedly informed him that he would have to buy a better quality suit if he hoped to avoid the attention of the police. This brash introduction immediately won Collins's confidence. Broy later recalled his first encounter with the Big Fella:

> I was filled with curiosity. Would this Michael Collins be the ideal man I had been dreaming of for a couple of years? Looking up the police record book to see what was known about him, I discovered that he was a six footer, a Corkman, very intelligent, young and powerful. There was no photograph of him at the time in the records book. . . . I had studied for so long the type of man that I would need to act efficiently, that the moment I saw Michael at the door, before he had time to walk across and to shake hands, I knew he was the man. . . . He was very handsome, obviously full of energy and with a mind quick as lightning. . . . I had a long talk with Mick from 8 o'clock until midnight. He thanked me for all the documents I had sent and all the information, and said it was of the utmost assistance and importance to them.[16]

Since Broy was in charge of the file room, Collins tasked him to provide copies of all confidential police reports. Broy complied by inserting an extra carbon into his typewriter as he transcribed the reports.[17]

Collins personally handled Kavanagh and Broy initially, but he was careful to keep the two cases compartmentalized so that neither asset was aware of the other's role for the IRA. Later, when IRA attacks on G Division began, it became necessary to inform the two detectives of each other's association with Collins in order to protect them from internal missteps.

Over time, additional police sources came under Collins's control. In addition to Broy and Kavanagh of G Division, Collins and his staff recruited police officers across the country. These included Sergeant Maurice ("Matt") McCarthy and Detective Pat Stapleton of the Belfast RIC. Also spying for the IRA were seven members of the DMP uniformed division: Sergeant Mannix and Constables O'Sullivan, Tim Neary, Patrick Byrne, T. J. McElligott, and two brothers named Culhane. Constables Jerry Maher and Patrick Casey of the RIC were also working with Collins, as was

Sergeant Thomas O'Rourke, a member of the RIC Crimes Special Branch based in County Kerry. Some of these officers were of special value to the IRA. McCarthy had access to the RIC codes and to documentary information along the same lines as Kavanagh and Broy in Dublin; his assistance later proved to be of critical value to Collins in eliminating the head of G Division. Frank Thornton of GHQ intelligence staff was McCarthy's handler. Constable Maher worked as a clerk in the Dublin District Inspector's Office, where he had access to the police codes. O'Rourke in Kerry was able to supply the RIC Crimes Special Branch code key. With such agents, Collins would often have a DMP or RIC message intercepted and decoded before the original message reached its intended recipients.[18]

Kavanagh was in ill health and would die within a year. Before he died, however, he recruited his own replacement, Detective Sergeant James MacNamara. Like Collins's association with Broy and Kavanagh, MacNamara's work for Collins was compartmentalized for his safety, until it became necessary to advise him about the other G Division penetrations.[19]

BUILDING MOMENTUM

The roundup of Sinn Fein leadership in May 1918 backfired. Most nationalists recognized the German Plot for what it was. This event, coupled with widespread disillusionment over delays in Home Rule, eroded the public faith in the British administration, even among moderates. Sinn Fein was the rallying standard for anti-British sentiment across the country; it organized demonstrations, established banks, courts, and other institutions of civil administration, in effect setting up a shadow government in many counties throughout Ireland. The populace increasingly refused to recognize the administrative and legal authority of the Crown and turned to Sinn Fein to settle civil matters.

The most essential element of any successful insurgency—that of winning hearts and minds—had been largely achieved by the end of 1918. The vast majority of the people of southern Ireland united in their resistance to the draft, in their eroding obedience to Crown authority, and in their selection of Sinn Fein candidates at the polls. It remained only to convince London to recognize Ireland as a separate country, and nationalist leaders, foremost among them de Valera, hoped this could be done through international political pressure. Ulster remained the sticking point in de Valera's plan. It was clear that the majority of people in the northernmost province would resist joining any independent Irish republic, even in the unlikely event it were to be mandated by a postwar political formula imposed by the Great Powers. Collins the realist and IRB members of similar mind understood this, and remained convinced that full independence could only be accomplished by war. Toward this end the IRB stepped up preparations, arming and training the IRA. IRA veteran Dan Gleeson, in a newly raised Volunteer company in Toomevara, County Tipperary, described the atmosphere there from May to December 1918, which was typical of developments across the country:

> England now made the mistake of increasing the momentum to fever pitch. Early in 1918, she threatened to impose conscription. It was the greatest boost we could have got. They all flocked in. I remember the massive demonstrations; I remember one in Nenagh, everyone wearing badges, *Death Before Conscription*. Priests, professional men, and everybody were on the platforms. There was a Father Gaynor . . . and I remember him declaring — "The right place for the bullet from an Irish rifle is in the heart of an Englishman." Needless to say, that went down well. From now on we were perfecting a proper military machine through training classes, raiding for arms, intelligence and arranging dumps, supplies and transport. We were gradually moving from a phase of uneasy peace to one of hostilities.[20]

It was not surprising to anyone but the British government, therefore, that Sinn Fein captured seventy-three seats from the Irish Parliamentary Party in the general election of December 1918. However, the Sinn Fein delegates (many of whom were in jail) refused to take their seats at Westminster and instead formed an "abstentionist" parliament, the Dail Eireann.[21]

The tension in London following Sinn Fein's December 1918 electoral victory was palpable. The Lloyd George cabinet was still engaged in pressing postwar matters. They had not been prepared for the draft resistance in Ireland the previous spring, they had not been prepared for the

Sinn Fein electoral sweep, and they knew precious little about the latest crop of Irish nationalists—Griffith, de Valera, Collins, and the rest.

On January 21, 1919, the new Dail Eireann government issued a Declaration of Independence of the Irish Republic. De Valera—still imprisoned in Lincoln Jail—was elected Dail Prime Minister. With the formal creation of the Dail government, the Irish Volunteers became, de facto, the Army of the Irish Republic or, more commonly, the Irish Republican Army (IRA).[22]

London had miscalculated. In the two years since the Easter Rising, British intelligence seems to have focused on the wrong targets. Instead of worrying about the IRB, the Irish Volunteers, or Sinn Fein, the British concentrated on tracking German agents and suspected Bolsheviks, seemingly oblivious to the tempest brewing within the Irish nationalist movement. Basil Thomson was receiving intelligence reports from Rex Benson—his man at Dublin Castle—that Sinn Fein was growing stronger. In Thomson's view, this was due to a lenient policy by the chief of the army's Irish Command since Easter 1916. In July of that year he had recommended the introduction of an entry permit system to prohibit foreign and Irish conspirators from reentering Ireland from the United States, believing, apparently, that the center of agitation still lay in Boston, New York, and Chicago. He was apparently too busy running agents in Holland, Norway, and even Africa to grasp that the Irish nationalist center of gravity had shifted, first to Frongach internment camp and later to Dublin.[23]

Thus, Sinn Fein's electoral sweep in December 1918, and the establishment of the Dail government and its Declaration of Independence the following month, came as a rude awakening to Lloyd George. It was an intelligence failure of the first order.

CONSOLIDATION OF POWER

The new Dail government lost no time in capitalizing on its electoral victory. As president of the Sinn Fein Party and Prime Minister, de Valera appointed a cabinet in April that included Cathal Brugha as Defence Minister and Michael Collins as Finance Minister. Behind the scenes, however, de Valera also appointed Collins Director of Information (intelligence)— formalizing a post he had already held in the Volunteer Executive for the previous two years. Significantly, when Collins was named to the cabinet, the IRB Executive concurrently elected him president of their Supreme Council. With that elevation, Collins— not de Valera—became the true and only authentic "President of the Irish Republic" in the hearts and minds of many of the most dedicated physical-force nationalists—the IRB.

By early 1919, therefore, Collins's four separate portfolios—finance, intelligence, adjutant general, and IRB president—provided him carte blanche to control the purse strings, conduct espionage operations, smuggle arms, and place trusted IRB cadre into key positions within the army. Political restraints prevented him from attacking the Castle spy system for the time being, however.

De Valera was the foremost moderate in the revolution and was a popular hero with enormous influence on the course of events. His departure for America in June for a one-year tour to lobby for U.S. political and financial support would leave control of the revolution in the hands of the physical-force element, foremost Michael Collins. De Valera had selected senior IRB man Harry Boland to go ahead of him to America to garner support from the Clan na Gael leadership in organizing the tour. With de Valera out of the picture, Brugha's authority over Collins waned. Collins thus became the most powerful leader of the revolution with virtually unlimited authority to direct day-to-day military operations. This latter authority did not bother Richard Mulcahy, the IRA's Chief of Staff (in effect, commander in chief of the Volunteers) who had just twenty-four months earlier tried to keep Collins from rising to a leadership post. Mulcahy, like Collins, was a realist who knew war was inevitable; and he had grown to trust Collins's judgment. The two became natural allies and this irritated Brugha, who grew increasingly resentful of Collins's growing influence. Collins's control over Ireland's most secretive organization— the IRB—and his concurrent management of Sinn Fein funds and IRA operations amounted to a consolidation of power unprecedented in Irish revolutionary history.[24]

De Valera realized that his role as president of Sinn Fein and prime minister—and that of any future elected Irish prime minister—would be tenuous so long as de facto power lay within the hands of IRB gunmen. To be sure, de Valera endorsed Collins's blueprint for armed warfare as a means of driving the British from Irish soil: a military means to achieve a political end. But de Valera also carefully distanced himself from the violence by arranging the American fundraising tour just at the very mo-

Liberal Party member Winston Churchill was a strong advocate for the creation of the Secret Service Bureau, based in part on his own experiences during the Boer War. *Imperial War Museum*

As secretary for war, Richard Burdon Haldane created the Imperial Committee on Intelligence, leading to the creation of the Secret Service Bureau in 1909. *Library of Congress*

Sir Vernon Kell,
Director of MI5,
1909–1940. *Hulton
Archive/Getty*

Sir Basil Thomson became
head of Special Branch in
1913 and served concur-
rently as director of Home
Intelligence from 1919 to
1921. *Hulton Archive/Getty*

The noted Irish athlete, Harry Boland, who, with Sam Maguire, recruited Collins into the secret Irish Republican Brotherhood.
Hulton Archive/Getty

Eamon de Valera, commander in chief of the Irish Volunteers, president of Sinn Fein, and prime minister of the abstentionist Dail Eireann government.
Hulton Archive/Getty

"The Big Fella." *Courtesy of the National Library of Ireland*

Thomas Ashe was president of the IRB after the Easter
Rising until his death in British custody in 1917.
Courtesy of the National Library of Ireland

Arthur Griffith, Irish journalist and founder of Sinn Fein.
Hulton Archive/Getty

Richard Mulcahy, chief of staff of the IRA, was suspicious of Collins initially but later became his ally on policy and strategy. *Courtesy of the National Library of Ireland*

L–R: Liam Tobin, deputy chief of the IRA Intelligence Staff, and Tom Cullen, one of his case officers, in uniform.
Hulton Archive/Getty

Hiding in plain sight. With a price on his head, Collins moved freely around Dublin masquerading as respectable businessman "John Grace" for more that three years. *Courtesy of the Irish Military Archive, Cathal Brugha Barracks*

ment that the IRA was taking the offensive. De Valera subsequently also distanced himself from direct negotiations with the British government in 1921, instead ordering Collins to London to lead the delegation. Realizing that Collins as president of the IRB Supreme Council was in effect the "de facto president" insofar as most of the IRA leadership was concerned, the British may well have pressured de Valera into naming Collins to the Irish negotiating team. Regardless of how de Valera came to that decision, in so doing, he manipulated Collins and the IRB into an impossible political entrapment that would eventually fracture and weaken the IRA, lead to Collins's death, and guarantee de Valera's political future.

6

IN THE SHADOW OF GUNMEN

Contrary to what is thought generally, the Irish are a peaceable people, but when roused they can be ruthless.

—*David Neligan, IRA-controlled double agent, 1968*

On the same day in January 1919 that the Dail issued its declaration of Irish Independence, IRA officers Dan Breen and Sean Treacy led a squad of the Third Tipperary Brigade in an ambush of two RIC constables guarding a shipment of explosives at Soloheadbeg, killing both. Neither Collins nor anyone on the IRA General Staff ordered this attack. Breen and Treacy were merely in a position to carry it out, and the time had come to liven things up a bit.[1] The attack had an electrifying effect on all nationalists. The opening volley of the Anglo-Irish War had been fired. Four days later, the Castle declared County Tipperary a "military area," giving notice that the army would now be assisting the police in keeping the peace. Ready or not, the Volunteers would have to go on the offensive. Collins's first move would be against the local British intelligence infrastructure.[2]

ON THE OFFENSIVE

Premature as it was, the Soloheadbeg attack showed the British that neither their police force nor armaments were secure from the IRA. For its part, the Castle clamped down with stringent security measures. In the coming months, the government outlawed Sinn Fein and declared Dail

Eireann an illegal body. The army and the RIC had conducted over 12,000 raids since 1917; by early 1919, it had arrested 18,000 citizens. The War Office increased British Army Irish Command from 20,000 to 37,529 troops.[3]

Soloheadbeg forced the hands of both the Dail and the IRA. Collins was preparing to go on his own offensive against G Division and the RIC, and had already accelerated efforts to obtain more arms and ordnance. After the government announced its intent to introduce conscription in May, the ranks of the Volunteers swelled. By the time of the Soloheadbeg incident in January, the Volunteer Executive was well along in training an army that had swollen to over 100,000.[4] The IRA was organized geographically by counties into brigades and companies. There were brigades in all four provinces, as well as in Britain and Scotland. Despite these impressive figures, only a fraction of the IRA was sufficiently armed to conduct active service operations. Consequently, brigade commanders could deploy only a small number of their men in the initial stages of the war.

The Soloheadbeg attack illustrated how little actual control IRA GHQ—and the IRB—exercised over brigade commanders in the outlying counties. As Hopkinson notes, in some provincial IRA units, the IRB was considered too timid by local commanders who were spoiling for action. As noted earlier, because so many IRA field officers acted independently, especially in Tipperary and Cork, IRA GHQ responded by dispatching liaison officers like Ernie O'Malley and Sean MacBride to the countryside. Some were accepted, while others were ostracized. In 1921, IRA GHQ would reorganize the army, subordinating the county-organized brigades to division-echelon command organized by region in a further effort to exercise more tactical control from Dublin and promote combined operations.[5]

Nevertheless, throughout the war many local commanders continued to act on their own initiative. In February for example, officers of the Third Tipperary Brigade issued a proclamation "ordering" all British Army and RIC out of south Tipperary under penalty of death. IRA Headquarters refused to endorse the proclamation, but it appeared on handbills throughout the county just the same.[6]

These leaders did not have to be told by Cathal Brugha, Richard Mulcahy, or Michael Collins that they stood no chance in a sustained stand-up battle against British Army regulars. Brugha, in particular, was acutely aware of the consequences, having been wounded fourteen times as a

Volunteer during the Easter Rising. That reality, and the fact that arms and ammunition were always in short supply, made hit-and-run tactics the only viable option. The IRA discarded its uniforms and began operations from their home areas. The initial attacks against the RIC were carried out by individuals or groups from local fixed-based Volunteer companies. By the summer of 1920, so many Volunteers were on the run that "flying columns" consisting of twenty to thirty men were formed. They lived on the run for months on end, striking the enemy and withdrawing into the countryside where they employed arms dumps and safe houses to safeguard their weapons and rest between operations. Despite their independence from Volunteer headquarters in Dublin, James Mackay has noted that IRA field units maintained good discipline even with inferior numbers and chronic shortages of weapons and supplies. Their intelligence was good, they fought on familiar ground, and their morale was high, imbued with the justice of their cause and following their own strict code of conduct.[7]

This entire effort depended on superior intelligence. Collins had already pulled together a regular and full-time intelligence staff complete with analysts, agent handlers, logistics personnel, couriers, and safe-house keepers. Supporting this organization, of course, was the traditional IRB information network. Starting in June or July of 1919 when Collins was elected President of the IRB Supreme Council, he instantly had at his fingertips a widespread clandestine network of IRB members, cooperative contacts, informers, and sympathizers spanning the length and breadth of Ireland, England, and Scotland. The network extended to all major English cities and had a presence in several continental European capitals, not to mention the United States. Sam Maguire, IRB center in London, was beginning to look and act like a head of station for Collins's organization. From his vantage point, Maguire carried out myriad intelligence-gathering, logistical, and exfiltration operations. Once information was collected by Maguire's people in Britain, it was delivered to Collins's Dublin headquarters via a courier network comprising merchant seamen, longshoremen, and railway employees. The IRB had thoroughly penetrated the postal system as well as the dock and railway unions. This made it possible for Collins to send intelligence dispatches based on intercepted British messages to IRA units in the outlying counties in the morning and receive replies and after-action reports from those same units the same afternoon. Each morning O'Reilly cycled to meet the incoming mail boat to retrieve overnight reports from London. Coogan relates that Coolevin's Dairy, situated close to Dublin's Amiens Street rail station, eventually served as a drop point for secret dispatches and messages carried by IRB railway workers, merchant seamen, and other couriers between Collins and his operators.[8]

The IRB presence within the British and Irish transport industries greatly facilitated exfiltration operations. Some Volunteers released from custody in Britain had to be secreted back to Ireland, while others had to be smuggled from Ireland to continental Europe and onward to the United States. IRA veteran Connie Neenan's experience in returning from Wormwood Scrubs Prison to rejoin his Cork Brigade illustrates how efficient Collins's escape and evasion network was. It also sheds light on the ham-handed surveillance tactics of Special Branch—openly provocative, thoroughly devoid of clandestine technique, and easily evaded:

I was due for release in February 1921. The morning I was due to go I saw two individuals near the gate, I asked a warder: "Who are they?" "They are two 'tecs'" [detectives] said he. I moved out. I could see I was being followed. I stayed well back from the tram stop. When the bell rang I made a rush for it and got away from them. I arrived at the Queens Hotel where a completely new rig-out awaited me, I put the old clothes in a bag and passed out again. No one could have recognized me. I went to London that night and I was in touch with Sam Maguire, O.C. [officer in command] Britain, the next day. Frank Thornton, from GHQ was there with him. I was given some work to do and remained there for three weeks, keeping a low profile of course. Collins must have had a marvelous organization for he knew when each of us was due for release, and he always had a job waiting for us. The only trouble on release was the ridiculous travel voucher. It practically ensured that you would be arrested before getting to your destination. "Buy them a ticket" I told them in H.Q. Subsequently, that is what they did. Sam Maguire was one of the most resourceful men I have ever met. He had a marvelous intelligence group. He got me up to Liverpool with Tadgh Sullivan, a Kerry chap originally but attached now to the Cork Brigade. We were in Liverpool for about five days, keeping well out of sight. We came back then as two stowaways in a coal boat. Tadgh was so sick I thought he would die. We were two days at sea. I was alright but the smell of the coal and the oil, and the rocking about of the old tramp in the February gales was too much for him. Poor chap, he was killed five weeks later in Douglas Street.[9]

Meanwhile the Dail was seeking support from the Irish-American community. The Irish Race Convention that convened in Chicago in February 1919 issued a statement calling upon President Wilson to support Irish self-determination at the Versailles Peace Conference. It appointed a delegation that met with Wilson in New York the following month. Wilson flatly refused to support the self-determination concept at Versailles but suggested that a League of Nations might be helpful to the Irish cause. In April, the delegation met again with Wilson in Paris; the president informed them he could do nothing publicly, but implied that he was pressuring Lloyd George privately. Shortly thereafter, however, the U.S. secretary of state issued a statement that the Irish case could only be aired at Versailles with the concurrence of the four major powers. This was a convenient excuse for Wilson, who, as mentioned earlier, had no intention of including the Irish in his much-celebrated campaign for the rights of small nations. The pressure of Irish Americans was illustrated by a nearly unanimous resolution passed by the U.S. Senate in June that expressed support for the airing of the Irish case at Versailles. The peace conference would never hear the Irish case, however.[10]

The rebellion gained momentum. On April 10, the Crown proclaimed the counties of Kerry, Cork, Limerick, Roscommon, and Tipperary to be in "a state of disturbance." On May 13, Treacy, Breen, and other members of the Third Tipperary Brigade mounted a brazen daylight rescue of one of their own from RIC custody on a train stopped at Knocklong, Limerick.[11]

In June, the Dail took a further step in boycotting the British government when it announced a system for courts, local councils, and a Republican police force. A Sinn Fein Land Bank was also established. An Irish Republican shadow government was rapidly taking shape in southern Ireland, and this shadow government became a key factor in the erosion of Crown authority there.[12]

CODES AND DISPATCHES

Collins, meanwhile, continued to expand his intelligence network, which commenced interception of coded British diplomatic and military dispatches at this time. While the RIC and DMP had always used police codes, Collins had solved that problem a year earlier with the recruitment of Kavanagh, Broy, Matt McCarthy, and other cops. Until 1919, however, the army command, including Sir Henry Wilson, Chief of the Imperial General Staff, communicated via unclassified dispatches through the ordinary British post and telegraph service. Lord French, the viceroy (and now a member of the cabinet), also sent his reports in open post channels. This lapse in security had allowed IRB sources in the London and Dublin post offices to intercept the military correspondence which Collins in turn passed to Brugha, Mulcahy, and members of the revolutionary cabinet.

By early 1919, however, the British began using codes to protect sensitive administrative and military communications. In February, Brigadier General John E. S. Brind arrived at Irish Command to take charge of army intelligence. Brind's deputy was Major (later Lieutenant Colonel) Stephen S. Hill-Dillon, an MI5 veteran whose job was to establish an MO4x secret service unit within the Dublin Military District.[13] Army intelligence headquarters was at Parkgate Street Barracks in Dublin and Collins early on had considered ways to penetrate Parkgate. The introduction of the code system provided the key. He soon found two invaluable agents. The first was Lily Mernin, a clerk-typist in the British Women's Auxiliary Army Corps (WAACs), who worked as Hill-Dillon's confidential secretary. She was a cousin of 1916 veteran, Dail member, and IRB operative Piaras Beaslai, and presumably it was Beaslai who teed her up for recruitment by Collins. Mernin purloined army reports from coded dispatches filtering to and from Hill-Dillon's office. As the army's Irish Command beefed up divisional, brigade, and battalion intelligence sections with IOs and as Hill-Dillon established an MO4x plainclothes unit in the months ahead, Mernin's importance increased exponentially. Each evening she visited a Dublin safe house where she typed up reports based on notes she had made during the day. After her departure, one of Collins's intelligence lieutenants retrieved the reports. Mernin never met the cutout. She would later undertake even riskier work identifying some of the plainclothes MO4x intelligence officers and their local agents for IRA GHQ intelligence staff.[14]

Later, in April 1920, when London replaced the Dublin Castle adminis-tration, Collins was able to penetrate a new civil service code system. Nan-cy O'Brien, a secretary employed at Dublin's General Post Office (GPO), was hired by the incoming undersecretary James MacMahon to handle the decoding and encoding of his official correspondence. It is unclear how the candidates were vetted—or indeed if they were vetted—because O'Brien was Collins's cousin. She had worked with Collins in the London post office years before and was apparently hired by MacMahon solely on her spotless civil service record. O'Brien took great risks in removing sensitive classified information from the office. She concealed documents in her underclothing and took them to the ladies' room where she pains-takingly copied them onto notepaper before returning the originals. The verbatim notes were then smuggled by O'Brien beneath her clothes and in her hair out of the GPO and handed over to Collins's staff. Later on, Collins tasked her to case other sensitive offices inside the GPO. She took great risks visiting offices where she had no business. Her espionage ac-tivities were never discovered.[15]

A third invaluable code agent at this time was Josephine Marchmont Brown, a secretary working at British Army Sixth Division Headquarters in Cork—scene of the heaviest fighting between the IRA and British forces throughout the war. Jo Brown was the daughter of an RIC constable and widow of a Welsh officer killed in France; she came to Collins's attention through Florrence O'Donoghue, Cork First Brigade intelligence officer. O'Donoghue learned that the woman had lost a custody battle for her son Reggie with her English in-laws and was extremely distressed. With the child in England, Brown had no opportunity to see him. Learning of this, O'Donoghue informed Collins, who in turn authorized O'Donoghue to kidnap the child. Collins put O'Donoghue in touch with Sam Maguire in London, and O'Donoghue lost no time leading a small team from the Cork intelligence section to England. They promptly brought the child to Cork where he was reunited with Jo Brown. From that day on, Brown faithfully supplied the Cork IRA with decoded dispatches containing in-formation on the British Army Order of Battle, troop movements, and the identities of army intelligence officers and their confidential informers. Jo Brown eventually rose to become chief secretary at British Sixth Division Headquarters, with almost unlimited access to sensitive army intelligence information.[16]

LIEUTENANT G

While he was engaged in stealing the police, military, and civil service codes, Collins sought a better understanding of how the Castle administration worked, how it spied on dissidents, and the threat level posed by G Division and the RIC. Reading intercepted dispatches and civil service cables would provide a tactical day-by-day picture, but understanding the Crown's strategic intentions required good human sources. Some of Collins's many police, intelligence, and army penetration agents obtained considerable access to Castle affairs by 1920, but he had recruited another valuable civilian agent there as early as 1919.[17]

At some point just after his ascendancy as Director of Intelligence, Collins developed a sensitive source with direct access to senior officials and also with contacts in British intelligence. He handled the case personally and never revealed the agent's identity, instead attributing the sourcing of the information to a mysterious "Lieutenant G."

Since most of what is known about the IRA intelligence service is derived from memoirs, definitive evidence of the existence and identity of Lieutenant G may never surface. David Neligan, Collins's agent in G Division and later in the British Secret Service, denied the existence of Lieutenant G, stating that "Collins had astonishing contacts, but one thing is certain; the mysterious Lieutenant referred to in a life of Collins did not exist. I have Liam Tobin's word for it."[18] Be that as it may, Neligan was certainly not privy to all of Collins's secrets, and the taciturn, tight-lipped Tobin was the soul of discretion. If in fact Tobin knew the identity of Lieutenant G, there was no imperative for him to violate the "need to know" principle of espionage by revealing it to anyone else—least of all to another access agent such as Neligan.[19] To do so would violate the elementary rule of compartmentalization employed by espionage services. Dwyer has speculated that Lieutenant G was a clerk-typist serving at army GHQ, leading still others to speculate that Lieutenant G was Lily Mernin, who spied on Colonel Hill-Dillon's intelligence staff.[20]

A case might very well be made that Lieutenant G was John Chartres, a British barrister, former British intelligence officer, and friend of Churchill who had met Collins in London in 1918 as a member of a group proclaiming sympathy with Sinn Fein. Chartres left the civil service in 1919 to accept a minor post in the Dail and became a very close confidante of and advisor to Collins (see appendix A).

Tim Pat Coogan states that a British civil servant named Thomas Markham was aiding Collins from inside the Castle, while biographer James Mackay has speculated that Markham was Lieutenant G. Coogan relates that Markham was likely the source of a report prepared for Collins in late 1918 or early 1919—later found in the papers of IRA Chief of Staff Richard Mulcahy—that outlined the philosophy and system of British control. According to this report, the British system was based upon three principal factors:

A) The grasp of human weakness and vanity.
B) A correct appreciation for the value and use of duplicity and Pecksniffianism.
C) A clear conception of the truth that success in governing depends on well-contrived antagonisms in the economic and social structure of the state. . . . The Royal Irish Constabulary [is] organized in counties, districts. . . . During his training [a constable]'s vanity, ignorance and intelligence were each subjected to the treatment designed to make the British Government his servant and his God. The RIC has something to do with every phase of government activity. The constable records everything in his diary. What he frightens from the child and coaxes from the cailin (young woman). What he sees, hears, infers. The sergeant transfers the constable's report, never abbreviating. It is not his part to select. The policeman moves in a social atmosphere, he writes down everything, gossipy servants, what the RIC pensioner says. A "someone" whose name is never written down. He's a "reliable source." He could be the publican. The rail spy could be the inspector. He frequently is. The road to the Castle is paved with anonymous letters, deriving from the besetting Irish sin, jealousy. The depth and widespread nature of this treachery would make a good Irishman despair. The local Loyalist could have a good post and be merely a disreputable Spotter . . . what was said at a Volunteer meeting; where the arms were kept; the Eavesdropping prison warder, the opening of letters in the post.[21]

Defeating the RIC would be a huge undertaking, but IRA Chief of Staff General Richard Mulcahy also directed that Dublin would be the center of military activity. This was based on the imperative that the IRA keep the capital under armed threat at all costs in order to demoralize the British administration and demonstrate nationalist strength and resolve to the world.[22]

Mulcahy's war strategy meant that Dublin's G Division detectives, as well as the RIC, would both have to be neutralized. Collins was already considering the possibility that he would have to attack them, and with Mulcahy's directive it now seemed inevitable.

Markham's report on the Castle administration was insightful and undoubtedly bolstered Collins's argument for use of force. He still needed to get a better idea of how much the political police knew about the IRA, the IRB, and Sinn Fein. He directed Broy to get him access to police files and, on April 7, Collins and Sean Nunan—an old friend and veteran of 1916 and Frongach—spent the night in the upstairs file room at G Division headquarters in Brunswick Street. Combing through classified files by candlelight, Collins realized that G Division and the RIC had amassed a huge amount of data on the movement and its leadership. Collins's sojourn in the police file room convinced him that he would have to commence imminent attacks on both G Division and the RIC.[23]

NEUTRALIZING THE CONSTABULARY

De Valera abhorred the idea of assassination and did not consent to Collins's proposal to attack the G men. Failing that, Collins undertook an alternative campaign of intimidation. Just two days after visiting the G Division file room, he issued a letter of warning in the name of the IRA to every detective. The letters admonished them to cease investigations and harassment of Sinn Fein and Republican sympathizers under penalty of death. This was merely the first of several written warnings that Collins would send to the G men over the next two months.[24]

The Volunteers were now attacking police in the countryside, but de Valera sought to restrain them, fearing the violence would destroy the legitimacy of the Dail government and possible diplomatic initiatives with the Americans. He called instead for a national campaign of ostracism against the RIC, referring to them as "the eyes and ears of the enemy." This campaign went into effect on April 10 and immediately had a major impact on the effectiveness of the force. Constables and their families were shunned throughout the country. Publicans, restaurant owners, and shopkeepers would not serve them, while neighbors avoided them. The morale of the RIC sagged while informers and would-be informers found it nearly impossible to communicate with their police contacts. Soon the RIC was plagued with hundreds of resignations. Those who remained on duty had to face the increasing threat of holdup and assassination.[25]

Collins introduced the next phase of this intimidation strategy by mounting a series of holdups. A selected unit that would become known as the Squad began surveillance of G men and accosted a few of them at gunpoint, tying and gagging them and issuing a verbal warning. This showed the detectives that the IRA knew exactly who they were and how to find them, and it had a chilling effect on G Division. A few of the detectives were convinced in this way to stand down from further investigation of Sinn Fein and the IRA.[26]

THE TWELVE ASSASSINS

When de Valera left Ireland for his American fundraising tour in June 1919, Collins again sought consent to begin armed operations against the police. This time he received it from Defence Minister Cathal Brugha and Chief of Staff Mulcahy. The IRA intelligence staff had assembled the list of targets but Collins had no men to carry out the attacks. Dick McKee, commanding officer of the Dublin Brigade, suggested drawing a small team of operatives from his command and ordered Mick McDonnell to begin the selection process. Contrary to popular perception, Dwyer notes that the Squad was built up incrementally, beginning with a nucleus of four Volunteers. Squad member Jim Slattery recalled that when a group of candidates from the brigade was assembled, the majority turned down the assignment when asked individually if they had any qualms about shooting enemy agents:

> The greater number of Volunteers objected for one reason or another. When I was asked the question I said I was prepared to obey orders. . . . I recall that two men, who had previously told Mick McDonnell that they had no objection to being selected for special duty, turned down the proposition at that meeting. . . . McDonnell seemed very annoyed at them and asked them why they had signified their willingness in the first instance.[27]

McDonnell built the unit up gradually from four to nine and then to twelve men, prompting Collins and others to refer to them as the Twelve Apostles. Before the end of hostilities, this unit—formally designated as the Special Intelligence Squad—had nearly twenty members. In addition to Slattery, the original members were Paddy Daly, Frank Saurin, Ben Barrett, Joe Leonard, Pat McCrea, Bill Stapleton, Joe Dolan, Tom Keogh, Vinny Byrne, and Charles Dalton. Subsequently Charles Byrne, Mick O'Reilly, Ned Kelliher, Bob O'Neill, Paddy Kennedy, Emmet Dalton—brother of Charles—James Conroy, Jimmy Dempsey, Sean Doyle, Joe McGuiness, and James McGuiness also saw service with the Squad. After Tipperary Brigade officers Dan Breen and Sean Treacy went on the run, Collins brought them to Dublin, where they participated in Squad operations. Most of the original members were in their teens or early twenties. All were single and most came from middle-class backgrounds, although the Dalton brothers came from a wealthy family. Each member was fully qualified with firearms, and Collins issued them .38 caliber revolvers. Squad members were among the few paid members of GHQ staff, each drawing £4 and 12s a week—excellent wages at the time and far more than a schoolteacher or a police constable could earn. The salary enabled the members to support themselves on the economy without undue risk of exposure.[28]

Emmet Dalton was one of the most distinguished members of Collins's Squad. He was one of several thousand National Volunteers who had followed James Redmond's call to enlist in the British Army in 1914. A commissioned officer, he served with distinction as a company commander on the Somme and in Palestine and was awarded the Military Cross. Upon his return in 1918, he joined brother Charlie as a full-time member of the Irish Volunteers. His leadership skills, sound judgment, coolness under fire, and military expertise made him a formidable member of Collins's Squad, and he became a close personal friend of Collins. In his final press interview in 1978, he said of Collins, "I loved him. I use no other word. I loved him as a man loves a man, with pure love."[29]

The exploits of Collins's Squad have been recounted in sensational fashion so many times that they now overshadow every other aspect of Collins's intelligence apparatus. This is ironic, as it was Dick McKee, not Collins, who came up with the concept for the Squad in the first place.

Although the Squad acted on Collins's orders and its operations served a counterintelligence function, its members were not intelligence officers per se and did not view themselves as such. They protected Collins's myriad other intelligence collection activities, to be sure, but their operations extended beyond assassinations of enemy agents. They regularly engaged in vehicle hijackings, raids on army depots, kidnappings, jail breaks, and physical protection of senior officials, including Collins himself. Squad members employed both alias and disguise and used sophisticated multitiered surveillance and countersurveillance techniques that they developed instinctively through a combination of street smarts, common sense, and experience evading G Division and RIC detectives. They were also meticulous in building effective cover; some of them had worked as painters, decorators, and carpenters in civilian life so Collins installed them in a safe house at the rear of a builder's yard just minutes away from police headquarters and the Castle. From there they mounted almost continual operations under the noses of the police without detection for two years. In sum, they were mentally tough, physically fit, sober, reliable, and disciplined. And they would prove to be ruthlessly efficient killers.

On June 23, Stapleton, one of the most experienced Volunteers, tracked down forty-six-year-old RIC District Inspector Michael Hunt, who had been investigating the Soloheadbeg killings of the previous January. Stapleton caught up with Hunt in the market square at Thurles, County Tipperary, and shot him dead in broad daylight. This operation preceded the formal establishment of the Squad by a few days, but Stapleton was soon operating as a member of the Squad under Collins's direct orders.[30]

The assassination of Hunt was followed a month later by the Squad's attack on G Division Detective Sergeant Patrick Smyth in the Dublin suburb of Drumcondra on July 30. Smyth was a bully who had arrested Piaras Beaslai on the charge of sedition. Known on the force as The Dog because of his mean countenance and threatening manner, Smyth had already received a written warning from the IRA to cease his prosecution of Beaslai, but he persisted. Two Squad members subsequently walked up to Smyth on the street and shot him with their revolvers. The bullets slowed, but did not stop Smyth, so the assassins fired several more bullets into him. The detective still refused to go down and managed to stumble some distance to his own house and bolt the door before collapsing on the floor in front of his wife. He lingered for four months before dying. Following this affair, Collins collected the Squad's .38 caliber revolvers and reissued them .45 caliber Webley military revolvers which, when fired at close range, were virtually guaranteed to inflict a fatal wound. Some members eventually acquired the powerful and reliable American-made 1911-model Colt .45-caliber semiautomatic pistol—an equally devastating handgun at close range.[31]

Hunt's assassination received much attention, but the killing of Smyth sent shock waves through G Division and the Castle. The entire political crimes branch consisted of no more than a dozen detectives. All of them now realized that Hunt's death was not an isolated attack, and that the IRA was fully aware of their identities and movements. The tension increased when Detective Daniel Hoey was gunned down near Dublin police headquarters on September 13. On November 30, Detective Constable John Barton was assassinated. Sean Treacy, vice commander of the Third Tipperary Brigade and one of the Soloheadbeg shooters, was on the run hiding in Dublin at that time; Collins directed him to join in the operation against Barton. Treacy reportedly fired the coup de grâce that brought Barton down, but it was a pitiful affair. Barton was a young constable who had only joined G Division two months earlier. His offense was that he had been assigned to investigate the murders of Smyth and Hoey, and he was making progress. Neither the first shot nor Treacy's second two rounds killed Barton immediately. The G man lay gravely wounded in the gutter, repeatedly moaning, "What did I do?" until he died. [32]

When interviewed by Coogan years later, Squad member Vinny Byrne described the Squad's modus operandi and credited Collins with instilling the discipline that made the unit effective:

> We were all young, twenty, twenty-one. We never thought we'd win or lose. We just wanted to have a go. We'd go out in pairs, walk up to the target and do it, then split. . . . On a typical job we'd use about eight, including the back-up. Nobody got in our way. One of us would knock him over with the first shot, and the other would finish him off with a shot to the head. Collins was a marvel. If he hadn't done the work he did, we'd still be under Britain. Informers and drink would have taken care of us. But our move-

ments were temperate. Collins would meet us from time to time and say, "You're doing great work, lads." There was no formality about him.[33]

In his memoirs, David Neligan reported that some of the Squad had specialties. Joe Dolan was "quick on the draw," while Pat McCrea was an expert driver. Saurin was a deadly accurate shot who normally went about the city so impeccably dressed that police and British Tommies alike dismissed him as an innocent businessman. Neligan related that young Dolan walked about the streets of Dublin with a lapel badge that read, "For King and Country." The prop reportedly fooled many a sentry into passing Dolan through checkpoints at all hours while engaged on dangerous missions.[34] Bill Stapleton recalled how the Squad coordinated activities with the intelligence staff:

> Tobin or Cullen would come down and tell us who we were to get.
> . . . Two or three of us would go out with an Intelligence Officer
> walking in front of us, maybe about ten or fifteen yards. His job
> was to identify the man we were to shoot. Often we would be walk-
> ing the streets the whole day without meeting our man. It meant
> going without lunch. But other times the Intelligence Staff would
> have their information dead on, and we would see our quarry im-
> mediately we came to the place we had been told he would be
> at. The Intelligence Officer would then signal to us in the follow-
> ing way. He would take off his hat and greet the marked man. Of
> course, he didn't know him. As soon as he did this we would shoot.
> We had to accept that General Headquarters knew the right men
> to shoot. We knew that very great care was taken that this was so.
> As a result, we didn't feel we had to worry. We were, after all, only
> soldiers doing our duty. I often went in [to church] and said a little
> prayer for the people that we'd shot, afterwards.[35]

Collins's goal of neutralizing the RIC was proving far simpler than anyone anticipated, thanks in large part to de Valera's ostracism cam-paign. Nevertheless, an increasing number were being accosted or shot down on a daily basis. As more flying columns were brought online, the IRA pressure on the RIC increased. The army responded by assigning detachments of regulars to outlying rural RIC barracks, but this only temporarily deterred the IRA. Meanwhile, resignations continued at an alarming rate.[36] The job of RIC constable, once one of Ireland's most respected occupations, was rapidly becoming a dangerous and undesirable profession.

The assassination of five G men by year's end convinced Castle authorities that the DMP was infiltrated with informers. They ordered G Division to relocate from Brunswick Street Station to the relative safety of the Castle.[37]

THE VICEROY REACTS

The Castle administration was under growing pressure to find a solution to the increasingly unstable security situation. The IRA was well on its way to neutralizing the RIC and the British Army would soon be tasked with assisting them in restoring order. The police were nevertheless conducting hundreds of raids in Dublin and elsewhere. Anyone suspected of membership in Sinn Fein or complicity with IRA gunmen was arrested and deported to an English prison. In London, the coalition government of Prime Minister Lloyd George was concentrating on the Versailles Conference and other postwar challenges. The cabinet was loath for political reasons to acknowledge that war had broken out in Ireland. Downing Street therefore downplayed events in Ireland, referring to them as an "insurrection." This only led to intensified criticism by political opponents in the House of Commons and the press. Behind the scenes, however, the cabinet began to study options.

Collins himself was nearly caught in a raid on Dail/Sinn Fein headquarters at 76 Harcourt Street in November. He avoided arrest by using an emergency escape route through the attic and across the roof of two adjoining buildings to a skylight on the top floor of a nearby hotel. The hall porter in the hotel had been instructed to leave the skylight unlocked at all times. While the police were busy rounding up suspects at number 76, Collins emerged from the front lobby of the adjacent hotel like any businessman going about his daily routine.[38]

But the raids were staggering in number, and hundreds of private houses were invaded while scores of suspects were being arrested and deported without charge. The Irish Council of Bishops condemned the massive raids, accusing the government of employing "the rule of the sword," and declaring the policy "utterly unsuited to a civilized nation."[39] It was the first of many propaganda victories that Sinn Fein would have over the course of the war.

The army had sent troops to reinforce the RIC earlier in the year; this was about all it could do under provisions of the Defence of the Realm Regulations (DRR), which restricted the military to assisting civil authorities. No official state of war existed and martial law had not been declared.[40] Lieutenant General Sir Frederick Shaw arrived in Dublin to take command of British forces in August, and on his recommendation several repressive measures were implemented, including the banning of Irish language classes, Irish football matches, and even dances, unless by permit. Instead of calming down, the population became even more rebellious.[41] Soon after his arrival, Shaw notified RIC Inspector General Joseph Byrne that the army would be unable to provide detachments to protect RIC barracks after December because of manpower shortages resulting from continuing postwar demobilization. Shortly thereafter, Byrne informed the undersecretary that if the army detachments pulled out, he would be compelled to abandon numerous RIC posts across the country.[42]

As summer turned into fall, the war intensified. In September, the Dail was declared illegal.[43] The same month, the County Cork IRA carried out the first direct attack against army troops when it ambushed fifteen unarmed soldiers on their way to attend church services in Fermoy. Only one soldier was killed, but this was just a taste of things to come. Later that month, the RIC began withdrawing from most of its isolated rural barracks and retreating to larger, fortified barracks in more strategic locations.[44] The constabulary nevertheless maintained a robust presence in Dublin, Cork City, Limerick, and other urban areas. Between January and the end of September, the police had conducted nearly six thousand raids. After further assessing the situation, Shaw suggested the RIC might be rebuilt through the recruitment of a reserve force of ex-servicemen. The cabinet endorsed the idea in October, and the following month the RIC was given authority to proceed. Press advertisements appeared shortly thereafter in English newspapers soliciting veterans to become police reserve constables in Ireland.[45] Concurrently, Collins, Chief of Staff Mulcahy, and Defence Minister Brugha met with Liam Deasy, adjutant of the West Cork Brigade, to discuss further efforts against the RIC in Munster Province. According to Deasy's memoir, the IRA leadership approved direct attacks upon RIC barracks to commence as of January 1. This would give the local column commanders at least sixty days to select their targets and make preparations.[46]

In early November, a special cabinet subcommittee studying implementation of Home Rule recommended that two separate parliaments be set up, one in Belfast and one in Dublin. The cabinet accepted the proposal and just before Christmas the government introduced the "Better Government of Ireland" bill.[47] London had still not come to the realization that it was confronting a revolution, not a rebellion.

Meanwhile, the British Viceroy, Lord John French, was growing more frustrated by the day. He summarily sacked RIC Inspector General Joseph Byrne, who had incurred French's wrath for, among other things, questioning General Shaw's recommendation to recruit British ex-servicemen as a paramilitary force to augment the rapidly dwindling RIC. In his place French appointed T. J. Smith, the Commissioner of the Belfast police whom he considered less intelligent but more likely to toe his line. T. J. Smith's appointment would be the first in a series of publicized appointments designed by the cabinet to replace southern Irish security officials—many of whom were Catholic and thus suspected of being sympathetic to Sinn Fein—with solid northern Irish loyalists, most of whom were dependable Protestant Unionists. For his part, Smith lost no time vowing to hunt down Michael Collins. Before year's end, he was quietly joined by Inspector W. C. Forbes Redmond, who arrived from Belfast to become Assistant Commissioner of the DMP. Smith and Redmond were supported by a third Belfast official, Magistrate Alan Bell, a highly respected former RIC inspector who arrived in Dublin in late November to become a low-profile intelligence advisor to the Castle. Indeed, Bell was likely recommended by Basil Thomson and had a hand in the selection of both Smith and Redmond. It would not be long before this trio of Belfast imports would find themselves under direct fire. Lloyd George approved these appointments, noting in particular that T. J. Smith was highly regarded by Sir Edward Carson. This point underscored Downing Street's principal concern at the time: Lloyd George was prepared to implement some form of Home Rule but he had assured Carson that he would preserve Ulster within the Union. If such a formula could be agreed upon, however, the prime minister might be able to quell the disturbances without direct military intervention.[48]

French then convened a special commission to study the impact of the IRA violence on British intelligence capabilities. The commission consisted of Assistant Undersecretary Sir John Taylor, T. J. Smith, and Bell. On December 7, 1919, it reported,

> An organized conspiracy of murder, outrage and intimidation has existed for some time past. Dublin City is the storm centre and mainspring of it all. We are inclined to think that the shooting of a few would-be assassins would have an excellent effect. Up to the present time they have escaped with impunity. We think that this should be tried as soon as possible.[49]

These findings set the stage for London's subsequent reorganization of security infrastructure. Inspector Redmond not only became assistant commissioner of police but also the new chief of G Division. He brought in additional—Protestant and solidly Loyalist—detectives from the Belfast Metropolitan Police whom he intended to be the nucleus of a revitalized secret police branch. It was clear that Bell (and by extension Basil Thomson) considered G Division penetrated, and Redmond's appointment was a pure counterintelligence move intended to isolate the unreliable and demoralized G Division veterans and to place intelligence within a compartmentalized circle of trusted Ulstermen.

Just days after the commission issued its report, the Squad attempted unsuccessfully to ambush French's motorcade near Dublin. It was the second assassination attempt on French in as many months. The angry and shaken Viceroy wrote:

> Our secret service is simply non-existent. What masquerades for such a service is nothing but a delusion and a snare. The DMP are absolutely demoralized and the RIC will be in the same case very soon if we do not quickly set our house in order.[50]

7

SPIES AT THE WINDOW

Without her spies, England is helpless.
—*Michael Collins, 1919*

The year 1920 has been referred to as "The Year of Terror" in Ireland. Ambushes of police constables escalated and IRA attacks on RIC barracks commenced. De Valera's call for a boycott of British institutions, and the corresponding establishment of Sinn Fein shadow governments in almost every county, were rapidly eroding Crown authority and demonstrating Irish resolve to the world. Across Ireland, taxes went unpaid. Juries increasingly could not be impaneled, and if they were, Sinn Fein and IRA suspects were acquitted. The Dail established Republican courts to settle civil disputes and set up its own income tax and banking system. The IRA formed a police force to settle civil disputes and enforce law and order in towns and districts abandoned by the RIC. All of these measures marginalized British institutions and contributed to the erosion of public support for them.

In London, the strong-willed David Lloyd George, with support from hard-liners in the cabinet and the military, was determined to implement a tougher policy calculated to cause so much misery in Ireland that the inhabitants would cease their disobedience to the Crown. This sentiment now mirrored the official policy at Dublin Castle. Lord French and Ian

Macpherson, newly appointed chief secretary, were of like mind in advocating much stronger security measures. As Hopkinson notes, Macpherson's fourteen-month tenure as chief secretary represents the zenith of British reactionary conservatism.[1]

STRUCTURING MILITARY SECURITY

It is significant that while the IRA had gone on a full war footing in January 1919, the British had not. Until the end of the year, Castle security forces—principally the RIC—were simply concentrating on restoring law and order. The army increased troop strength in Ireland at the end of 1919 to nearly forty thousand men, and reorganized them into two new divisions comprising seven brigades each. Commanded by General Sir Hugh Jeudwine, the Fifth Division, garrisoned at the Curragh Camp near Dublin, had one brigade in Dublin and one in Belfast; the Sixth Division, commanded by General Sir Peter Strickland, was headquartered in Cork. In recognition that the IRA was concentrating operations in Dublin, however, Jeudwine's command was soon further reorganized; his Dublin brigade was upgraded to a third separate division, the Dublin District Division. General Gerald Boyd assumed command of the Dublin District.[2]

In the absence of a declaration of martial law, however, the army was restricted to providing support to the civil authorities. As the military soon learned, however, police intelligence as practiced by the RIC and G Division was woefully inadequate. To their credit, Irish Command anticipated early on that the IRA would adopt guerrilla warfare tactics. But it moved slowly to strengthen its own tactical intelligence-gathering capabilities, not realizing for some time just how paralyzed the police intelligence system had become. The army would have to improvise.[3]

By mid-1919, General Brind was organizing the intelligence structure for Irish Command. Colonel S. S. Hill-Dillon, Brind's deputy and chief of MO4x, had ambitious plans for a secret service branch and was searching for suitable officers and ex-officers to staff an undercover unit of one hundred men. Most of these men, however, would first have to be trained in clandestine operations, interrogation and elicitation of information from sources, cover, recruiting, surveillance and surveillance detection, impersonal communications, debriefing and interrogation, and myriad other tradecraft skills. Creating a clandestine service task-organized specifically for Ireland was a slow process and MO4x faced many disadvantages, not least of which was development of suitable cover.

Cover is always the most important element for successful clandestine operations; it is also the most difficult problem to solve, requiring planning, backstopping resources, and time. MO4x was underfunded at the outset, and as the IRA accelerated its operations in 1919, time became a precious commodity. Simply put, the army case officers would either have to be native Irish, they would have to learn how to speak and role-play as native Irish, or they would have to develop cover jobs as salesmen or other British business profiles that would give them a natural cover for being in Ireland. Tourist cover was impractical as it offered only short-term cover. Moreover, trying to pose as a tourist in Dublin in 1920 was akin to trying to pose as a tourist in Baghdad or Kabul in 2003. Official cover—affiliation with some department of the government—was initially seen as a good option, but that rapidly faded as Sinn Fein effectively created a shadow government in almost every county of southern Ireland by early 1920, so posing as a government worker only invited close scrutiny. Crown officials, from constables to tax collectors, magistrates, and corporation employees, were all subject to harassment, abduction, or execution.[4]

Moreover, although Brind and Hill-Dillon envisioned that once the plainclothes branch was developed it would be dispersed throughout Ireland to support army maneuver units, the acceleration of IRA activity in metropolitan Dublin compelled them to abandon that goal. During the First World War, maneuver units enjoyed robust secret service support from the national community—NID, MI5, MI1c, and Special Branch. In the colonies, where local police special branches were expected to fulfill the secret service function, the need for this national assistance was not foreseen. Perhaps more significant, British security officials did not comprehend the changing mood of the country or the depth and refinement of the IRA intelligence network until it was too late. MO4x, meanwhile, reached out to the War Office for recruits and also began to develop its own registry of suspects, patterned perhaps after MI5's famous Central Registry.[5]

Army intelligence had to build the Irish files from the ground up. It naturally turned first to the RIC Crimes Special Branch for information, but as the army postmortem notes, army intelligence officers discovered an obsolete card registry and an information-sharing policy mired in obsessive secrecy that impeded coordination:

> The Crimes Special Branch depended much more on personal and local knowledge than on organization and methodical reporting. The clerical personnel at Headquarters consisted of three RIC sergeants and constables, all said to be excellent clerks and very keen. But they were entirely absorbed in the duties of registration, filing and indexing, and were hardly ever available for typing. The card "index" was really a series of "history" cards alphabetically arranged. The cards were well and carefully kept, but such "potted" records, unless produced by persons of the utmost precision and powers of concentration, are not by themselves reliable documents. The branch was all so secret that no one was allowed to know anything about it. So much was this the case that most communications for the officer in charge were addressed to him personally and were not opened except by him. The reason, no doubt, was the loathing with which any informer has always been regarded in Ireland and the realization of his fate were his name to be discovered. It should however have been possible to overcome this difficulty. There are many offices in London in which secrets of the highest importance were received and where there was no leakage. . . . As it was, even to the very last, it was exceedingly difficult to obtain information from any RIC man unless he were seen and examined by an officer whom he knew and trusted.[6]

On the night of January 30–31, 1920, army units assisted the police for the first time in conducting coordinated raids in Dublin and Cork. Hundreds of private homes were entered without warrants and some ninety IRA suspects were arrested. Within two weeks they were charged with sedition under the Defence of the Realm Act and deported to English jails to remain in limbo, guilty until proven innocent, according to British law. The action was unprecedented and raised eyebrows in Parliament. The criticism escalated when many of the IRA men went on hunger strikes.[7] In preparing for these raids, army IOs were surprised to learn how little actionable intelligence was in the RIC files:

It was not . . . understood how completely the RIC service of information was paralysed until it was decided to arrest, about the end of January 1920, a large number of Sinn Feiners in the hope that the deportation of a few hundred would put a stop to the Sinn Fein movement. It was then found that the local RIC could give little reliable information about such persons beyond a statement that so and so was "a bad boy" or "a bad article." The police lists were out of date and to them every Sinn Fein Club was a battalion. The lists were eventually compiled with their assistance, but the IRA status of the person who it was proposed to arrest was in all cases supplied by military intelligence officers.[8]

At the end of February, a curfew was imposed in Dublin from midnight (later on, 10:00 p.m.) until 5:00 a.m. More raids followed, and by the middle of April, more than 317 IRA suspects were in custody. The army had captured documents in the earlier raids that had implicated dozens of IRA battalion and brigade officers.[9]

But exploiting captured documents, interrogating prisoners, and conducting house raids were one thing. Penetrating the inner circle of the IRA command–and-control structure was quite another. With the IRA's campaign against the RIC in full swing, the British mounted a series of operations designed to do just that. The first case, managed by G Division, developed as the result of an unexpected walk-in who offered his services to the Castle. Subsequently, MO4x and Special Branch would launch more focused efforts.

THE IRREPRESSIBLE HARRY QUINN

Magistrate Alan Bell, who had arrived in Dublin from Belfast the previous November, was advising the Castle on intelligence matters. He had very likely recommended the appointment of Inspector General T. J. Smith and Forbes Redmond as commissioner and assistant commissioner of police, and there is no question that Bell and Redmond collaborated closely. It is also probable that Bell was in close coordination with Basil Thomson of Special Branch on specific operations. Redmond vowed to hunt down Collins and eliminate the IRA. Collins sent Frank Thornton to Belfast to gather traces on Redmond and the others. Belfast RIC Sergeant Matt McCarthy sneaked Thornton into the file room as Broy had done earlier in the year for Collins in Dublin. Thornton got a look at Redmond's personnel file from which he lifted a photo of the inspector. Concurrent with Thornton's success, Collins had another stroke of luck when the popular and gregarious Detective Sergeant James MacNamara—one of his G Division penetrations—was assigned as Redmond's assistant, guide, and confidential clerk.[10]

Shortly before Redmond's arrival in Dublin, an ambitious if hapless would-be double agent who went by the name Harry Quinn walked in and offered to spy for the Castle. Quinn—whose real name was either Timothy Henry Quinlisk or Henry Timothy Quinlisk—was an ex–British Army noncommissioned officer. A native of County Waterford, Quinn had been captured by the Germans on the Western Front and while a POW had joined Sir Roger Casement's Irish Brigade prior to the 1916 Easter Rising. His military experience made him an attractive volunteer candidate and Collins took him on as a training officer. Quinn would soon be lobbying to raise his status—and his fortunes.[11]

Coogan has written that the Harry Quinn affair was one of the most important counterintelligence threats facing Collins at the time.[12] Although Quinn's treachery may have been responsible for a police raid that nearly captured Collins, his counterintelligence importance is exaggerated. To begin with, Quinn was a rank amateur and a bold opportunist—an informer—not a professional agent. His motivation for turning against the IRA was a combination of ego, ambition, and money. Nevertheless, G Division took an active role in cultivating Quinn—a decision they would soon regret.

Quinn's acceptance into the IRA was not unusual; some of the IRA's best men were experienced combat veterans of the British Army. Their knowledge of weapons and tactics proved invaluable to the columns. But Quinn had an irrepressible ego and an air of arrogant assurance. He tried to give the impression to anyone who would listen that he was a close confidante of Collins. After successfully badgering Collins into giving him money for new clothes, he went about Dublin dressed like an aristocrat while angling for additional handouts. He envisioned a more important role in the IRA and, after weeks of showing up at IRA GHQ to pester Collins about this, Joe O'Reilly was ordered to keep Quinn at arm's length. O'Reilly was an effective gatekeeper, and the incensed Quinn made the fateful decision to turn informer. He wrote a letter to the undersecretary in late November 1919 calling Collins a "scoundrel" and offering to spy for the Castle. By this time, a £10,000 reward had been offered by the Crown for information leading to the apprehension of the killers of G Division officers, a strong motivation for Quinn's treachery.[13]

In due course, Quinn was brought to the Castle, where he was interviewed by Police Superintendent O'Brien and G Division detectives. Ned Broy typed up the report and passed it to Collins; his intelligence staff conducted a damage assessment, concluding that Quinn may have been responsible for the October raid on Dail headquarters in Harcourt Street that almost snared Collins. The report from Broy sealed Quinn's fate. Not aware he was already under investigation by the IRA intelligence staff, Quinn told his IRA contacts that he had visited the Castle to apply for a passport. Collins feigned acceptance of this explanation but decided to try to gain some advantage from Quinn. He ordered his staff to try to arrange an ambush of O'Brien; disguising his voice, Tom Cullen telephoned the superintendent, pretending to be Quinn. Cullen requested a second meeting—this time outside the Castle—and insisted that O'Brien himself must make the rendezvous. The Squad staked out the site but when O'Brien and a group of policemen approached, they spotted the surveillance, suspected a setup, and quickly withdrew.[14]

Quinn now came under suspicion by the DMP and found himself entangled by the classic double-agent conundrum of being distrusted by both sides. To extricate himself, Quinn wrote a letter to a newspaper in which he accused Castle authorities of attempting to bribe him into working as an informer. The letter was never published, but Collins obtained a copy. He decided not to take action against Quinn, but when Quinn again approached IRA GHQ, O'Reilly told him that Collins had gone to Cork. Quinn was directed by G Division to follow Collins to Cork, try to locate him there, and report back. Upon his arrival in Cork, Quinn resumed his modus operandi, bragging about his past with local IRA brigade members and claiming that he could assist them in smuggling arms. The Cork City IRA then learned from sources in the local post office that an important letter would be forthcoming from Dublin intended for a British agent in the city. Florrence O'Donoghue personally held up the postman and obtained the letter, which implicated Quinn. Brigade men then reached out to Quinn, telling him that they were interested in his arms proposition and that they would show him one of their arms dumps. Luring the unlucky spy to a lonely lane, they executed him.[15]

Notably, the Cork City IRA acted against Quinn on its own authority, without coordination with Collins or IRA GHQ. It would not be the last such incident. The Quinn killing followed a pattern by the Cork IRA to shoot first and ask questions later. Peter Hart claims that the Cork City IRA conducted 131 indiscriminate attacks against civilians, including ex-British servicemen, in 1920–1921. Moreover, Hart raises the issue of sectarian violence, accusing the Cork IRA of attacks on Protestants simply because they were Protestants. John Borgonovo has challenged these findings. Basing his own assessment on IRA brigade records, police and army reports, and local newspaper accounts, Borognovo has accounted for only 31 such victims, 18 of whom he assesses had no apparent connection with Crown forces. Other historians, most notably Brian P. Murphey and Niall Meehan, have vigorously challenged Hart's assertion of IRA sectarian murder.[16]

Connie Neenan, the commanding officer of the Cork City Brigade's Second Battalion in 1921, was convinced that an "anti–Sinn Fein society" of loyalist citizens was actively engaged in espionage activities against the IRA there. According to Neenan,

> The sad thing was, that although we had good intelligence contacts, we did not know until it was nearly too late, that there was an anti-Sinn Fein murder gang in existence. Information on our lads was passed along from certain business people and loyalists living a low profile existence. It was not until September 1920 that we laid a trap and caught this clerk in the main post office. He was the main channel through which the notes were passed. He confessed everything. We now had twelve names, some of these very prominent people. One by one they were shot dead, except one fellow who made off to London, but he, we were told, committed suicide on the train. That made a terrific impact. There were other forces against us too.[17]

Borgonovo notes, that while many Cork IRA veterans shared Neenan's conviction that a loyalist "murder gang" existed, there is no conclusive evidence that the "anti–Sinn Fein society" per se was anything more than a British propaganda creation designed to incite loyalists to fight back against the IRA in Cork City. Nonetheless, the number of executed persons suspected of collaboration with Crown forces appears to be around thirteen, including Harry Quinn, a confirmed spy.[18]

West Cork was a different matter, perhaps. In his detailed memoir, Tom Barry, the commanding officer of the IRA West Cork Brigade Flying Column, steadfastly maintained that there was a large organized British network of loyalist informers in his operating theater, which encompassed the large area of County Cork west and south of a demarcation line between Macroom to the north and Kinsale to the south. By the opening of 1921, County Cork was occupied by nearly nine thousand British Regulars of the Sixth Division, including three full infantry regiments, the most aggressive of which was the Essex Regiment, whose regimental IO, Major Arthur E. Percival, had organized an extensive network of intelligence agents. Barry placed these British spies into three categories: unpaid civilian informers, paid civilian loyalist informers, and retired British Army officers who willingly volunteered their services to the Crown. Barry relates that his column commenced direct counterintelligence strikes in the spring of 1921, executing a total of sixteen British spies, and opined that the IRA made a grave mistake in waiting so long to take action against them.[19]

From this debate we may safely conclude that the victims of IRA counterintelligence operations included innocents and that there was a higher percentage of these in Munster, but Hart's high numbers are problematic.

Cork IRA intelligence chief Florrence O'Donoghue recalled that up until that time intelligence coordination between Cork and Dublin was very informal, meaning that the Cork IRA did not clear everything in advance with Collins. On the contrary, O'Donoghue and the IRA intelligence staff in Munster Province developed their own tactics and operations and normally informed GHQ in Dublin after the fact. For his part, Collins went along with this arrangement and, to be certain, whenever his staff had valuable information for O'Donoghue, it was sent to the Cork command without delay. As spectacular as Collins's efforts against Dublin's G men had been, the Cork IRA conducted many more attacks on the RIC and British Army intelligence than did Collins's Squad—especially from November 1920 until the truce.[20]

HILL-DILLON'S GAMBIT

A second counterintelligence case confronted Collins in March 1920 when MO4x's Hill-Dillon mounted a penetration operation against the IRA senior command. Hill-Dillon had served in MI5 during the war and was experienced in developing such operations. He had commenced organizing a clandestine plainclothes branch in the summer of 1919, but work had proceeded slowly and by fall of that year his bench was still pretty thin. This may be why he selected Army Sergeant Fergus Bryan Molloy as his agent provocateur. A native Irishman, Molloy was a "red cap," or military policeman, who had volunteered to undertake secret service work, despite having no apparent prior experience in clandestine service. Hill-Dillon's plan called for Molloy to approach the IRA and say that the army had directed him to join the secret service, but he was a reluctant spy because he was secretly sympathetic to Sinn Fein. In due course, Molloy made contact with Batt O'Connor, one of Collins's closest friends. Molloy ran down his pitch to O'Connor, telling him that he was well positioned to supply arms and intelligence on the British Secret Service. O'Connor agreed to see what he could do and in short order arranged for Molloy to meet with Liam Tobin, Tom Cullen, and Frank Thornton, Collins's deputy and two principal case officers. Over a period of weeks, Molloy promised to supply arms but never followed through. Then Molloy made a costly error. He wrote a letter to a sister in the United States saying that if anything happened to him, Liam Tobin would be responsible. Lily Mernin, Collins's agent on Hill-Dillon's staff, learned of the document and sent a warning about Molloy.[21]

Now alerted, Tobin, Cullen, and Thornton handled their meetings with Molloy with the utmost caution. Molloy next offered to sneak them into the Castle so they could copy classified documents. They turned the tables by asking Molloy to help them ambush Hill-Dillon. The following morning the colonel unexpectedly moved from his apartment to a more secure accommodation. Molloy continued to meet Tobin and soon asked him to write down the names of prominent Sinn Fein and Dail Eireann members on Dail stationery so he could show his British handlers that he was making progress. At this juncture, an alarmed Tobin recommended to Collins that Molloy be eliminated. The next evening, March 25, the Squad caught up with Molloy and shot him outside the Wicklow Hotel.[22]

BASIL THOMSON TRIES HIS HAND

Basil Thomson had won the counterintelligence turf battle with Vernon Kell in February 1919, and he was expected to produce results—especially in Ireland, traditional Special Branch territory. The cabinet, the military, and the Castle all looked to him for a solution. The thought of failure never entered his mind. He had been offering advice to the Castle since Lord French convened the security review in November. He had dispatched Special Branch men to Dublin, and commenced development of an agent network there. Thomson probably had a hand in bringing magistrate Bell out of retirement to handle some of Special Branch's agents in Ireland. With Bell's assistance and coordinating his steps with Inspector Redmond at G Division, he put into play a clever dangle operation intended to locate Michael Collins and penetrate his organization.[23]

The short, overweight, forty-something secret agent with piercing black eyes and ruddy complexion chosen by Thomson to establish a Special Branch spy network in Dublin in November 1919 employed the alias "John Jameson." The British agent did have an exotic past and numerous rumors about it have appeared as fact in Collins biographies—including such Bond-esque fiction as that he was an experienced secret service pro who had done intelligence work in India before the Great War and had undertaken amazing secret missions behind German lines during the war. The reality was much less spectacular and thus more typical of an access agent.

London born, Jameson had twice served in the British Army, reportedly including routine, nonintelligence postings in India and the Far East. Between hitches, he had worked as a plumber. He had not spent the Great War behind German lines but in backwater posts in the Mediterranean and had documented his overseas travel with delicately rendered oriental tattoos. He was reportedly fond of Edgar Wallace mysteries and told stories about the American Wild West, most likely inspired from dime novels. He kept birds as pets.[24]

Precise details of Jameson's introduction to Basil Thomson are unknown, but there is a plausible scenario. In 1916, with MI5 fully engaged in wartime efforts against German spies and saboteurs, Vernon Kell asked Thomson to take over complete responsibility for monitoring domestic labor unrest—an assignment the ambitious assistant police commissioner eagerly accepted. Special Branch quickly selected twelve detective sergeants from Scotland Yard CID and secured an £8,000 annual budget to form a labor squad. Not long after the armistice Thomson's labor squad extended its operations to the Soldiers', Sailors' and Airmen's union (SSAU) that was taking root within the forces. Thomson's men likely spotted the politically active ex–Sergeant Major Jameson shortly after his discharge from service in mid-1918 and recruited him for secret service work at that time.

Concurrently, the army's general staff formed a morale branch under Lieutenant Colonel Ralph Isham to develop a motivational program for servicemen. But the enterprising Isham eventually extended his efforts to security functions, including investigations of disgruntled military personnel, as well as selected civilian targets, including labor radicals and other potential subversives. The SSAU soon also became one of A2's priorities. At some point while Thomson's and Isham's men were stumbling over each other in pursuit of the SSAU, Isham became Jameson's handler. Given Thomson's ambitions, it is plausible that Thomson saw an opening to unofficially subsume A2 functions under his own control. All he had to do was lend Jameson to Isham to formalize that relationship. It was a win-win for Thomson on the one hand, who could now exercise some control over A2's intelligence activities. And on the other hand, Colonel Isham could enhance his cloak and dagger credentials by aligning himself with Special Branch.

Jameson had also been a key government agent penetration of British police union circles, and reported on the leaders who had orchestrated the London Metropolitan Police strike. While on that assignment, Jameson met an ex-RIC constable named Thomas J. McElligott. McElligot was one of Collins's agents who had tried to form a similar union in the RIC and had been fired for his inflammatory remarks. In 1918 Collins had dispatched McElligott to London to try to foment discord within the police union there, which, interestingly enough, was hardly a counterintelligence function and more accurately a covert action measure by the IRA intelligence staff. In addition to his contact with McElligott, Jameson was in contact with IRB member Art O'Brien of the Irish Self-Determination League, a Sinn Fein propaganda front that was also undoubtedly on the Special Branch radar screen. When Isham's unit was shut down in February 1919—not to be replaced by MO4x until seven months later—Thomson appears to have formally brought Colonel Isham into the new Home Intelligence Directorate.[25]

Art O'Brien was a key Republican operative, active in fundraising and propaganda as well as facilitating introductions for nationalists in Britain, and he was in close contact with Collins on financial matters. Jameson and O'Brien were soon discussing Ireland and the IRA's need for weapons, but Jameson insisted he would discuss the acquisition of arms only with the responsible parties. O'Brien was convinced of Jameson's bona fides and passed the message on to Collins. Thus, the established Jameson-O'Brien nexus was the perfect means to target Collins. However, Thomson later claimed that his original intention was merely to use Jameson as an influence agent to try to convince Irish nationalists to refrain from shooting police officers. According to Thomson, it was the Irish side that moved to involve Jameson more deeply by inviting him to Dublin to assist in their efforts to corrupt the police. Thomson was thus presented with an unanticipated opportunity to run a penetration operation.[26]

Jameson had already established the legend of a disgruntled ex-serviceman and radical activist. Thomson now rounded out a more complete cover story, according to which Jameson had been born in Limerick and was a disaffected ex-soldier sympathetic to Sinn Fein, Bolsheviks, and unions, who earned his living as a sales representative for the London-based Keith Prowse Agency, a theater ticket distributor. The cover was intended to provide Jameson with access to Dublin District Barracks, ostensibly to do business with the motion picture theater operator there, but likely this was to facilitate secure meetings with his handler(s) and possibly with other agents. It would also provide Jameson with an escape-and-evasion mechanism in the event that he became compromised as a Special Branch agent. Jameson's age and short, paunchy appearance were an ideal match for his cover.[27]

O'Brien recommended that Collins meet with Jameson, and recalling McElligott's glowing report of the previous year, Collins agreed, interested no doubt in learning what Jameson could bring to the table in terms of arms and other support. The first meeting appears to have taken place near London during one of Collins's periodic whirlwind visits to England. It is doubtful that Collins's true identity was revealed to Jameson at this first meeting. Collins was satisfied with Jameson's bona fides after their first encounter and agreed that they should stay in contact. Special Branch may very well have attempted to place the meeting under surveillance, but Collins and other intelligence staff always traveled under aliases, routinely ran surveillance detection routes, and undoubtedly took the usual security precautions. As a result of that first meeting, subsequent meetings were planned for Dublin.[28]

Jameson duly arrived in Dublin in November 1919 and immediately began making the rounds in pubs, building his cover as a traveling salesman. Against the advice of his own staff, which had not had time to fully vet Jameson, Collins held a follow-on meeting with the British agent over dinner at a Dublin safe house some days later. Jameson was blindfolded and taken by one of Collins's lieutenants to the safe house, while the escort informed him that the man he was meeting was the "greatest man Ireland had ever produced, greater even than de Valera." This second meeting also went well, and Collins concluded that Jameson was a decent fellow who might be valuable to the cause. Undoubtedly Jameson now realized that the Irish rebel he had been speaking with was one of the most important leaders, if not the most important leader. For his part, Collins was satisfied, and on December 9, 1919, Collins wrote to O'Brien, "Jameson has duly arrived and been interviewed by 3 of us. I shall report developments later on."[29]

According to Thomson, Jameson had informed his Irish contacts that he had a friend who worked in the army adjutant general's office, and the insurgents asked Jameson if he could use that connection to lay his hands on the secret War Office communication code. Thomson consulted the Home Secretary on the case, and after some convincing, was able to obtain permission to proceed. As the case had now moved partly within the realm of War Office jurisdiction, Thomson's decision to bring Colonel Isham along to handle Jameson had proven to be a wise move. Bell, meanwhile, as Thomson's man in the Castle, was able to provide Isham and Jameson with local support. During a planning session in England, Jameson was very insistent that should a decision be made to attempt to seize Collins or other senior IRA leaders while he was with them, the arresting party must also shoot him, preferably in a "nonvital" place. Jameson was reportedly adamant on this, noting that his life would not be worth "an hour's purchase" otherwise. Thomson found this to be a "very inconvenient stipulation," but he apparently agreed to it, for he proceeded to craft a batch of bogus "decoded" War Office messages for Jameson to hand over to Collins.[30]

Liam Tobin, Tom Cullen, and Joe O'Reilly never trusted Jameson; all were frustrated when Collins dismissed their concerns. Evidence soon mounted against Jameson, however. Two more meetings were arranged, the last in the home of friends where Collins frequently lunched. During that encounter, Collins promised to introduce Jameson to IRA Chief of Staff Richard Mulcahy and Defence Minister Cathal Brugha the following day. Collins's agreement to introduce Jameson to two of the most important leaders in the movement shows how far he had been drawn in by this dangle. Tobin and the rest of the staff grew increasingly uneasy. Only when G Division mole James MacNamara subsequently reported that the police had placed the luncheon site under surveillance did Collins realize the trap.

Although IRA intelligence was already very busy handling the Molloy case, Jameson became a counterintelligence priority. The IRA intelligence staff promptly assigned him the code name CORRY and acted swiftly to dig up everything it could about him. Tobin's staff soon confirmed that CORRY/Jameson had no relationship with the Keith Prowse Agency. Beyond that, Collins knew by this time from another source that Special Branch was trying to set up a trap. He soon received corroborating information from that source and wrote to O'Brien on January 20:

> Jameson: What I have to say with regard to him will probably be somewhat of a thunderbolt to you. I believe we have the man or one of them. I have absolutely certain information that the man who came from London met and spoke to me . . . reported that I was growing a moustache to Basil Thomson. I may get some more information.[31]

This note, found among Collins's papers after his death, is clear evidence that Collins could and did reach out to a source with direct access to Thomson's Home Intelligence Directorate—a remarkable feat for a revolutionary intelligence service operated by an underground chief and staff on the run. Indeed, as contemporary photographs reveal, Collins had grown a moustache, probably in an effort to age his appearance. Had "Lieutenant G" tipped off Collins? We may never know who the source was, but Collins clearly had a highly placed agent within British intelligence, perhaps in the Castle, or within Scotland House.

After disappearing for a month—to return to London to confer with Thomson and Isham—Jameson returned to Dublin and soon made contact with Tom Cullen, who apparently was not expecting the visit. Jameson told Cullen that he had been away in England organizing a secret union among the police forces. To prove his story, the agent handed over a heavy suitcase filled with handguns. Suspecting a setup, the quick-thinking Cullen walked Jameson down O'Connell Street carrying the grip. As they approached Kapp and Peterson's tobacco shop, Cullen turned to Jameson and said, "I'm going to take these guns in here as it is [an arms] dump for us." With that, Cullen said good-bye to Jameson and simply walked through the front of the shop and out the back, later concealing the guns at a separate location. That evening the police raided the shop. Chief Inspector Redmond—with James MacNamara at his side—showed up personally to supervise the raid. Finding nothing, the police retreated. Collins did not need further proof of Jameson's true vocation.[32]

The next act of this drama occurred a few days later, when Chief Inspector Redmond berated a G Division detective for lack of initiative. In an egregious lapse of judgment, Redmond angrily yelled, "You were supposed to have been looking for Collins. You have been after him for months and never caught sight of him, while a new man, just over from England, met him and talked to him after two days." MacNamara overheard the remark and reported it to Collins, who now had conclusive proof that Jameson was a British spy. Moreover, Collins now knew that Redmond had a hand in running the agent or, at a minimum, was cooperating closely with Special Branch on the case. Such involvement represented a considerable escalation of G Division intelligence activities, and just when the IRA believed it had thoroughly demoralized the force. Collins moved first against Redmond, perhaps concluding that the best way to deal with a snake would be to cut off its head. The chief inspector lived outside the Castle walls and walked to and from his job without escort, and the Squad laid plans to ambush him. Broy and MacNamara reported that the chief inspector wore a steel protective vest under his suit, so when the Squad caught up with him outside his flat on January 24, they aimed for his head. The first shot smashed his jaw and Redmond went for his revolver. The second shot was a fatal hit in the forehead. A few days later,

Redmond's crew of detectives cleared out and returned to the relative safety of Belfast.[33]

THE STAR CHAMBER

While Collins and his intelligence staff were preoccupied with the Jameson/CORRY affair, they were confronted with an equally serious threat from the Castle. One of Alan Bell's priorities was the discovery of Dail Eireann's National Loan funds. According to Neligan, these funds amounted to £378,858, and another $5.8 million collected by de Valera on his American tour.[34] Bell assembled a team in the Castle to investigate bank accounts. On March 10, he subpoenaed the managers of Ireland's two largest banks to appear before him and reveal the names of the account holders. Neligan recounted,

> He set up a kind of Star Chamber in the Castle. In March 1920, he was given power, under an ancient statute known as the Crimes Act, to send for and interrogate bank managers and others in order to lay his hands on that money.[35]

As Finance Minister, Collins was responsible for safeguarding the funds, and according to Neligan he had converted a portion of the money to gold and concealed this in a vault beneath the floor of Batt O'Connor's home. Collins persuaded some wealthy Sinn Fein sympathizers to deposit the remainder in several private accounts.[36] Bell's threat to Dail funds was the most immediate reason he was targeted by the IRA; however, it was becoming increasingly clear to the IRA that Bell was also Basil Thomson's man in the Castle, and had been working closely with Inspector Redmond on a variety of intelligence matters, likely including the Jameson effort. It is unclear whether the IRA intelligence network was fully cognizant of everything Bell was doing but Bell's agent-running activities notwithstanding, his subpoena of bank managers was enough reason to become a prime target, and Collins ordered the Squad to shoot him.[37]

Bell lived in the far Dublin suburbs and never varied his route to or from the Castle, always riding the same tram. On March 26, therefore, Squad members easily intercepted Bell at the Merrion tram stop, dragged him off the tram, and shot him in broad daylight. The killing of the elderly magistrate was widely reported, resulting in an outcry of revulsion

throughout England and abroad. The act only strengthened London's resolve to take firmer steps against the IRA.[38]

Despite the assassination of Redmond and Bell, neither Thomson nor
Isham made an executive decision to pull Jameson out of Ireland after
Bell's death. Both of them, and no doubt Jameson himself, realized that
the British agent was in grave peril. Thomson and Isham foolishly allowed
Jameson to continue his masquerade, and a week after Bell's killing, the
Squad lifted Jameson from his flat at the Granville Hotel on O'Connell
Street and drove him to an isolated spot in Dublin's Glasnevin Cemetery.
One of the Squad reportedly apologized to their prisoner, saying, "We
know you are a spy and you are going to die. We are only doing our
duty." The British agent reportedly replied, "And I have done mine. I shall
love to die for my country. God save the King!" With that, "John Jameson"
snapped to attention, saluted his foes, and was shot dead.[39]

As a footnote to this episode, Tom Cullen went through CORRY's personal effects in his hotel room the day after the Squad assassinated him
and discovered notes indicating that he had been running a network of
agents. This may have been the reason that Thomson and Isham allowed
their agent to remain in place for so long; at any rate, Cullen's discovery
was too late, for the other members of the Jameson network had slipped
out of the country the night before. Their true identities have never been
revealed, but CORRY's came to light a few days later when his corpse
was claimed by his wife—Mrs. John Charles "Jack" Byrnes of Romford,
England.[40]

When the cabinet was briefed on the case a few weeks later, First Lord
of the Admiralty Walter Long—a close confidante of Basil Thomson—
commented that Jack Byrnes "had been the best secret service man we
had."[41]

In retrospect, while Byrnes overplayed his hand, Thomson nearly succeeded in trapping not only Collins but key political and military leaders.
The exposure of Jameson/CORRY was a good piece of counterintelligence work by Collins's lieutenants. But in a broader sense it was inevitable, and no real surprise to Collins, that Special Branch would eventually
come after him once G Division was crippled. Still, there was considerable
finger pointing within the intelligence staff and between Collins and Art
O'Brien. More significant, however, was the killing of Redmond, which
effectively marked the end of British efforts to rebuild the G Division,

and this helped to convince London that a change in security policy was essential. As for Basil Thomson, there is no telling how much operational intelligence he developed on Collins from this case—very likely a good deal. The Castle, meanwhile, announced a £10,000 reward for information leading to the arrest of Redmond's killers.[42]

The Jameson/CORRY case is yet another of the most sensationalized episodes of the Anglo-Irish War. Historian Hart offered some interesting new details based upon his discovery of the A2 operational files, and while Hart assesses that Collins and the IRA generally scored a "hattrick" against British intelligence, he seriously underestimates the importance of the Jameson/CORRY case, noting merely that the British agent was suspected from the start and did no real damage.[43]

The case was much more important than Hart seems willing to admit and his assessment is based solely on the IRA's timely exposure and elimination of this spy. There is rarely an inconsequential development in a counterespionage case. In the realm of human intelligence, events *always* have consequences. The steps taken today—or not taken—may influence other intelligence operations or even government policy for years to come. The case was a reality check for Collins that strengthened his security awareness and confirmed that he was now up against not only G Division but also Special Branch—a far more formidable foe. If the IRA tightened operational security as a result of this case—and it appears that this was so—then it did affect the outcome of the war. Moreover, the case is significant for showing that Collins had successfully penetrated Thomson's organization, perhaps at a very high level, and perhaps as early as the fall of 1919.

Perhaps more importantly, it seems clear that Basil Thomson obtained invaluable personal assessment information on Collins from Jack Byrnes that the British had heretofore been unable to obtain. That information would soon be of great tactical assistance in revealing to Special Branch the security tradecraft used by Collins and his officers. On a strategic level, Byrnes's detailed description of Collins's personality, demeanor, likes, dislikes, tastes, personal preferences, and idiosyncrasies would prove invaluable to Lloyd George and the cabinet when it subsequently sought to open a secret channel of communication with the insurgent leadership to explore peace talks. Even more importantly, it was personality assessment data that could aid the British immensely in trying to manipulate and out-maneuver Collins, should he participate in any future peace negotiations.

Finally, the entire Special Branch/Home Intelligence effort against Collins and the IRA lay in shambles as a result of the case. In eliminating Byrnes/Jameson, Bell, and Redmond, Collins not only killed a large snake but he cut off its head. Thomson had no choice now but to try to rebuild a clandestine collection system in Ireland.

The demise of the British spies Quinlisk, Molloy, and Jack Byrnes by April 1920 marked the end of the first phase of the intelligence war, and the IRA emerged the clear winner. It was evident to the cabinet that serious intelligence reforms were needed for Ireland, not least the establishment of a properly organized and coordinated clandestine service.

BACK CHANNELS

On April 9, 1920, in the wake of the Jameson fiasco, Basil Thomson made the acquaintance of American journalist and war correspondent Carl Ackerman, who had been reporting on the Irish rebellion for the *Philadelphia Ledger*. Two weeks later Thomson recontacted Ackerman and told him that the British side was interested in discussing peace and, perhaps disingenuously, that the Crown did not know the right person with the authority to represent Sinn Fein. Was this the "Pecksniffian" subterfuge that Lieutenant G had warned Collins about, or was it genuine? Basil Thomson had known full well as early as November 1919 via Jameson that Michael Collins was the driving force behind the IRA. Indeed, by the spring of 1920 Lloyd George himself had singled out Collins as the most influential rebel leader, while publicly vilifying him as a "gunman" and labeling Sinn Fein and the IRA as a "murder gang."[44]

Thomson's overture was genuine. He may have been Britain's domestic spymaster, but Sir Basil had begun his career in the diplomatic service. After watching one dangle operation after another end in disaster, Thomson and some cabinet members probably realized that peaceful resolution was worth pursuing if an agreement could be achieved on London's terms. Home Rule had almost been a reality in 1914 and now the government was prepared to implement it—albeit with partition of Ulster. Regardless of his personal views, Thomson was almost certainly acting under cabinet instructions in approaching an intermediary. He told Ackerman and other journalists that Lloyd George's inflammatory public remarks should be ignored, because behind the scenes there was a genuine interest in peace at Downing Street. Thomson also realized— undoubtedly from Jameson's clandestine reports—that in private, Collins could be a quiet, intelligent, genial man, and much more reasonable than the bloodthirsty gangster portrayed by British propaganda.

Ackerman subsequently briefed Martin Glynn, a U.S. congressman from upstate New York and a fellow newspaperman. Ackerman arranged for Glynn to meet Lloyd George, and Glynn spent three hours stressing to the prime minister the strong support of Irish Americans for Sinn Fein, convincing Lloyd George that the special relationship between the United States and Great Britain depended to an extent on a peaceful resolution of the conflict. All parties in these backdoor discussions knew that the Ulster Unionists would never agree to be part of an Irish Republic. Therefore the key question for Basil Thomson—indeed for Lloyd George—was whether Michael Collins and the Dail would accept partition as a prerequisite for peace talks. Ackerman set out to find out.[45]

Maire Comerford, who was close to Collins throughout the Anglo-Irish War, described the dual-track policy that the British pursued with Collins. She dated the commencement of the back-channel contacts to the beginning of 1920, but her claim that there was a "hot line" between Collins and the Castle is a bit melodramatic:

The British Government was unsure what to do about people who were supposed to be politicians but who were also engaged in fighting them. They did not ban Dail Eireann until September 1919. Griffith was openly around and could have been picked up any time. They had a bad description of Collins; they did not know he was as dark as he was. They thought that he was fair. From the beginning of 1920 when Cope was appointed Under Secretary for Ireland, Collins was in touch directly with the Castle. There was a hot line between them. . . . In a war such arrangements sometimes exist. . . . So while the Upper Yard was having its dealings with Collins, the Lower Yard was having dealings of another sort. It was after him with the murder gang. He was however a very cool customer with plenty of nerve.[46]

This was a significant development in British policy. Despite urgings from the military to declare martial law and attack the insurgents on all fronts, from at least April 1920 onward, London would pursue a dual-track policy: brutalize the Irish people to compel their loyalty on the one hand and secretly reach out to the insurgents to find a peaceful resolution on the other hand. This was a tricky gambit, for the government first had to convince the Irish leadership to accept a partition in order to reach accommodation with hard-liners in London and with Ulster Unionists. Such a geographical division of the country was completely opposite the independence proclamations of April 1916 and January 1919, and unlikely to ever be accepted by the most ardent physical-force nationalists.

8

UNIFICATION BY FORCE

My own view is that to win a war of this sort you must be ruthless.
—*Major Bernard Law Montgomery, British intelligence officer
during the Anglo-Irish War, 1923*

The war intensified significantly at the opening of 1920. British Army intelligence had been combing through old RIC records, resulting in more
than 1,000 raids in January, including the joint army-police operation on
the last day of the month that netted some 90 IRA officers and men. In
February, 4,000 raids were carried out, resulting in a further 296 arrests.[1]
The IRA also stepped up its activity, moving from assaults on individual
constables to attacks against RIC barracks and army patrols. As counterinsurgency pressure increased in the spring and summer, the Volunteers
were no longer safe operating from stationary bases. Flying columns of
twenty to thirty men now operated on the run in almost every county.
Lloyd George and his cabinet would explore many options in the next
twelve months, but the one they would implement followed a hard line. A
shake-up in the Dublin administration seemed increasingly likely.

IRA attacks on constables had been under way for a year. Its barracks
campaign opened on February 14 when the IRA captured the RIC barracks at Ballytrain, County Monahan. That same day, Cork IRA elements
captured the barracks at Castlemartyr. Between February and April, the
IRA burned some 350 abandoned barracks in districts that had been ced-

ed by the RIC and dozens of tax offices were also destroyed. This escalation would bring a strong response from London.[2]

ENTER THE PARAMILITARIES

The proposal by General Shaw the previous November to recruit ex-servicemen for the RIC was proving successful. Hundreds of unemployed ex-Tommies were responding enthusiastically to the prospect of a job 'with adventure and decent pay.

The purpose of the Royal Irish Constabulary Reserve Force (RICRF) that arrived in Ireland in March 1920 was to bolster the constabulary, which had been debilitated through an average of two hundred resignations a month since the first of the year. The force quickly took on a sinister character. The recruits were exclusively ex–enlisted men, most with combat experience on the Western Front. They knew how to kill and destroy things, but they had no police or intelligence skills whatsoever. Because of shortages in police uniforms, they were outfitted in the dark green caps and tunics of the RIC with army khaki trousers. The public quickly began calling them Black and Tans, or simply "Tans." Their behavior would make them infamous, yet it was not their brutality but their lack of intelligence and police skills that would soon lead hard-liners in the cabinet to seek a better solution.[3]

By late spring, Churchill developed the idea for a new force comprising a better caliber of men with better leadership qualities and initiative and an appreciation of intelligence and military tactics. From this concept was born the Auxiliary Division, a force of ex–commissioned officers. Because of anticipated delays in integrating these officers into individual RIC units, London decided to deploy them as a separate paramilitary division. Although they were supposed to undertake police functions, they were only nominally part of the RIC. The Auxiliaries were organized and equipped like a mobile light infantry regiment. Army Brigadier General Frank Crozier was appointed to command them, but Irish command provided only general direction and oversight of their actions; in practical terms, while they coordinated their operations with the army, they maneuvered quite independently. This Auxiliary Division of 2,214 men was far more cunning and dangerous than the Black and Tans. Some 280 of them had been decorated for gallantry in the Great War, including three Victoria Cross holders.[4]

Moreover, each Auxiliary company had its own intelligence officer to coordinate information with the army and the RIC. This would pose a more serious threat to the IRA than the Tans. Churchill and Crozier envisioned it as an elite unit, and Mackay has provided a good description of their background and high esprit de corps:

They wore their medal ribbons with fierce pride, and included many a Military Cross and Distinguished Service Order. They were the product of the finest English public schools and a good percentage of them came from old Anglo-Irish families; but otherwise they differed only from the Black and Tans in their ruthlessness and ferocity. Utterly fearless, especially when cornered, they often earned the respect of their opponents; but they also included a sinister sprinkling of sadists and psychopaths who delighted in devising ever more fiendish methods of torture, mutilation and death.[5]

Highly paid at the rate of £7 per week and heavily armed, each Auxiliary officer (also known as Temporary Cadet) carried two .45 caliber Webley revolvers strapped to his hips, as well as a carbine; some wore their pistols slung low on their hips, prompting one Auxiliary officer to remark that they appeared to be emulating Texas cowboys.[6] They also mounted machine guns in their Crossley Tender and Lancia armored cars. Dubbed "Auxies" by the Irish, they were instantly recognizable by their distinctive Glengarry caps.[7]

The Black and Tans and Auxiliaries introduced an atmosphere of stark terror in Ireland. The two forces have often been confused, but it was the Auxiliaries who perpetrated most of the outrages between June 1920 and July 1921. Cunning, intelligent and better armed than an ordinary infantry unit and with the arrogant conviction that might makes right, the Auxiliaries resembled a sort of English *Freikorps*: a close fraternity of jobless veterans with few skills except the profession of arms, comfortable within a military structure, fiercely loyal to the government, and out for adventure. Significantly, unlike the Black and Tans, who were officially the RIC Reserve, the Auxiliaries were generally not held accountable for their actions to either military or police authority. Ostensibly, their mission was to restore law and order, but instead of attempting to stabilize the situation or pacify the people, they were employed to punish the Irish and damage the local economy in an effort to destroy the IRA's base of support. Their methods included clearing out towns and burning and looting of houses, farms, factories, and dairies while rounding up and shooting or arresting unarmed citizens and sending them to internment camps. There was little valor in their behavior, and as distasteful as it may seem to British partisans, their modus operandi was not unlike the special "police actions" carried out by the German Order Police battalions against Jews in Lithuania, Poland, and the Ukraine in the summer of 1941. The highly mobile, truck-mounted British Auxiliaries conducted more than a dozen disturbingly similar clearing actions in Irish communities between July 1920 and July 1921.[8]

While condemning both sides in the conflict, the American Commission on Conditions in Ireland, which investigated human rights abuses in Ireland in 1920–1921, offered chilling testimony—and photographic evidence—of atrocities committed by the Auxiliaries and Black and Tans. These included floggings of juvenile males suspected of complicity with the IRA and other forms of physical torture. The commission further focused on raids in rural areas, particularly the practice of arresting and shooting male family members and, in some instances, the wholesale murder of entire families. The report dryly noted one particularly effective method that the paramilitaries had devised for minimizing resistance and panic during raids on farms; they apparently learned from experience that the executions of family members tended to result in a great deal of screaming and panic, particularly by frightened younger children. According to the commission's findings, in a flash of cool military efficiency, the Auxiliaries adopted the practice of placing cream buckets over the heads of the smaller children prior to shooting family members. Collins knew that penetrating such a hardened group would be difficult. Up to now, most of his star agents had been walk-ins or volunteers; he had not recruited any significant "hard targets," or loyalists. Nevertheless, his deputy Liam Tobin succeeded in recruiting an Auxiliary, Major J. C. Reynolds, whose principal motivation was money. Reynolds belonged to F Company, based in metro Dublin. Although Reynolds could never be fully vetted or completely trusted by the IRA, the agent reportedly provided valuable information on his fellow officers. Later on, when Reynolds was transferred up-country, Tobin recruited a second F Company cadet named McCarthy to replace him.[9]

The excesses of the paramilitaries soon led to international criticism of the British government. While it privately pursued a relentless hard-line policy, however, the cabinet continued to deny publicly that a rebellion had broken out in Ireland.

THE ARMY RESPONSE

British Army field commanders were growing increasingly frustrated by the lack of actionable intelligence from the RIC and they were further hamstrung by existing legal statutes, which made court prosecutions extremely complicated. They had been participating in joint operations with the RIC since late January, but from an intelligence point of view, the police records left much to be desired. The army intelligence staff later wrote:

> From the experience gained while these arrests were being made it became clearer than ever that military intelligence must depend on itself if results were to be obtained. Very considerable information about the organization of the IRA was collected; the framework of the Order of Battle was built up and it was realised that it was essential to keep up-to-date what was already known and also to discover a great deal more about those individuals who kept the spirit of rebellion alive.[10]

Further handicapping counterinsurgency efforts were the amnesties granted to detainees since December 1916. On April 14 another amnesty was granted to the prisoners who had been arrested at the end of January. Due to an administrative mix-up, however, ninety of the most hard-core men who had gone on hunger strike were released, including thirty-one who had been convicted for membership in the IRA. The army command noted that the action was a serious setback for army intelligence:

> On the 14th of this month the release of the men who had been arrested since January and who had gone on hunger strike was a severe blow to Intelligence in Ireland. It decreased still further the moral [sic] of the RIC and correspondingly raised that of the IRA, whose organization was expanded and improved. Informers, who had begun to come forward in the preceding months, now became afraid to do so and military intelligence grew both more necessary and harder to obtain.[11]

In London, meanwhile, the cabinet set up a special committee on April 18 to review the conduct of the Castle administration. The study was chaired by Sir Warren Fisher, who had recently become head of the British civil service. In less than a month, Fisher reported that the Dublin administration was in complete disarray and recommended the appointment of a "powerful" civil servant to lead a reorganization effort.[12]

The first ten days of May were marked by a series of IRA attacks on police barracks in Tipperary.[13] Between May 14 and 16, each member of Dail Eireann not in custody received a threat letter printed on Dail stationery reading, "An eye for an eye, a tooth for a tooth, therefore a life for a life." A glance at the stationery confirmed it was from the same stock seized by Crown forces during the October raid on the Dail's Harcourt Street headquarters. A few days afterward, Arthur Griffith assembled reporters and announced that the note was on paper captured by the police and he denounced the British government for inciting the assassination of the legally elected representatives of the Irish people. It was another Sinn Fein propaganda coup, and Griffith and the Dail Propaganda Bureau would enjoy several more.[14]

Within the month, the Irish Transport and General Workers Union (ITGWU) announced that dock workers and railway employees would no longer operate trains carrying British troops or load and unload ferries or ships carrying British armament or supplies. This profoundly affected the conduct of the war. Troops and equipment were stranded at rail heads and docksides around the country. By late September 1920, the strike had forced the Great Northern Railway Company to shut down 563 miles of main lines and trunk lines in Ireland.[15] Unable to deploy troops or resupply them by rail or sea, the army was compelled to rely on motor transport. This situation, in turn, presented ideal conditions for guerrilla warfare along the twisting, unimproved single-lane roads in much of rural Ireland. The IRA capitalized on this, setting up ambush points for British Army and Auxiliary police vehicles. Killing zones were established by felling trees and digging trenches ten feet deep by ten feet wide to block the roads. With local IRA scouts watching for the approach of British vehicles, flying columns moved into position adjacent to the kill zones, concealed behind stone walls, hedges, trees, and fences. A motorized convoy turning a bend in the road would suddenly be halted by a roadblock;

given the single-lane roads and rough country, it was next to impossible to turn the vehicles around. Once the British were blocked in the kill zone, the IRA began the attack. IRA units always focused on first incapacitating the lead vehicle; this was accomplished with sniper fire, by setting off a mine, or by lobbing a hand grenade into the driver compartment. After the driver was killed, the IRA would open fire on the passenger compartment with Lewis machine guns—if they had them—or with well-placed rifle, shotgun, and revolver fire. As the Tommies or Auxiliaries scrambled in panic to exit their vehicles to return fire, they were picked off one by one.

Henceforth, the army also had to improvise counterambush tactics and adopt its maneuver doctrine to match its restricted lines of communication and supply. It was compelled to escort each convoy with troops and in some cases the ambushes developed into prolonged running firefights conducted on foot over very rough terrain. In general, however, the IRA was not only fighting on its own turf, it was defining the place for battle; British forces became far more vulnerable than ever before. Irish Command established a guerrilla warfare school for troops arriving in Ireland, but as with intelligence, it was an ad hoc effort. As officers of the army's Fifth Division noted:

The country (except the Bog of Allen) is covered by a haphazard network of narrow second and third class roads. The narrowness of the roads, and the many patches of bogland over which they cross, have assisted Sinn Fein greatly, since Christmas 1920, to interrupt our road communications by blowing up bridges, cutting trenches and trees, and also to select suitable places for ambush on lorries and convoys. . . . It was not until the spring of 1921 that, owing to the increase in the number of rebel ambushes and road mines, it was found unwise to allow lorries to travel singly in the country, and as a precaution against a single lorry being destroyed, it was ordered that not less than two lorries should proceed in company, the escort being between them so that half the party had a good chance of taking on the ambushers. It was, however, essential that a certain distance (300 yards) should be kept between lorries to prevent both being overwhelmed at the same spot.[16]

THE DUBLIN DISTRICT SPECIAL BRANCH

By the spring of 1920, British security authorities on the ground in Ireland recognized that the insurrection was evolving into a full-scale rebellion. While publicly they (and hard-liners in London) referred to Sinn Fein and the IRA as a "murder gang," they realized privately that they were facing a well-organized insurgency with a well-organized and efficient intelligence and counterintelligence capability. The failure of piecemeal British intelligence efforts to penetrate the IRA since late 1919 was ample proof. Whatever agents or informers remained in place were in disarray, and Bell's financial investigation into Dail funds had been halted in its tracks. Special Branch's promising Jameson network had been disrupted, and G Division had ceased to be a factor after the assassination of Forbes Redmond and the departure of his Belfast detectives.

After the demise of his agent, Molloy, Colonel Hill-Dillon had accelerated efforts to expand his secret service branch. The War Office pulled strings to locate personnel with intelligence experience or those who might volunteer for such service. The success in forming the Auxiliary division showed that there were thousands of unemployed ex–army officers eager to risk the dangers of Ireland in return for a paycheck. Hill-Dillon's plainclothes unit was a mix of such veterans, some of whom had served in IO billets with the Field Intelligence Corps in occupied Germany, in Russia, and in the Balkans as well as recently separated officers with no experience. A secret service training school was established at the War Office Technical School at Hounslow Barracks, west of London, under MI5 auspices, and the first groups of army case officers began to arrive in the spring of 1920. In May, Lieutenant Colonel Walter Wilson arrived in Ireland to take over direct command of the expanded unit. Seven men had arrived by June, including some of the veterans; by August, seventy-five more were on the ground. Wilson continued to add officers until its strength peaked at ninety-seven in November. MI5's training left its mark on the freshly minted army operators, for upon their arrival in Dublin, some of them began referring to themselves as "Hush-Hush" men.[17]

The army planned to deploy these case officers in teams in Dublin and also eventually in the outlying provinces to support Fifth and Sixth Division operations. Initially, however, it decided to activate them within the Dublin District, where curfew and stringent government security measures gave them a freer hand and also, no doubt, time to acclimate themselves to Ireland and build up their various covers. Another reason for retaining the branch in metro Dublin was the fact that it was the most important theater of operations, where rebel gunmen now roamed the streets with impunity. Consequently, MO4x designated its plainclothes unit the Dublin District Special Branch (DDSB). Over the spring and summer, DDSB was divided into operational cells and deployed to various neighborhoods in Dublin.[18]

Not all of the members of Wilson's unit were rookies. Several were recently demobilized officers who had gained hard experience in intelligence operations during the World War and afterward. A few were MI5 veterans. Most had been given "special employment" with the rank of Temporary Captain and were placed on the openly publicized War Office General List—revealing that they were paid from other than War Office funds. That in itself was a giveaway, inasmuch as the British Secret Service budget in those years was drawn variously from the Foreign Office, Home Office, and even the Admiralty. The core leadership of DDSB included a handful of officers who had worked in Germany, Russia, Poland, Holland, and Egypt.[19]

Cover was a continuing problem. Nearly one hundred of them were in country, yet there were only so many plausible traveling salesman stories. Even without solid cover, however, they could at least spread out and lower their profiles more easily in metro Dublin than in a rural district, where they stood out. According to Captain Robert D. Jeune, a member of the branch, some of the first officers to arrive posed as members of the Royal Engineers, apparently under the mistaken theory that this would give them sufficient cover to wander freely throughout Dublin entering buildings at random and making inquiries of complete strangers. They may also have reasoned that posing as harmless engineers made them somehow less threatening than other British troops, diverting suspicion and protecting them from reprisal. This notion was likely based on a widely held belief early in the conflict that if one was not seen as a combatant, the IRA would leave them alone. So widespread was this conviction that, according to the wife of a British infantry battalion commander, officers living off-post in Ireland were advised not to have weapons on their persons or in their lodgings. Nevertheless, DDSB officers habitually went armed and kept automatics in their lodgings. Some favored the reliable high-power Colt .45 semiautomatic pistol over the British Army–issue Webley revolver.[20]

Jeune noted that the DDSB officers soon dropped the pretext of being Royal Engineers, donned plain clothes, and began direct surveillance of suspected targets. Some of the officers did succeed in gaining nonofficial cover, however; one worked as a shop assistant, and another as a garage mechanic, for example. They carried out their sub-rosa activities at night, often after curfew.[21]

The DDSB case officers were supposed to recruit and handle agents, or sources. In addition, since the majority of DDSB officers were operating under non-official cover, it was necessary for MO4x to employ some of them as "inside officers," or couriers for the street operators. An inside officer's job is to meet and debrief the street officers, retrieve any documentary intelligence the case officers may have obtained, and pass on new intelligence priorities and tasking. The inside officer is also responsible during clandestine rendezvous for paying the case officer his salary and passing operating funds and any equipment—a camera, for example—that a street operator requires.

This system enables the street operator to avoid official facilities, enhances his commercial cover, and offers significant protection. At the same time it is incumbent upon the inside officer to be assiduous in his street tradecraft to avoid drawing surveillance upon himself and, by extension, to the street officer. Likewise, street officers must take care not to attract surveillance that would endanger their assets. To be sure they are not followed, officers and their agents run predetermined surveillance detection routes to and from rendezvous sites. If the case officer is running three sources, for example, he in turn must instruct his three assets in the same clandestine tradecraft and insist that they follow the same security precautions.

A case officer's life thus becomes a continual seven-day-a-week cycle of running surveillance-detection routes; putting on disguises; meeting assets; meeting the inside officer; submitting reports, both verbal and documentary; and handling operational funds. On top of this, the case officer must put in extra hours to work at his cover job, leaving little spare time for sleep. In wartime conditions, a case officer may work as many as eighteen or twenty hours a day. It is exhausting and stressful, yet strangely exhilarating, especially when an agent delivers key information. According to one source, DDSB had four inside officers serving as couriers or go-betweens. David Neligan, the IRA-controlled penetration agent who joined MO4x in the spring of 1921, was also met regularly by an inside officer.[22]

Although the foregoing outlines the way that clandestine operations are supposed to function, what developed in DDSB was decidedly subpar. As the army's postwar report stated:

> The Special, or D Branch was a peculiar organization, as secret service organizations usually are. It was built up in the first instance by enthusiastic amateurs who neither knew or cared about the difference between I [Intelligence] a or I b. It was partly pure intelligence and partly executive. It had its own "constitution" and in the event of its official head taking actions to which the original creators objected, they did not hesitate to raise their objections in unmistakable fashion. Persons accustomed to police or detective work, where objectives are usually limited and definite, might and did regard the personnel as amateurs.[23]

The "executive" function alluded to in the report is a polite reference to lethal covert action—assassination. Officers of the DDSB were clearly empowered to conduct espionage or to stalk, detain, or execute suspected IRA members without arrest, arraignment, or trial. This was consistent with the government's policy of reprisal and in line with the recommendations of Lord French's security committee.

By the end of the year, the British would place DDSB under Castle management and amalgamate it with other civil and police elements under a new central intelligence chief. The reorganization would not resolve the dual army and police management of intelligence resources, however.[24]

Concurrent with Lieutenant Colonel Wilson's arrival, the divisional intelligence staffs were increased by one officer, while additional general IOs were appointed at brigade and battalion level. Since the MO4x officers were to focus for the time being on the Dublin District, funds were distributed to the Fifth and Sixth Divisions to expend on their own intelligence collection efforts. Now it was the divisional commanders who would have to improvise.[25]

THE SECRET WAR UP-COUNTRY

Although few of the officers appointed to intelligence duties within army maneuver units in the provinces were professionals, several displayed talent and skill. Four who later achieved fame were Major (later General) Sir Kenneth Strong, Major (later General) Arthur E. Percival, Major (later Field Marshal) Bernard Montgomery, and Major (later General) Colin Gubbins.

In 1920, Strong was a brigade intelligence officer in County Offaly. With no prior training or experience in undercover operations, he was given a budget of £5 per month and told to recruit intelligence sources. Years later Strong remembered:

> I never to my knowledge managed to catch a single Sinn Feiner of any importance. . . . They had, they had said, been in our net, but because of our ignorance or the unwillingness of witnesses to identify them for fear of reprisals, we had let them go. . . . To get to [agent] rendezvous, I would disguise myself as the owner of a donkey cart, but my accent was against me and I had several narrow escapes.[26]

Despite his self-effacing remarks, Strong remained in intelligence and later became MI5 defence security officer (RSO) in Malta and then Chief of Joint Staff Intelligence for General Dwight D. Eisenhower's command at Supreme Allied Headquarters during World War II. Strong was twice considered for nomination as director-general of MI5 in the late 1940s and early 1950s; he made the short list both times but never ascended to that post. It was the government's loss, considering the questionable skills of some of MI5's postwar leaders.[27]

Major Montgomery was responsible for establishing a regional intelligence center in Cork. He would go on to command the Allied Expeditionary Forces in Europe in World War II.[28]

Percival stands out primarily for his violent, sadistic behavior toward IRA prisoners, suspects, and innocent civilians while serving as IO for the Essex Regiment. He reportedly relished personally interrogating and torturing prisoners. He also participated in reprisals, burning farms (including Woodfield, Collins's ancestral family estate) and businesses in response to IRA attacks. Percival's outrages and excess so angered the IRA that Collins tried to have him assassinated and nearly succeeded. Members of the Squad failed to get Percival in Ireland, so they followed him to England when he went on leave in March 1921. Percival either detected the surveillance or was tipped off, for he spent his entire leave in a military garrison. The Squad lay in wait to shoot him on the platform at Liverpool Street Station when he arrived from camp, but they were apparently detected by a Special Branch security team. The Squad spotted the countersurveillance and was compelled to withdraw from the station just before Percival's arrival, narrowly avoiding a full Special Branch raid.[29]

After three frustrating years of trying to track down a faceless army that shot from behind hedgerows and placed mines in country lanes, Major Colin Gubbins got the hang of guerrilla warfare. By then he had learned how much mayhem could be caused by a disciplined and shadowy army of operatives fighting on their own territory and employing hit-and-run tactics. Gubbins survived his tour in Ireland and by 1939 was assigned as training officer for Britain's new super-secret unconventional warfare and sabotage agency, the Special Operations Executive (SOE). By 1944, General Gubbins had ascended to chief of SOE, in charge of all anti-Nazi sabotage and guerrilla operations from Norway to Yugoslavia. Gubbins was an admirer of Collins's tactics and considered Collins the master of guerrilla warfare. He applied the lessons he'd learned in Ireland twenty years earlier most effectively in SOE.[30]

Other army intelligence officers operating undercover were not so fortunate and did not survive the Anglo-Irish War. In Cork, the combined presence of the Auxiliaries, Black and Tans, and military, along with a staunchly loyalist element in the business community willing to take active measures to support numerous arrests and murders of nationalists, prompted IRA retaliation. Florrence O'Donoghue, head of IRA intelligence in Cork, operated a ruthlessly efficient counterintelligence organization against the Army Sixth Division. Whereas concealment was a great problem for undercover men in Dublin, it became absolutely critical to survival in Cork, Limerick, and smaller cities and towns. Establishing a plausible cover for status or action when one had an English accent was extremely difficult. IRA intelligence in Cork City was already targeting Loyalists and ex–British Army veterans fairly indiscriminately, apparently on the theory that they were automatically suspects given their backgrounds and that it was easier to shoot a known Loyalist or ex-Tommy than it was to vet their sympathies.

As noted earlier, while the Cork IRA may have executed more innocents than the IRA in other operational areas, there appears to be no hard evidence to support Hart's broad assertion that the IRA in Cork followed a deliberate sectarian policy or that it indiscriminantly murdered hundreds of non-combatants. Hart did discover, however, that it is not uncommon for both sides in a low-intensity conflict to employ deliberate and sometimes indiscriminate killings as a means of coercion. This phenomenon was not limited to Ireland; it is what contemporary intelligence officers sometimes refer to as the Guatemala Solution, based upon the counterinsurgency strategy employed in Guatemala in the 1980s. In its most extreme form, it operates on the principle of mass murder. If the government forces estimate that there are a thousand rebels in a particular district, they round up and deport—or kill—two thousand people in that district to ensure they have eliminated all of the disloyal ones. Conversely, guerrilla leaders may suspect or confirm that someone in the village is cooperating with the authorities, so they kill the adult males in the village to ensure they have cauterized the leak. It would hardly be fair to attribute this principle to Guatemala alone, however, for the same tactics have been used by everyone from Mao, to Che Guevara and Fidel Castro (who together murdered some thirteen thousand political opponents) to the Viet Cong, and from the Sandinistas to the Taliban. Small wars—low-intensity conflicts—are much more personal than conventional warfare, and are always marked by deep personal hatred, paranoid suspicion, and lethal revenge. And they always leave a legacy of bitterness and division. Most historians agree that Cork was an especially dangerous operating environment in the Anglo-Irish War and what took place there between 1919 and 1921 appears to have been based on the same principle but on a much smaller scale. Ireland is far from an isolated phenomenon.[31]

Added to this is the fact that as a general rule, irregular troops often lack fire discipline, are poorly or marginally trained and are led by amateur officers; individual units thus tend to become trigger happy, especially under the strain of combat. It is assumed that the IRA had better fire discipline than most guerrilla armies, if only because of the constant scarcity of ammunition. Nevertheless, mistakes were made, excesses occurred, and innocent non-combatants were killed by the IRA. This is the reality of war.

Moreover, an irregular guerrilla unit living off the countryside and constantly on the move can ill afford to take prisoners. Guerrilla leaders learn quickly that the safety of their own men depends on stealth and speed; retiring from an ambush site with prisoners in tow slows the withdrawal of the guerrilla unit and greatly increases the vulnerability of the unit to envelopment, counterattack, capture, or annihilation. This was true in Ireland as well. Cork IRA intelligence chief Florrence O'Donoghue wrote,

> The absence of any facilities for detention of prisoners over a long period made it impossible to deal with the doubtful cases. In practice, there was no alternative between execution and complete immunity. That made it imperative to obtain the clearest proof of guilt before a man was executed. . . . This was never an easy matter.[32]

British Army IOs had a relatively short life expectancy, as attested by IRA officer Martin Corry. Corry recalled two British officers who were trying to operate in the suburbs dressed as tramps. They approached a house to check the names on the door, were arrested by the IRA, and immediately shot, no questions asked. Lieutenants Brown and Rutherford of the Royal Artillery were pressed into service as brigade IOs. Both were arrested and executed by the IRA after being spotted near Macroom, County Cork, posing as tourists. Captain Thompson, an IO in the Manchester Regiment, placed himself within easy reach of the IRA by traveling to work on the same route day in, day out, and at the identical time each day. Thompson was gunned down by an IRA team in November 1920. Major Compton-Smith was a highly regarded IO serving with the Welsh Fusiliers. He was apprehended while visiting Blarney dressed as a fisherman. Florrence O'Donoghue personally interrogated Compton-Smith before he was executed by firing squad.[33]

Employing cover as a tramp or a tinker appears to have been a common ploy of British IOs, prompting the IRA to commence attacks on homeless and transient men in County Cork. The steadily increasing number of executions of suspected civilian informers and British officers in Cork and other outlying counties caught the attention of IRA GHQ, which learned of most of these killings through unofficial channels. Although GHQ tried to exercise control over executions, in practical terms the decision to execute a civilian suspect or a British prisoner continued to rest with the local column commander. As Tom Barry explained,

> Despite suggestions to the contrary, the Brigade never sought GHQ sanction for any of these executions. How could it? We had no jails to hold these men. And we dare not put all our evidence in writing because it might be captured en route or at GHQ and expose to certain death our own informants. GHQ during all the conflict never knew of the killing of an informer in West Cork until it read of it in a newspaper. How could those staff officers in Dublin judge better as to the guilt of an informer than the officers who had effectively to combat in the field the nefarious results of the traitors' activities?[34]

A British intelligence report tells the story, obtained from a captured IRA document, of one David Walsh who was arrested for espionage, interrogated, tried, and executed by the IRA:

> Some idea of the method of extracting information by threats of violence is demonstrated in the case of a man named David Walsh, a detailed account of whose treatment was found in a captured documents. He was arrested by the I.R.A., for being a "suspicious person of the tramp class" and he was detained for two days, during which time no information could be obtained from him. In order to remedy this, he was removed to a lonely mountain, and was confronted with the parish priest and an empty grave, and informed that he was to be shot forthwith, unless he supplied them with full information concerning himself and his accomplices. If this was forthcoming, the Captain guaranteed him a free pass to Australia. The unfortunate man, with the prospect of imminent death staring him in the face, invented a bogus story as to his having met a military party on the way to Cork, and having given them information concerning a camp at Clonmel. The way in which the I.R.A. Captain fulfilled his guarantee is told in the final paragraph of the document, which reads "David Walsh was subsequently tried by Court Martial for espionage, found guilty and sentence[d] to be shot. The finding was duly confirmed and the sentence duly executed."[35]

In County Kerry, an Auxiliary company commander named McKinnon incurred the wrath of the local IRA with his interrogation tactics and outrageous behavior. IRA veteran John Joe Sheehy, who led a section of Kerry Volunteers, described the IRA operations there and the killing of McKinnon in May 1921:

> Constant harassment was now our motto. . . . The Tans were here and the Auxiliaries, they occupied the jail and the Technical School. Every night they patrolled the town but we took awful chances, dangerous chances because in the curfew there was nobody about, and if they saw you they were certain to shoot. They were getting tougher and tougher. We availed of every opportunity that was presented to us. It was all short arms of course. That suited the sort of urban fighting we specialized in. But it would be difficult to get hold of a rifle anyway. In fact, we had to borrow the one that shot Major McKinnon. Connie Healy, an ex-British Army man from Boherbee, did that. . . . McKinnon became so bold and brazen that he went around the countryside with a machine gun on his shoulder. He was a terror. In fact, on one of those raids near Ballymacelligott . . . he called to this house . . . on Christmas night, 1920. It was the home of John Byrne . . . a key man in our organization. . . . There were two Volunteers there, Mossy Reidy and John Leen. McKinnon went in and shot them dead.[36]

Volunteer Con Casey provided additional details:

> It was not long before I was picked up by the Auxiliaries, the English recruited police. They had taken over the Technical School down the road from here. The man in charge of them was the infamous Major McKinnon. He interrogated me anyway. I lied like a trooper and pleaded innocence. I told him I was in Sinn Fein but he would not listen to me. He drafted me into the local jail here. . . . I was then Courtmartialled and they gave me three months for being a member of the I.R.A. . . . I was released from Cork Jail in May 1921. . . . I should tell you now that Major McKinnon too was dead. He had been playing golf on the links here; our fellows ambushed him there. That was the same time, the month of May. We

were going full pelt. The I.R.A. never felt stronger. John Joe Sheehy can give you details on that one; he was actually in charge of the affair.[37]

The experience of Lieutenant Colonel Evelyn Lindsay Young, an army IO with the Connaught Rangers from 1920 to 1922, further illustrates how dangerous the intelligence "game" was:

> The collection of intelligence was one of the most interesting and risky games over there. Our intelligence was not too intelligent and methods employed were sometimes unorthodox; the only rule for this work was "get the information"—the means of procuring it were left to the individual. . . . Several times I was detailed to take despatches to GHQ in Dublin. Its [sic] not such a very nice job to arrive in North City at midnight in the winter, and to have to make one's way on foot from Broadstone to Parkgate when there's shooting about. I looked as rough as possible in mufti with hat pulled down over the eyes as, with the dispatches fixed to the inner part of my leg, I trudged onwards. I lost my way and had to adopt the somewhat risky procedure of asking the way to the nearest landmark—the quays—from which point direction I knew the way. . . . On a night like this every lonely individual in the streets might have been a mobile arsenal . . . or possibly each had a dozen notches in his gun. . . . Parkgate was reached without further mishap; entry seemed surprisingly easy, for I passed the guard without being challenged and climbed up the dusty stairs to the duty room to report. I entered the room unannounced—the tired looking officer on my entry made a furtive grab for his pistol; then withdrew his hand leaving the weapon on the table with the butt pointing politely towards me. I received a receipt for my package and then lingered a little, bemused. "I'd like to say" said I "that although I admire your second line of defence, I passed your guard at the gate and came up here unchallenged. "Good God!" cried the tired one. "Impossible." He seized the telephone, almost terrified at the thought that he might possibly have been assassinated, and proceeded to make exhaustive enquiries. The guard turned out and all below seemed in uproar in the yard. I am rather sorry I had told him—I had some difficulty getting out."[38]

Not every British intelligence officer came up empty-handed. As Hart points out, the diary of Lieutenant R. M. Grazebrook indicates that he was running numerous agents in Cork, including three members of the local IRA.[39]

The severe cover disadvantages eventually prompted the British to commence recruiting native Irishmen in Britain to serve as operatives. Moreover, there was no centralized intelligence center to collect all-source information from various police and army sources or to direct and de-conflict operations. That sort of effort required a central authority, an established and effective clandestine service, an organized system for document exploitation, and rapid dissemination of interrogation reports. These would be addressed as part of a major reorganization of the Castle administration.

SETTING THE HOUSE IN ORDER

Increasingly frustrated with the lack of progress against the rebels, and acting upon the findings of the Fisher Committee, Lloyd George sacked the Castle administration and replaced it with new blood in the spring of 1920. In May, General Neville Macready, who had served previously as commissioner of the London Metropolitan Police, replaced Shaw as head of Irish Command. Macready had recommended that a strong personality be brought in to command the RIC, with a deputy who would concentrate on managing intelligence. By May 20, General Hugh Tudor arrived in Dublin as "police advisor." Within days, this was formalized when Tudor was officially named commissioner of police. Tudor was a line artillery officer with a distinguished battle record, but he had no particular expertise in police matters. He was, however, a great friend of cabinet hard-liner Winston Churchill and shared Churchill's views on Ireland.[40]

Two days later, Sir John Anderson and James MacMahon were appointed joint undersecretaries at Dublin Castle. Mark Sturgis and Alfred (Andy) Cope were named as assistant undersecretaries. Anderson was the more forceful personality and he eventually dominated Castle administration.[41] The Castle began using the new civil service code at this time and, as confidential secretary to MacMahon, Collins's agent Nancy O'Brien had access not only to MacMahon's classified correspondence, but very likely also that of Anderson, Sturgis, and Cope. The latter two were moderates who were tasked with exploring a peaceful resolution.

Basil Thomson's peace overture had been delivered to intermediary Carl Ackerman just weeks earlier, and O'Brien was critically placed to offer Collins most valuable intelligence on London's strategy and intentions.

Just nine days after taking over at the Castle, Anderson and his team, joined by army representatives, met with the cabinet to discuss options for dampening the enthusiasm of the Irish people for independence. The hard-liners prevailed, recommending the harshest possible economic sanctions. They reasoned that, if food and employment were scarce, it would cause enough misery to force the Irish into submission. It was the decision made at this conference, asserts Coogan, that led to the unofficial policy of reprisal, resulting in the destruction of grist mills, bacon factories, and creameries.[42]

"O"

General Tudor had been selected to strengthen the backbone of the RIC and had no doubt been briefed by Thomson and the army about the dismal state of police intelligence. Reorganizing that would be a huge undertaking and called for experience and a thorough understanding of clandestine collection techniques. Yet this was not to be. Tudor instead chose an old army crony from the field artillery corps as his number two and chief of intelligence. Colonel Ormonde de L'Épée Winter, KBE, CB, CMG, DSO, arrived in Dublin in May, officially as assistant police commissioner, but this was merely a cover title. His true mission was to set up a Combined Intelligence Service (CIS) to establish central command for all civil/police intelligence activities, to streamline coordination between the army and the police, and to establish an effective secret, or clandestine, service.

Although lacking a traditional intelligence background, except for a three-month assignment as a divisional intelligence officer during the Gallipoli Campaign in 1915, Winter was educated, fearless, and bold. What he lacked in formal intelligence training he made up for with overconfidence. Nevertheless, Winter was bright, sophisticated, and imaginative. All these qualities should have made him a worthy opponent of Michael Collins.

Above all, Winter was from the army, and it was clear that Commander in Chief Macready preferred that an army man take over police intelligence matters. Winter was action-oriented and undoubtedly viewed the offer as a great opportunity, and preferable to the tedium of peacetime garrison life. He'd had enough of that during ten years' prior service in India.

A career officer, Winter was born in 1875 and commissioned in the Royal Field Artillery in 1894. He spent his pre–World War I career in India, where he became a noted and published authority on breeding race-horses. His shrewd racing investments and horse trades provided him with a standard of living far exceeding that of his army peers. He was devoted to horses and was himself a peerless rider. Described as a bon vivant by colleagues, Winter was an interesting conversationalist on a wide range of topics, a wine connoisseur, and an authority on cuisine. He spoke Russian, French, and Urdu. Ironically, all of these qualities would have endeared him to Sir Vernon Kell, who actively sought well-rounded army officers with aristocratic connections and exotic language skills for the gentlemen's club that was MI5.[43]

Winter had a temper every bit as strong as that of Michael Collins. This regularly got him on the wrong side of his superiors. In 1903, while visiting England to cram for the Staff College entrance exams, for example, Winter attacked a youth who had thrown stones at him as he was rowing, beating him to death with an oar. Winter was arrested, tried, and acquitted of manslaughter. The incident appears to have cost him a place at Staff College and he sat in grade for years, but later boasted of his acquittal. His 1912 fitness report described him as "a smart and talented officer, excels as a horseman, a horse-master and a Vet, per contra, is not at all times reliable in some respects." Characteristically, Winter spent a year getting this remark expunged from his service file, and likely did not ingratiate himself with his superiors in the process.[44]

By August 1914, Winter was a thirty-nine-year-old major commanding a field artillery battery at Barrackpore, India. He failed repeatedly to be transferred to the Western Front; when his battery was finally mobilized, it was attached to a division that was sent to Gallipoli. Winter served in the Dardanelles Campaign from its commencement to evacuation and was division intelligence officer from October to December 1915—his only experience in intelligence affairs and one he did not enjoy, but which earned him the Distinguished Service Order (DSO). When his division was redeployed to the Western Front, however, Winter came into his element. He served with considerable distinction and documented bravery at the battle of the Somme, as well as Arras, Ypres, and Cambrai. He was elevated to command an artillery brigade, and, from 1916 to 1917, his unit was in the thick of the action. During attacks, Winter usually took up his position with the forward artillery observation officer on the front line. On one occasion, he took the initiative in leading an infantry attack against a heavily fortified German position from horseback. On another occasion, he refused to carry out a fire support mission when he realized that the infantry attack he was going to support was through layers of un-cut wire and would have been suicidal. Threatened with disciplinary action, Winter displayed admirable courage by standing up to his division commander and succeeded in getting the attack cancelled, thus saving British troops from slaughter.[45]

He was also personally brave, as illustrated by an incident in France in July 1917. When an ammunition dump caught fire, Winter fearlessly ran into the dump and, with a fellow officer, succeeded in extinguishing the flames. This won him the universal admiration of his men and fellow officers and a second bar on his DSO. Years later, Lieutenant General Sir Thomas Hutton, who had served under Winter in the war, wrote of him:

> He was, I think, the bravest man I have ever known, he really seemed to enjoy war and yet was one of the most considerate of commanders. In the attack he usually arrived on the final objec-tive before his forward observation officer. . . . He has many of the qualities of a gentleman adventurer of the Middle Ages, who feared neither God nor man, who had no mercy for his enemies but who would die happily for a friend or a cause in which he believed. With all these qualities he combined a brilliant and original mind which made him a most inspiring commander and gained the af-fection and respect of all who served under him.[46]

On December 26, 1917, Winter was brevetted to brigadier general and placed in temporary command of the Eleventh Division, where he per-formed admirably. His leadership undoubtedly contributed to the British capture of Cambrai, and Winter was mentioned six times in dispatches.[47]

Upon his arrival at Dublin Castle, Winter certainly cut the figure of a dashing man of mystery with his slicked-back hair, patrician monocle, and English oval cigarettes, which he chain-smoked with panache. Upon seeing Winter for the first time, Mark Sturgis, an administrative assistant in the Castle, wrote that he resembled "a wicked little white snake . . . probably entirely non-moral." The mystique was further reinforced by Winter's insistence that subordinates refer to him as "O" — copying the practice of SIS's Mansfield Cumming (C) and MI5's Vernon Kell (K). Despite Winter's egotistical traits, IRA-controlled double agent David Neligan described him as "a dapper little fellow" who was "friendly enough."[48]

The IRA intelligence staff quickly learned of Winter's appointment, and Collins hoped to eliminate him. Winter was an elusive target and it was more than a year before the Squad got an opening. Shortly before the cessation of hostilities, as Winter drove to pay a courtesy call on Lord French, the Squad fired several bullets at his car, one of which passed through his hand as he was placing a cigarette in his mouth, narrowly missing his head. The bullet caused a painful wound and injured his thumb. It was just another day in wartime Dublin.[49]

Winter's charter was to set up a centralized service to bridge the gap between the RIC and army intelligence, but he was too active a man to be satisfied with being a desk-bound bureaucrat. He sought a quick operational success; since he was not given authority over the army's DDSB case officers upon his arrival, he took matters into his own hands. With a flair for the cloak and dagger, he personally engaged in a number of "hush-hush" escapades. While he eventually organized a Central Raid Bureau and established centers in the provinces, he claimed shortages of both staff and space to organize a proper file system and registry. Instead, his strategy was to mount a succession of quick undercover operations directed at the IRA leadership in metro Dublin. If he could nab Collins or Mulcahy, he might quickly cut off the head of the snake and end the entire thing in one spectacular swoop.

Lieutenant Colonel John C. Carter, a former MI5 officer, was Basil Thomson's deputy at Special Branch and served as Thomson's liaison to Winter. Joining Winter at the Castle from Special Branch was Captain (later Major) Jocelyn Lee Hardy, DSO, MC. Hardy appears to have been recruited by MI5 at the close of the Great War and, like Carter, he transferred to Special Branch after the intelligence reshuffle of 1919. A tough-minded veteran, Hardy was young, dedicated, cunning, and ruthless. His no-nonsense attitude soon earned him a notorious reputation as an interrogator. His vilification by nationalists appears justified, and his unsavory reputation raises speculation that Hardy was one of the officers that Eric Holt-Wilson had not considered "suitable for retention" by MI5. Hardy's close colleague at the Castle was Major W. L. "Tiny" King, the intelligence officer of K Company Auxiliary Division. Of King little is known except that he had apparently spent most of his army career in South Africa before joining up as a temporary cadet for Irish service. King and Hardy soon earned the reputation of being vicious and sadistic. While he did not relish assassinations, Collins did not give British officers implicated in torture any quarter and he wanted Hardy and King dead.[50]

Coinciding with the reorganization of the local British administration and the arrival of Winter in Ireland in May 1920, G Division Detective Constable David Neligan resigned his job. Neligan had joined the RIC in 1918 just out of secondary school. In due time, he had been invited to join the depleted and demoralized ranks of G Division, which allowed him more salary and an escape from the tedium and petty internal politics of RIC barracks life. After serving in the G for over a year, Neligan resigned for ideological reasons and returned to his parents' home in the country. He subsequently contacted local Sinn Fein members to offer his services to a guerrilla column. Within a few days, word reached Collins and he summoned Neligan to a sit-down. Concerned about security and cover for the trip to Dublin, Neligan agreed to the meeting only if the IRA would mail some threatening letters to him, thus providing him an ostensible reason to return to report the threat to authorities. The letters duly arrived in Neligan's mailbox; armed with these, he was on his way to meet Collins, escorted to a safe house by Joe O'Reilly. Neligan recounted his first meeting with Collins in his memoirs:

> A tall, handsome man of about thirty who was alone rose from his chair and greeted us. This was my first glimpse of the famed Michael Collins. He was about six feet tall. Sturdily built, a ready laugh and cheerful manner. He had a trick of turning his head swiftly and then the resolute line of his jaw showed. He was a friendly man with the fortunate manners of putting one at ease. He was dressed in an ill-fitting tweed suit which had cycling clips on the pants. An old soft hat and a cheap dust-coat were thrown on a chair. Shaking my hand with a firm grip he said: "I know you and your brothers are all right (i.e., friendly to the revolution). . . . You

shouldn't have been let resign—there was a misunderstanding. I want you to go back to the Castle to work for us." "Mr. Collins," I said, "there's nothing I should hate more than to go back there; I'll do anything else for you; join a flying column or anything." "Listen Dave," he said, "we have plenty of men for columns, but on the other hand no one can fill your place in the Castle, for they trust you and we trust you." Only the two of us were present at this conversation. After some further talk I agreed to go back.[51]

Neligan went immediately from his meeting with Collins to see his old employer at the Castle. After Neligan showed Chief Inspector Bruton the bogus threat letters, Bruton immediately concluded Neligan had just cause for rejoining the force and rehired him on the spot.

GOVERNMENT BY REPRISAL

The presence of the Black and Tans and the Auxiliary Division, which had arrived by July 1920, was beginning to be felt across Ireland. In April, the town of Thurles, Tipperary, was twice sacked by the RIC. This was followed through the summer and fall by the sacking and looting of Balbriggan, Tuam, Upper Church, Limerick, Miltown, Lahinch, Templemore, Malbay, Carrick on Shannon, and Trim.[52]

As for Michael Collins, he managed to remain free if not entirely anonymous. He took a fair amount of chances but his charming manners and charisma saved him during a number of close encounters. Compounding the problem of his own security, however, Collins frequently frustrated his staff by deliberately approaching policemen and army personnel whom he would engage in casual conversation. Collins's ego thrived on telling tales of his run-ins with the enemy, and these contributed in no small manner to the legend. For example, Collins enjoyed telling a favorite story about an encounter he had with three Auxiliaries in a central Dublin pub. As the story goes, Collins stood at the bar having a drink with the three officers making small talk. Suddenly Collins exclaimed to no one in particular, "That man Collins! I wish I could nail him!" To which one of the Auxiliaries reportedly looked straight at Collins and replied, "Don't worry, his days are numbered!" Once after recalling the incident, Collins reportedly held up a calendar, laughed, and asked his aide Joe O'Reilly, "See here, how many days have I got left, Joe?"[53]

Collins stood out in a crowd because of his size and it did not hurt his security that he was often accompanied on the street by a few members of the Squad. On one occasion he was stopped by one of Basil Thomson's detectives who demanded to know his name and see his identification papers. Collins reportedly stared hard at the detective and advised him to take a look around. When the detective turned, he saw four young men with their right hands inside their coat pockets fingering pistols. Without another word the detective walked away.[54]

Collins maintained pressure on the secret police. On April 14, the Squad shot and killed Detective Constable Henry Kells of G Division. Kells's colleague Detective Constable Laurence Dalton was gunned down just six days later.[55]

By summer 1920, the majority of G men avoided trouble by remaining inside the Castle. David Neligan noted the depth of police demoralization at that time:

> Often I was sent on duty with an elderly detective inspector and detective sergeant. They were supposed to be investigating the killing of Barton, Smyth and Hoey. They spent each day on a pub-crawl and did no investigating, as they wanted to stay alive. They drank steadily from 10 am until 6 pm—all whiskey—with an interval for lunch. . . . Regularly they had to submit reports on the progress of their "investigation." This task they had to face in the morning when their heads were jumping off. So they used to call on me to help and lend colour to an otherwise bald and unconvincing narrative. I cannot now recall the deathless prose we used, but I recollect the last sentence which ran: "Every effort will be made to apprehend the perpetrators of this dastardly outrage." The Castle had to be satisfied with this Johnsonian pearl and that is as far as they got. Those two old men were charming fellows.[56]

When J. J. Purcell was appointed to replace the assassinated Forbes Redmond, Purcell took the unprecedented step of calling a press conference to announce that he had been transferred to G Division against his will. Moreover, Purcell announced he would concern himself solely with nonpolitical criminal investigations, making it clear that he intended to sit out the war. It was a signal of capitulation by the once-feared political police.[57]

TESTING LOYALTIES

The brutal reprisal operations carried out by the Black and Tans and the Auxiliaries commencing in the spring of 1920 brought international condemnation of British policy. At home, a war-weary British public was also sickened and disgusted by the actions of these mercenary militia, and criticism mounted. Two of the most vocal critics were General Sir Henry Wilson, chief of the Imperial Staff, and General Neville Macready, commanding officer of British Forces, Ireland. Both were concerned that the undisciplined paramilitaries would have a negative impact on military discipline.

The declaration of martial law in Dublin and parts of Cork and Tipperary in the spring of 1920 was a promising start at restoring order, but it fell short because of legal constraints. To overcome the legal loopholes that enabled prisoners to obtain parole, hard-liners in the government pushed for the passage of a new bill that would make it easier for the police and military to engage the IRA.[58]

Irish Command had been advocating general martial law throughout the country since 1919, and now pressed the argument as IRA columns commenced direct attacks on the forces in mid-1920. Martial law would allow the army to undertake raids and arrests without the requirement of having an RIC officer present, and to try suspects by courts-martial. Moreover, the army intelligence structure was designed to function under condition of martial law, whereby all civil police and intelligence would be placed under a single, unified army command.

In late July, the cabinet convened a second conference with the new Castle administration to review Irish policy. Not surprisingly, hard-liners such as Sir Henry Wilson and Churchill advocated the most extreme security measures, while Sir John Anderson, Andy Cope, and General Macready expressed doubt that such measures would succeed. Shortly thereafter, Lloyd George's secretary summarized the options as "the rigorous application of force by means of courts-martial, the suspension of civil government, the stoppage of trains and motors, the withholding of pensions and generally the infliction of a rapidly increasing paralysis on the country or an immediate attempt to conclude a pact with the leaders of Sinn Fein and the revolutionaries."[59]

On August 9, Parliament approved the Restoration of Order in Ireland Act (ROIA). Essentially, it suspended trial by jury and allowed the use of military tribunals in jurisdictions where the IRA was most aggressive. Army units could now convene courts-martial to mete out swift sentences. A suspect could now be arrested, tried, and sentenced without recourse to civil barristers, judges, or jurors. Not surprisingly, courts-martial in the county districts were soon reporting a sharp rise in convictions.[60]

The hard-liners declared victory, but it would prove to be only a political triumph. As reprisals against innocent civilians escalated through the summer and fall of 1920, the world press reflected almost universal condemnation of the British government, thus handing another important victory to Dail Eireann's propaganda department.

9

WITHIN THE GATES

Law and order have given way to a bloody and brutal anarchy .
. . England has departed further from the standards even of any
nation in the world, not excepting the Turk and the Zulu, than has
ever been known in history before!
　　　　　　　—*General Sir Hubert Gough, British Army, March 1921*

The intelligence war between the Castle and Michael Collins escalated
during the second half of 1920. The army's Dublin plainclothes unit,
DDSB, pursued Sinn Fein and IRA suspects relentlessly, if not always
professionally.

With his own networks in shambles following the Jameson affair, Basil Thomson supported the creation of Winter's Combined Intelligence
Service at Dublin Castle. It was far preferable to Thomson that the reins
of intelligence be held within the police services than give further open-
ings to the War Office. Unlike Major Price's Special Intelligence Service
that reported to Irish Command during the First World War, Winter held
a civil appointment. Tudor's selection of Winter nevertheless seemed a
good compromise with the army. Commander in chief Macready, who
had previously served as commissioner of the London Metropolitan Police, knew something about police intelligence and he hoped a forceful
military personality like Winter could make CIS a success.

Winter's efforts to get CIS up and running were hindered through the summer while adequate office space was located in the Castle. His charter was to set up a central office to collect, analyze, and distribute all-source intelligence information to bridge the intelligence gap between the police and army. What he established was a multitiered bureaucracy that operated completely independently of the army's intelligence infrastructure:

- One tier consisted of Special Branch detectives and whatever street assets in their stable were left over from Basil Thomson's earlier efforts. Colonel J. F. C. Carter, an ex-MI5 veteran, was Winter's principal liaison with Thomson, while assorted Special Branch detectives worked with the RIC and the Auxiliaries to mount raids, arrest suspects, and interrogate them.[1]
- A second tier consisted of a special plainclothes unit, officially known as the "Identification Company" and made up of senior RIC men from outlying counties led by Chief Constable Eugene Igoe. The IRA referred to this unit as the Igoe Gang, and it would soon learn that the unit's mission went well beyond intelligence collection and surveillance to include lethal covert action—what the British Army had termed "executive responsibilities."[2]
- A third tier—and Winter's pet project—was a London-based Secret Service Bureau. This consisted of civilian Anglo-Irish agents recruited, trained, and deployed from London. Two top professionals from the Indian Colonial Police Special Branch, Inspector Charles A. Tegart and Inspector Godfrey C. Denham, were brought in from Calcutta to take charge of this unit. Training of agents included a secret writing course so that the agents could file their reports to a London address via impersonal communications.[3]

Winter later described the program, acknowledging that it was only partly successful:

In order to minimize, if not eliminate, the risks incurred by agents, a Bureau was formed in London, with an officer in charge who had considerable experience in dealing with espionage through the war. In England, Irishmen are easier to approach, and when suitable people were found, they were provided with a secret ink which was considered, for all practical purposes, immune from discovery. To each was allotted a particular task, all available information on the subject was placed at his disposal, a suitable cover was given to him and, once he had left for Ireland, he corresponded with no Government official, except the head of the London bureau, writing his information in the secret ink and sending his letters to a cover address. This went far to inspire a sense of security amongst those engaged on this difficult work. The risk they ran was the possibility of their becoming suspect and being planted with wrong information which, if acted on, might have disclosed their position. Fortunately, only one of these agents met with a violent end, and this was undoubtedly the result of his own carelessness for, amongst his effects . . . some notes were found in ordinary ink and it is more than probable that he was betrayed by one of the attendants at the hotel at which he was staying. It is not, however, easy to recruit people for this work and, during a period of some eight or nine months, only sixty, in all, were transported to Ireland. Of these, many proved unsatisfactory and had to be discarded.[4]

Tegart and Denham soon found Winter's operation simplistic and amateurish. Both believed that some investment in developing files and a target list would be time well spent, while Winter decided to bypass the spade work in favor of scoring a quick success with "secret service," which, alas, he knew very little about. Consequently, Winter spent much of his time whisking around Ireland in a fast chauffer-driven auto or by airplane in order to personally involve himself in raids and other tactical operations. As the results indicate, this would have been time better spent setting up a unified central file room and targeting branch, or coordinating more closely with army intelligence headquarters.[5]

In addition to these official British intelligence units, Neligan claimed that the Castle also employed a gang of freelance assassins against the IRA whose primary motive was revenge:

Another man resigned from the RIC, rejoined, and became an active enemy of the Volunteers. He was promoted rapidly. He formed a squad of policemen who had been fired or otherwise ill-treated, and they buzzed about Dublin in two Ford cars. They wore steel waistcoats and woe betide any Volunteer they laid their eyes on. The Dublin Brigade lined the Northern quays one day in an effort to annihilate them, only to see them flying down the Southern quays. Next day they lined the latter but the Fords chased down the Northern quay. It took on the elements of a farce. In the event, they escaped unscathed. A Volunteer named J. [Jimmy] Conroy, waited outside the Castle for them. When three of them emerged he shot them. It turned out though that they were three poor devils of dispatch riders in the RIC, one of them a brother of Detective Sergeant Hoey, shot earlier.[6]

The existence of such a freelance group, as well as the tactics of the Igoe Gang, were clear signs that all British intelligence elements—official and unofficial, military, and civilian—were given a free hand to track down and murder Sinn Fein and IRA Volunteers on sight. This was what the Castle's intelligence advisory committee had recommended in December of 1919. It was far more than merely the collection of information—it was covert action, even if not conducted covertly at times. While Hamar Greenwood and Lloyd George publicly ranted about the Sinn Fein "murder gang," Whitehall had deployed several lethal murder gangs of their own, over and beyond the Black and Tans and the Auxiliaries.

Cumulatively, therefore, the British would address intelligence shortcomings by deploying many more case officers, informers/agents, and Special Branch detectives on the street while failing to coordinate these clandestine efforts with the War Office. On the other end of the spectrum was army intelligence, acting independently of Castle direction. While it was theater commander General Macready who originally suggested that the CIS be created, Macready had Major Ivor Price's Castle intelligence section of 1914–1919 in mind when he made that recommendation. Indeed, the army's own intelligence structure from 1919 onward had been based upon the assumption that the military would eventually assume central command of all intelligence operations under nationwide martial law, and that the Castle's intelligence commander would be transferred or subordinated to the army. Martial law was not universally declared, however, and intelligence activities proceeded in unilateral army and police channels, with little attention to coordination or shared intelligence. The net result was the deployment of four separate British Secret Service efforts managed under two separate military and civilian commands.

Figure 3. Restructuring of Crown Intelligence in Ireland 1914–1921

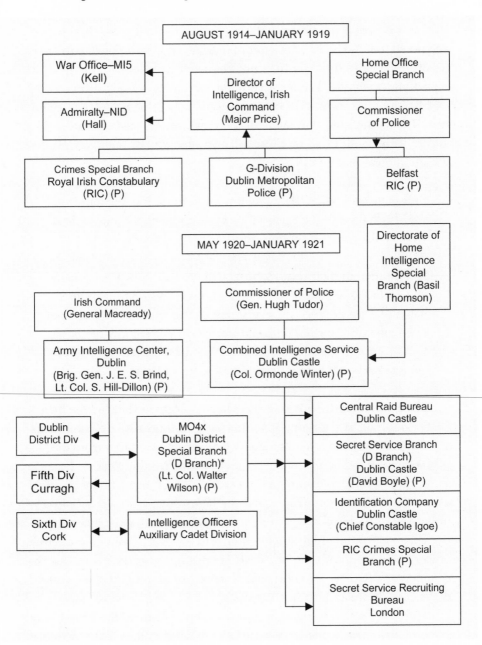

* Transferred from British Army to Dublin Castle control December 1920
(P) Penetrated by IRA intelligence

THE UNDESIRABLES

The precise number of secret service officers and agents who entered Ireland at this time is unknown, but Neligan estimated it to be "hundreds," and noted that "so many worked for the British it was impossible to counter all." Neligan's estimate may not be far off the mark. In his postwar report and memoirs, Winter accounted for ninety-seven officers in the DDSB alone, and sixty additional agents in his London Secret Service Bureau. It was rumored that some of the most experienced operators, like Tegart, were handpicked by Churchill (see appendix B).[7] Neligan recalled the situation at that time:

> As I have said, when the G men were more or less demoralized, the British flooded the place with secret-service men. Some of these were civilians, some serving British officers, some ex-officers and NCOs and some professional agents. Most were Anglo-Irish or British, though their head, Count Sevigne, may have been French and certainly looked it. Of course, those fellows had a different name and cover story for every day of the week, so unless one knew one from birth, one could not be sure of his identity. I am told that the first intimation the relatives of some had of their occupation was when their dead bodies were sent home.[8]

Since the Anglo-Irish War, writers have collectively labeled the British DDSB unit the Cairo Group, or Cairo Gang. Authors disagree on the origin of this moniker, but it is agreed that it was derived either from the fact that some of them had previously served in the Middle East, or because some of them liked to congregate at Dublin's Café Cairo.[9] It may be safely assumed that insofar as Collins and the IRA were concerned, all of these undercover officers posed a potential threat, regardless of their respective chains of command. It mattered little to the IRA whether a particular officer spied for the Castle, for Basil Thomson, or for the army. But the situation underscores the confusing system of dual command and control that existed in Ireland during the war.

Moreover, while Neligan accurately estimated that "the British sent some of their crack operators here," many writers have extended that compliment across the board to all of the British agents operating in Dublin. That is fiction, and it has helped to spawn the myth that British intelligence was "eliminated," "annihilated," or "wiped out" on November 21, 1920, when that was not the case.[10]

SOLICITING INFORMERS

As these various units were assembling in the summer and fall of 1920, Winter turned to another pet project. In mid-September he collaborated with Special Branch to implement a program intended to rebuild the system of informers that had collapsed with Collins's attacks on the police. Like previous efforts to solicit information in exchange for large monetary rewards, however, the new scheme failed to attract any informers. It did bring replies from several practical jokers; in hindsight, it appears to have been a desperate measure and an embarrassing failure, despite Winter's subsequent effort to justify it:

> In the month of September 1920, GHQ, assisted by Scotland Yard, formulated a scheme to obtain information by correspondence. Anyone desirous of giving information was invited to do so by sending a letter to an address in London. This resulted in a quantity of letters being received but they were practically all written either by irresponsible jesters or active rebels, and led to no satisfactory results, being, for the majority, merely accusations against well-known loyalists. The experiment was, however, well worth the attempt, as, indeed, is any experiment when faced with so many outstanding difficulties. Many other anonymous communications were received through various sources, but the vast majority contained false information, intended only to mislead.[11]

According to Neligan, Collins immediately countered the Thomson-Winter scheme to solicit informers by ordering the Castle mails seized:

> The British had thought of many schemes for getting information about the rebels. One was that a letter could be dropped into any letter-box and would find its way to a post office in London specially ear-marked to receive it. Notices to this effect were published by the Castle in all the newspapers on 15th September 1920. This gave rise to frequent raids by the IRA on mail bags. The Irish Post Office was certainly one of Collins's most useful services. Nothing

there was hidden from him or from his agents. Nearly all the rank and file were ardent sympathisers and everyone knows the inquisitive village postmistress. She is interested in everything passing to and fro and little escapes her. A Corkman named Pat Moynihan was a sorter in Dublin and a Sinn Fein Sympathiser. One of his jobs was to sort the Castle mails which were the subject of extraordinary precautions. The poor British Tommies whose job it was to escort them from the sorting office to the Castle were very chummy with Moynihan and often offered him a lift in their armoured car. He accepted it one day. With him was a suitcase which contained the much-guarded Castle mails. He got off just outside the Castle. As he told it, by sleight-of-hand he had substituted a bag full of old papers for the Government bag. Another day armed men took the Castle mails in a hold-up. Consternation reigned in the Castle. I've never seen such panic. A thousand houses in Dublin were searched that day and for a week following. The raids went on day and night. They discovered nothing. Moynihan was not suspected. The Tommies were dumb of course about their breach of regulations and certainly did not suspect the cheerful Pat. To this day I've never discovered what was in those bags or if they contained any earth-shaking revelations. I suspect that it was not worth the energy wasted, but it was great fun at the time.[12]

It is worth noting at this point that guarding the official mail was one of the most important contributions of the Royal Flying Corps in Ireland during the Anglo-Irish War. The 141st Squadron based outside Dublin performed a number of missions, including scouting for the ground forces, dropping propaganda leaflets, and transporting senior officers between garrisons. Until 1921, their Bristol fighters were unarmed. Since the IRA knew this, they generally did not fear the fast, sleek planes that swooped down on them from the clouds. Later, after the British mounted machines guns and bombs on their aircraft, however, the flying columns had to contend with a serious new threat. These aircraft also carried mail across the country, reducing IRA opportunities to hijack official dispatches in transit. Once on the ground, however, the mail was still vulnerable to intercept by the rebels, thanks to collaborators like Moynihan.[13]

Meanwhile, the IRA intelligence service began to report the arrival of a small legion of intelligence officers. The British had significantly raised the stakes, and Collins knew he was no longer dealing with vulnerable Irish cops who could be scared off or intimidated into resigning. Many of the imported spies were experienced operatives who had worked in Germany during the occupation or who had been part of the British Secret Service's well-organized efforts to topple the Bolshevik government in Russia and counter Bolshevik advances in Western Europe. At least one had operated with the British Army of the Black Sea, and another had served undercover in Holland. One had allegedly been part of MI1c's successful influence operation in Spain during the war. An IRA man who had been interrogated by one of the newcomers reported that he was a perfect gentleman who smoked Egyptian cigarettes. Most of these operatives joined the Irish Command's clandestine branch, the DDSB. A good number of them were Irish or Anglo-Irish, but for the most part, these men did not have local family ties that might impede their efficiency. Thomson also contributed more Special Branch officers in pressing the hunt for Collins and other leaders. The next seven months would be marked by deadly action and counteraction pitting the IRA intelligence service against these British agents.[14]

PENETRATING THE SECRET SERVICE

The expansion of the army and Castle intelligence resources were of deep concern to Collins. He nevertheless still enjoyed some significant advantages on the intelligence front. His stable of penetrations and assets was in fact growing, and paramilitary outrages continued to erode popular support for the Crown. In response to the arrival of the undesirables, Collins took a number of proactive counterintelligence measures.

The IRA now had no fewer than three agents inside G Division, although by the time Neligan joined the force in May 1920, it was already nearly moribund. Moreover, when the G was relocated to the Castle in late 1919, its files were left at the old Brunswick Street Station and Broy remained there, essentially cut off from the rest of the branch. He still had access to the documentary reports that crossed his desk every day, but he now had limited interaction with fellow detectives or senior police officials. The value of the G Division moles was further reduced with the army's establishment of DDSB and Winter's own secret service branch in mid-1920. It was clear to Dave Neligan that the colonial secret police were being replaced by British intelligence officers. The shrewd Neligan began to make acquaintances with some of the arriving British officers, and Collins directed his staff to start building dossiers.

In mid-1920 Collins got timely access to the secret service when he recruited William "Willie" Beaumont. An ex–British Army officer, Beaumont had served on the Western Front. Now demobilized, he returned to Dublin unemployed. Beaumont despised Sinn Fein and began to make dangerous comments in public, threatening to capture Michael Collins and collect the reward. Willie's brother Sean—thoroughly sympathetic to the Republican cause—grew concerned for Willie's safety. One day a group of Auxiliaries stopped a streetcar on which Willie Beaumont was riding and began to question him and the other passengers. Although Beaumont carried a notebook documenting his honorable service in the Royal Dublin Fusiliers in France, the Auxies gave him a hard time and Beaumont was incensed at their abusive manners. Relating the incident to Sean, Willie angrily volunteered to shoot any Auxiliaries he encountered in future.

Sean Beaumont knew Dan O'Donovan, one of Collins's Finance Ministry employees, and O'Donovan advised Sean to suggest to his brother that, instead of shooting the Auxiliaries, he pass a list of their names to Sinn Fein. O'Donovan subsequently received a written note from Willie Beaumont, which he duly passed to Collins. Collins realized that Beaumont was thoroughly disillusioned and ripe for recruitment. Cutting O'Donovan out of the case, Collins asked Sean to set up a meeting with his brother. What came of this meeting is a testimonial to the power of Collins's charismatic personality; within a few minutes Collins had not only charmed Beaumont but had also convinced him to join the cause.

Collins had an even more important agenda. It was a poorly kept secret at that time that the army was seeking ex-servicemen to undertake intelligence work in Ireland; Beaumont had not only served honorably in the army, but he had already publicly proclaimed his violent hostility toward Collins. He was the perfect candidate. On Collins's orders, Beaumont approached the Castle about joining up and was soon sworn in as a member of His Majesty's Secret Service. It was a major intelligence coup for the IRA. Given the influx of British intelligence officers and agents from abroad, and Winter's buildup of the CIS, Beaumont's recruitment was timely. He began to learn the identities of some of his undercover colleagues and where they spent their time after hours. Collins soon began to get a picture of what he was up against.[15]

That picture became much clearer in April, when the IRA intelligence staff intercepted some letters from British Army intelligence officer Captain Frederick Harper-Shove. One letter revealed not only that the British Secret Service men had been given a free hand to deal with IRA suspects as they saw fit, but that they were also planning to carry out some type of spectacular operation against the rebels. Ignoring communications security, Shove conveyed his thoughts on this via regular postal correspondence to a colleague in London:

> Have duly reported and found things in a fearful mess but think they will be able to make a good show. Have been given a free hand to carry on and everyone has been very charming. Re: our little stunt, I see no prospect until I have got things on a firmer basis, but still hope and believe there are possibilities.[16]

The IRA intelligence staff was convinced that the "little stunt" Shove contemplated was the assassination of Dail, IRA, or Sinn Fein leaders. It was essential that Collins take an aggressive counteraction to throw the British Secret Service off its game.

KIDD'S BACK

Many of the British intelligence officers arriving in Ireland in the summer of 1920 employed aliases and commercial cover. Nevertheless, with their distinctive British accents it was extremely difficult for them to move around the city unnoticed. The army's DDSB officers were perhaps the most vulnerable, as most of them had no prior experience and had received only perfunctory training. Anglo-Irish agents recruited under Winter's London Bureau perhaps fared better, but they too had limited training in operational tradecraft.

As noted, several of these officers congregated after hours at the Café Cairo. Two other watering holes favored by the British operatives were a venerable pub known as Kidd's Back and Rabiatti's Saloon in Marlborough Street. Learning this, Collins directed his moles—foremost Beaumont and policeman Neligan—to start associating with the agents at these venues. Night after night, they sat drinking with the British officers at Rabiatti's and Kidd's Back. On a few occasions, Neligan brought Collins's lieutenants, Tom Cullen and Frank Thornton, along with him and successfully introduced them to British Army MO4x case officers George

Bennett and Peter Ames as two of his local Irish "sources." The British officers never realized their friendly drinking companions were two senior members of the IRA intelligence staff.[17]

Neligan had a mixed impression of the British intelligence officers flooding into Ireland at the time, pointing out their bravery on the one hand and their poor judgment on the other:

> The secret service was extremely busy at this time. The British sent some of their crack operators here. I must say they were brave men who carried their lives in their hands. As is well known (to me at any rate), a spy leads a lonely and dangerous existence full of perils, in the midst of enemies, never acknowledged by his masters, at the end thrown on the scrap-heap, if he is lucky enough to see the end. They shadowed suspects continually and kept meeting-places under surveillance, carrying out all of the functions of a secret police. Working in close co-operation with the military and Auxiliaries, they had some victories. Some had seen service in other parts of the Empire. I saw a report from one dated on a Saturday which was the vigil of a Catholic feast. He said, "A big operation must be imminent (the natives are restless), the R.C. churches were crowded all day."[18]

Through these efforts, and with further assistance from such agents as Nancy O'Brien at the GPO, Lily Mernin decoding army intelligence messages in the Castle, and probably the mysterious Lieutenant G, not to mention a virtual legion of sympathetic maids, hotel porters, taxi drivers, streetcar employees, and saloon keepers, the IRA intelligence staff assembled dossiers on as many British officers and agents as they could identify.

A MISSED OPPORTUNITY

One British contract agent was apparently foisted upon Winter's special London bureau by Basil Thomson and surfaced in Sinn Fein circles in September 1920. The case was another of Collins's counterintelligence successes as well as a propaganda coup for Sinn Fein, but evidence suggests that his handling of the matter may have denied him his greatest opportunity.

J. L. Gooding was serving time for forgery and fraud in an English prison in August 1920 when he wrote a letter to Lord French at Dublin Castle claiming to have information on Sinn Fein and IRA arms dumps. Gooding's offer was forwarded by the impatient French to Basil Thomson in London, but the latter was understandably skeptical of any claims of a convicted felon. Gooding was serving time for good reason, and his promises were entirely self-serving. Nevertheless, Thomson found some reason to accept Gooding and he was sworn in as an agent of the CIS London Bureau—apparently without the endorsement of the two ICP inspectors on loan to Winter—Tegart and Denham—or of Majors Cameron and Jeffries, who later replaced them and took over management of the program. Thus Gooding became one of the sixty Anglo-Irish agents recruited as part of the buildup. Armed with an operational alias, Gooding arrived in Dublin in September as "Digby Hardy" and began to seek contacts in Sinn Fein and the IRA.[19]

The IRA intelligence staff, meanwhile, had intercepted Gooding's August letter to Lord French, and so Collins was forewarned about Gooding's treachery. By the time of the agent's arrival in Dublin in September, Tobin and his crew had apparently discovered Gooding's operational alias prior to his arrival in Ireland, for he was almost immediately located and placed under surveillance. Gooding appears to have possessed considerable street smarts—acquired perhaps during his criminal past or because of countersurveillance training, because Frank Thornton's account of the IRA surveillance operation indicates Gooding was very deliberate in his movements and appeared to be running surveillance detection routes:

> I picked up one of our intelligence officers who pointed him out to me. My orders were just to watch him and follow him, to find out with whom he made contact and also the places he visited. I can tell you I was footsore and weary walking around the city after him. I remember we walked to Westland Row station, turned back, waited outside the Queen's Theatre for a considerable time, then up to Grafton Street, dilly-dallying all the way and back across town. He went into the Hamman hotel in Sackville Street and, as I was about to enter the hotel, he came out again and started walking aimlessly about the town. I was not sorry when I was relieved early that evening.[20]

Gooding eventually made contact with Arthur Griffith. Although he was acting president of the Dail in de Valera's absence, Griffith moved about Dublin freely at that time and made no effort to conceal his location. Griffith was a journalist with numerous contacts in the Irish, British, and American press, and he was the figurehead leading Sinn Fein's propaganda war against the British. His close contacts with the predominantly anti-British press corps provided him with some degree of immunity, at least at the beginning. Because of this high profile, Griffith was the most accessible rebel leader. Gooding sought a way out of his commitment to the British Secret Service and apparently decided the best way would be to betray them to the IRA, who might reward him or at the very least offer him protection. Gooding confessed to Griffith that he was a British agent and claimed that he had been personally recruited by Basil Thomson. Gooding further claimed that he could identify Thomson for the IRA and asked Griffith to put him in touch with senior IRA or Sinn Fein leaders.

Gooding was playing a dangerous game; his actions defied common sense, except perhaps to an ex-convict trying to give his handlers the slip. Nevertheless, Griffith relayed the information to Collins, who suspected another British dangle operation. With the memory of CORRY, Molloy, and Harry Quinn fresh in his mind, Collins looked for an opportunity to expose a double agent and embarrass the British in a single stroke. He asked Griffith to expose Gooding and reveal the agent's criminal background to the press corps. Griffith duly contacted Gooding and told him he had arranged a secret gathering of senior Sinn Fein officials and that Gooding would get his audience with them on September 16. Unbeknownst to Gooding, Griffith gathered a room full of international reporters, promising them a juicy story. Meeting with the reporters in advance of Gooding's arrival, Griffith told them that the man they were soon to meet had already admitted his affiliation with the British and had asked to meet some of the leaders of the Sinn Fein movement. Griffith's only request of the reporters was that they not reveal their true identities until after the man finished briefing them.

In due course Gooding arrived and—believing he was addressing Sinn Fein leaders—announced that he was a British Secret Service agent and that he was under instructions from Basil Thomson to find Michael Collins. He offered to arrange another meeting with Thomson in Dublin so the IRA could assassinate him. Gooding also claimed he could lead

Auxiliaries into ambushes and perform other valuable services for the IRA. Significantly, Gooding told the reporters that Basil Thomson controlled all British Secret Service efforts against Sinn Fein. He concluded by stating that if they would give him the address of Michael Collins, he would sit on the information a few days, turn it over to his British handlers to impress them, but that "no harm would come to Mick." At this point Griffith interrupted, stating, "Well, gentlemen, you have heard this man's proposal and you can judge for yourselves." Griffith then produced Gooding's letter to Lord French, denounced him as an agent provocateur, and exposed the fact that Gooding had a criminal record. Griffith then turned to Gooding and mentioned that a boat was leaving Dublin at nine o'clock that evening and advised him to be on it and never return to Ireland.[21]

The resulting newspaper stories received international attention; happily for Sinn Fein, the entire episode was a propaganda victory. The only problem was that Gooding was a bona fide defector as noted by Ormonde Winter in his after-action report. Winter was careful to note that neither Gooding nor a second agent killed by the IRA had been engaged by his own CIS representative in London. It was a petty point, to be sure, and typical of a man who once spent a solid year getting one critical word removed from a fitness report:

> The notorious F. Digby Hardy proved himself a villain of the first water, but, in attempting to betray the organisation that had engaged him, his story was disbelieved, and he was treated with some contumely by the redoubtable Michael Collins, who denounced him, in front of a lot of journalists, as "the spy unmasked." He was ordered by the IRA to leave Ireland forthwith, lost, at the same time, his luggage and his appointment. Incidentally, neither this man nor the man who was murdered were engaged through . . . the officer now in charge of the London bureau.[22]

Given Winter's candid admission, the possibility exists that Gooding may well have been able to deliver Sir Basil into IRA hands. Such a development could truly have broken the back of the British intelligence system. But Collins was likely too preoccupied with countering the dozens of other British agents and did not have the time to work with an ex-convict whose reliability could not easily be confirmed and over whom control would be difficult to establish. Collins had much bigger problems to deal with.

THE DMP SURRENDERS

By October 1920, the detectives of G Division had had enough. Through Sinn Fein intermediaries, the commissioner of the DMP sent an offer to the IRA: the detectives would stop carrying weapons in return for a guarantee of safety. Collins was consulted, and he agreed to these terms, provided the G men would also cease their support of the British military on house raids. The commissioner agreed to that point, and henceforth the DMP ceased to be a factor of concern for the IRA.[23]

This amounted to total capitulation by G Division, although the reinforced RIC was certainly not out of the fight. With the influx of the Black and Tans and Auxiliaries, the force had reached its highest personnel level in fifteen years by October 1920; it was exerting tremendous pressure on the IRA. But this came at a price. Hamar Greenwood reported to the House of Commons in mid-October that there had been 667 Republican attacks on RIC barracks in the first ten months of 1920, and that the RIC had suffered casualties of 100 killed and 160 wounded. He further reported that in the same period the army had suffered casualties of 18 killed and 66 wounded. On the positive side, however, 194 suspects had been convicted by courts-martial in the first three weeks of October.[24]

TIGHTENING THE NOOSE

While G Division was opting out of the fight, Winter was making progress. IRA officers Daniel Breen and Sean Treacy were being sought by the British for leading a series of bold strikes, and Collins brought them to Dublin where they could join the Squad and be better protected. Winter countered by bringing RIC constables from Tipperary to Dublin to identify them; a CIS team commanded by two senior RIC inspectors soon had both under close surveillance. On the evening of October 11, Winter organized a raid of Professor Carolan's residence in north Dublin where Treacy and Breen were believed to be holed up. The two RIC inspectors commanding the raiding party entered the house at one o'clock in the morning with weapons blazing, shouting for Breen and Treacy to surrender. Treacy quickly escaped out a bedroom window with a minor scratch, but Breen remained behind and engaged the raiders with his semiautomatic pistol. He killed the two inspectors and wounded a third police officer, while suffering no fewer than seven gunshot wounds himself in the melee. Though seriously wounded, Breen climbed out of the bedroom onto an adjoining roof, smashed a skylight, and dropped to the floor. Suffering severe loss of blood from his many wounds, he nevertheless shot his way through the police cordon surrounding Carolan's residence. Breen eventually reached another safe house some miles away, and Dick McKee of the Dublin Brigade brought a car to spirit Breen away to Mater Hospital where he was admitted under an alias and treated by sympathetic hospital staff. With just a minor wound, Treacy began to plan his escape from Dublin. Toward that end, he procured a bicycle with the intent of cycling his way home to Tipperary via back roads and cross-country trails to evade army and police checkpoints ringing Dublin.[25]

A few days later IRA intelligence staff learned that senior government officials would be attending the public funeral procession for the two killed RIC inspectors. Collins ordered an attack on these officials. According to Frank Thornton, several members of the Headquarters Intelligence Staff and the Dublin Brigade had assembled for that purpose on the morning of October 14:

> Our information was that Hamar Greenwood, General Tudor and several prominent officers would take part in the funeral procession and it was decided that an attempt would be made to shoot them en route. With this purpose in mind, Liam Tobin, Tom Cullen, Dick McKee, Frank Henderson, Leo Henderson, Peadar Clancy and I met in the back of Peadar Clancy's clothing shop. Receiving information that none of those whom we sought were taking part in the funeral, the job was called off.[26]

Treacy, however, attended the funeral of the two inspectors. A devout Catholic, Treacy had a custom of praying for his victims, but in this instance it was a costly breech of security. Afterward, he cycled to the safe house behind Clancy's clothing store where Frank Thornton and the others had assembled. Collins had cancelled the operation in the meantime, and Thornton and the others had dispersed by the time Treacy showed up. Treacy had not taken proper security precautions and was spotted and followed to Clancy's shop by a surveillance team consisting of Major

Frank Carew, Captain Gilbert A. Price of the DDSB, and Sergeant Frank Christian, an Auxiliary Intelligence Officer. Captain J. L. Hardy may also have been present as the Special Branch member of the surveillance team and Winter's representative.

Learning that Collins had cancelled the attack on the funeral procession, Treacy likely decided that the heavy security focus on the funeral procession might create enough diversion to enable him to make his escape from Dublin by cycling around checkpoints on back streets and bike trails. Growing concerned that their prey would elude capture, the secret service officers prepared to apprehend Treacy the moment he emerged from the shop. Eventually Treacy stepped out onto the sidewalk, but before he could mount his bicycle, Cadet Frank Christian drew his weapon and pointed it at Treacy. Treacy shot Christian dead, then turned to face Captain Price. Price had drawn his revolver and fired at Treacy but missed. When Price closed in, the two men struggled and Treacy succeeded in wrestling away Price's revolver. At that moment, a squad of British Tommies heard the gunfire and turned into the top of Talbot Street where they saw two civilians struggling on the sidewalk. Treacy, now armed with two revolvers, pointed one of them at the soldiers, who defended themselves with a volley of rifle fire, instantly killing Treacy, Price, and two civilian bystanders. Treacy and Price were both just twenty-five years old.[27]

The postscript of this tragedy is equally gruesome. Two more RIC sergeants were summoned from Tipperary to identify Treacy's corpse and to assist in the search for Dan Breen, who was still at large. Neligan was assigned to accompany the two sergeants to a hospital where they suspected Breen was hiding. Looking at one man lying in bed, one of the RIC men declared, "That's not Dan Breen. I'd know that ugly mug anywhere." Neligan dutifully passed this report to Collins. Two days later on October 17, Neligan was chatting with the two sergeants on the Dublin quays when he noticed a couple of members of the Squad watching from across the street. Neligan put two and two together and quickly crossed over to try to wave them off, but the Squad members told him they were under orders. They brushed past Neligan, crossed the street, drew their revolvers, and shot one of the RIC sergeants dead, while the other ran for his life. Neligan was in shock after witnessing the killing, which he considered unjustified. Moreover, he was outraged that Collins would endanger him, particularly as the escaped RIC man had seen Neligan speaking with the gunmen just before the incident. Neligan was summoned before an official inquiry convened by the RIC Inspector-General and questioned about his actions. He denied having spoken to anyone before the killing, a weak defense considering the eyewitness was a fellow cop. He was excused with no further comment but in a matter of days he realized that he too was under surveillance. Coogan, who interviewed Neligan many years later, has written that the latter finally took matters into his own hands. Faced with the prospect of arrest on charges of treason, Neligan allegedly led his police stalker into an alley one evening, turned upon him, and shot him dead.[28] On balance, Collins's decision to have the Squad shoot one of the RIC sergeants looking for Breen shows that he was prepared to risk exposing Neligan to protect Breen, begging the question of what steps he would have taken to protect Neligan had the latter been arrested and charged as an accessory to murder. It was one of the most ill-advised operations ever ordered by Collins, but it shows how concerned he was over the increased pressure of the Crown's intelligence services.

British intelligence, the Auxiliaries, and the military had substantially increased the pressure on the IRA, and October had been a bloody month for both sides. The tracking and cornering of Treacy was a clear sign that British intelligence was getting better. On October 19, four days after Treacy's death, the British arrested eighteen-year-old medical student Kevin Barry for his part in an IRA attack that killed three soldiers. Barry was convicted by court-martial and sentenced to death, causing a national uproar. Collins examined options to rescue Barry to no avail. Some five thousand people gathered outside the jail to demand clemency and pray. The tension increased on October 25 when Terence McSwiney, the mayor of Cork and commanding officer of the Cork City Brigade, died in Brixton prison after seventy-four days on hunger strike. Dail Eireann declared October 31 a national day of mourning, focusing world attention on the conflict and winning another propaganda victory when McSwiney's coffin was paraded with an Irish tricolor through British streets on its return to Cork. On November 2, despite widespread appeals for mercy, the British hanged Kevin Barry. IRA GHQ responded with a general order to all units to initiate armed attacks. Within twenty-four hours, the IRA in County Kerry had shot sixteen RIC constables and a Royal Navy radio operator in Tralee. Seven of the constables died and another was beaten so savagely that he committed suicide. In reprisal, the Black and Tans went on a rampage, occupying Tralee, firebombing houses, holding up citizens, destroying businesses, and closing others. A Canadian newspaper declared to the world in a bold headline, "Tralee Is Paralyzed," followed by the subtitle, "Town Near Starvation, Conditions Desperate."

Against this backdrop, Collins's three senior intelligence deputies, Tobin, Cullen, and Thornton, were all arrested. Tobin and Cullen were detained in a raid at Vaughn's Hotel, an overused Collins safe house, but they managed to talk their way free. Thornton was interrogated for a harrowing ten days before being released. On November 10, another raid nearly resulted in the capture of Chief of Staff Mulcahy, but he escaped through an attic. However, a large number of important documents were recovered that contained highly sensitive information, including the names of more than two hundred IRA Volunteers and operational plans. It was a disaster for Collins, who knew that more raids were inevitable, and more operatives would be at risk. Even more serious, the British now had some idea of his plans.[29]

THE OPERATION

The IRA intelligence staff had been compiling dossiers on each British agent that had been identified. By mid-November, with British raids growing more accurate, Collins needed to buy time to protect his operations and his operators, and to organize further offensive measures. He was also certainly concerned about the "little stunt" that the British Secret Service was planning.

Given the very large number of British agents and intelligence officers that Neligan reported operating in Dublin, it is extremely doubtful that the IRA had ferreted out even half of them, much less assembled actionable biographic intelligence on them. The most professional were some of the DDSB men who had arrived from foreign posts since May. Experienced in the tradecraft of espionage, the best of these were embedded in aliases and maintaining various commercial covers.

Nevertheless, assembling a short list of targets was plausible as Neligan, MacNamara, Willie Beaumont, Liam Tobin, Cullen, and Thornton were rubbing elbows with several of them nightly at Kidd's Back and Rabiatti's Saloon. Some of the officers were cocky and careless; they associated with prostitutes and drank with strangers, perhaps trying to develop quick recruitments. Regardless, Collins knew that his best option would be to mount a spectacular attack by killing several of the British agents simultaneously.[30]

He would have to take them by surprise all at the same time to achieve maximum impact. Isolating them and taking them out one by one was not an option. Shooting G men and RIC constables individually over a period of eighteen months was one thing; trapping and shooting two dozen or more armed British officers was quite another matter. It was a proposition beyond the capability of the Squad alone. Substantially more manpower would be needed to ensure success, as would be stealth, operational security, and precise timing. Collins would also need a large dose of good luck.

DMP Sergeant Jerry Mannix of the Donnybrook Station, one of Collins's agents, had obtained a partial list of names, which he duly passed on to Collins. Lily Mernin, Collins's mole inside MO4x, offered corroborating information about the DDSB officers. Maids and hall porters were co-opted to report on the comings and goings of the strangers. All of this information flowed to Frank Thornton, who was tasked to assemble a master target list. Thornton remembered his assignment as "presenting my full report to a joint meeting of the Dail cabinet and Army Council, at which I had to prove that each and every man on my list was an accredited Secret Service man of the British Government."[31]

Lieutenant Colonel W. Woodcock was a British officer who would later be mistaken by the IRA as an intelligence officer. In fact, he was the commanding officer of one of the British infantry battalions based in Dublin and resided with his wife, Carolyn, in a top-floor flat at 28 Upper Pembroke Street. Mrs. Woodcock was aware that four intelligence officers resided in the same building, although it is unlikely she was aware that the premises housed one of many army secret service cells in Dublin. Weeks before Bloody Sunday, the Woodcocks had taken leave to visit Scotland. Upon their return and in the days leading up to November 21, Mrs. Woodcock recalled the foreboding atmosphere in Dublin and the suspicious behavior of the house staff:

> Nearly every night there was firing now, usually just a shot or two, but sometimes a full volley. The whole atmosphere was more than ever hostile, and I struggled with my depression and told myself it was just because I had been so thoroughly spoiled in Scotland. But

it was no good. I was just miserable. Even the servants in the house seemed different; certainly one of them did. I thought, too, that I was followed home once or twice, and could not understand why such an unimportant person as myself should be watched. But I realise now that they watched every one who went to and from that ill-fated house.[32]

Lieutenant G reportedly suggested to Collins that November 21 was the optimal date to carry out the operation. Dick McKee, commanding the Dublin Brigade, was in overall charge of the operation and provided additional men to augment the Squad. With Frank Thornton in tow, Collins met Mulcahy and Brugha on the afternoon of November 20 to lay out the operation and present the target list for final approval. It is believed that Collins originally brought a list of thirty-five names to Mulcahy and Brugha, including the army DDSB officers who had been socializing with Neligan, Tobin, and Cullen and others suspected of intelligence affiliation. At least one civilian informer was on the list, as were two army court-martial officers. After close questioning, Brugha was convinced that some of the names did not belong on the list. He ordered Collins to revise the list, which was done on the spot. It now contained only names of officers whom Tobin, Cullen, Thornton, Beaumont, Neligan, or Lily Mernin could personally identify or who were personally known to other IRA members.[33]

At this point it is useful to address the varied backgrounds of the men who would become casualties on Bloody Sunday. Historians have disagreed on whether they were drawn primarily from the ranks of the Imperial Security Service (MI5), from the Secret Intelligence Service (SIS, or MI1c), or from Special Branch. In fact, most of the men targeted were army case officers assigned to DMI/MO4x, operating in Ireland as the DDSB (later "D Branch"); a few of these had served previously in Poland and Holland and may have had prior service with MI1c and MI5. Others on the list included Special Branch officers (some who had served in MI5 during the war) and army officers involved in court-martial proceedings. The affiliation of a few others remains shrouded in mystery, and one of them may have been a serving MI1c case officer or may have recently resigned from that service. Although a complete list has never surfaced, the following twenty-three names are believed to have been on the IRA's final list of twenty-five targets:

- **Temporary Captain Leonard Price** of MO4x/DDSB had four years of secret service work under his belt, having been specially appointed to the General List in September 1917, indicating that Price had served previously with the Field Intelligence Corps on the Western Front during the war. Price was one of the few who stuck with the original Royal Engineers cover story. He appears to have been among the very first DDSB officers to arrive in Dublin and likely had seniority — if not officially, then certainly by date of appointment and street experience.

- **Temporary Captain George Bennett** of MO4x/DDSB had formerly served as an army intelligence officer in Turkey from April to August 1919 and received his appointment for Ireland on November 16, 1919. Bennett appears to have been one of the first of the MO4x special branch to arrive for duty in Ireland. Bennett and Temporary Captain Peter A. Ames were introduced to IRA double agent David Nelligan at Kidd's Back saloon in the weeks leading up to the operation of November 21, 1920.

- **Temporary Captain Henry R. Angliss** of MO4x/DDSB — a native Irishman who employed the operational alias "Paddy Mahon" — had received his special appointment to the General List in October 1918, indicating that Angliss had been an IO in the Field Intelligence Corps during the war. He had most recently been working in Russia before arriving in Ireland, possibly in support of British Expeditionary Forces there who were cooperating with the White Russian Army to topple Lenin's regime.

- **Temporary Captain Donald Lewis MacLean** of MO4x/DDSB had allegedly served in Cairo during the war and reportedly smoked Egyptian cigarettes, from which the moniker "Cairo Gang" may have been derived. It is certain that MacLean had also previously been based in Holland. He was specially employed on the General List for Ireland in June 10, 1920. Inasmuch as Holland was a primary center for MI1c operations in Western Europe between 1914 and 1940, it is plausible that MacLean had some prior experience working with Cumming's department. In Ireland he was on the MO4x payroll.

- **Temporary Captain Peter Ashmun Ames** of MO4x/DDSB received his special appointment in June 1920 for Irish service. Ames was born in Pennsylvania and reared in New Jersey. He traveled to Britain in 1912, became a British subject, and subsequently joined the Grenadier

Guards. At age thirty-one, Ames was one of the older intelligence officers on the list. This, and the fact that Ames frequented Kidd's Back saloon along with Captain George Bennett—where both were cultivated by IRA agents David Nelligan and Willie Beaumont—may be the reason that IRA intelligence staff believed Ames was one of the leaders of the secret service contingent.

- **Captain Robert D. Jeune**, MO4x/DDSB. Jeune had recently come to Dublin after service with the British diplomatic delegation in Poland—possibly a cover for anti-Bolshevik intelligence work.

- **Lieutenant Randolf George Murray**, MO4x/DDSB. Murray received his special appointment to Ireland in May 1920 and was Captain R. D. Jeune's roommate. His previous intelligence service, if any, remains unclear.

- **Major C. M. C. Dowling**, MO4x/DDSB, was a highly decorated soldier who had commanded combat troops on the Western Front and had been twice wounded in battle. He received his special appointment to the General List for deployment to Ireland on April 16, 1920, and this appears to have been his first employment in intelligence work.

- **Lieutenant Colonel Hugh Montgomery**, Royal Marines. A Royal Marine captain (later major), Montgomery appeared on wartime Naval Intelligence Division lists, and it is possible that this was the same Lieutenant Colonel Hugh Montgomery who arrived at Irish Command in 1920. There is evidence that Lieutenant Colonel Montgomery had been attached to the Department of Military Intelligence since 1916. Perhaps the most convincing evidence of Montgomery's intelligence affiliation was his listing as one of two general service officers 1 (GSO 1) directly under General J. E. S. Brind, MO4x Chief on the Irish Command General Staff. Significantly, the other GSO 1 serving under Brind and alongside Montgomery at Parkgate Barracks was Lieutenant Colonel S. S. Hill-Dillon, an ex-MI5 officer who had established the MO4x's DDSB in the summer of 1919 and ran it until the arrival of Lieutenant Colonel Walter Wilson in the spring of 1920. It was Dillon who had mounted the Fergus Bryan Molloy dangle operations against Collins beginning in the fall of 1919. It is very likely, therefore, that the experienced Hugh Montgomery was managing some aspect of M04x operations; it is also likely that Montgomery had come to

Thornton's attention courtesy of IRA penetration agent Lily Mernin, Hill-Dillon's confidential code clerk.

- **Captain William Noble**, MO4x/DDSB. Noble was a decorated war veteran who joined DDSB at the beginning of June 1920.
- **Temporary Captain Charles R. Peel,** MO4x/DDSB. At age forty-four, Peel was probably the oldest man on the list. Born Carl Francis S. Ratsch in London in 1885, he had served a lengthy career as an enlisted petty officer in the Royal Navy where, among other things, he had once served as a firearms instructor. In 1916, he appears to have changed his name to the more Anglicized "Charles Peel." By 1917 he had transferred to the Army Labour Corps. He received his special appointment to the General List for Irish service in August 1920.
- **Temporary Captain John J. Fitzgerald**, MO4x/DDSB, was an ex–RIC sergeant. He had previously been kidnapped and shot by the IRA but upon his recovery joined the DDSB. He used the operational alias "Fitzpatrick."
- **Captain Geoffry Thomas Baggally**, Legal Staff, Irish Command. Baggally was a court-martial officer.
- **Lieutant William Frederick Newbury,** Legal Staff, Irish Command. Newbury was also a court-martial officer.
- **Captain Jocelyn Lee Hardy,** Special Branch/Home Intelligence Directorate. A former officer in the Connaught Rangers, Hardy was a POW during the First World War. Upon his repatriation, he appears to have worked for MI5 during the closing months of the war, possibly in debriefing fellow escapees to obtain intelligence information, or perhaps managing escape-and-evasion networks for other British servicemen caught behind enemy lines. Hardy claimed to be employed by Special Branch while in Ireland, and he was closely associated with Major W. L. "Tiny" King, the intelligence officer of K Company of the Auxiliary Division. As mentioned earlier, Hardy was notorious for his brutal interrogations of IRA prisoners and was high on Collins's hit list.
- **Major William Loraine "Tiny" King**. Born in London, King had served most of his army career in South Africa. By November 1920, King was a recently demobilized officer serving as the Intelligence Officer for K Company, Auxiliary Division. K Company was responsible for augmenting police security in the Dublin Military District and as such it carried out dozens of raids, arrests, and interrogations in the city.

King worked closely with Captain J. L. Hardy of the Castle, and was wanted by the IRA for his investigations and brutal interrogations.

- **Major Frank Murray Maxwell Hallowell Carew** had served in the Tank Corps and was decorated for bravery on the Western Front. He was appointed to MO4x for intelligence duties with the DDSB on June 1, 1920, and was one of the four intelligence officers who cornered Sean Treacy in Talbot Street in October of that year. Carew's DDSB colleague, Captain Gilbert Price, died in the shoot-out with Treacy, as did Auxilliary Intelligence Officer Sergeant Frank Christian.

- **Lieutenant Colonel Jennings.** Jennings was a known associate of Major King, and may have been an Auxiliary intelligence officer, like Major King, or a member of MO4x.

- **Major Callaghan.** Also an associate of Major King. Callaghan may have been an Auxiliary intelligence officer, like Major King, or a member of MO4x.

- **Captain Frederick Harper-Shove.** Shove was a member of MO4x/ Dublin District Special Branch and may have been in charge of other officers. He received a "special appointment" on March 1, 1920. By April 1920, Shove was in Dublin and had written a London colleague advising that he was preparing to carry out "a little stunt." The IRA believed this referred to the simultaneous assassination of Dail leaders.

- **Ex-major Patrick McCormack,** Royal Veterinary Corps. McCormack's precise role has never come to light, but he appears to have been on the IRA target list. As noted below, while Collins later claimed that the targeting of McCormack was a mistake, this may very well have been a lie to protect extremely sensitive IRA operational equities. After several weeks of living in Dublin's most expensive hotel, the Gresham, McCormack was scheduled to depart Dublin for Egypt on Monday, November 22, ostensibly to take up employment at a Cairo racecourse. Egypt was at that time the center of considerable British espionage activity.

- **Ex-lieutenant Leonard Aldie Wilde.** Likewise, the targeting of Wilde remains a mystery, although an unsubstantiated claim has surfaced that he was a British Secret Service officer who had previously served in Spain during the war. If so, Wilde likely had been an MI1c (SIS) officer. In addition, at thirty-five, Wilde was quite a bit older than most of the officers on the list, and he too had been living for some time at the luxurious Gresham Hotel, further telltale signs of his possible intelligence affiliation. As noted below, there is the possibility that Wilde had recently resigned from the secret service, or was contemplating resignation, at the time of his death.

- **T. H. Smith.** Civilian informer and the landlord at the address where DDSB officer Temporary Captain D. L. McLean and his wife lodged.[34]

While Collins had suspicions about many more British officers, at the end of the day, he could not make incontrovertible connections for several suspects in spite of Thornton's research, and he was compelled to settle for the short list. The IRA would fail to get even half of those men on Bloody Sunday. Of those killed, only seven were later acknowledged to be engaged in secret service work. This fact, and Collins's uncertainty, suggests that many more British agents evaded IRA detection than were caught on November 21.

A total of eight hit teams comprising Dublin Brigade men assembled, each team led by Squad officers. Collins set the time for the operation at precisely 9:00 a.m. Sunday morning, giving specific orders that the actions not begin a minute before 9:00. Precision timing was critical, for Collins knew that the psychological impact of multiple, simultaneous assassinations throughout Dublin would be enormous. Collins reportedly told the team leaders, "It's got to be done exactly at nine. Neither before nor after. These whores, the British, have got to learn that Irishmen can turn up on time."[35]

The operation proceeded on Collins's timetable, but it was not carried out with the professionalism often attributed to it. On Sunday, 9:00 a.m. sharp, the IRA teams descended upon seven separate private residences as well as the Gresham Hotel. They were each armed and also carried sledge hammers to force open doors. Completing their gruesome task at the first seven venues, they moved on to the Eastwood Hotel and to a guesthouse in Fitzwilliam Square. Of the twenty-two targets the IRA located, nine were shot and killed, four were shot and wounded, while nine escaped. Two of those shot were infantry officers who had no connection whatsoever with intelligence. They shared the same lodging house with several DDSB officers and were apparently shot because they blundered into the gunmen on their way to breakfast.[36]

At 28 Upper Pembroke Street, the IRA shot Dowling, Price, Murray, and Montgomery. At the same address, infantry battalion commander W.

J. Woodcock was in full uniform, preparing to report to his barracks as duty officer for a Sunday morning church parade. As he walked downstairs from his third-floor flat, he encountered gunmen standing outside the door of Colonel Montgomery. Woodcock shouted a warning to Montgomery, but the Marine opened his door and was immediately shot and mortally wounded. The IRA gunmen then ordered Colonel Woodcock to turn around and shot him in the back. Seriously wounded, Woodcock tried to scurry up the staircase and was shot twice more in the arm and back. Somehow he managed to stumble back to his flat where he collapsed in front of his wife. The assassins did not pursue him further. Although seriously wounded, he later recovered, as did the battalion's adjutant, Captain Keenlyside. Dowling, Price, Murray, and Montgomery all perished, the latter two in the hospital.[37] Captain Jeune, who shared a room with Murray, had been on a raid the evening before and recalled the scene that greeted him at 28 Upper Pembroke Street upon his return Sunday morning:

> In the evening of Saturday 20 November, I received orders to collect my fellows and search the railway yards at Inchicore, where it was thought that ammunition might be stored. We went there and searched for several hours, but there was obviously nothing to be found, so we slept in railway carriages, and in the morning I telephoned the Castle and asked whether I was to be relieved. Our Adjutant, Hyems, said, "I am sorry to say that there have been some raids by the Shinners and I am afraid that they have got some of our fellows." So it was agreed that we should return to our lodgings. I was at that time sharing a flat at 28 Upper Pembroke Street with a colleague, Murray, and on getting back there I found a very distressing scene. In the flat next to Murray's and mine, I saw the body of my friend "Chummy" Dowling, a grand ex-guardee [veteran of the Grenadier Guards], wounded three times in the war, lying full length on the floor. As he was to have relieved me he was in uniform and had obviously been shot in the heart, probably by a small Sinn Feiner because there was a bullet hole in one corner of the ceiling. In the doorway of the bathroom was Price's body. Murray had already been taken to the hospital. Colonel Woodcock, commanding the 1st East Lancs, had been shot three times, but sur-

vived. Likewise Captain Keenlyside, Adjutant of the same battalion. Colonel Montgomery had been shot on the stairs as he came up after breakfast. He died some time later.[38]

Court-martial officer G. T. Baggally, was located at 119 Lower Baggott Street and shot dead by Thomas Whelan, James Boyce, and three others, including Sean Lemass, who would survive the war to become a future prime minister of the Irish Republic. At 28 Earlsford Terrace, Temporary Captain John Fitzgerald—an ex-RIC sergeant working under the alias "Fitzpatrick"—was gunned down. At 92 Lower Baggott Street, Paddy Daly and Bill Stapleton, along with six or eight others, were admitted by the maid; they located the room of court-martial officer Captain W. F. Newbury, whose wife tried to block the door. They broke in, brushed past her, and shot Newbury dead as he attempted to escape out a window, leaving his riddled corpse dangling from the window ledge.[39]

Things got very messy at several locations because many of the assassins had never been involved in point-blank executions and they fired nervously and wildly, wounding but not killing some of the victims. Moreover, as some of the British officers were caught in bed with their wives or girlfriends, considerable delays ensued and the hysterical screaming of spouses and partners unnerved several Volunteers, including some of the most hardened Squad members. Volunteers burst into 22 Lower Mount Street in search of two intelligence officers, C. R. Peel and another known to the IRA only by the alias "Paddy Mahon." Peel was believed to have been officer in charge of the DDSB cell at 22 Lower Mount Street, while "Mahon" was Temporary Captain Henry R. Angliss, who had recently been on intelligence assignment in Russia. Both were at home when the Squad showed up but Peel survived by barricading himself in his flat; IRA gunmen fired numerous bullets through the door at him, but he escaped uninjured. Angliss, a veteran of MO4x, was executed without incident. Hearing the shooting at the address, Auxiliary officers Frank Garniss and Cecil Morris, on patrol nearby, closed in on the apartment house, while a third Auxiliary ran to summon reinforcements from Auxiliary headquarters at Beggar's Bush Barracks, a few hundred yards away. As Garniss and Morris entered the premises, an intense gunfight ensued; the two Auxiliary officers were killed and Volunteer Frank Teeling was seriously wounded in the leg and soon captured by Auxiliaries arriving on scene. One cadet placed his revolver to Teeling's head and was counting to ten when General Crozier arrived and put a stop to the execution. Teeling was spirited away in custody for medical treatment.[40]

A few blocks away, at 38 Upper Mount Street, where the IRA team had entered in search of Temporary Captain George Bennett and Peter A. Ames, the team found itself under fire from the house across the street at 28 Upper Mount Street. Major Frank Carew, who had recently moved to a new flat opposite number 28, was himself on Frank Thornton's hit list for having been on the surveillance team that cornered Sean Treacy two weeks earlier. Alerted by the commotion across the road, he now opened fire on the IRA team with his revolver. Not realizing that the gunfire was coming from the intrepid Major Carew, the IRA evaded him and moved on, but not before Carew got a good look at the assassins. At 117 Morehampton Road, Volunteers cornered Temporary Captain Donald Lewis MacLean and shot him dead, then killed his brother-in-law, T. H. Smith, the informer on Collins's list. Before departing the premises, the Volunteers also shot Mrs. MacLean's brother, ex–army officer John Caldow, who was visiting Dublin to interview for a job with the RIC and who had no known intelligence connections. Although grievously wounded in the chest, Mr. Caldow survived.[41]

At the Gresham Hotel, Paddy Moran, Paddy Kennedy, and a small team went searching for two alleged spies; they were registered under the names L. A. Wilde and Major Patrick McCormack. The missions of Wilde and McCormack have never been clarified, and their deaths sparked a great deal of speculation over the years. It has usually been assumed that one or both were killed in error, and in McCormack's case, Collins stated as much.

Wilde's background is mysterious, and his status as an intelligence operative remains uncertain. He resided alone at the posh Gresham Hotel and does not appear to have been connected with any of the DDSB cells. Most mysterious is the fact that he had written a letter to a Labour Party politician, published in London a day after his death, in which he said he had been "an eye witness" to events in Ireland for some time and therefore was in a good position to know that Britain's coercive policy was wrongheaded and would never bring peace. Wilde stated that he was now interested only in promoting democracy and that he looked to the Labour Party to lead that effort. He wrote that his change of heart came after discussions with the Roman Catholic clergy.[42]

This was certainly not the sentiment of a hardened veteran of His Majesty's Secret Service. Yet it may have reflected the sentiment of a burned-out case officer disillusioned and ashamed of his role as an instrument of brutal coercion that caused the deaths of Irishmen and was destroying the economy of the colony. An alternative theory is that this letter may have been a cover mechanism intended to ingratiate Wilde with Sinn Fein and IRA contacts à la Jameson/Molloy/Quinn. But other circumstantial evidence suggests that Wilde was looking for an escape from the nerve-wracking profession of espionage. No fewer than five secret service officers working for Winter became so despondent that they committed suicide—was Wilde also despondent or suicidal?

Further, Wilde is an anomaly since he was named publicly as "Lieutenant Wilde" during a stormy House of Commons session on November 22nd, yet his corpse was not honored with a solemn escort to Westminster for a hero's funeral as were those of Bennett, Ames, Angliss, Fitzgerald, Price, Dowling, Newbury, and Baggally. Was Wilde considered a traitor to the secret service? According to an undocumented source, Patrick Doyle, manager of the Gresham Hotel, later alleged that he had been told by Archbishop Patrick Clune that Wilde was a British agent who had been expelled from Spain during the war and that Doyle had assumed that this was true. How Clune may have come by such information is uncertain—unless he got it from Wilde himself.

What is certain is that Clune had been in Dublin to meet discreetly with Arthur Griffith to propose a cease-fire prior to Bloody Sunday. Was Archbishop Clune the "Roman Catholic clergy" that Wilde mentioned in his letter? Was Wilde's change of heart genuine, and might this have resulted from discussions with Clune while both were staying at the Gresham? Had a deeply troubled Wilde admitted his secret service background and activities to Clune during those discussions—or perhaps in the confessional? Had Clune counseled Wilde to quit the service, reform his life, and work toward peace? Had Clune later warned Griffith about Wilde when the two met in early November?

The answers may never surface, but what seems certain is that Leonard Aiden Wilde (if indeed that was his true name) disappeared from history after November 21, 1920, anonymous in death as in life—nameless, faceless, and placeless—as befits a deep-cover intelligence officer lost in action. If Doyle's testimony is accurate, it seems quite plausible that Wilde may have come to Ireland after serving with MI1c in Spain, and that he was on loan to Winter at the time of his death. Whatever Wilde's true identity, on that fateful Sunday morning an IRA team forced open the door to his room with a sledgehammer, discovered him standing in his pajamas, and shot him dead.[43]

After dispatching Wilde, the Volunteers forced the door of room 22 at the Gresham and discovered ex-major Patrick McCormack, late of the Royal Veterinary Corps, sitting up in bed, where he had been reading a racing form. He was shot six times, including a round to the head. Tom Bowden has suggested that McCormack may have been in Dublin either to penetrate the IRA and feed it improper technical data on how to develop bacteriological cultures, or to investigate whether the IRA was attempting to develop this capability on its own. This theory stems from the fact that when Richard Mulcahy's room had been raided two weeks earlier, a document discovered among his papers was a detailed explanation of how the IRA could develop a germ culture that could be introduced in milk to spread typhoid in British units and also how to develop a culture to spread the disease glanders in horses and mules. Ormonde Winter considered the document so important that he immediately sent it by courier directly to London. When it was raised in the House of Commons on November 18, Irish opposition party members denounced it as a forgery, but there is no convincing evidence that this is the case. In addition, McCormack had been living at the Gresham—Dublin's most upscale and expensive hotel—for several weeks and, as mentioned, was scheduled to leave for Egypt on Monday, November 22—allegedly to be employed at a local racecourse. Ostensibly he was in Dublin to purchase mules. Not only was it unusual for an ex-officer on a short pension to be able to afford digs at the Gresham for several weeks, but Egypt was then the focus of much British intelligence activity. This is all circumstantial evidence, to be sure, and the fact that Collins later acknowledged that McCormack's death was an error seems to close the case.

But does it? The wilderness of mirrors that is the domain of intelligence operations is purposely deceptive and intended to distort or obfuscate the truth; things are very often not what they appear to be. Collins may well have lied to distance the IRA from the germ warfare scheme. The Mulcahy document had already been rather aggressively labeled a forgery by several opposition MPs sympathetic to Sinn Fein, and there was no gain whatsoever in revealing why McCormack was singled out. The opposite is true—it would likely expose the truth about the IRA germ warfare plot or at a minimum perpetuate a story that the IRA would like to bury. Its public revelation would have shocked most Irish, British, and American citizens, and it would have overshadowed any outrages committed by the British side in the conflict to date. Moreover, it would have jeopardized de Valera's mission to get official U.S. recognition. The IRA would have been branded as ruthless barbarians instead of oppressed freedom fighters. If the IRA was laying plans to use germ warfare and if McCormack was on a sensitive mission to investigate or expose the threat, then Collins would have had little choice but to lie in order to dampen speculation about the McCormack killing and bury the bacteria development initiative. Significantly, Daniel Breen, who operated twice with Collins's Squad in metropolitan Dublin during the war, asserted in his 1924 memoirs that McCormack's mule-buying story was merely a cover and that his execution was no mistake.[44]

At least six additional officers on Collins's list escaped. Five or six Volunteers led by intelligence officer Dan McDonnell and squad member Joe Dolan went looking for Captain William Noble at 7 Ranleagh Road. Discovering that Noble was not at home, the team dispersed. One officer had gone to early Mass, while some others stayed with girlfriends the evening before. Three of them—Colonel Jennings, Major Tiny King, and Major Callaghan—had spent the night in a brothel, while Captain J. L. Hardy of Special Branch was apparently on duty at the Castle that morning—later to be joined by a wobbly, sleep-deprived Major King. On balance, there was more than a little sloppiness on the IRA's part in this attack.[45]

The IRA also suffered casualties. Collins had given orders that his operatives were to avoid the streets and to stay away from their normal haunts and pubs on Saturday night before the operation. Nevertheless, Dick McKee, OC (commanding officer) of the Dublin Brigade, and Peadar Clancy were involved in last-minute planning on Saturday evening. Both were picked up by Auxiliaries at Vaughn's Hotel—well known by the police as a Sinn Fein establishment and hangout—and jailed at Beggar's Bush Barracks overnight. The following day, after news of the shootings began to spread, their interrogators—Hardy and King—went into a rage, perhaps after learning that their own names had been on the hit list, McKee and Clancy were killed, either by Hardy and King, or by other Auxiliaries from F Company who were present. This was also the fate of an innocent young man named Clune who had been picked up at Vaughn's a few days earlier. Although Clune had no connection with the IRA, he was a member of Sinn Fein and was charged as a suspect; he died with the two others. The prisoners were reported to have been shot while attempting to escape. Collins dispatched Neligan to learn their fate and Neligan confirmed their deaths, but denied later rumors that the three had been bayoneted or that their bodies had been mutilated. The wounded Frank Teeling, Paddy Moran, and Thomas Whelan, along with James Boyce, were all implicated in the killing of Baggally. Major Carew was called to testify but could not positively identify the suspects. Teeling later escaped, James Boyce was acquitted, and Moran and Whelan were hanged.[46]

In hindsight, Collins's operation, although executed with imprecision, was a shock to British intelligence but quite limited in scope. Contrary to popular romantic nationalist mythology, British Intelligence was not "wiped out" or "annihilated." The IRA succeeded in eliminating only a small fraction of the legion of British intelligence operatives, although there is no question that a few of those assassinated were among the more experienced and aggressive operators. The IRA appears to have succeeded in identifying about thirty-five targets and received permission to attack perhaps twenty-five. Not counting two army regimental officers who were shot by mistake, at the end of the day IRA gunmen killed seven confirmed intelligence officers, two legal officers, one informer, and two Auxiliary temporary cadets, while wounding four more suspected spies.

In the days that followed, six of the corpses were sent to London where they received a state funeral at Westminster Abbey. Neligan termed the operation a "body blow" to the British Secret Service and it achieved the desired result of causing panic in the Castle. Some intelligence officers were hastily withdrawn from Ireland within days (among them Charles Tegart, who had been on Winter's staff). As for the DDSB, the remaining officers and the Special Branch contingent were pulled out of their dispersed undercover locations; they set up their headquarters at Jury's Hotel and the Hotel Central in a matter of days. Now guarded day and night by armed soldiers, their effectiveness was clearly crippled, at least for the time being.[47]

Several of the British intelligence officers killed on November 21 were tough and experienced customers, but most practiced poor tradecraft that directly contributed to their demise. Instead of keeping the low profile demanded of their profession, some of them arrogantly roamed around the city, making the same rounds night after night in the same pubs, and discussing sensitive information with Irish cops, including Neligan. According to Lily Mernin, Henry Angliss—alias Paddy Mahon—had a serious drinking problem and talked too much. Others showed poor judgment in sleeping with local girlfriends and prostitutes. With well-placed moles at Parkgate and the Castle, it was a simple matter for the IRA intelligence staff to purloin copies of their service records and photographs and match names with faces. In addition, some of the officers performed clandestine surveillance operations in mufti and then led raids in full military uniform—immediately compromising themselves. A number of them went about the city armed while in civilian clothes, another telltale giveaway. Given the hundreds of sympathizers and informers working for Collins, these inconsistencies would certainly not have escaped the attention of the IRA.

In sum, it would seem that the DDSB officers followed a modus operandi and outlook that had been shaped during wartime conditions in Germany, the Middle East, and Russia, where the pace of military operations required intelligence officers to cut corners, dispense with vetting procedures, and cold-pitch informers in order to meet army demands. Many failed to appreciate the meaning of secret or clandestine work and became complacent, and all completely underestimated the depth or breadth of the IRA counterintelligence network. The officers assassinated on Bloody Sunday had no inkling they had been compromised until the second before their assassins pulled the trigger. Their swaggering, high-profile behavior, lack of concern for compartmentalizing sources and information, loose lips, and indiscreet liaisons may have caused little concern for intelligence officers in wartime Germany, Holland, Turkey, or Russia, but it brought disaster in Ireland. This was a sad episode in the history of British intelligence that British Secret Service officers are reluctant to discuss even today.[48]

Collins was satisfied with the results, stating of the victims:

> My one intention was the destruction of the undesirables who continued to make miserable the lives of the ordinary decent citizens.

I have proof enough to assure myself of the atrocities which this gang of spies and informers have committed. Perjury and torture are words too easily known to them. If I had a second motive it was no more than a feeling such as I would have for a dangerous reptile. By their destruction the very air is made sweeter. That should be the future's judgment on this particular event. For myself, my conscience is clear. There is no crime in detecting and destroying in wartime the spy and the informer. They have destroyed without trial. I have paid them back in their own coin.[49]

But privately, Collins grieved over the loss of Dick McKee, who had been his close ally in setting up the Squad and a right hand in orchestrating arms transfers, jail breaks, and countless other operations. Neligan remembered:

McKee, a printer by trade, was a grave loss to the Dublin Brigade as he was a very able man; the leadership following his was not the same. He was really irreplaceable.[50]

The day's carnage was not over. Just after 3:00 p.m., a combined force of Auxiliaries and army troops surrounded Croke Park, where an important Gaelic football game was in progress. The authorities were aware that several of the Tipperary team's players had Sinn Fein and IRA connections, and acted on the assumption that the assassins, or some of them, might be members of the team or that they were hiding in the crowd of spectators.

There were plenty of eyewitnesses to the attack. The troops apparently moved in with the intention of questioning the adult males and checking for weapons, but as the Auxiliaries approached the stadium gates, shots were fired, causing a panic in the grandstand. This was answered by general firing from the Auxiliaries and from a machine gun mounted in an armored car opposite the main entrance. When the shooting stopped, fourteen civilians had been killed, including one of the football players, while another civilian succumbed to a heart attack. Two more civilians were crushed to death by stampeding spectators.

The British claimed they were fired upon first, and almost ninety years later, the controversy surrounding the incident has still not been resolved. Even the recent release of the heretofore classified British inquiry dated

December 8, 1920, does not shed much light on how the shooting began, but it makes clear that the raid was a carefully planned joint army-police operation personally approved by General Boyd, commanding officer of the Dublin District Division. More than one Auxiliary officer testified that a group of young men rushed into the park ahead of the Crown forces and fired at the police first. While this is denied by the Republican side, there is a strong possibility that IRA men who had entered the park fired shots into the air to cause panic and create a diversion for their getaway. Regardless, the classified inquiry found that the police and army had fired 228 rounds of small arms ammunition and 50 rounds of machine gun ammunition; it concluded that the Crown forces fired without orders and that their actions were unjustified.[51]

In summation, Collins's November 21 attack was intended as a stop-gap measure to eliminate some agents, scare off more, achieve maximum psychological impact with simultaneous killings, buy time, and preempt the DDSB from pulling off their "little stunt." All of these goals were achieved, but the cost had been terribly high. The attack and the slaughter at Croke Park made world headlines, many of them negative. Eamon de Valera sought to counter the negative press in a long press release of his own on November 23, which he concluded by writing:

> The Irish people have learned again the old lesson that so long as the patient will suffer the cruel will kick; and having no other av-enue of redress they naturally pursue individually of those forc-es who are responsible for the outrages and are, as enemy spies among them, rightly deserving of death, for they provide an alien Government with the knowledge and the strength to persecute and inflict misery upon a whole nation.[52]

Within weeks, de Valera would be condemning Collins for assassina-tions in behind-the-scenes Dail cabinet meetings, and ordering the IRA to switch to open confrontation with the British Army.

Round two of the intelligence war concluded on Bloody Sunday, and for the time being the IRA still held the advantage. As for the British side, many more MO4x officers had escaped the November attacks than had fallen, and the DDSB survived to spy and raid again under Winter's direct command.[53]

AFTERMATH

The Year of Terror was not quite over. On November 28, Commander Tom Barry's Flying Column lured two trucks carrying nineteen officers from C Company of the Auxiliaries into an isolated killing zone at Kilmichael, County Cork, and wiped them out, killing seventeen and seriously wounding two. Of the two survivors, one suffered debilitating brain damage, while the other managed to crawl to a nearby cottage. He was discovered there later by local IRA scouts, who executed him and dumped his body into a bog. Barry's column suffered three killed.[54] Shortly thereafter, the remainder of C Company was transferred from Macroom to Dublin and replaced by K Company, which had been supporting the Dublin Military District since the previous August. Authorities apparently believed that K Company, with its record of aggressive raids and arrests in Dublin, would be better able to suppress the insurgents in Cork.

On December 10, two weeks after the Kilmichael ambush, the Crown extended martial law to Counties Cork, Tipperary, and Limerick, declaring

> that a state of armed insurrection exists, that any person taking part therein or harbouring any person who has taken part therein, or procuring, inviting, aiding or abetting any person to take part therein, is guilty of levying war against His Majesty the King, and is liable to conviction by a military court to suffer DEATH.[55]

Just one day after martial law was declared, however, the IRA reacted by ambushing a patrol from K Company at Dillon's Cross, outside Cork City. One cadet was killed while eleven others were wounded. That evening, the enraged members of K Company went on a bloody rampage in Cork, sacking, looting, burning, and shooting up the central business district. When pressed in the House of Commons, Hamar Greenwood, who had replaced Macpherson as undersecretary, denied that Britons were responsible and then equivocated in response to harsh questions from the opposition.[56] In a letter to his mother, however, a K Company officer identified only as "Charley" subsequently gave a more accurate account of events:

> My darling Mother,
>   We cam [sic] here from Cork and are billeted in a workhouse—filthy dirty. Half of us are down with bronchitis. I am at present in

bed . . . recovering from a sever [*sic*] chill contracted on Saturday night during the burning and looting of Cork in which I took a reluctant part. We did it all right never mind how much the well intentioned Hamar Greenwood would excuse us. In all my life . . . I have never experienced such orgies of murder, arson and looting as I have witnessed during the last 16 days with the RIC Auxiliaries. It baffles description. And we are supposed to be officers and gentlemen. There are quite a number of decent fellows and likewise a lot of ruffians. On our arrival here from Cork one of our heroes held up a car with a priest and a civilian in it and shot them both through the head without cause or provocation. We were very kindly received by the people but the consequences of this cold-blooded murder is that no one will come within a mile of us now and all shops are closed. The brute who did it has been sodden with drink for some time and has been sent to Cork under arrest for examination by experts in lunacy. If certified sane he will be court-martialled and shot. The poor old priest was 65 and everybody's friend. The burning and sacking of Cork followed immediately on the ambush of our men. I, as orderly sergeant had to collect 20 men for a raid, and then left the barracks in motor cars. I did not go as I was feeling seedy. The party had not got 100 yards from barracks when bombs were thrown at them over a wall. One dropped in a car and wounded eight men, of whom one has since died. Very naturally the rest of the Co. were enraged. The houses in vicinity of the ambush were set alight. And from there the various parties set out on their mission of destruction. Many who witnessed similar scenes in France and Flanders say that nothing they have experienced ever compared to the punishment meted out in Cork. I got back to barracks at 4 a.m. Reprisals are necessary and loyal Irishmen agree, but there is a lot that should not be done.[57]

Damages to the Cork economy were estimated at £3 million. But not every Auxiliary officer felt pangs of conscience. On December 12, several members of K Company proudly wore burnt corks attached to the crest of their Glengarry bonnets.[58] One IRA officer who witnessed the destruction of Cork later told journalist James Gleeson, "We could have shot most of them that night if we had wanted to . . . and we wanted to all right, but it would have ruined the whole show. They were doing all they could to help us."[59]

THE FIREBOMB CAMPAIGN

For some time IRA Chief of Staff Mulcahy and Dail Defence Minister Brugha had proposed a campaign to attack the British economy and thus bring the war home to the English people. The IRA in England was an extension of the robust IRB organization that had existed there for decades, led by Sam Maguire. IRA units had been organized in most major British cities and now comprised motivated Volunteers itching to get into the fight. The previous year, Collins had sent them £2,000 for the purchase of arms, while explosives were purloined from mining districts. The Liverpool IRA had mushroomed from three dozen men to 150 men by November 1920.[60]

Brugha had been advocating the assassination of the entire British cabinet for some time. It was an overly ambitious scheme prior to Bloody Sunday, and afterward it would have been a suicide mission, as all British government offices, Downing Street, and residences of key policymakers were placed under armed guard by uniformed London Metropolitan Police and CID detectives. The IRA settled for a campaign with more realistic goals: destroy the docks at Liverpool and sabotage the Manchester power plant. A third project involved intimidation of the Black and Tans, Auxiliaries, and their relatives in England. All three objectives had important intelligence dimensions: casing, surveillance, countersurveillance, covert acquisition of explosives, surreptitious entries, collection of biographic intelligence, and research. The pervasive presence of the IRA intelligence network and its value to Collins in being able to gather biographic data on British targets was revealed years later by one particularly well placed Volunteer who had served during the war with the Dublin Brigade:

> In 1918 I joined H Company of the First Battalion. I was then stationed at Richmond Hospital in North Brunswick Street. This was a very useful place to be, as the Auxiliaries—who came later—were stationed nearby in the North Dublin Union. Their records were available to me in the hospital. I was able to go through these, take the English addresses and pass them on to the battalion Intelligence Officer. From there they were fed to . . . O.C. of operations in England.[61]

Mulcahy dispatched the IRA's Director of Engineering, Rory O'Connor, to Britain to advise the local IRA units, but a raid on Mulcahy's office by Winter compromised a list of names of Volunteers in Liverpool and several key men were arrested. Nevertheless, a few days after Bloody Sunday, 115 warehouses at Liverpool and Boole were set on fire, resulting in £250,000 worth of damage. The Manchester attack was cancelled. Subsequently the IRA set off incendiary bombs at several locations in London and elsewhere in the spring of 1921, which did little physical harm but had a major impact on British public opinion. Desultory and isolated firebomb attacks in Britain continued until the end of hostilities. We do not know what impact IRA operations to intimidate and frighten Auxiliary relatives in England may have had.[62]

CARROT AND STICK

Before year's end, the British responded with hundreds of roadblocks and checkpoints and thousands of arrests, including that of Arthur Griffith on November 25. Collins became Acting President at Griffith's arrest and was diverted from war making to deal, however reluctantly, with peace initiatives, several of which had been put forth by the British side since October.

The principal effort was brought forth by none other than retired Brigadier General George Cockerill. As deputy director of DMI at the War Office in 1903, Cockerill had established the first British clandestine service under William Melville, and he later became first director of MI9. Having retired from the army, Cockerill was now a Conservative MP. He wrote a letter to Lloyd George—later published in the *Times*—suggesting that a conference of British and Irish delegates meet to negotiate peace with no preconditions. Arthur Griffith responded to Cockerill through Art O'Brien, saying that Dail Eireann was prepared to participate at any time in a conference with no preconditions. *Chicago Tribune* reporter John Steele and London-based Irish businessman Patrick Moylett, who acted unofficially for the cabinet, began shuttling back and forth between Lloyd George and Griffith. A second effort was the public call for extension of full Dominion status at the earliest possible moment by former prime minister Asquith. The famed Irish poet and painter George Russell ("AE") also met with Lloyd George seeking a formula for a cease-fire.[63]

Collins was dismissive of these efforts. When Carl Ackerman, the reporter who in April was asked by Basil Thomson to track down the leaders of Sinn Fein, finally caught up with Collins, the latter was adamant about negotiating with the British. In a published interview, Collins was unequivocal:

> There will be no compromise and we will have no negotiations with any British government until Ireland is recognized as an Independent Republic. I see you think we have only to whittle our demand down to Dominion Home Rule and we shall get it. The talk about Dominion Home Rule is not promoted by England with a view to granting it to us, but merely with a view to getting rid of the Republican movement. England will give us neither as a gift. The same effort that would get us Dominion Home Rule will get us a republic.[64]

When Lloyd George made an inflammatory speech in October declaring that the government "had murder by the throat," Collins cynically asked, "I wonder what these people with their hypocritical good intentions and good wishes say to L. George's speech yesterday? So much for the peace feelers."[65]

Collins's reaction was natural. He was president of the IRB, which vowed by secret oath to create an independent republic, and as such he had been publicly branded a murderer by the government. Griffith represented the political faction of Sinn Fein in de Valera's absence, and his pacifist past made him especially attractive to Downing Street as a vehicle for a truce. But with de Valera out of the country, Collins held the real power. Thus had the Dail responded to Britain's carrot-and-stick approach with its own dual track strategy: while Griffith met with Downing Street's emissaries, Collins relentlessly attacked British forces.

But after Griffith's arrest, Collins was acting head of state for four weeks, and he could no longer dismiss the peace emissaries. Moylett returned to Dublin in November and Griffith met him; after being arrested, Griffith encouraged Collins to stay in touch with him. Then Archbishop Clune appealed to both sides to implement a cease-fire and embarked on sensitive negotiations, meeting Griffith in jail. Griffith warned Collins not to meet with the archbishop, for fear that the British Secret Service would place any such meeting under surveillance. Collins and his staff worked out the security issue, however, and Collins met secretly with Clune in

December, when he handed the archbishop the Dail's general outline of terms for a truce:

> If it is understood that the acts of violence (attacks, counter-attacks, reprisals, arrests, pursuits) are called off on both sides, we are agreeable to issue the necessary instructions on our side, it being understood that the entire Dail shall be free to meet [in public] and that its peaceful activities not be interfered with.[66]

The Clune initiative was unexpectedly disrupted when Sinn Fein members of the Galway County Council unilaterally appealed to London to end the war, and when Sinn Fein Vice President Father Michael O'Flanagan wrote to Lloyd George seeking terms. The Dail had not sanctioned these moves, but the timing of them complicated Clune's secret efforts, sidetracking them for the time being. Collins made certain that the press was informed that O'Flanagan had acted unilaterally, writing in disgust, "We must not allow ourselves to be rushed by these foolish productions or foolish people, who are tumbling over themselves to talk about a truce, when there is no truce."[67]

Eamon de Valera had delayed his return from America. He was disappointed that Collins was made acting president in November instead of Cathal Brugha. With apparently genuine peace feelers in evidence, de Valera was sure that he alone possessed the intelligence and statesmanship to handle negotiations with the British. Moreover, de Valera very much disapproved of Collins's ambush tactics, and he had conveniently avoided association with these dirtier aspects of the conflict by going to the United States and extending his stay there. But de Valera had little to show for his overseas mission; he had failed to get official American support for the Irish Republic, he had alienated the Clan na Gael and important Irish American members of Congress, and he was therefore in danger of becoming marginalized entirely so long as he remained in America. He was determined not to miss what would perhaps be his last opportunity to make his mark as statesman. He was also convinced that the Dail government could not achieve legitimacy unless he exerted tighter control over Collins and placed the IRA war strategy on a more conventional (and, to him, more honorable) footing. Perhaps then he could win a favorable political settlement with Britain. He sailed for home, arriving secretly and without fanfare, aboard a steamer in Dublin on December 23, 1920.

That same afternoon, Parliament had passed the Better Government of Ireland Act, which provided for the partition of the country with dual home parliaments in Dublin for three of Ireland's four provinces, and in Belfast for Ulster. The notion of partition was as distasteful to Unionists as it was to Nationalists, and it seriously complicated peace negotiations.

As for Collins, he remained skeptical of the peace overtures. Despite London's hydra-headed peace initiative of the past four months, there was no sign whatsoever that the British Army was ready to throw in the towel. Quite the contrary, the army up to now had been restricted to a defensive "police action" supporting the RIC. General Macready was anxious to unleash the full fury of his forces upon the guerrillas, and he bristled when the politicians restrained him. Thus far the RIC—or more accurately, their mercenary colleagues, the Black and Tans and the Auxiliaries— had borne the brunt of the fighting. In the months to come, Commanding General Macready would receive the authority to dramatically escalate the military response.

Ormonde Winter, meanwhile, was already on the offensive. Temporarily stunned by Bloody Sunday, British intelligence was far from neutralized. It ended the year with a major success when Winter orchestrated a New Year's Eve raid on the residence of Eileen McGrane, a college professor, prominent Sinn Fein member, and Collins confidante. McGrane's flat was the storage site for sacks of old IRA intelligence files, including documents identifying names of Volunteers and some of the carbon-copy G Division reports that Ned Broy had been passing to Collins since the fall of 1918. It was an intelligence windfall that would have dire consequences for the Nationalists.[68]

10

ENDGAME

It is my considered opinion that in the fullness of time history will record the greatness of Michael Collins and it will be recorded at my expense.

— *Eamon de Valera, President of Ireland, 1966*

The attacks by Collins on the British Secret Service had a dramatic but temporary impact on Crown intelligence operations. Over the next six months, the determined Ormonde Winter redoubled his efforts to neutralize the IRA, and enjoyed a series of successes both in Dublin and in the southernmost counties, where IRA units were most active. The war escalated to new levels of violence as open insurgency in the countryside led to a number of mid- to large-scale combat actions between the IRA and the British Army. Beginning in January 1921 and continuing until the cease-fire in July, both sides would suffer the highest casualties of the war. The return of de Valera would signal a temporary but disastrous change in IRA tactics but renewed efforts to seek a peaceful settlement. With all of these developments, Collins would be hard-pressed to sustain the guerrilla campaign. What emerged in early 1921 was a new dual strategy: The IRA fought on with dwindling resources; de Valera and his allies slowly began to rein in IRA activity as they moved toward a political solution. By mid-year, a truce would be in place.

SORTING THINGS OUT

The government extended martial law to all of Munster Province on January 5.[1] This fell far short of what the military wanted, but it freed Macready to react swiftly in arresting and trying suspects in that part of the country where the IRA had been most aggressive. In the absence of total martial law, however, Winter's CIS would remain an independent effort under civil control at the Castle. The problem of army-police intelligence coordination, which had hamstrung the British from the beginning, would not be resolved.

In the wake of Bloody Sunday, Winter pressured the army to transfer DDSB to his control, which the army reluctantly did, in January 1921. Whether Winter decided on this takeover or whether Basil Thomson encouraged it is unclear, but it bore the mark of the turf-conscious director of Home Intelligence. Winter and Thomson may have made the move in an effort to professionalize the army unit and to deconflict and streamline targeting efforts; it would have been a positive development had not the army contingent resisted the move.

The first impediment was Lieutenant Colonel Walter Wilson, who resigned as head of DDSB rather than work under Winter. Winter appears not to have been fazed in the least by this rebuff, likely because he was very fortunate to get an experienced intelligence officer to replace Wilson, David Boyle. Boyle had most recently served as number two to Major Norman Thwaites, the head of MI1c's undeclared station in New York City. The MI1c station operated semiclandestinely under diplomatic cover at the British mission in Manhattan and had been investigating various radicals arriving in New York from abroad—including IRB radicals—throughout the First World War. Afterward it shifted collection focus on economic intelligence using the same justification with U.S. immigration officers to gain access to frequent interrogations of business travelers arriving in New York, questioning them about their products, services, and clients. Boyle took command as acting head of station (HOS) when Thwaites left New York for London in January 1920 (not before communicating to Cumming his views that Sidney Reilly, then living in New York, should not receive a staff appointment in MI1c). Security concerns, apparently resulting from complaints by U.S. immigration officers to the Justice Department about the intrusive British "diplomats," prompted MI1c to lower its profile considerably. In March 1920, Boyle closed the MI1c station at the British Mission and departed the United States for Canada. Within a short time, however, he was quietly replaced by a Captain De-Graz, who reopened the station under nonofficial cover at a new commercial address, resuming operations with Boyle's old staff and, apparently, Boyle's same stable of recruited American-citizen assets. By the start of 1921, Boyle was in Dublin to replace Wilson and take over management of the DDSB for Dublin Castle.[2]

With Boyle's arrival, Winter amalgamated DDSB with his own secret service program and appointed Major Jeffries and Captain Cameron, two of Wilson's men, to go to London to take over from Tegart and Denham, who had already handed Winter their resignations. The combined force, now ostensibly under Boyle's overall command in Dublin, henceforth became known simply as D Branch.[3]

Despite the consolidation, there was confusion within the army about how this shotgun wedding should function. Although the army's case officers were now officially on Winter's civilian table of organization, they continued to view themselves as a de facto operating unit of the army's Dublin District Division. This would have been frustrating enough for Boyle, who should have been given authority to establish a formal "center" or station at the Castle, which would have enabled him to manage the army case officers without interference from Winter. Because of his civil appointment as deputy police commissioner and chief of combined intelligence, however, Winter was the senior intelligence authority at the Castle; he could overrule Boyle on operational matters, and apparently did. Consequently, it appears that no formal secret service station was established. Instead, Winter subsumed that vital function into his role as head of service for the Castle. Given the crisis at hand, and Winter's almost total lack of experience in intelligence management, analysis, and operations, this arrangement was programmed to fail. Under the circumstances, even a senior operational manager of many years' experience would have been severely challenged. Winter simply did not have the background or experience to make the scheme work. The army apparently agreed. Their postmortem strongly criticized the manner in which this transfer of its case officers took place, the failure to establish a proper intelligence station, and the manner in which Winter himself "usurped" the role and functions of head of station:

Early in 1921, the [Dublin District] Special Branch with its records was handed over to the Chief of Police and amalgamated with Police Intelligence, which already had a service of secret agents directed from London. The Director of Police Intelligence was thus responsible for the organization, henceforth known as "D" Branch, which had become partly intelligence, partly executive, and the Central Intelligence Office usurped functions which were properly those of a Local Centre, Dublin, which was never created. This transfer of what was in fact the military intelligence system was a grave mistake. For personnel reasons it was wholly unpopular among the personnel . . . and unfortunately personal considerations can rarely be left out of account in questions connected with secret service. The organization continued to work for the army but was responsible to a new master, the Chief of Police, consequently the driving power behind the agents gradually diminished. The G.O.C. [General Officer Commanding] Dublin District remained responsible for intelligence in an area where he had not a sufficient organization and ceased to control the agents working in his command. Consequently, duplicate organizations both to check the police information and to act as a liaison became necessary. The result was delay in taking action, overlapping in work and a registry created on the lines of compromise and satisfactory to neither military or police.[4]

Although Bloody Sunday had the desired shock effect on the secret service that Collins had intended, it was also somewhat of a wake-up call, strengthening the resolve of British intelligence officers. While there was undoubtedly unhappiness over being seconded to the control of the civilian intelligence office, the army postmortem may have exaggerated the issue, since many of the army case officers remained upbeat about their work and optimistic about the prospects for success.[5]

At some point in early 1921, Winter was also fortunate to get the services of Lieutenant Colonel Maldwyn M. Haldane. Haldane was a former assistant director of MI5 who had been responsible for building up and managing Kell's H Branch—the section responsible for administration and management of the famous Central Registry that had enabled MI5 and Special Branch to pounce on German spies and would-be saboteurs at the outbreak of the war. Interestingly, these additions to staff came as Winter was starting to receive criticism for his methodology, or lack of it. It is no wonder, when respected operators like Tegart and Denham walked out on him, that Winter received flak from London that likely included an imperative to get on with organizing a proper file system. With the arrival of Boyle and Haldane, Winter now had professional help, but it was too little, too late; the war in the countryside was escalating daily with British regulars now fully engaged in battle with IRA flying columns. The demand for actionable intelligence was far greater in the spring of 1921 than it had ever been.[6]

Moreover, regardless of this infusion of expertise, the dangers to the men of D Branch and Special Branch rose exponentially after Bloody Sunday. Concerned for the safety of these officers, Winter ordered them out of their private lodgings and set them up in solidly loyalist Dublin hotels. If anything, this move only made the officers more vulnerable. The IRA knew that any man going in or out of those hotels was connected with intelligence, and the Dublin Brigade stalked them relentlessly. The diary of Army Private J. P. Swindlehurst, assigned to guard the entrance to Jury's hotel, provides a glimpse of the extremely dangerous atmosphere that existed in central Dublin at that time:

13 January
I have been detailed for guard duty in Jury's Hotel in Great Dame Street, our party, ten of us take over after dinner tomorrow. It is the headquarters of Dublin CID the lads say it is a hot place, we shall have to see.

16 January
The time is 5 pm of the 16th, we on the Jury Guard have just had tea, incidents have been quiet and murderous in turn. . . . The days and nights have been a constant repetition of comings and goings, Secret Service men and detectives kept us on alert to admit them, the pass word on the first day was "Gin" and altered every few hours to every drink that could be thought of. Prisoners were brought in occasionally, a few looked about all in, covered in blood, minus teeth, and numerous other injuries. After a grilling in one of the upper rooms, we could hear groans and curses coming

down the stairway, a dull thump indicated someone had taken a count, they took them off to Mountjoy Prison on the outskirts. . . . Early this morning I was on sentry at the main entrance behind the iron gate, when the noise of a motor and running footsteps caused my pal and I to look out for trouble. We got it, the runner was a secret service man being pursued by Sinn Feiners in the car. They dropped him with a fusillade of shots, when he was about two yards from the doorway. His impetuous roll knocked us into the hall, when we were going to reply to them. In a few seconds they were gone, leaving a bomb in the roadway which failed to explode. The victim was luckily only slightly wounded, one through the leg and another through his hand. We don't know where he had been but a big party of men moved out armed to the teeth at dawn, so he must have got some information which was acted upon. It appears the Sinn Fein element hide out amongst the hills, and come into the city by various routes after dark, bent on some errand of murder, revenge or raid. They can get in easily enough, but it's the getting out that causes the trouble. Our men, Black and Tans, police and CID all hunt them down, when the deed has been done.[7]

Winter's organization may have looked good on paper, but it was clear nine months after the creation of CIS that coordination of intelligence had not been achieved. Sir Warren Fisher, who had conducted the earlier survey of the Castle administration the previous year, issued a second report on February 11, 1921, in which he noted that the Castle, police, and military were more in competition than coordination. Fisher's report ended with a call for a unified intelligence command system in Dublin. It would not be achieved.[8]

It was after DDSB's reorganization at the first of the year that David Boyle welcomed another army IO, Captain Cecil Lees, to D Branch. Lees had most recently been assigned to the British Chinese Labour Corps on the Western Front. An IRA source reported Lees's arrival and also that he was considered a crack operator who had a reputation as a torturer. The source discovered that Lees had checked into the St. Andrew Temperance Hotel, and provided a description of the six-foot three-inch officer. Tom Keogh and Ben Byrne of the Squad placed the hotel under surveillance for several days without success. Eventually they spotted a man matching Lees's description entering a movie theater. Following the film, Keogh and Byrne followed the man and noted that he entered the St. Andrew Hotel. Anticipating that Lees would head to the Castle at around 9:30 a.m., Keogh, Byrne, and two others waited outside. When Lees emerged in the company of a woman, five shots were immediately pumped into him, instantly killing him. The hit team escaped down a nearby alley.[9]

Winter's best intelligence was coming not from agents but from captured documents. Shortly after the first of the year, his Central Raid Bureau was up and running at the Castle. In order to have a record copy of documents on file at his headquarters, Winter insisted that all documents be forwarded to the bureau to be reviewed and a finished intelligence report prepared. Captured documents were funneled upward from field units to a team of "epitomizers," or reports officers, whose job it was to collate them and draft finished intelligence summaries. This took days; if the documents contained time-sensitive data, it was often useless by the time army units got a look at finished summaries. Moreover, the epitomizers at headquarters did not always appreciate conditions in the field, and thus they did not always recognize key data in the captured documents, sometimes omitting significant points in their finished summaries. The days it took to transport the information to the Castle or regional center and the time spent drafting the summaries essentially had the effect of converting important, time-sensitive, actionable information into historical archives. If anything, Winter's records scheme tended to undermine opportunities to mount follow-up operations and military staffers roundly criticized the system:

> At the Central Police Intelligence Office in Dublin, where documents were of greater importance than in the country, a sub-office was formed with a staff of epitomisers in order to deal with captured documents. This sub-office was named the Raid Bureau. Its creation further illustrates the complication of intelligence in Ireland. For purposes of evidence, all the documents found on the person or in the house of an individual were kept together, while, to enable various branches of intelligence concerned to extract such information as was required, an epitome, often consisting of over a hundred typed pages, and containing a mixture of complete quotations and lists of letters were compiled. This meant that every

branch had to read the whole of every epitome and then, where necessary, ask for a copy of the original.[10]

In fairness to Winter, his centralized reports-processing system followed the accepted practice of professional intelligence services (and indeed, may have been suggested by Colonel Haldane). The gulf between headquarters staff and field operations officers is a common problem in most services and is normally reduced by training and some cross-fertilization of the two disciplines of analysis and operations. However, such training and orientation requires time and a full complement of experienced reports officers and operations officers. Winter had neither.

For its part, British Army Irish Command—not least Commander in Chief Macready, Winter's biggest critic—was accustomed to dedicated national intelligence support such as they had received during the Great War. With the extension of martial law in early January, the Irish Command had gone on a full war footing in anticipation that it would be extended throughout the country, and it expected that Winter's department would soon be transferred to their control. They were frustrated when that did not happen. In hindsight, the army's critique of the Raid Bureau appears motivated as much by the military's general underlying dissatisfaction with civilian control of intelligence as it was by the actual output of the Central Raid Bureau. Indeed, army intelligence had established a similar centralized "I" staff under Hill-Dillon at Parkgate a year earlier.

Concurrent with these changes, Tudor and Winter decentralized the RIC organizational structure, appointing regional superintendents and establishing CIS centers in the countryside to better coordinate intelligence. The first regional center was established at Belfast, followed by Cork, Limerick, Kildare, Galway, Clonmel, and Dundalk.[11]

Winter's New Year's Eve windfall of IRA intelligence documents soon began to pay dividends. A new campaign of police and army raids kicked off in January. Now that the army was empowered to arrest and try suspects in a large sector of the country, arrests increased tenfold, and it became necessary to open internment camps to accommodate the massive numbers of suspects. According to Hopkinson 1,478 suspects were interned at the end of January 1921, 2,500 by the last week of March, and 4,454 through July 16. Many key IRA leaders were among those in-

terned and tried by courts-martial, and this was due in no small part
to the capture of IRA intelligence documents at Eileen McGrane's flat a
month earlier.[12]

TERRORISM AND ANTI-TERRORISM

Another of Winter's subdepartments was an undercover team known officially as the Identification Company. Led by Chief Constable Eugene
Igoe from Galway, the unit comprised veteran RIC constables from outlying counties who could recognize leading IRA men by sight. It was their
mission to patrol the streets of Dublin searching for IRA men on the run
who had come to the city. Operating in mufti, Igoe and his team moved
relatively freely about the city, and it took some time before Collins's intelligence staff discerned the identity and purpose of the unit. As Neligan
pointed out, the British had encouraged unofficial groups of private gunmen to pursue the rebels, so Igoe's team could easily have been mistaken
for a mercenary murder gang.[13]

Although intended as a special identification and surveillance team,
the Igoe Gang's modus operandi soon changed from surveillance to stalk-
ing and shooting; the intent was to give the IRA a taste of its own medi-
cine. Igoe and his men played a lethal cat-and-mouse game with Collins's
Squad and members of the Dublin Brigade as they hunted each other on
the dark streets and back alleys of Dublin. Igoe used provocative foot
surveillance tactics: when IRA teams spotted the gang and placed them
under surveillance, Igoe and his crew would turn a corner or duck into
an alley and wait in ambush. Other times, they would double back to
confront their stalkers, guns drawn. This was a dangerous foe, and on
one occasion, the Squad and Igoe's men faced off on opposite sides of
Parliament Street, leading to a running gunfight that left three of the RIC
men wounded. As these groups of trigger-happy men stalked each other,
a new level of mayhem seized Dublin. In one effort to undermine popular
support for Sinn Fein, Igoe is alleged to have come up with the idea of
shooting a few innocent civilians, leaving bogus IRA notes reading "death
to spies and informers" on the corpses, making the murders appear to be
the work of the IRA.[14]

The Igoe Gang was a sustained, tactical threat to the IRA from the
spring of 1920 up to the cessation of hostilities. In his memoirs, IRA officer
Daniel Breen asserted that it was this unit that identified him and Sean

Treacy upon their arrival in Dublin, leading to the shoot-out at Professor Carolan's home and, ultimately, to the death of Sean Treacy. Breen suggests that Igoe's men had been working with army prosecutor Baggally and army MO4x officer MacLean—both victims of Bloody Sunday—at the time. The IRA never succeeded in neutralizing this unit. Eventually, Igoe also led some Auxiliary raiding parties, so his unit did perform an intelligence function. Although he survived the war, when the truce came he was compelled to leave the country for good and give up a Galway farm. Some time later, when Igoe applied for a British pension after the war, it was clear that he continued to work for British intelligence elsewhere abroad following his resignation from the RIC. His whereabouts and specific assignments following his work in Ireland are unclear, but Igoe appears to have undertaken several similar assignments abroad for the British.[15]

While the Igoe Gang was a serious and ongoing tactical threat to IRA operatives in Dublin, it was not a strategically effective counterterrorism effort. Igoe's unit was created because the Castle was having so much trouble identifying key IRA officers. However, the effort clearly was not intelligence driven and relied on blind patrolling and personal identification to find the foe. Thus, while it might have become a solid preemptive counterterrorism tool, it deteriorated into a reactive force.

On February 9, members of N Company of the Auxiliaries looted and burned a bar in Trim, County Meath. General Crozier, the commander of the division, immediately investigated the incident, resulting in the dismissal of twenty-one men and the arrest of five more to await trial. Commissioner of Police Tudor, Churchill's friend and the hardest of the hard-liners in Ireland, had supported every transgression committed by the police, Tans, Auxiliaries, and secret service. He now intervened to reinstate the men that Crozier had dismissed, leading to Crozier's resignation.[16]

ESCALATION OF HOSTILITIES

The extension of martial law throughout Munster Province enabled General Macready to unleash his army regulars against the IRA at the beginning of 1921. Cork, Limerick, Tipperary, and later Kerry soon witnessed regular engagements between the IRA and the Army's Sixth Division under command of General Peter Strickland. IRA columns were also active in Mayo, Clare, Armagh, and other western and northern counties by the end of January 1921.

Ireland's rugged terrain and limited transportation infrastructure shaped army tactics, which centered upon mobile patrols and security sweeps from regional garrison towns. Typically, the British operated in platoon or company-sized elements of 30–150 men mounted in trucks. Their mounted patrols were increasingly subjected to sudden, deadly ambushes from IRA flying columns. The British had already learned to spread out their vehicles so that if the front of the column was ambushed, additional forces could move up from the rear echelon as reinforcements, or vice versa. Although IRA columns lacked experience, their discipline was good and they fought on familiar ground. They struck suddenly and without warning, then disappeared just as suddenly, moving cross-county on foot to evade pursuit by the road-bound British troops. Dumping their arms in hidden cache sites—frequently no more than crude dugouts in the countryside—the Volunteers took refuge in the towns and country farmsteads where they were assured of aid and support. Local IRA units acted as scouts, couriers, intelligence, and logistics personnel for the flying columns, while local civilians offered concealment, food, and medical assistance.

As noted earlier, Florrence O'Donoghue was adjutant and chief of intelligence with the Cork First Brigade from 1919, but it took more than a year for O'Donoghue to refine his intelligence operations to effectively support combat operations. As O'Donoghue later recalled:

> We were completely ignorant of the enemy, except in the most general and fragmentary way. We never made any attempt to study closely his organization, routine, morale, equipment and personnel. Was there any reason why we should continue to remain in so dense a state of ignorance? We thought not. Out of these ideas our intelligence service was born; or rather I should say, was born locally, because Collins was developing similar ideas in Dublin, though we did not know it then. . . . I became more and more impressed by the need for putting the collection and evaluation of information on some organized basis. We had then nothing more than a few individual men in the General Post Office who brought up an occasional copy of the police message in cipher—messages

that we were not always able to decode. I though we needed a basic organization in every Company and Battalion, with men specially detailed to study the area and its possibilities from the Intelligence point of view, as well as a wide development of such sources as Post Offices and Telephone Exchanges.[17]

Collins and O'Donoghue did not begin to collaborate formally or closely until March 1920—the month that the Black and Tans entered Munster Province. After that, they routinely shared information.

Collins and I, each without the knowledge of each other, were trying to build up something similar, but with this difference. I put down the basic organization in the Companies and Battalions but had made no progress in the espionage aspect at that stage, where he had practically no basic organization, but had made very considerable progress on the more valuable espionage aspect. Working in Dublin, and with contacts in London, his opportunities in this regard were much more extensive than mine. Out of the Quinlisk case there arose a comparing of notes and a mutual cooperation and close contact that proved valuable. . . . This efficiency was due to neither chance nor to the exclusive abilities of one man. It was due to three things: First, to a keen appreciation on the part of GHQ at the time of the value of Intelligence; Second, to the efficient organization and exploitation of sources of information; and, Third, to the fact that every member of the Defence Forces [IRA] at that time—and to a large extent every loyal citizen also—regarded it as a paramount and personal duty, promptly and at all times, to pass on to those in authority every item of enemy information that resulted from his constant watchfulness. And of these three contributory sources, the last was by far most important.[18]

One of Collins's most important services was to pass on to O'Donoghue the RIC police cipher keys for Cork. O'Donoghue organized a team to intercept RIC messages as they passed through the local telegraph office, to decode them, make copies, and transmit them to Brigade Headquarters. Collins also eventually provided funds to O'Donoghue to support local intelligence operations in Cork.[19]

IRA operations in Munster Province accelerated dramatically in late 1920 and into 1921. As mentioned earlier, Tom Barry's November 28 ambush of a company of Auxiliaries at Kilmichael marked a profound escalation of the conflict, and it demonstrated that the IRA was now capable of mounting regular company-sized actions. As a result, British Army regulars—many of them combat veterans—were unleashed; IRA columns were aggressively hunted by large-scale army sweep-and-destroy operations. IRA operations that had heretofore been desultory and irregular now followed a more organized and regular pattern, particularly in Cork, Waterford, Tipperary, and Limerick. The Munster IRA leaders continued to operate fairly autonomously and bristled at directions or suggestions from Dublin.

In Cork, the scene of heaviest fighting, the IRA leadership was critical of headquarters "pen pushers" with their regulations and organizational formalities. Mulcahy and Collins had their idea of how the war should be prosecuted, while Cork guerrilla leaders like Tom Barry had theirs.

A veteran of the British Army who had served in Iraq and Egypt from 1915 to 1919, Barry was instrumental in organizing, training, and leading the West Cork Brigade's flying column, which at times numbered as many as 104 men. Barry's knowledge of weapons, reconnaissance, patrol security, tactics, and military discipline enabled him to transform the raw recruits of his column into one of the most feared IRA units during the war. Indeed, with a few exceptions, the men who executed the highly successful Kilmichael ambush had no prior battle experience and little weapons practice, but Barry had carefully trained and disciplined them just days before that action. Neither Column Commander Barry nor his superior officers waited for orders from Dublin to launch bold and effective strikes against RIC and Auxiliary units and later against the experienced troops of the British Army's Essex Regiment in Cork.

Over time, a rift developed between the Dublin and Cork IRA that was never fully resolved. Barry and his superiors believed that maintaining momentum against the British was of utmost importance, even when the Dublin General Staff may have preferred the Cork Volunteers to maneuver on its timetable. At the end of the day, however, all concerned recognized that the local flying column commander knew local conditions best.[20]

The inexperience of the Volunteers was made up for by their flexibility, mobility, and above all, their ability to improvise in combat situations—

a quality the British Tommy did not always exhibit. Tom Kelleher described his experience as a section leader in Barry's flying column during a major engagement with elements of two British infantry battalions from the Sixth Division at Crossbarry, County Cork, during a British sweep operation on March 19, 1921. The British deployed 800 men in an attempt to envelop Barry's 42-man column by sending separate convoys of mounted infantry from three directions. Kelleher attributed his own survival to the ability of his men to improvise and the inflexible tactical doctrine employed by their British opponents:

> We heard the lorries leaving Bandon at 2 am. They were coming and stopping, coming and stopping. Tom Barry was in bed. . . . I said, "You better get up quickly, they are coming along very near. . . . They are coming along, coming and stopping." He got ready quick and we made down the road. . . . We were locating our scouts, all local men, strung out in all directions. That was our mission. . . . We had to hop lively. They were moving slowly however, because they were raiding as well. We could hear them distinctly coming into Kilpatrick. The night was very calm. A strange thing happened then. They arrested a man there by the name of White. He was a prisoner, I would say, in the second lorry. There were 24 lorries in the sweep. I had a scout counting them. There were nine, seven, five and three. Of the first convoy, the nine, only three got into the fight. A soldier in the fourth lorry spotted a man with a rifle at a window, and the rest stopped. Tom Barry used [to] always criticize that man, but I clap him on the back because if the nine lorries got in, the occupants of the nine lorries would make a fight and we had only three sections there to face them. . . . Three time fourteen is 42 men; begod 42 men could never fight nine lorries. That was my opinion; Barry was of a different opinion but I had mine. The man, White, who was captured at Kilpatrick, jumped out of the lorry as soon as it entered the ambush, got inside the gate and there a rifle was put in his hands rightaway. . . . We had however dealt with the column trying to encircle us from the west. There were still about 600 men in the lorries approaching from Cork, from the northeast. . . . There was a third facing us to the south along the Cork/Bandon railway line—not there now. They were all under

Consolidation of power: Minister of Finance, Director of
Intelligence, Adjutant General of the IRA, and President of the
IRB Supreme Council Michael Collins. *Hulton Archive/Getty*

The Viceroy Sir John French was one of the principal
architects of Britain's hard-line policy. The IRA launched
twenty attempts to assassinate him. *Library of Congress*

Britain's brutal paramilitary order police, the Auxiliaries. This company is standing inspection by a regular army officer at the Phoenix Park Depot, Dublin, but typically there was little army oversight of their operations.
Courtesy of the National Library of Ireland

Brig. Gen. Sir Ormonde Winter, or "O," was chief
of Combined Intelligence at Dublin Castle
from 1920 to 1921. *Reproduced from*
Winter's Tale, *Richards Press, 1955*

During the last twelve months innumerable murders and other outrages have been committed by those who call themselves Members of the Irish Republican Army. Only by the help of self-respecting Irishmen can these murders be put a stop to.

It is possible to send letters containing information in such a way as to prevent their being stopped in the post.

If you have information to give and you are willing to help the cause of Law and Order act as follows :

Write your information on ordinary notepaper, being careful to give neither your name nor your address. Remember also to disguise your handwriting, or else to print the words. Put it into an envelope, addressed to :

D. W. ROSS,
Poste Restante,
G.P.O., LONDON.

Enclose this envelope in another. (Take care that your outer envelope is not transparent). Put with it a small slip of paper asking the recipient to forward the D. W. ROSS letter as soon as he receives it. Address the outer envelope to some well disposed friend in England or to any well known business address in England.

You will later be given the opportunity, should you wish to do so, of identifying your letter, and, should the information have proved of value, of claiming a **REWARD**.

The utmost secrecy will be maintained as to all information received.

Advertisement for informers, 1920

The men in this portrait that was purloined by the IRA have often been identified as the British Cairo Gang. More likely they were the RIC surveillance team of Ormonde Winter's Identification Branch, the so-called Igoe Gang, or possibly members of an RIC Auxiliary Company in Mufti. The photo was clearly analyzed by the IRA for intelligence purposes. *Hulton Archive/Getty*

VICTIMS OF "THE MURDER GANG": OFFICERS KILLED IN DUBLIN.

PHOTOGRAPHS BY BENDER AND LEWIS, NEWSPAPER ILLUSTRATIONS, LAFAYETTE, I.B., PARISIAN STUDIOS (GILLINGHAM), PHOTOPRESS, AND VANDYK.

MAJOR C. M. G. DOWLING, GRENADIER GUARDS.

CAPT. W. F. NEWBERRY, 4TH QUEEN'S (ROYAL WEST SURREY) REGIMENT.

CAPTAIN P. McCORMACK, R.A.V.C.

LIEUTENANT D. L. MacLEAN, LATE RIFLE BRIGADE.

CADET FRANK GARNISS,

LIEUT. H. ANGLISS, D.C.M. INNISKILLING FUSILIERS.

LIEUTENANT G. BENNETT, LATE R.A.

CADET C. A. MORRIS, AUXILIARY R.I.C.

CAPTAIN LEONARD PRICE, M.C., LATE MIDDLESEX REGIMENT.

LIEUTENANT A. AMES, LATE GRENADIER GUARDS.

CAPTAIN G. T. BAGGALLAY (EXTRA REGIMENTALLY EMPLOYED).

On the day following the Sinn Fein murders in Dublin (on Sunday, November 21), Sir Hamar Greenwood, Chief Secretary for Ireland, said in the House of Commons : "I hope that this series of cold-blooded and carefully planned atrocities will bring vividly before the House and the public the cruel reality of the Irish situation. We are fighting an organised band of paid assassins, whose plans, recently discovered, include the destruction of life and property in this country as well as in Ireland. . . . Now I shall read the details of, I think, one of the most foul tragedies in the history of our Empire. There have been 14 deaths and 6 injured, including 1 assassin, and 3 assassins captured red-handed with arms." We have not space here to give the details referred to, even in outline, nor have we been able to obtain portraits of all the murdered officers. The list of killed included also Capt. Fitzgerald, Mr. T. H. Smith, and Mr. L. Wilde. In earlier published accounts Lieut. Angliss was mentioned incorrectly as Lieut. Mahon. We have just heard of the mistake, too late to alter it on pages already gone to press.

London press coverage of the secret service officers, court-martial officers, and two Auxiliaries slain by the IRA on Bloody Sunday 1920.
The Illustrated London News/Mary Evans

The IRA West Mayo Flying Column. Their grim demeanor betrays the experience of combat and the stress of life on the run. In a series of firefights between January and July 1921, this column killed ten and captured sixteen British regulars and Auxiliaries while losing nine of their own killed in action. *Courtesy of the Irish Military Archive, Cathal Brugha Barracks*

the command of Major Percival. . . . We were attacked from the north. . . . Bob Hales was in front of me and this fellow who was shot in the ankle was just behind my back. In other words, and you can take it this way, they were running away from the firing. I got them over the fence. I said, "Look here, I have orders to shoot the first man that runs." . . . They were exposed before but we had cover now. . . . Our two men in the Castle [snipers] once they had the enemy in line opened up and shot two officers. Grand job. They surrounded the Castle and to look at them they were like bees in a hive. You could not miss them. . . . I said to my squad, "Section ready! Volley fire!" I repeated that order, and then I said rapid fire. . . . What did the British do? They came at the northern side of the fence. . . . Do you know what was beating them? They were going according to plan. If they had not gone according to plan but had moved over the fence we would have been destroyed. Anyway, I had my two men. And I am sorry to say they were not two good men. The man on the left I don't think he fired a shot. I had ten in my magazine and one up the breech. That was eleven. I fired eleven and eleven fell. I reloaded with five and five fell. I reloaded again and five more fell. That was twenty-one. The man on my right had his rifle pointed away at the horizon, and pulling away, wasting ammunition. I stood back and gave him a toe up the tail. "Can't you fire?" I said, and he did. That fellow did very good after. . . . They were all laid out there, the twenty one of them. "No, no," said Tom, "We are not going for their guns. We have more than we can carry including a machine gun." "Splendid," says I. I was mad for guns. "Let us take the lot." "No," he said, "We haven't got time." And I didn't realise time at all, but he did. He had a weather eye cocked for the inevitable reaction from the British. . . . And the 21 dead men were lying there all the time. And we left them there too, guns and all.[21]

A CHANGE IN STRATEGY

Eamon de Valera's mission to America had achieved mixed results. He failed to gain official U.S. recognition for the Irish Republic but he managed to solicit about $6 million in donations from the Irish-American community. While initially greeted with fanfare at coast-to-coast receptions organized by the American Clan na Gael, de Valera soon offended the most powerful clan leaders with his plain talk and demands for their financial and political support. Although he met with many prominent American politicians, de Valera secured no official U.S. backing from the Wilson administration, and he alienated no small number of prominent Irish-American political leaders.

De Valera's return to Ireland was followed almost immediately by a resumption of peace feelers from London. An exchange of notes was initiated by Archbishop Clune and continued for months. Meanwhile, de Valera was determined to bring Collins under control and exert his personal authority over the IRA. De Valera was back in Ireland only one day when he told IRA Chief of Staff Richard Mulcahy:

> Ye are going too fast. This odd shooting of a policeman here and there is having a bad effect, from a propaganda point of view, on us in America. What we want is one good battle a month, with about 500 men on each side.[22]

This was quite a reversal from de Valera's late November press release in which he had applauded and justified Collins's Bloody Sunday operation. It is doubtful that he was completely at sea about the realities of the previous eighteen months, but he blamed his failure to gain American recognition of Ireland on the absence of a conventional IRA military presence. It is quite remarkable that de Valera would order large engagements, and that Brugha would support it. Both had experienced the folly of 1916, when woefully undergunned Irish Volunteers had route-marched through Dublin's streets to take on British regulars in pitched battle. Nevertheless, Brugha and de Valera now criticized Collins for his tactics in open cabinet meetings.

De Valera knew all too well what he was asking of Collins. In retrospect, his order for a conventional attack was likely intended to make headlines, underscoring the points he had argued in America and perhaps deflecting criticism from Nationalists at home who held him responsible for the failure to win American and international recognition of Irish sovereignty. De Valera also tried gentle persuasion. In a long, flattering letter to Collins he pointed out that a new American president would take office on March 4, and explained his view that a major conventional battle would perhaps move the new American administration to recognize the Republic. It was even suggested that Collins go to America to rest and then pick up the political campaign where de Valera had left off. This, and the strident rebukes Collins had suffered in cabinet sessions, convinced Collins that de Valera was trying to move him out and reassert control over the IRA. Collins nonetheless held the purse strings, had a precise record of how many arms were on hand, and knew how many Volunteers were actually available for active service. Furthermore, only Collins appreciated the continuing threat posed by the British Secret Service. With scarcely 2,500 men under arms, he knew the IRA was no match for the 43,000 British regulars then occupying the country. Moreover, the British were making it extremely difficult to smuggle arms and ammunition from Europe to sustain operations. Every bullet had to count. To Collins, therefore, de Valera's order was madness; he delayed, commenting bitterly, "That long whore won't get rid of me as easily as that."[23]

Collins's chief ally, Chief of Staff Richard Mulcahy, also rejected de Valera and Brugha's strategy change, but de Valera maneuvered the cabinet to gain its formal approval, and he ordered Mulcahy to make an attack on the Customs House in Dublin. Collins considered the plan harebrained but agreed to release the Squad to support the Dublin Brigade in the operation. The plan was to send a raiding party of men into the building under cover of a larger security detail posted outside, set it on fire, and withdraw. The Volunteers were under orders not to shoot unless fired upon, and they carried only pistols with five rounds of ammunition apiece.

Within minutes after entering the building, Black and Tans and army units converged on it, resulting in a running gun battle in the streets. The shoot-out was a total fiasco for the woefully out-gunned IRA, resulting in the loss or capture of more than eighty Volunteers from the Dublin Brigade, one of the IRA's best units. It was a loss that Collins could ill afford, but the results were a vindication of his guerrilla warfare strategy. De Valera and Brugha quietly dropped their demand for further conventional attacks, leaving Collins free to resume unconventional warfare; meanwhile they continued their efforts at dialogue with London. Recognizing that his organization was stretched to the limit, Collins endorsed these peace overtures.[24]

De Valera and Brugha continued to put pressure on Collins. In cabinet meetings Brugha continually questioned Collins about his financial activity, suggesting falsely that Collins was guilty of creative accounting methods. Then the Squad—heretofore an independent unit under Collins's direct command—was amalgamated with the Dublin Brigade to create a larger organization known as the Guard. The expanded unit became a sort of Praetorian Guard for the Dail cabinet, which continued to meet secretly in cellars.[25]

THE CROWN CLOSES IN

Collins, meanwhile, was being relentlessly hunted by Winter. The British enjoyed a small coup when Winter's men apprehended an IRA officer named Vincent Fourvargue in March 1921. The son of French parents, the young Fourvargue had joined the IRA and risen to command a company in the Third Battalion of the Dublin Brigade. Under interrogation—and allegedly under torture—however, Fourvargue revealed to Winter the names of the members of his entire company, and Winter lost no time rounding them up. Realizing he was now a doomed man, Fourvargue sought help from Winter, who had the prisoner whisked off to England under the protective custody of Special Branch. Remarkably, some days later Special Branch issued a bulletin reporting that Fourvargue had "escaped" while being transferred in a car under escort of four armed detectives. Neligan intercepted the bulletin at DMP headquarters. The escape account strained credibility and was quickly seen by the IRA as a British ruse to mask Fourvargue's collaboration and disappearance. Worse, Collins and his staff now had to consider the very real possibility that Fourvargue had been a British penetration from the outset. Collins notified Sam Maguire, his IRB Center in London. Maguire's local IRA team soon located Fourvargue in hiding and, on the evening of March 21, Reggie Dunne, one of Maguire's best operatives, shot and killed Fourvargue on a golf course outside London.[26]

Regardless of whether or not Fourvargue was a British double agent from the beginning, Collins took no pleasure in ordering the man's execution. Yet, many IRA men had undergone horrendous physical torture at the hands of the British, and a number of them had paid the ultimate price rather than give information to the enemy. Indeed, Cork Volunteer Tom Hales, a brother of one of Collins's closest friends, had been brutally tortured in custody the previous October, and managed to smuggle a message out to Collins informing him that his fingernails had been pulled out with pincers by Black and Tan interrogators. An example had to be made for other IRA officers.[27]

One of Collins's best officers in County Limerick, Tomas' O'Maoileoin (Thomas Malone)—alias Sean Forde—narrowly escaped death while in the custody of Auxiliaries in Cork City. O'Maoileoin was the younger brother of Seamus O'Maoileoin, an IRA intelligence officer in Limerick. Tomas' was among the few Irish Volunteers who participated in the 1916 Easter Rising outside of Dublin and, after confinement in Frongach, he returned to Limerick and helped organize the IRA East Limerick Brigade. He was one of the most active IRA officers during the conflict, rising to become Vice Commandant of the Brigade and participating in some of the most celebrated attacks on RIC barracks and firefights with British regulars. In the spring of 1920 he was wounded during an attack in East Clare. A party of Black and Tans from Cork apprehended him on Christmas morning, 1920. Knocked unconscious with a blow from a rifle butt, O'Maoileoin awoke in handcuffs on the floor inside Union Quay Barracks, Cork, surrounded by RIC constables and Auxiliary officers who had been drinking.

One of the policemen lunged at O'Maoileoin and kicked him in the mouth, knocking out most of his teeth. With mouth and tongue swollen and bleeding, he was dragged from the barracks and transferred to Bridewell prison. That afternoon he was dragged to an interrogation room where a pair of blacksmith's tongs was heating on a coal fire. When the questioning began, O'Maoileoin answered with a "cock and bull" account. Eventually his interrogators asked him if he knew Sean Forde. Realizing that the more distance he could put between himself and the outlaw Sean Forde the better, O'Maoileoin attempted a credible answer, saying that he had met Forde twice. He gave a false description of Forde. At that point, one of the interrogators stood up, grabbed the red-hot tongs, and announced, "We will begin again and this time you will tell the truth." The shirt was ripped from his body and the red-hot tongs were rubbed up and down his back. Collapsing on the floor, O'Maoileoin struggled to his feet only to have the three inquisitors lunge at him and beat him to within an inch of his life. They threatened to shoot him, but eventually dragged him back to a holding cell where he lay near death for some hours. O'Maoileoin eventually was incarcerated at the Spike Island detention camp, from which he escaped to rejoin his column. His story was evidence that a man could resist torture and survive to fight again.

The IRA leadership simply could not afford disloyalty, particularly from its officers who were responsible for the safety of IRA rank and file.[28]

Collins suffered another blow shortly after the Fourvargue affair when Detective James MacNamara was summarily dismissed from the police without explanation. According to Neligan, MacNamara's dismissal should have come as no surprise. While Winter was busy turning Fourvargue, a secret dispatch arrived in General Tudor's office at the Castle. MacNamara was serving as confidential clerk to the Assistant Commissioner of the DMP and he obtained a copy of the dispatch, which apparently originated from the Admiralty's NID. The dispatch noted that some American sailors had handed over arms to the IRA and directed that all U.S. sailors were henceforth to be considered suspects. Instead of keeping the intelligence to himself, Collins passed it to the Dail Propaganda Department, which had the letter published. This in turn prompted a formal British démarche to Washington. The letter had been closely held and its leak to Sinn Fein implicated a narrow group of suspects, the most likely being MacNamara. It was one more serious counterintelligence lapse that cost Collins a valuable agent. No charges were brought against MacNamara, possibly because he was widely respected and had many friends in high places on the force. Indeed, Neligan warned him not to go home that evening for fear the secret service would attack or arrest him. With no job and no income, MacNamara joined the IRA and went on the run. He participated in some Squad operations. But his dismissal from the DMP left Ned Broy and David Neligan as Collins's two remaining police spies in the Castle.[29]

Yet another calamity befell Collins when Winter raided his intelligence office in April 1921. Collins never visited the clandestine office of the IRA intelligence staff in Crow Street, but instead kept a private intelligence office in a flat at 5 Mespil Road, where he often worked alone into the wee hours of the morning. Collins left early with the intention of returning later but changed his plans. That evening a British raiding party entered the Mespil Road flat and discovered all of Collins's personal intelligence documents, including all of the codes for members of the Dail cabinet and other sensitive material. Winter's busy epitomizers at the Central Raid Bureau went to work exploiting the documents. And when Collins established a new personal intelligence office in Mary Street, Winter raided it on May 26, narrowly missing Collins a second time. He had been working at Mary Street when he decided to step out for lunch. He normally returned to the office at 2 p.m. but had a strange feeling—what Neligan described as a sixth sense—and decided not to return. Later that afternoon Auxiliaries raided Mary Street. Two days later, one of Collins's couriers, a teenager named Bob Conlon, was arrested and taken to the Castle where thumb screws were employed in his interrogation.[30]

Winter was close on Collins's heels. On June 1, Collins wrote to de Valera, "I may tell you that the escape of Thursday was nothing to four or five escapes I have had since. . . . They ran me very close for quite a good while on Sunday evening." It was unclear how long the IRA could sustain offensive operations.[31]

Collins was nevertheless contemplating some bold operations. During the conscription fight of 1918, Brugha had advocated sending a team of Volunteers into the House of Commons to shoot as many cabinet members as possible. Brugha now resurrected the idea; a skeptical Collins tried to refine the plan, considering that it might be possible to kidnap several members of Parliament. Moreover, by now he had amassed an even larger file of secret service dossiers and was planning to carry out a second Bloody Sunday attack, this time with a target list of sixty British agents.[32]

WINTER NABS A SPY

There was more fallout from the McGrane raid. Winter had focused on a collection of official G Division carbon-copy intelligence reports that had been recovered from that raid, and realized they could only have been obtained by someone with access to the police file room. It was a simple matter to pull the originals from the G Division files and match them up with the carbons to discover who had typed them. With evidence in hand, Winter had Ned Broy arrested at his office in March. Broy was remanded to Arbour Hill prison—a dungeon-like facility that was Dublin's equivalent of the Tower of London.

Rumors circulated in the Castle that Broy would be tried and executed for espionage. Anticipating that Collins would immediately contemplate a jailbreak to save his star agent, Neligan visited Arbour Hill on the pretext of police business to case the premises. He reported to Collins that the jail was guarded by experienced troops with four machine guns guarding the gate and all approaches. It could not be breached; a jailbreak was out of the question.[33]

Two plans were devised. The first, suggested by Neligan and Sergeant MacNamara, called for simple intimidation of the prosecutor. A backup plan called for Collins to deliver a forged confession signed by an ex–G Division detective who had been Broy's predecessor in charge of the file room and who had resigned his post to emigrate to the United States. In short order, Neligan and MacNamara learned that Broy's court case would be prepared by Broy's supervisor, Chief Inspector Joseph Supple. Neligan and MacNamara knew that Supple and his family regularly attended Mass together, and Collins agreed to a plan to confront Supple while he was exiting the church with his wife and daughter. It is unclear who delivered the threat to Supple; it may have been Collins himself. As Neligan recorded in his memoirs,

> As [Supple] was leaving church the next morning, a polished gentleman who happened to be passing beckoned to him. . . . He asked the urbane beckoner what he could do for him. "You can do nothing for me, Mr. Supple," he replied. "But I have a grave warning to give you! It concerns someone called Broy, of whom I know nothing. I am to tell you that if you go on with the case against him, you will be shot!" If Joe had not been grabbed by his wife and daughter, he would have fallen on the spot. Muttering to the man who had transmitted this somber signal, he was frog-marched home by those devoted ladies.[34]

Chief Inspector Supple made the decision to live. He delayed, procrastinated, took sick leave, and generally dithered while the case gathered dust, undoubtedly to Winter's consternation. Broy was nevertheless held in custody for the duration of the war and his days as a spy were over.[35]

ONE MORE PENETRATION

By the spring of 1921, G Division was essentially doing nothing, and it had long since lost the confidence of British intelligence. Neligan therefore informed Collins that he wanted to attempt to join the British Secret Service. Collins was skeptical that Neligan would be accepted; to his surprise Neligan was welcomed by D Branch and quickly sworn in with the following oath:

I . . . solemnly swear by Almighty God that I will faithfully perform the duties assigned to me as a member of His Majesty's Secret Service: that I will obey implicitly those placed over me: that I shall never betray such service or anything connected with it even after I have left it. If I should fail to keep this oath in every particular, I realise that vengeance will pursue me to the ends of the earth. So help me God.[36]

Assigned code identification number 68, Neligan was issued a pistol and taught a sign of recognition similar to that used by Freemasons. Neligan was ordered to work in the Kingstown area and took up residence there posing as an insurance agent. There he was met regularly by both his inside officer with pay and instructions, and by Collins's lieutenants with their taskings. When Neligan's British handler showed up for the first meeting, he was dressed very conspicuously in a neat English suit. Neligan protested, directing his British contact to wear the oldest coat and hat he could find in future encounters.[37]

Neligan was no longer in the Castle, and while he could provide useful information on his secret service associates, his access to more strategic information was severely restricted. At the end of May 1921, Neligan's effectiveness as a core collector was less than it had been when he was a police detective, but he soon proved equally valuable as a disinformation agent.

COVERT ACTION: PSYCHOLOGICAL
OPERATIONS AND DIRTY TRICKS

Paralleling the shooting war in Ireland was a vigorous and vicious propaganda war. As early as the 1918 conscription fight, it was apparent to both sides that propaganda would play an important role in the struggle. Dail Vice President Arthur Griffith, a career journalist, and Desmond Fitzgerald of the Dail propaganda department waged a clever propaganda effort from 1919 onward. Their principal publication was the *Irish Bulletin*, an underground news sheet produced by Erskine Childers, an Englishman who had helped the Volunteers smuggle arms in preparation for the 1916 Easter Rising. The *Bulletin* exposed details of Auxiliary, Black and Tan, and army outrages and setbacks, and it was distributed widely in Ireland and Britain to opposition members of Parliament, foreign diplomats, and journalists; it soon developed more credibility than the cabinet's official pronouncements. The government constantly found itself on the defensive, answering charges and accusations appearing in the *Irish Bulletin* on the floor of the House of Commons. Lloyd George and Chief Secretary Hamar Greenwood so detested the *Irish Bulletin* that they tried to suppress it; by March 1921 it was operating from its ninth underground location. The propaganda department had a field day with the J. L. Gooding/ Digby Hardy spy case, and there were many other propaganda victories. When Griffith and Fitzgerald were finally arrested, the talented Austin Stack, another Englishman, stepped in to replace them, keeping the pressure on.[38]

To counter this, the British imported Basil Clarke—a propaganda specialist who had made his reputation as a newspaperman embedded with the British Army on the Western Front. By 1920, he was listed in *Who's Who* as "late Director, Special Intelligence Branch, Ministry of Reconstruction," and he subsequently became director of the Public Information Branch (PIB) at Dublin Castle. Clarke was a proficient journalist who understood military operations, and was a good choice for the job, but by the time he arrived, the propaganda momentum had already swung in Sinn Fein's favor. While Clarke's PIB spread disparaging stories about Sinn Fein and IRA leaders in local newspapers, the *Irish Bulletin* countered them with details, facts, and testimonials. Clarke's efforts to garner favorable publicity for Crown forces were also undermined by the bumbling chief secretary, Hamar Greenwood, whose dissembling and half-truths on the floor of the House habitually destroyed the government's positions.[39]

Despite Neligan's relatively limited access to Castle information, Collins had another equally important mission for his agent, namely, disinformation operations. Collins fed Neligan scripted reports that the latter in turn passed to his British superiors portraying a robust and determined IRA with high morale, growing strength, and a steady supply of arms and ammunition.

Not long after filing a series of these reports, Neligan uncovered a British dirty tricks operation. Reacting to one of Neligan's reports detailing the IRA's robust weapons and ammunition holdings, a British officer mentioned one day that one of the reasons the IRA was so well equipped with ammunition was because, "We are helping them." The officer went on to explain that modified rifle ammunition had been seeded into IRA stocks.

Meanwhile, reports had arrived at IRA GHQ of several Tipperary Volunteers suffering lost fingers and portions of their hands while using revolvers. Neligan managed to elicit details and learned that the head-stamps on the modified bullets contained the letters ZZ. Further investigation revealed that some hand grenades procured from British stocks had their timers altered to cause the grenades to explode instantly when the pin was pulled. Ammunition and ordnance modification is a highly effective counterinsurgency tactic. Modified ammo is usually either rendered inert so it will not fire or rigged to explode in an insurgent's weapon, hopefully causing debilitating injury or death. Once it is covertly introduced into the insurgent's supply system, it wreaks havoc within the enemy camp. Neligan learned later that the IRA had examined some of the ZZ ammo and discovered that it had been modified by removing the gunpowder and replacing it with gun cotton surrounding a vial of fulminate of mercury—a highly explosive cocktail. The modified ammunition originated from an army barracks in Tipperary, and at least one Volunteer had been injured before Collins issued a warning to IRA units across the country.[40]

Later on, Neligan scored a major success when he suggested to D Branch managers that compartmentalizing the work of the branch was actually counterproductive. Neligan argued that better results might be achieved if they could all come together at a conference to compare notes. Incredibly, management agreed, and Neligan soon found himself in a room with twenty-five other undercover case officers, who were introduced to each other by operating district. The conference enabled Neligan to identify British operators, scoop up information from every district in the city, learn valuable information about sources and methods, and assess the morale of D Branch. It was another clumsy violation of security principles by the British, resulting in a windfall of valuable counterintelligence information for the IRA.[41]

TRUCE, TREATY, AND TRAGEDY

Meanwhile, the earlier peace feelers led to cautious dialogue, and eventually face-to-face meetings between de Valera and Lord Derby, acting as an unofficial representative of the cabinet, on April 21, 1921. A truce and cease-fire were announced on July 21. The Irish leadership soon learned that as difficult as waging war with the British had been, forging a peace agreement with Lloyd George would be even more difficult. By this time, however, peace was far more preferable to a continuation of hostilities. The cost of the struggle had been high; since the beginning of hostilities the British had suffered 600 killed and 1,200 wounded, while the IRA's losses had been 752 killed and 866 wounded.[42]

De Valera's series of meetings in London likely convinced him that the British would simply not give the Nationalists their "Irish Republic" and that the best that could be hoped for would be a partitioned Ireland, still under British control, albeit with Dominion status. With this knowledge, de Valera cajoled Collins into leading the Irish peace delegation—which included former British intelligence official John Chartres acting as legal counsel—to London. For his part, Lloyd George believed that no terms could be reached unless Collins was part of the Irish delegation, since Collins, not de Valera, controlled the IRB and had de facto control over the IRA. De Valera realized this, of course, but his decision not to participate in the treaty talks appears now, ninety years on, to be one of the most cowardly political acts in history. While supporting his peace delegation from Dublin, de Valera consistently encouraged Collins, Griffith, and other delegates to seek a compromise formula. Such a formula would certainly mean that Ireland would remain part of the British Empire. Even Collins recognized that this was all they could expect under the circumstances, and the Irish delegation subsequently agreed—under considerable pressure from Churchill and other British hard-liners—to exactly such a compromise on December 6, 1921. What the delegates brought home to Dublin was an agreement that closely paralleled the latest version of the Home Rule Bill:

1. There would be dual parliaments in Dublin and Belfast; the province of Ulster would remain an integral part of the Union with boundaries to be decided by a commission;
2. Southern Ireland would have Dominion status under the Empire;
3. The southern government, to be known as The Irish Free State, would have the right to maintains its own armed forces;
4. All citizens of the Free State would be required to acknowledge the authority of the English Crown.

By now Collins had been well exposed to British authorities, so his effectiveness as an underground leader and intelligence chief was compromised. Thus, for him, there was no going back to war. He would live with the treaty that created an Irish Free State, he would go along with partition of the northern counties for the time being, and he would agree to take an oath of allegiance to the Crown. Distasteful as the latter seemed at the time, Collins and all who negotiated in London considered it to be merely a first step toward full Irish independence, and none of the negotiators ever implied or stated otherwise. The treaty delegation's zeal for an Irish Republic had not ebbed; their enthusiasm for war had. Griffith, Collins, and the other delegates had spent weeks across the negotiating table and in some social gatherings with their British adversaries; they recognized that Lloyd George was hamstrung to a great extent by his own political problems and that his proposal to make Ireland a Dominion was a major concession at that moment. Incomplete though this settlement seemed, the Irish delegates recognized it as a major advancement to their cause and an administrative stepping-stone to full independence. But they also recognized that this final step would take more time. Collins was probably the most conflicted of the Irish delegates to affix his signature to the treaty. After signing the document, Lord Birkenhead turned to Collins and said, "I may have signed my political death warrant tonight," to which Collins replied, "I may have signed my actual death warrant."[43]

Such terms could have been established at any time since 1914. Thus, for thousands of Irish separatists, this was a stab in the back. De Valera no doubt also recognized these realities early in his exchanges with the British, but he simply could not face up to bringing such an agreement home to the Irish people, which is why he sent Griffith, Collins, and the others. Now he attacked them privately and publicly, declaring his vehement opposition to the treaty terms and condemning Collins and the other delegates as traitors.

This led, inevitably, to a face-to-face showdown in the Dail. When the treaty was put to a vote, on January 7, 1922, the Dail approved it by a narrow margin of 64 to 57, prompting de Valera and Cathal Brugha to viciously denounce Collins before leading the anti-Treaty faction in a walkout. Arthur Griffith was elected president to replace de Valera, and Collins was elevated to Commander in Chief of the Free State Army, soon to be equipped with British-supplied armored cars, machine guns, and artillery.

The treaty still required ratification by popular vote, and as both sides presented their case to the Irish people, a fissure developed in the IRA leadership. The rift widened when an anti-Treaty IRA faction, led by Rory O'Connor, Liam Mellowes, Tom Barry, and others, began to occupy public buildings around the country, including the Four Courts—an elegant eighteenth-century Dublin showcase that was the symbol of Irish legal administration. At an IRA organizational convention in the Four Courts, Tom Barry stood up and introduced a resolution calling for the withdrawal of all British forces from Ireland within seventy-two hours. This was essentially a declaration of war on Britain; it circumvented the authority of the Dail, and it caused further confusion within the IRA's ranks. In the tense weeks ahead, there continued to be communication between the anti-Treaty and pro-Treaty factions. In fact, Collins worked with Mellowes and O'Connor to accelerate arms deliveries to IRA units in Ulster in the hope they could destabilize the same Unionist government that he had agreed to accept with the Treaty. Sean MacBride, who was Mellowes's partner in covert arms acquisitions operations for Collins and who followed Mellowes into the anti-Treaty faction, recalled the situation at the time:

> Did we feel . . . that we were on a collision course? No, we did not. The pro-Treaty side was known to be divided; one section was friendly to Republicans. There was a good deal of collaborating in the transfer of arms between Collins and Rory O'Connor. This collaboration continued right up to the hour of the attack on the Four Courts. They had been transferred from Beggar's Bush Barracks to Charley Daly and Sean Lehane in Donegal. This was being done to impede the new Six County government and as a counterblast to the Belfast anti-Catholic pogroms then in full spate and in which many hundreds of defenceless people were killed. I do not think this collaboration with Collins was in any way a sham, or intended to mislead. Collins thought that way.[44]

London, meanwhile, pressured the Dail to act against the rebels, threatening to resume full-scale war. After considerable efforts to negotiate with the Four-Courts dissidents proved unsuccessful, Collins finally ordered the Free State Army to retake the public buildings. The Four Courts burned during the firefight, signaling the outbreak of civil war. The anti-Treaty forces went on the run, seizing large areas of the south and west and attacking Free State troops and facilities on a wide scale.

O'Connor's faction had laid its hands on a cache of explosives, hand grenades, and some Thompson submachine guns. There was fighting in the streets of Dublin, and the number of victims mounted.

Cathal Brugha, the honored veteran of 1916, the simple, straightforward man who was never cut out to be a politician and who had resigned as Dail Defence Minister, honorably reenlisted in the anti-Treaty Volunteers—now called Irregulars—as a private soldier. Cornered in a Dublin street, Brugha essentially committed suicide when he advanced on a barricade manned by Free State soldiers, brandishing his weapons and ignoring repeated calls to lay down his arms. Recognizing Brugha, the Free Stater soldiers fired at him, aiming low. A bullet severed Brugha's femoral artery, however, and he later bled to death in the hospital. Collins wept when he learned the news, and wrote:

> Many would not have forgiven, had they been in my place—Cathal Brugha's attack on me January 7th. Yet I would forgive him anything. Because of his sincerity I would forgive him anything. At worst he was a fanatic—though in what has been a noble cause. At best I number him among the very few who have given their all that this country—now torn by civil war—should have its freedom. When many of us are forgotten, Cathal Brugha will be remembered.[45]

Harry Boland, the dynamic and charismatic leader who had recruited Michael Collins into the IRB and who served at his side during jailbreak operations and in Sinn Fein political struggles, had also rejected the Treaty. He went on the run and was hunted down by Free State troops at a seaside hotel in Skerries, north of Dublin. Boland was acquainted with a local yachtsman there, and may have been trying to arrange his escape to England. Troops burst into his room at 2:00 a.m. on August 1 and shot him, mortally wounding him. After three hours' delay, an ambulance arrived to take him to Dublin. Although he was in intense pain from extensive internal bleeding, the escort refused to stop at a hospital along the route, instead taking Boland straight to Portobello Barracks. There, another three hours elapsed before Boland was seen by a physician. He died at 9:00 p.m. that night. In a last conversation with his sister, he requested to be buried next to Cathal Brugha. When his funeral procession passed through Dublin, Free State troops grounded their weapons, removed their caps, and stood at attention. Collins was grief-stricken, writing to his fiancée, Kitty Keirnan:

> Last night . . . My mind went to him lying dead and I thought of the times together, and whatever good there is in any wish of mine he certainly had it. Although the gap of 8 or 9 months was not forgotten—of course no one can forget it—I only thought of him with the friendship of the days of 1918 and 1919.[46]

On August 12, 1922, an exhausted Arthur Griffith—founder of Sinn Fein, president of the Free State, and one of the leading lights of the revolution—succumbed to a stroke.

Eight days later, Collins embarked on an official visit to Counties Kerry and Cork in an effort at reconciliation with anti-Treaty leaders—including some who had been his close allies in the struggle against the British. They now considered the Big Fella a scoundrel and their bitterness knew no bounds. His staff argued that such a trip was far too dangerous. Despite the fact that he was running a fever and had a bad cold, Collins was determined. The man who so ruthlessly prosecuted a campaign of terror against the British now showed a different side. He desperately wanted to put an end to the fighting between his countrymen and was willing to face any personal danger to achieve that result. He dismissed the concerns of his aides, convinced that his enemies would not attack him in Cork, his home county. Once again, he had faith that his wit and charm would protect him from his enemies.

On August 22, while traveling in convoy with a heavily armed escort that included an armored car with mounted machine guns, Collins's entourage was halted by a roadblock near Béal na mBláth, not far distant from Woodfield, his childhood home. The escorting section of troops, including Emmet Dalton, the decorated ex–British officer who served with the Squad, noticed a cable stretching across the road, the sign of a concealed mine. Ordering the vehicles stopped just in time, Dalton knew they had driven into an IRA ambush site and immediately ordered the vehicles turned around. Dalton then called for the wheelmen to "drive like hell." Although realizing they were in a carefully selected kill zone, Collins countermanded the order, preferring to give fight. As they dismounted the cars to take cover, shots rang out. Collins's party returned fire. Some forty minutes into the firefight, Collins was struck behind the ear by a ricocheting rifle bullet. The guerrillas broke contact, enabling Dalton to start back for Dublin with their commander in chief, who lingered in a coma. Bad road conditions and a vehicle breakdown impeded their return after nightfall, and by the time they reached Dublin in the morning, Collins was dead.[47]

The genius of the Irish revolution, the man who planned and orchestrated the war against the British, the man who sustained it through its darkest hours, and the man who secured the peace, had slipped into eternity. Collins was gone at age thirty-one, but the legend was born.

11

CONCLUSION

> The Secret Service holds much that is kept secret even from very
> senior officers in the organization. Only M and his Chief of Staff
> know absolutely everything there is to know.
> —*Ian Fleming, former British Intelligence Officer and spy novelist, 1964*

The full extent of Collins's intelligence network will never be known. What we continue to discover about it year after year comes principally from memoirs and diaries, which are likely to remain the principal source of information. Yet despite these occasional discoveries, the complex maze of Collins's various professional relationships —including those with members of British intelligence—will never be fully revealed. His career is full of inexplicable contradictions. Here was a ruthless revolutionary intelligence chief who employed a former British Secret Service officer, John Chartres, as a key advisor, a leader who could and did reach out to important contacts working in sensitive policy jobs in the Castle, and who at the very least had cooperative contacts if not a direct penetration of Basil Thomson's Home Intelligence Directorate in London. Here was the man who, as Maire Comerford has related, was on the run from British agents dispatched from the lower Castle yard while concurrently exchanging communications with Assistant Undersecretary Andy Cope in the upper yard.

Likewise, it is highly unlikely that the complete story of British intelligence efforts against the IRA during 1919–1921 will ever be known. As David Neligan reported, the British burned many of their secret files and sealed the remainder when they left Ireland in 1922.[1] Except for a few contemporary memorandums, the handful of official documents released from classification controls in the past ten years were written after the events; they offer a neatly organized and interesting overview of the British intelligence effort, but prepared with the benefit of 20-20 hindsight.

But the all-important operational files—those containing the identities of case officers and their agents, collaborators, cooperative contacts, penetration operations, records of surreptitious entries, covert actions, surveillance reports, operational aliases, locations of safe houses, interrogation reports, target lists, operational codes, debriefing notes—those records that are the guts of day-to-day espionage, the sources and methods—undoubtedly went up the Castle chimney when the English conducted their burn-down.

As McMahon reports, the British had no plans for a stay-behind network when they left the country, expecting that the new Free State government would cooperate as Dominion partners in security matters.[2] When that proved not to be the case, the British were hard-pressed to restart an intelligence effort. Winter stayed on for a while, but his organization was broken up. MO4x, which had provided most of the manpower for clandestine collection, was withdrawn.

While the army's postmortem on intelligence operations and Ormonde Winter's memoirs make fascinating reading, they reveal more about bureaucratic warfare—complete with excuses, finger-pointing, careerism, and survivalist posturing—than they do about the daily business of espionage and counterespionage, its challenges, and its frustrations. These official intelligence postconflict analyses are not much different from what one might expect to read by any branch of government attempting to explain a fiasco.[3]

BRITISH COUNTERINSURGENCY PERFORMANCE

Against what standard can we objectively measure British counterinsurgency performance in Ireland? A contemporary guide for counterinsurgency theory and doctrine developed by an interagency task force of American security and policy agencies in 2009 is based on the analysis of dozens of insurgencies around the globe from the nineteenth century to the present, and it offers an excellent baseline for measuring British performance. This guide advances the theory that four elements are necessary for a successful counterinsurgency: a security function, a political function, an economic function, and an information (intelligence) function. Further, this theory recognizes two fundamental approaches to counterinsurgency:

- A military-centric approach wherein primary concentration is upon defeating the insurgency militarily. Success in this approach is determined by control of the population through a combination of military presence/operations, political conciliation, economic development, and intelligence. This approach emphasizes defeat of the enemy as its primary task and other activities as supporting efforts. There are many variants within this approach, including "soft" vs. "hard," direct vs. indirect, violent vs. nonviolent, and decapitation vs. marginalization strategies. This approach can be summarized as "first defeat the enemy, and all else will follow."
- A population-centric approach where the primary concentration is on maintaining or recovering the support of the population. While direct military action against the insurgent organization will definitely be required, it is not the main effort; this approach assumes that the center of gravity is the government's relationship with and support among the population. It can be summarized as "first protect and support the population, and all else will follow."[4]

We believe most observers of events in Ireland between 1916 and 1922 would agree that Britain followed a military-centric approach to counter the insurgency there, and thus the military-centric model will guide this performance analysis.

As we have seen, in 1916 the British government's system of governance in Ireland followed a strictly colonial policy and its security system was based on control of the population through a colonial police intelligence mechanism consisting of the RIC and G Division of the Dublin Metropolitan Police. Although Britain held out the prospect of political and economic reform to Irish nationalists in the form of the Home Rule Bill, it had unwisely acquiesced to threats by a minority of ultra-Unionist and reactionary northern Ireland extremists and, upon the outbreak of war on the continent, quickly suspended Home Rule, frustrating Irish nationalist ambitions and providing an opening for Irish physical force nationalists. Instead of recognizing the implications of the 1916 Easter Rising, however, the British government failed to make reforms to its security policy. At the same time, London exacerbated popular discontent by introducing a conscription bill in 1918, further undermining popular support for the government. In this way the ill-advised Lloyd George government itself created ripe conditions for insurgency. Once that insurgency surfaced openly in January 1919, the same government chose to follow a military-centric approach in countering the IRA, but by that time—aside from granting periodic amnesty to republican prisoners—the political conditions for control had been seriously eroded by Sinn Fein's election victory of 1918. Furthermore, the introduction of the paramilitaries in early 1920 carried out a deliberate policy of economic destruction in an ill-conceived effort to make life so miserable for the Irish they would welcome a restoration of British rule. In sacking and burning creameries, bacon factories, pubs, and shops, the paramilitaries destroyed the economy.

With the political and economic elements of a military-centric counterinsurgency thus nullified, Britain's campaign in Ireland revolved upon only two of the four counterinsurgency ingredients: intelligence and military force. Only when the military conflict escalated substantially in the spring of 1921, bringing international condemnation of British policy, did Lloyd George seriously pursue a political agreement. And he had to overrule hard-liners in his cabinet to do that.

Lloyd George and a cabinet dominated by hard-liners thus pursued a brutal war against the insurgents. The responsibility for physically securing the country and exercising control over its subjects devolved upon an army that was trained and experienced in conventional warfare and a security and intelligence infrastructure that was outdated and inadequate to cope with conditions of sustained low-intensity comflict. With the RIC and G Division neutralized by mid-1920, the British military once again found itself in the situation of having to improvise.

The postmortem histories of the British Army maneuver units that are also contained in the official War Office report on this period reveal far more about the overall counterinsurgency struggle than do the aforementioned intelligence assessments.[5] In fact, these narratives explain precisely what the military knew going into the struggle and what they experienced in the field; this in turn provides a much more realistic picture of the intelligence failure by placing it in the overall context of counterinsurgency. The narratives, as well as the memoirs of army officers and enlisted personnel who served during the conflict, generally portray a calm, reasoned, and objective assessment of events, and they by and large avoid the incessant finger-pointing of the intelligence-specific postmortems. They lay out the problems facing the military in Ireland—terrain, weather, attitudes of the population, religious considerations, logistics, and so forth—and explain the steps that Irish Command took to overcome them.[6]

After sitting more or less on the sidelines for a year after the armistice with Germany, Irish Command had plenty of time for battlefield preparation. They knew from the beginning that it would be guerrilla warfare, and they established a guerrilla warfare school, at least within the Fifth Division, in 1920. Troops arriving in country after October 1920 were required to attend it. When the IRA's ambush methods became clear, the army developed a manual of standard operating procedures to be followed for responding to them, and their records indicate that this tactical doctrine reduced casualties—although as Tom Kelleher's account of Crossbarry suggests, the British may actually have suffered higher casualties in that major battle because they lacked flexibility and individual initiative.[7]

In addition, the military had the foresight to request troop increases on the assumption that martial law would be declared across the entire country sooner or later. Irish Command's strategy was to unleash full-scale war on the IRA as soon as the politicians in Westminster authorized them to do so. And with some 43,000 combat troops on the island, General Macready likely assumed that, if need be, he could suppress the rebellion with overwhelming numbers and firepower, even if it meant he had to place an infantry company, an artillery battery, and a machine gun company in every town in Ireland and arrest and imprison every male over the age of fourteen. He had the troops to do so, but the political authorization never came. Thus the British Army was forced to fight a war that was part combat and part police action. And the army had to do it blindly with poor intelligence and with one hand tied behind its back by the cabinet, which continually paroled prisoners of war and which after mid-1920 secretly pursued negotiations with Dail Eireann.

In the final analysis, British military forces (which must include not only the army but also the two distinct paramilitary forces supporting the RIC comprising ex-military personnel) never got past the first phase of a counterinsurgency mission, which is to control and stabilize the battle-field. Without that control, the follow-on phases—pacification and res-toration of civil institutions and authority—cannot proceed. And as we have seen, the excesses of the paramilitaries utterly destroyed any hope for political and economic reform and, by extension, any hope for pacifi-cation of the population and stabilization of the country. The British fail-ure to control the battlefield in Ireland may be attributed to many causes, but the two main causes were inadequate intelligence and a conventional military mindset.

THE ROOTS OF FAILURE: ASSESSING BRITISH INTELLIGENCE PERFORMANCE

At the theater level, British intelligence failures in Ireland fall into two cat-egories: tactical or operational mistakes, and strategic or administrative mistakes. The operational failures were legion, and have been described in the preceding chapters of this book:

- Inadequate cover;
- Poor operational security;
- A weak record and file system;
- Fraternization, including close and continuing contact with prostitutes;
- Improper use of covert communication systems;
- Inadequate training in interrogation techniques;
- Failure to compartmentalize information;
- Failure to properly vet sources; and
- Alcoholism and low morale.

Administrative failures were equally serious. These included the fol-lowing:

- The failure to establish a single unified intelligence "center" or station in Dublin to command and control both police and army intelligence activities.

- A complete underestimation of the enemy's intelligence capabilities.
- A shortage of operating funds for employing sources.
- Lack of professional training of intelligence officers.
- Poor coordination among army and police agencies, particularly the failure to establish a joint military-police intelligence targeting branch and subject registry.
- Stove-piping of communication channels.
- A fundamental misunderstanding by both civil police agencies and army staff of the distinctions between "police" and "military" intelligence. By extension, a culture gap between the police and the military that resulted in confusion over the difference between information gathered for the arrest, prosecution, and conviction of criminals and that clandestinely obtained to support long-term counterterrorism operations. As the army postmortem noted, "Consequently, the systems which evolved grew up haphazard and without coordination."[8]

Significantly, while these theater-level failures cannot be overlooked, both official British Army maneuver unit reports and testimony by British veterans attribute the overall failure in Ireland to strategic intelligence shortcomings as much as to theater shortcomings. They point to the failure of intelligence to keep the political leadership informed about the situation on the ground, and the resulting disarray in security policy. As the officers who wrote the Fifth Division's postwar assessment noted:

Discussing what can be learnt from the occurrences in Ireland of 1919–1921, it is impossible altogether to omit policy, since military measures must be framed on and supported by policy. . . . It follows, therefore, that ministers must be fully cognizant of the true situation in order that they may frame their policy, and possess convincing arguments by which to persuade the country of its necessity and induce the Empire to support it. Only by such convictions, as was found in the late war, can the support of the Empire be obtained and the policy carried into execution, if need be by military action. The Army is only the spear point; it is the shaft of the spear and the force behind it that drives the blow home. During the last two years it would appear that the true state of affairs in Ireland was not realized in Great Britain, at all events, until it was too late. Consequently, the want of a suitable and clear policy was felt and sufficient importance was not, perhaps, attached to convincing the country of the need for putting one into force. . . . The first lesson we learn, therefore, is the necessity for a thoroughly good intelligence system so that the Government advisors may be in a position to appreciate the situation justly and to put it squarely, fully and honestly before the Cabinet.[9]

It is easy some ninety years after the events to critique the British intelligence effort from the comfortable armchair of some university library, but given the disarray that existed in the British national strategic intelligence community in 1919, one might argue that the officers sent to Ireland between 1919 and 1921 to conduct espionage and mount counterterrorism operations did as good a job as could be expected. The reshuffle of that national community in January 1919 had as much to do with the loss of Ireland as did any mistakes made by Ormonde Winter or British Army intelligence.

Moreover, the appointment of a career law enforcement officer to become supreme director of national intelligence and principal home security officer—and the corresponding gutting of MI5—resulted in a "brain drain" of strategic management, not to mention clandestine expertise, that denied Irish Command and Dublin Castle the much-needed single coordinating authority to manage the overall intelligence effort. With Basil Thomson dominating the "Secret Service" (and broadcasting that fact to the world in British newspaper stories), it is no wonder that the handful of experienced clandestine operators remaining at MI5 had as little to do with the Irish crisis as possible.

Wisely, Churchill authorized the creation of MO4x within the DMI in late 1919. With MI5 down to only a dozen personnel, including secretaries, and robbed of a realistic operating budget, the War Office envisioned that army-specific intelligence would suffer. The creation of MO4x was intended to fulfill that gap, and it was the right thing to do at the time.

Military intelligence is very much a specialty. It combines the expertise of intelligence collection and exploitation with a knowledge of military organization, strategy, and doctrine. It tends to be very tactical in nature and thus is a very arcane science. Civilian personnel are quite capable of performing these functions, if they have a proper military background (such as MI5 and MO4x officers generally had), or at least a thorough appreciation of the needs of a theater commander in chief, or of a divisional or brigade commander.

Likewise, civilian espionage and counterespionage are specialties that focus on civil and political intelligence, also unique disciplines that generally require no expertise in military affairs. In Ireland, the traditional collectors of political intelligence were the police. When Ormonde Winter arrived as chief intelligence officer at Dublin Castle in 1920, he made the mistake of following the Castle administration's desire to reinvigorate and preserve the police intelligence system. Consequently, the system of police intelligence in Ireland, which had already been shown to be ineffectual against the IRA by late 1919, was perpetuated by Winter and his Castle bosses.

Police officers have a culture all their own and do not generally speak the language of classical intelligence. While one might argue that Basil Thomson and Special Branch had an advantage over most police organizations with their years of international experience and foreign contacts, the end goals of police services are different from those of classical intelligence services. Police services usually run informers just long enough to spot, arrest, and prosecute a target who has committed a crime, or to prevent the target from committing a crime, and they seek to do this as quickly as possible. For the Special Branch inspector, it was the chase, the arrest, and the laudatory headlines that made the game interesting. Classical, clandestine intelligence is more of a long-term proposition; it seeks to penetrate the enemy camp with reliable sources who will work in place as long as possible to gather the maximum amount of information possible. For a clandestine service officer, anonymity is everything.

As Home Intelligence Director from 1919 until 1921, Basil Thomson demonstrated how to disrupt a proven, established, and cooperative counterintelligence community by adding extraneous bureaucracy. The civil intelligence organization that Thomson set up at Scotland House to oversee all home security matters could not have worked effectively since it was not all-inclusive; it ignored and bypassed the expertise built up over many years within the War Office intelligence departments, MI5 and MI1c. There was no fusion of intelligence specialties, although as this narrative documents, the army made a greater effort to achieve fusion than did Thomson (or Winter at the Castle). If anything, Thomson's organization created a superfluous layer of bureaucracy through which all intelligence had to be filtered from the experts through an opportunistic semiprofessional intelligence chief, to British policymakers. In Thomson's case, once his penetration operation resulted in disaster for agent Jameson, he appears only to have dabbled in the Irish problem. And if the military found in 1922 that the policymakers were ill-informed about conditions in Ireland, as the army postmortem charges, that is an indictment of Basil Thomson.

One might draw from this the lesson that national intelligence directors appointed in the face of a perceived threat (in Thomson's case, the so-called "Red Menace"), and in a highly politicized atmosphere, are not apt to serve either the policymaker or the theater customer very effectively. Thomson's failed tenure should stand as a stark warning to American politicians and policymakers, inasmuch as it is precisely these factors—partisan political maneuvering and budget slashing—that seem to habitually handicap the U.S. intelligence community every decade or so.

In July 1921, Sir Warren Fischer—whose investigation of the performance of the Dublin Castle Administration led to the wholesale sacking of Castle management a year earlier—issued an audit report on Basil Thomson's Home Intelligence Directorate. Fischer's report found not only that Thomson's Scotland House organization was wasteful but also that it duplicated the work of other agencies and—perhaps most serious of all—was guilty of issuing misleading intelligence. The Commissioner of the London Metropolitan Police wasted no time in calling for the return of Special Branch and Thomson to the control of the Criminal Investigation Division, calling the "independence of the Special Branch" under Thomson "a standing menace to the good discipline of the force." Thomson refused to comply with the Commissioner's demands and he was summarily dismissed from his post by the prime minister. His dismissal abruptly brought the Directorate of Home Intelligence to an end. British policymakers had learned their lesson and chose to discard the needless bureaucracy of a national intelligence director. Although it continued to suffer from budget and manpower shortages through the 1920s and early 1930s, MI5 rebounded from near-extinction, thus restoring stability to Britain's national intelligence community prior to World War II.[10]

ASSESSING THE IRA INTELLIGENCE SYSTEM

Any revolutionary or terrorist group could learn a great deal from Michael Collins, and more than a few have, for Collins advanced revolutionary strategy to a new level. He was perhaps the first revolutionary to combine guerrilla warfare tactics and ruthless political assassination with relentless political agitation that included nonrecognition of the existing political system, proactive formation of a shadow government to replace it, and a highly effective propaganda offensive.

As we have seen, Collins's tactics so impressed some British intelligence officers that they influenced the direction of future British special operations tactics during the Second World War. But Collins's influence has extended far beyond Great Britain.

There is an urban legend that in 1920 a young expatriate Vietnamese named Nguyen Ai Quoc, working as a pastry cook in a London Hotel, broke down and wept when he learned of the death after seventy-four days on hunger strike of Terence McSwiney, the Irish Republican mayor of Cork City. Distraught over McSwiney's death, Nguyen is alleged to have tearfully declared, "Such a people will never be defeated!" If indeed the man we now know as Ho Chi Minh ever actually uttered these words, it was not from London, for he had departed England for France in 1919.

What is certain, however, is that Ho later followed the Michael Collins playbook to perfection in his thirty-year revolutionary struggle against the French and the Americans. He launched the Viet Minh (later Viet Cong) guerrilla army to mount hit-and-run operations, assassinate government officials, and terrorize the civilian population, and he established a shadow government system in Vietnam's southern provinces. He also put in position a highly successful international propaganda offensive that — with the undeniable help of a sympathetic American news media — sharply divided American public opinion and undermined American resolve in Vietnam in much the same way that IRA and Sinn Fein propaganda turned British and international public opinion against London's Irish policy.

Collins, the self-educated west Cork farm boy with a sheepish grin, gregarious personality, and broad country accent was an unlikely intelligence mastermind. But Collins was financially astute, charismatic, and an organizational wizard capable of quickly assessing a problem and acting decisively. He knew from his careful study of Irish revolutionary history that British informers and spies had betrayed all past rebellions; his apprenticeship in the IRB taught him the importance of secrecy and stealth. Collins's objective from the beginning was to "put out the eyes of the British." He took stock of the British intelligence system arrayed against him, accurately identified its vulnerabilities, and attacked it ruthlessly and relentlessly.

Collins was the first to realize that British reliance on Irish informers and its dependence upon Irish civil servants was a vulnerability, and he was the first to capitalize on it. Although Irish secret societies had existed since the seventeenth century, their efforts had all petered out after a single show of force. The British system of informers and a loyal Irish civil service had always betrayed them. By 1916, Irish men and women were an integral part of the British civil service; they staffed the post and telegraph system; they served as policemen, magistrates, and tax collectors. Collins exploited that situation to the fullest. They had waited patiently for Home Rule for years; they were disappointed when it was suspended in 1914. They were later enraged when the British tried to introduce the draft in 1918. Unlike previous revolutionary movements, conditions were ripe for seizing the hearts and minds of the populace. Certainly a number of Irish civil servants like Broy, Kavanagh, MacNamara, and Neligan were volunteers; many others like Lily Mernin were easily recruited out of loyalty to Ireland. But when Collins could not solicit cooperation with an appeal to patriotism or other idealistic grounds, he resorted to bribery to recruit British spies. He also used extortion, kidnapping, and assassination to silence informers, which induced many others to help him who might not otherwise have done so. This ruthless approach went far beyond anything ever attempted by previous Irish secret societies and it made the difference between success and failure.

In low-intensity conflict where an insurgency's success or failure usually depends on the survival of one or two key leaders, counterintelligence takes on even more importance, and human source intelligence, or HUMINT, is arguably the most important element in counterintelligence. In Ireland the British strategy was based on the assumption that capturing Collins and other key IRA leaders would cause the rebellion to collapse. But they were compelled because of a vacuum at the national level to improvise their HUMINT effort and adjust their tactics to fight a small war on the IRA's terms and turf. Collins, however, knew that counterintelligence was key to survival of the nationalist movement, and he seized the initiative in the summer of 1919 with direct attacks on the colonial secret police. He managed to maintain the upper hand in the intelligence struggle into mid-1921—just barely.

Thus denied their system of informers, and surrounded by civil servants whose loyalty was questionable, the Crown's intelligence professionals were simply unable to neutralize the key leadership of the IRA. And when the British resorted to the army and imported paramilitaries from England, they were forced into an ugly and unfamiliar guerrilla war punctuated by mass arrests, blind reprisals, torture, and terror. As the number of innocent Irish victims mounted throughout 1920 and 1921, Prime Minister Lloyd George's policy of force invited vigorous condemnation at home and abroad. Faced with eroding political support, international pressure, and mounting casualties, Lloyd George finally called off the military campaign in July 1921.

There is no question that Collins was a natural intelligence officer and political genius. But he was also a desperate physical-force nationalist and determined warrior who exploited a weak British security policy to wage a ruthless and bloody intelligence contest and guerrilla war. Collins's greatest achievement, therefore, was to maneuver the British into this hopeless political dilemma, not in eliminating British forces. Unfortunately, Collins has all too often been portrayed as the invincible intelligence operative who brought the British to their knees at gunpoint. As we now know, British arrogance, insensitivity to a distinct Irish culture, reorganization, disorganization, bureaucratic infighting, and plain ineptitude played a major role in their defeat. Collins's genius was to recognize and exploit these conditions to the fullest. In so doing, he managed by the skin of his teeth to maintain the upper hand for much of the conflict.

Collins outworked and outwitted British intelligence. His intelligence apparatus was not, as has often been declared, a one-dimensional counterintelligence service. It was much more than that. While intelligence is generically a defensive activity, many functions carried out by the IRA intelligence service do not fall under the title of counterintelligence per se. Between 1918 and 1921, the Collins espionage organization undertook multiple functions:

- Recruitment of police and intelligence sources for defensive (counter-intelligence) purposes;
- Recruitment of political and military sources for discerning the enemy's political and military strategy;
- Influence operations, including the tasking of agent McElligott to try to foment disloyalty within the British police;
- Disinformation operations, including the scripting of intelligence reports containing misleading information passed to the British Secret Service by agent Neligan;
- Communication and code intercept to assist in prosecuting the offensive guerrilla war and to provide early warning of British penetration operations;
- Lethal covert action to directly eliminate threats from various British intelligence services, including G Division, the RIC, Special Branch, MO4x, divisional and brigade IOs, Auxiliaries, and civilian informers.

Collins painstakingly recruited and developed key penetrations in virtually all British institutions in Ireland, including the British Secret Service, and adroitly used this information advantage to unleash ruthlessly effective hit-and-run guerrilla attacks never before seen in modern warfare. In so doing, Collins forged a political-military strategy that would serve as a blueprint for subsequent revolutionary movements from Bengal to Palestine, from Cuba to Vietnam. And yet, Peter Hart, who rarely concealed his contempt for the profession of intelligence, got it only partly right when he wrote,

> Opinions were, and are, mixed as to which side had the upper hand. Whoever can be said to have won the struggle, however, the verdict is nearly unanimous that British intelligence were patent and inglorious losers. Indeed, "British intelligence"—out-witted and out-spied—emerges from most accounts of the revolution as a contradiction in terms: a disastrous compound of misdirection, malice and ignorance. In the Great War, His Majesty's secret services had triumphed over their German adversaries to great acclaim. This time, it was the revolutionaries who were the Kims, Hannays and Drummonds, led by Michael Collins as the Scarlet Pimpernel, while the defenders of the realm were reduced to the role of bumbling pursuers.[11]

The "bumbling pursuers" were in fact—with notable exceptions identified throughout this study—dedicated young Englishmen, most of whom had already served their country with distinction. They willingly placed their lives at risk for their country and they were thrust into a nearly hopeless and extremely hazardous operating environment with very little preparation by a government that denied them professional training, support, operating funds, and cover. Even David Neligan, whose double agent activities sent many of these officers to their deaths, acknowledged the great hazards they faced and did so with a hint of admiration. It therefore seems intellectually dishonest to sarcastically critique British street officers and agents for losing the intelligence war when the greater blame lay with incompetent administrators at the Castle and dithering and duplicitous politicians in London.

LESSONS OF THE BRITISH COUNTERINSURGENCY EFFORT

Winston Churchill, the hard-liner in Lloyd George's cabinet who promoted Thomson so ardently in January 1919, simply hated the Irish rebels. Churchill not only wanted his favorite man in charge of chasing the Bolsheviks and Fenians, but he also wanted these threats treated brutally and without quarter. In Ireland, this meant putting the population under the bootheel of the British Army and the mercenary order police, the Auxiliaries and Black and Tans. And that translated into tough police raids, brutal interrogations and torture of prisoners, summary execution of suspects without trial, wholesale destruction of private and public property, aggressive prosecutions, and concentration camps. The most sinister methods of physical torture were applied to IRA and Sinn Fein prisoners, and torture was certainly considered fair play as far as Churchill was concerned. But Collins frustrated Churchill time and again with a classic intelligence modus operandi, showing that it is sometimes easier to defeat a foe by building rapport with him and recruiting him rather than by simply killing him. Collins was well aware that in an open fight the British would outnumber and outlast the IRA. Therefore, he adopted the best tactic available to him—eliminating the colonial political police through intimidation, ostracizing, and assassination—and then penetrating the British Secret Service and forcing it to sharpen its tactics. And yet, fully seventeen months elapsed after Sinn Fein declared independence before the British fully realized what they were up against.

The British no doubt learned many lessons from their struggle with Collins. The following realities emerged from their experience in Ireland.

There is a big difference between "antiterrorism" and "counterterrorism."

Antiterrorism is primarily a tactical and short-term response in reaction to an incident or series of incidents. It is largely the domain of police forces. Counterterrorism, however, is a strategic, long-term, preemptive effort to head off an incident or series of incidents. It requires much more than an alert and motivated police force; it requires timely and focused intelligence to identify specific threats and the people equipped and available to carry out those threats. It requires a file system and an action list of high-value targets. Before 1920, British security policy in Ireland was based largely on its colonial police force and was very much in a *reactive response* mode. While it is true that the deployment of the infamous Igoe Gang to ferret out and kill Collins and his men in mid-1920 was a proactive step, it lacked centralized and focused intelligence support and in that sense was essentially also a reactive effort. It was also characterized by ham-handed street techniques that lacked the sophistication of a classic surveillance operation. After 1920, British efforts became more preemptive with the establishment of Winter's Central Raid Bureau to serve as a central clearinghouse for document exploitation. While Winter is harshly criticized by contemporaries and historians for not catching Michael Collins, his work put considerable pressure on Collins and the IRA. Despite the IRA's success on Bloody Sunday 1920, for example, Winter enjoyed an often unheralded string of successes in the eight months from October 1920 to July 1921:

- Located and eliminated Sean Treacy, one of Collins's most important operatives.
- Located and apprehended the high-value targets Dick McKee, commandant of the Dublin Brigade, and his deputy brigade commander, Peadar Clancy—a major blow to the morale and effectiveness of the IRA's most important brigade.
- Unmasked Ned Broy as a spy.

- Identified every member of a Dublin Brigade company through the arrest and interrogation of Fourvargue.
- Unmasked James MacNamara as an IRA collaborator and suspected spy.
- Pinpointed and successfully raided Collins's two personal intelligence offices, as well as the office of IRA Chief of Staff Richard Mulcahy, netting a cache of important documents, including the Sinn Fein and IRA codes and the identities of hundreds of Volunteers. In the second of his raids on Collins's offices, he missed nabbing Collins by a few minutes.

As U.S. policymakers and national security planners struggle to cope with the heightened domestic terrorism threat since 9/11, they would be well served to recognize the difference between antiterrorism and counterterrorism. Beefing up local police departments and identifying so-called "first responders" is a laudable but limited measure that is only as strong as the weakest cop on the beat.

A conventionally organized and trained military is a poor choice for combating political crime or fostering government stability.

U.S. military planners contemplating further extensions of American military muscle abroad in the twenty-first century—whether to attack terrorist safe havens, effect regime change, or participate in peacekeeping missions—would benefit from a study of the British performance in Ireland from 1919 to 1921. It is a perfect example—in the words of Irish scholar T. Ryel Dwyer—"of how not to wage peace." Generally speaking, soldiers are not trained to cope with an insurgency embedded among a civilian population, and their presence can generate even greater resistance and political instability. Moreover, military organizations tend by their vary nature to be inflexible and thus slow to detect and react to changing political conditions. The British Army Command in Ireland was trained to engage a conventional enemy force in open combat. They were completely unprepared to engage a shadowy army that enjoyed the support of a significant percentage of the local population, or to wage a propaganda war with Sinn Fein. In the countryside, the British Army was forced to stick to the roads, towns, and villages; it was neither equipped nor trained to pursue IRA flying columns that made use of hit-and-run attacks, and whose reliance upon living off the land was its stock-in-trade.

Regardless, the British Army was ubiquitous in Ireland throughout the Troubles. It supplied its officers to Special Branch and the secret service (the DDSB), and most of these detailees were veterans of the Western Front. Even when the DDSB was transferred to civilian control in January 1921, the new man in charge of it at the Castle was an old army artillery-man with a thoroughly military outlook. Beyond this, the army occupied a sizable portion of the country with its 43,000 combat troops. Moreover, ex–British Army servicemen and officers were recruited exclusively to fill the ranks of the Black and Tans and Auxiliaries.

Thus, the entire British counterinsurgency effort in Ireland was thoroughly shaped by a conventional military perspective. The result was almost complete reliance upon force, which resulted in stiffened resistance by the Irish population and a significantly enhanced support base for Sinn Fein and the IRA. Heavy-handed initiatives under Lloyd George's reprisal policy led to shock and revulsion in Britain and abroad, followed by a domestic political backlash for the Lloyd George government. And because much of this happened as Great Britain was attempting to redraw the map of Europe in Versailles, Britain's handling of the Irish problem was viewed by much of the international community as disingenuous at best, and violently reactionary at worst. Even in America—especially in America—the outcry was loud and sustained. Ireland became a quagmire for Lloyd George. Collins may not have been able to win an open contest with British regulars, but he certainly won the guerrilla and propaganda war that, at the end of the day, compelled Lloyd George to seek a political accommodation.

Despite the availability of large numbers of well-trained, well-equipped, well-fed, and combat-experienced British infantry, artillery, cavalry, armored, engineering, aircraft, and service units to combat the growing strength of IRA guerrilla columns from 1920 onward, London's military strategy as it applied to counterinsurgency was flawed and thus doomed. As West Cork Flying Column Commanding Officer Tom Barry observed after the war,

> Standing against this large field force was that of the Irish Republican Army, never at any time exceeding three hundred and ten riflemen in the whole of County Cork. . . . Those figures, showing

the Irish Republican Army outnumbered by over forty to one in armed men and to a far greater ratio in firepower before the Truce, may justly cause one to wonder why the British did not succeed in exterminating the small Irish field force in 1920 and 1921. The answer, of course, is that in the last analysis the struggle never was between the British Army and a small Irish force of Flying Columns and Active Service Units. Had this been so, the few Flying Columns operating would not have existed for a month, no matter how bravely and skillfully they fought. This was a war between the British Army and the Irish people, and the problem before the British Army from mid-1920 on was not how to smash the Flying Columns, but how to destroy the resistance of a people, for, as sure as day follows night, if a Flying Column were wiped out in any area, another would arise to continue the attacks on, and the resistance to the alien rulers. The Irish people had many weapons which the British lacked: their belief in the righteousness of their cause, their determination to be free, their political structure as declared in the General Election of December 1918, and a strong militant body of youth, who, though as yet unarmed, were a potential army of great possibilities.[12]

Bureaucratic infighting and reorganization of the national intelligence community has a debilitating impact on morale and operational effectiveness.

The MI5–Special Branch combination in force in Britain and the colonies from 1909 to January 1919 was a proven formula for management of domestic security matters. As events proved, the experiment of elevating Special Branch's Basil Thomson to lead a new Home Intelligence Directorate in January 1919 was an unmitigated failure. The timing of this power play by Thomson and his cronies could not have been worse. Not only did it add another layer of bureaucracy to the domestic security infrastructure, it angered and alienated MI5, which held considerable expertise in intelligence matters. Thomson spent the next two years throwing occasional resources against the IRA in a piecemeal fashion, to no great effect. Fortunately, Thomson's reign as Britain's security czar did not last long. The Directorate of Home Intelligence was abolished and smarter heads at MI5 soon reclaimed responsibility for Britain's domestic security. This enabled Vernon Kell and his successors to create in MI5 a counterintelligence and counterterrorism apparatus that today serves as the premier model for domestic security services around the globe. A well-trained political police force (Special Branch), subordinated to a strategic cadre of trained (and anonymous) intelligence professionals (MI5), is a devastatingly effective counterintelligence/counterinsurgency/counterterrorist combination. How differently events in Ireland might have turned out for the British side, had the professionals of MI5 not been sidelined for most of the period, and had the tactical core intelligence collection and counterintelligence effort in Ireland not devolved upon the D-list paraprofessionals of MO4x and Ormonde Winter's civilian department in the Castle.

Only a handful of determined terrorists is required to spread mayhem and fear.

The IRA demonstrated that, even when the insurgents are poorly armed, they can sustain their efforts indefinitely so long as they are disciplined, their intelligence is good, and the government's intelligence effort is fragmented, disorganized, and weak. As noted earlier, Britain learned this lesson in spades in Ireland. Having had the experience of trying to neutralize the IRA in the Irish countryside for three years, British Army intelligence officer Colin Gubbins became an admirer of Michael Collins and his methods. Years later, when he commanded Britain's Special Operations Executive (SOE) during the Second World War, Gubbins endorsed these same methods in his support of anti-Nazi resistance movements from Norway to Yugoslavia.

Native-born agents are the most effective tools for penetrating insurgents/ terrorist groups.

As we have seen, Michael Collins recognized that a sizable proportion of the British Civil Service was composed of sympathetic or vulnerable Irish-born natives who could be recruited or otherwise induced—or coerced—into supporting and assisting his secret intelligence efforts. The British, on the contrary, found a dearth of native-born Irish subjects with which to mount penetration operations against Sinn Fein and the IRA. When Collins's Squad began shooting constables and detectives in the summer of 1919, the pool of Irish police informers dried up. When the RIC and the army rounded up dozens of IRA officers in the December 1919 raids, the informers reappeared, and the government's subsequent granting of amnesty to those IRA cadre once again devastated the informer system. Although they tried, the British were never able to reestablish that system, particularly after the Commissioner of the Dublin Metropolitan Police negotiated a truce with the IRA in 1920. London responded by importing an enormous cadre of secret service officers, but these resources simply could not move about the city unnoticed the way an Irish native could. The results were disastrous. As Ormonde Winter lamented in his 1921 after-action report:

> The recruitment of agents was a matter of the greatest difficulty. Englishmen could be found who volunteered for the service, but Englishmen operating in Ireland were at a serious disadvantage. Irishmen could be found in England, but the majority of these had lived out of Ireland for some time, and had few facilities for gaining inside knowledge. The question of time was an important factor. To build up an Intelligence organization for the investigation of political crime in a few months is, practically, an impossibility. . . . The wholesale murder of practically all the members of the Dublin Metropolitan Police Detective Force employed on political work reduced that Force, exposed as they were to duty on the streets, to a complete cessation of activities as far as this class of work was concerned. The Intelligence Service, therefore, [was] bereft of the aid of those who knew the leading rebels by sight, and who were in a position to give information and effect arrests, had it not been a life hazard to do so.[13]

Finally, at a more strategic level, the events in Ireland between 1919 and 1921 should offer a chilling warning to contemporary intelligence professionals, military planners, policymakers—and law makers—currently engaged in counterinsurgency/counterterrorism operations, planning, and strategy. The overall failure of the British counterinsurgency/counterterrorism effort in Ireland happened within the following context:

- Deployment of 43,000 combat troops to defeat a well-organized and embedded insurgency and to restore order. These experienced troops were well-trained veterans with superior arms and a vast resupply network. But they were hamstrung by a confusing and contradictory policy that was the result of poor strategic intelligence and weak tactical intelligence that enabled their enemy to attack and ambush them relentlessly and almost at will with small arms and improvised explosive devices, resulting in 1,800 casualties.

- A demoralized and defeated proxy police force that was thinned to total ineffectiveness by assassinations, ostracizing, and intimidation. Police stations were firebombed and overrun in nearly every province in the country. Resignations of policemen averaged 200 per month at the height of the war.
- The introduction of 6,500 professional contractors to bolster the police force, to protect civil institutions, and to help in the hunt for the insurgents.
- An intelligence community in disarray, crippled by bureaucratic infighting following the appointment of a national intelligence director, competing among itself for turf and responding to acts of terrorism in a piecemeal and uncoordinated fashion.

Even if these events strike a chord with only a handful of future intelligence leaders, aspiring general officers, or would-be policymakers, this study will have served a purpose.

The most hard-core of British policymakers learned some lessons from the Anglo-Irish War. Churchill, who relished reading field reports detailing British reprisal operations, met Collins continually over the course of the treaty negotiations and came to respect him. In his memoirs, he dispassionately described Collins:

> Successor to a sinister inheritance, reared among fierce conditions and moving through ferocious times, he supplied those qualities of action and personality without which the foundation of Irish nationhood would not have been re-established.[14]

Collins was certainly the brightest and most charismatic revolutionary leader to emerge in the political vacuum left by the disastrous 1916 Easter Rising. His success as finance minister for the Dail Eireann government, and his organizational skills as adjutant general and Director of Organization of the Irish Republican Army, would in themselves have guaranteed Collins a prominent place in Irish history. But it was Collins's work as the IRA's intelligence chief that enabled his other efforts to bear fruit. His intelligence successes were fundamental to achieving the political settlement with London that eventually led to full Irish independence.

APPENDIX A

SINN FEIN'S SUSPICIOUS COUSINS

In December 1918 Michael Collins—still an obscure figure to the British despite his fugitive status at home since skipping bail in April—accompanied a delegation of prominent Irish nationalists and men of letters to London. The delegation sought a meeting with U.S. President Woodrow Wilson to petition him for inclusion of Ireland under terms of the Versailles Treaty as an independent nation. Wilson's moralistic speeches about the rights of small ethnic minorities notwithstanding, the President—ever the Anglophile—refused to meet the Irish delegation.

On December 14, however, the Irish delegation was unexpectedly invited to attend a holiday party and reception hosted by a very ad hoc group of British socialites calling themselves the Friends of Ireland Committee. One member of the committee, John Chartres, had been in intermittent contact via letter with Sinn Fein's founder, Arthur Griffith, since 1917, offering support for the movement and hoping to play a more meaningful role in the Sinn Fein cause. Another member of the committee in attendance at the party was the prominent libertarian writer Auberon Herbert. Both Chartres and Herbert—men much older than Collins and Griffith—had worked as journalists and in a variety of government postings throughout their careers. Both were also, coincidentally, veteran British intelligence officers.

Little was known about John Chartres at the time of the Anglo-Irish war, and he has remained a mystery man ever since. Born in 1862, he was an attorney by training who specialized in workmen's compensation cases. He had worked as a journalist for the *Times* and likely began his secret service career working under *Times* cover, for he subsequently ran the *Times* intelligence department—a quasi-official adjunct of the British Secret Service—for many years. In 1915, Chartres was appointed chief of intelligence section for the War Office Armaments Output Committee and was subsequently transferred to the Ministry of Munitions—then under Churchill. Chartres is known to have spent some time in Cairo during the war.

In 1918, Auberon Herbert was a prominent Liberal Party leader, newspaper publisher, and well-known social commentator. His moralistic essays examining the rights of man versus the rights of government had indeed been sympathetic toward the Irish cause. However, early in his career Herbert had also worked for the *Times* as a foreign correspondent covering the Boer War, and certainly knew Churchill—also a journalist dabbling in intelligence assignments in South Africa at the time. During the World War, Herbert served on secret service assignments in Egypt and Albania. Following the war, Herbert was elevated to the peerage, gaining the title Lord Lucas.[1]

While there is no evidence that these two were actively engaged in espionage against Sinn Fein at the time they met the Irish delegation in London in 1918, it seems incomprehensible that both Chartres's and Herbert's membership on this blatantly improvised "Friends of Ireland Committee" was a coincidence. On the contrary, their sudden appearance as supporters of Sinn Fein is highly suspect. Certainly their professional backgrounds and connections to Churchill cannot be ignored.

Moreover, the behavior of Chartres and his Italian wife, the playwright and socialite Annie Vivanti, over the next two years is highly suspicious. Following the war, Chartres moved from the Munitions Ministry to Dublin Castle as the British Labour Ministry representative. But in 1919 he suddenly resigned his civil service post to accept an appointment from de Valera to head the Irish White Cross—a Dail Eireannn organization set up to assist the families of imprisoned Republicans. This was quite a remarkable development. It is safe to say that middle-aged, senior, and well-connected British civil servants with security clearances do not normally abandon their comfortable, well-paid careers to take obscure, poorly compensated posts within a radical outlaw underground political movement that operates from cellars in what was then the most dangerous city on the planet. Equally suspicious is the fact that while Chartres was reportedly offered an OBE for wartime service, he refused it. Some suspect this refusal may have been directed by the secret service in order for Chartres to maintain a low profile during his subsequent intelligence career.[2]

Chartres's communications with Dail Eireann's secretary of agriculture, Robert Barton, is particularly suspicious. Robert Barton was the only member of de Valera's revolutionary cabinet not to have served on the Irish side in the 1916 Easter Rising. On the contrary, Barton had been an officer in a British Army regiment stationed in Dublin that fought the Irish Volunteers during Easter week. Although Barton did not receive a particularly sensitive post in the revolutionary government, he was privy to Collins's financial and fundraising data, and Barton clearly passed some of this sensitive financial information to Chartres. British intelligence went to extraordinary lengths to seize Collins's operating funds, with only limited success. Yet in 1921, Col. Ormonde Winter — Chief of the British Combined Intelligence Service in Ireland — personally entered a metro Dublin bank in alias and heavy disguise and successfully removed £4,000 of IRA funds.

As for Chartres's wife, Annie, she subsequently went with an Irish delegation to Versailles in 1919 to seek recognition of Ireland by the Allied powers. That came to nothing. Not only did Vivanti's background as an Italian poet and playwright make her manifestly unqualified to serve as a member of the Irish nationalist delegation to Versailles, but her later offer to procure weapons for the IRA in Italy was an even bigger stretch. While Chartres as a former Ministry of Munitions civil servant would have been qualified for this assignment, his wife was not. It did not matter in the long run, for no weapons were ever procured through Vivanti's efforts. And though Special Branch may have had mixed results in its efforts against Collins in Ireland, MI6 had considerable success foiling IRA arms smuggling schemes on the continent throughout the Troubles — perhaps with the help of Chartres and Vivanti.[3]

Maire Comerford, a member of Cumman-na-mBan (the Irish Women's League that served as a paramilitary auxiliary to the Irish Volunteers) and a committed Sinn Fein activist, was close to the Dail and IRA leadership throughout the Anglo-Irish War. Collins asked her to accompany Chartres as a social companion, but she found him distasteful and soon begged off this assignment. She made an interesting observation about Chartres during an interview with writer Uinseann MacEoin:

> I am convinced that John Chartres, the Englishman who joined us at that time, and who accompanied the Treaty delegation as a secretary, was a plant by the British. His wife accompanied Sean T. O'Kelly in the Peace delegation to Paris in early 1919, which, if he was a plant, would make her position an unusually significant one. They went out of their way to promote the reputation of Michael Collins far beyond what he seemed to deserve.[4]

Although Maire Comerford and others warned Collins about Chartres and Vivanti, he appears not to have had even the slightest concern about either. Rather, Collins appears to have accepted Chartres as a reformed Englishman who was now completely dedicated to the cause of Irish independence.

If indeed the appearance of Auberon Herbert, John Chartres, and Annie Vivanti was a carefully laid British Secret Service operation, then Chartres's later appointment as legal counsel and personal secretary to Collins and the Irish Peace Treaty delegation to London in 1921 was a genuine British intelligence coup. One may only speculate whether Chartres was secretly betraying the Irish delegation's strategy to Lloyd George and his hard-line delegates. If so, this might well account for the highly effective "good guy, bad guy" strategy adopted by Lloyd George and Winston Churchill that wore down the Irish delegation and convinced them to sign treaty terms that were highly favorable to the British government, and which precipitated the Irish Civil War.

But lacking firm evidence, there is also the distinct possibility that, at least in Chartres's case, he was a genuine defector to Sinn Fein and was assisting Collins with strategic information. Chartres's prior posting as chief of the Intelligence Section at the Ministry of Munitions under Churchill meant that he almost certainly worked closely with Basil Thomson of Special Branch, who was providing security briefings to Churchill from 1915 onward.[5] It is therefore entirely plausible that this former British civil servant who was so mistrusted by Collins's closest assistants, this Englishman with whom Collins was completely relaxed, was the strategic source who provided Collins with such valuable political and intelligence information, the mysterious Lieutenant G.

APPENDIX B

ON HIS MAJESTY'S SECRET SERVICE

Among the intelligence professionals sent to Ireland during the Anglo-Irish War were two prominent members of the Indian Colonial Police, Charles A. Tegart and Godfrey C. Denham. When the British government overhauled the Dublin Castle administration and installed Col. Ormonde Winter as chief of the Combined Intelligence Service in May 1920, London requested that the Indian High Commissioner release Tegart and Denham for temporary service in Ireland to bolster Winter's effort.

Tegart and Denham had years of service with the Criminal Investigation Division of the Bengal Police. Their experience in successfully tracking terrorists in Calcutta was thought by Whitehall to be an ideal preparation for establishing an efficient secret service effort against the IRA, particularly in the urban environment of Dublin, Cork, and other Irish cities.

A native Irishman, Tegart had been born in Ulster and raised in the south. He joined the Indian Colonial Police (ICP) in 1901. By 1906, he was acting Deputy Police Commissioner in Calcutta, aiding in the suppression of Bengal revolutionaries. In 1913, Tegart became chief of the newly created Intelligence Branch of the ICP, where he developed effective informer networks that led to the arrest and prosecution of Indian terrorists. By 1917, Tegart was an acknowledged counterterrorism specialist and his reputation had won him an appointment to the Rowlatt Committee, which was charged with investigating revolutionary crime in India.

Tegart was comfortable and effective in undercover roles and was a master of disguise. His skills were so keen that he often worked in the worst districts of Calcutta posing as a Sikh taxi driver. One ICP sergeant recalled seeing Tegart one evening in a red light district disguised as a Bengali gentleman and speaking to pimps and prostitutes. His confidence inspired fellow officers and informers alike. David Petrie—who served closely with Tegart and Denham in these early years and who later became Director of Intelligence for the Indian government—and subsequently Director-General of MI5—considered Tegart's recruiting and handling skills superior. Tegart kept the identities of his informers so secret that his colleagues often complained. He never took notes, preferring to maintain his files in his head. A former Indian colonial official described Tegart:

> Imperturbable in the face of danger which beset him for many years. . . . He was one of those men who radiate confidence, and the sight of Tegart driving through the streets of Calcutta . . . did more than almost anything else to keep up the morals [sic] of those who were fighting the revolutionary movement. Those who worked with him felt that somehow he could not fail.[1]

But when guile and tradecraft failed, Tegart was quite capable of resorting to violence and brutality. He especially liked to lead raids and handle his own interrogations, even as a senior officer. Owing largely to his employment of torture during interrogations, Tegart became one of the most hated men in India and survived several assassination attempts by Bengal radicals; in one instance an innocent British citizen was mistaken for Tegart and shot dead. In 1918, Tegart was implicated in a charge of police torture brought against the Bengal Police and publicly singled out for slapping and punching suspects and threatening to shoot a suspect with a revolver. These charges were never proven, but some fellow officers admitted to an investigating committee that Tegart's methods were "unconventional and daredevil," and that he was "not beyond circumventing the law to achieve results."[2]

The scandal and publicity accompanying this investigation may have contributed to Tegart's decision to take leave of absence from the ICP and report to England to join the ranks of the secret service in 1918. Tegart undertook assignments first in England and then in France, where he was rumored to have done exceptional service in counterespionage work against the Bolsheviks. By 1920, Tegart was considered one of the best and most experienced officers in the secret service. Tegart's cunning, aggressiveness, and unorthodox methods made him a favorite of Winston Churchill, who is believed to have personally recommended him for service in Ireland.[3]

G. C. Denham was Tegart's colleague in India and by 1920 was considered one of the top officers of the Indian Police. As Deputy Superintendent of CID in Calcutta between 1908 and 1911, Denham had survived an assassination attempt and traveled to the United States to provide testimony in the trial of a prominent Indian radical.[4]

Tegart and Denham reunited in Ireland in mid-summer 1920 to take charge of a new Secret Service Bureau comprising Irishmen recruited in England for Winter. The two were unimpressed with Winter's amateurish cloak-and-dagger escapades and instead urged him to set up a registry and file system similar to that kept by MI5 as a basis upon which to develop an organized targeting strategy. Personalities and ego came into play, and by November both Tegart and Denham had resigned their posts and departed Ireland.[5]

Things had come to a head about the same time as Collins launched his Bloody Sunday operation to assassinate British intelligence officers. In addition to the friction with Winter, therefore, Tegart and Denham may have departed Ireland for their own safety since Whitehall ordered several other operatives out of the country at that same time. Their superior undercover skills (and Tegart's near-paranoid security precautions) may have enabled them to elude IRA detection.

Following his work in Ireland, Tegart returned to India to become Commissioner of the Calcutta Police. In 1925, he met with Mahatma Gandhi to discuss the release of political prisoners. He was knighted the following year. On August 25, 1930, a member of the Bengal Revolutionary Party threw a bomb at Tegart as the latter was crossing Dalhousie Square. Though shaken by the attack, Tegart survived.[6]

Tegart retired shortly thereafter and became active in Anglo-Irish institutions. In 1933, he was awarded an honorary LLD from the most notable of these, Trinity College. It was ironic that Tegart, who had worked to crush the revolutionary Irish Republic, should receive this honorary degree in the company of several ardent Irish nationalists, including Dr.

Douglas Hyde, founder of the Gaelic League. Although an Ulsterman by birth, Tegart detested Lloyd George's partition of Ireland's six northern counties in 1921, and he had no sympathy for the fanatical ravings of rabid Ulster Unionists.[7]

In 1937, the Colonial Office asked Tegart to become Inspector-General of the Palestinian Police but he declined the offer. He ultimately did accompany MI5 Director-General David Petrie—his old colleague from ICP days—on a security survey to Palestine in 1938; Tegart stayed on to become consultant to the Palestinian Colonial Special Branch, which was then trying to cope with escalating Jewish and Arab violence that had resulted in the murder of dozens of British soldiers, police, and private citizens. In addition to providing training in interrogation, Tegart came up with the idea for a sixty-mile-long electric fence to seal off Palestine from Lebanon and Syria to hinder infiltration of Arab terrorists and weapons. The fence was bolstered by high-walled stone guard posts every few miles which were dubbed "Tegart fortresses." The entire project became known as "Tegart's Wall." Tegart survived another attempt on his life in Palestine in 1938.[8]

In 1939, just weeks before the outbreak of World War II, Tegart was instrumental in relaying an offer of assistance from the Zionist underground organization Hagana to the British Secret Service in common cause against Hitler. Tegart brokered an introduction of Hagana to an Admiralty NID officer in Romania; this led to an operational liaison between Hagana and Britain's wartime sabotage and special operations agency, SOE.[9]

June 1940, with the Nazi blitz pummeling Britain and fear of a German invasion gripping the country, Churchill tasked the secret service to investigate German fifth column activity in the neutral Irish Free State, and reputedly specifically requested Tegart for the assignment. SIS officer Valentine Vivian, who had served with Tegart in the ICP and who would become Deputy Director of SIS during World War II, personally asked Tegart to undertake the assignment. Tegart made several trips to Dublin, but the information he gathered was primarily on the loyalist dinner party circuit and these sources naturally were convinced that Nazi agents were working throughout the Free State preparing for an invasion; they also firmly believed that the (by now outlawed) IRA was coordinating with the German agents and were preparing to re-emerge from the shadows to launch a full-scale rebellion. Tegart's alarmist reports were just part of a stream of similarly exaggerated intelligence assessments flowing into 10 Downing Street in 1940 and apparently even Churchill found this too much to believe. While no fifth column activity could be substantiated, Irish fascists—the Blue Shirts—had made no secret of their admiration for Hitler. MI5 reportedly assembled a five-foot file on Irish suspects and was clearly prepared to orchestrate a massive roundup of Irish citizens, had Britain decided to occupy Ireland during the war. Tegart worked for the Ministry of Supply in the early days of the war and later became chief of the Intelligence Bureau for the Ministry of Food, combating illicit black market activities. In spite of heart disease and arthritis, Tegart remained on the job until his sudden death in April 1946.[10]

In 1923, Denham became inspector-general of the Singapore Police, and completed his police career there in 1925, subsequently joining MI5. In 1933, he became joint managing director and later chairman of the Anglo-Dutch Plantation in Java (later Indonesia). His private sector career was interrupted by World War II, when Denham appears to have returned to MI5.[11]

At the outbreak of the war, when Sir William Stevenson set up a joint British intelligence office in New York City, he established direct liaison communications with the White House. This offended FBI Director J. Edgar Hoover, who sent a note to MI5 Director-General David Petrie requesting that MI5 post a permanent wartime representative to Washington to work directly with the FBI. Petrie dispatched Denham on a fact-finding visit, and Denham recommended against Hoover's suggestion, believing that it would only confuse existing lines of coordination. Petrie informed Hoover that the locus for MI5-FBI coordination would continue to lie within Special Branch headquarters in London. Hoover, who had bullied presidents and congressmen for two decades, failed to bully Denham, and intelligence remained within intelligence channels during the war. Denham died suddenly in London on October 12, 1956, at age seventy-three.[12]

APPENDIX C

BRITISH INTELLIGENCE OFFICERS AND OTHER VICTIMS,
November 21, 1920

Name and Rank	Assignment / Likely Parent Organization	Result
1. Temp. Capt. Peter Ashmun Ames[a]	DDSB/DMI/MO4x	Shot/killed
2. Temp. Capt. George Bennett	DDSB/DMI/MO4x	Shot/killed
3. Temp. Capt. Donald Lewis MacLean	DDSB/DMI/MO4x	Shot/killed
4. Temp. Capt. John Fitzgerald[b]	DDSB/DMI/MO4x (ex-RIC)	Shot/killed
5. Temp. Capt. Leonard A. Price	DDSB/DMI/MO4x	Shot/killed
6. Temp. Capt. Henry R. Angliss[c]	DDSB/DMI/MO4x	Shot/killed
7. Lt. Col. C. M. C. Dowling	DDSB/DMI/MO4x	Shot/killed
8. Reserve Lt. R. G. Murray	DDSB/DMI/MO4x	Shot/wounded
8. Temp. Capt. C. R. Peel[d]	DDSB/DMI/MO4x	Escaped
9. Lt. Col. Hugh Montgomery, Royal Marines	DDSB/DMI/MO4x	Shot/killed
10. Ex-Lt. Leonard Aiden Wilde[e]	Possibly MI1c	Shot/killed
11. Temp. Capt. William Noble	DDSB/DMI/MO4x	Escaped
12. Capt. G. T. Baggally	Court-Martial Officer/ Legal Staff	Shot/killed
13. Capt. William F. Newbury	Court-Martial Officer/ Legal Staff	Shot/killed
14. Capt. Jocelyn Lee Hardy	Special Branch/ Home Intelligence (ex-MI5)	Escaped
15. Maj. William Lorraine "Tiny" King	Intelligence Officer/ K Company/Auxiliaries	Escaped
16. Maj. Frank M. H. Carew	DDSB/DMI/MO4x	Escaped

17. Temp. Capt. Robert D. Jeune	DDSB/MO4x	Escaped
18. Temp. Capt. Frederick Harper-Shove	DDSB/MO4x	Escaped
19. Maj. Callaghan	Unknown	Escaped
20. Col. Thomas J. Jennings	Unknown	Escaped
21. Maj. Patrick McCormack	Unknown (Ex–Royal Vet. Corps)	Shot/killed
22. Thomas Herbert Smith	Informer/civilian	Shot/killed

Mistaken Identity/Collateral Victims

23. Lt. Col. W. J. Woodcock	First Battalion, Lancashire Regiment	Shot/wounded
24. Capt. B. C. C. Keenlyside Adj.	First Battalion, Lancashire Regiment	Shot/wounded
25. Mr. John Caldow	Nephew of T. J. Smith	Shot/wounded
26. Capt. John S. Crawford	Army Service Corps	Detained/ released
27. Temp. Cadet Frank Garniss	Auxiliary Officer	Killed in firefight
28. Temp. Cadet Cecil A. Morris	Auxiliary Officer	Killed in firefight

---

a. Ex–Grenadier Guards, specially employed on General List, age thirty-two.
b. Fitzgerald was a former Detective Sergeant in the RIC. Upon joining the DDSB, he operated under the alias "Fitzpatrick." Age twenty-two.
c. Angliss operated under the alias "Paddy Mahon." Age twenty-seven.
d. AKA Carl Francis S. Ratsch. Age forty-four. The IRA mistakenly believed that "Charles Peel" was an operational alias used by this officer, but he had legally changed his name to the more Anglicized Charles Ratsch Peel in 1916.
e. Age thirty-nine.

NOTES

Foreword

1. The quote was attributed to the Roman statesman Terentius, but I later learned the more likely author was some anonymous disgruntled British soldier during World War II, which only serves to illustrate the universality of the experience and sentiment.
2. This quote may also be attributed to a Roman statesman, but if so his name was Yogi Berra.

Preface

1. Jack Lane, "Peter Hart Digs a Bigger Hole," Indymedia Ireland, 2009.
2. Brian P. Murphy, OSB, and Niall Meehan, "Troubled History" (Millstreet, Ireland: The Aubane Historical Society, 2008).

Chapter 1. England's Troubled Colony

1. J. C. Beckett, *The Making of Modern Ireland, 1603–1923* (London: Faber and Faber, 1966), 268–83.
2. Donnghadh O'Corrain, "Prehistoric and Early Christian Ireland," in *The Oxford History of Ireland*, ed. R. F. Foster (Oxford: Oxford University Press, 1989), 30–43.
3. Beckett, *Making of Modern Ireland*, 247–59.
4. Katherine Simms, "The Norman Invasion and the Gaelic Recovery," in *Oxford History of Ireland*, 44–87; William Irwin Thompson, *The Imagination of an Insurrection* (New York: Harper Colophon, 1967), 58–59.
5. Beckett, *Making of Modern Ireland*, 284, 376–77.
6. Ibid., 247–59.
7. David Neligan, *The Spy in the Castle* (London: Prendeville, 1999), 43–44, 179. To illustrate the multigenerational stigma attached to Irish informers, Neligan relates the story of an old policeman who once said of a colleague on the force,

"Sure he couldn't be good, his great grandfather was reared in the Informer's Home."

8. Beckett, *Making of Modern Ireland*, 285.
9. Ibid., 334–50; "Peel's Cabinet Memorandum, November 1, 1845," in *The Age of Peel*, ed. Norman Gash (London: Edward Arnold, 1968), 125–28.
10. Beckett, *Making of Modern Ireland*.
11. Ibid., 358–62. During the American Civil War, the IRB encouraged Irish immigrants to enlist in both the Union and Confederate armies with the aim of cultivating a secret Fenian army of trained combat veterans. The Irish served with distinction on both sides in the war between the states, and Thomas Francis Meagher—one of the leaders of the 1848 Rising—ascended to command the famous Irish Brigade of the Union Army of the Potomac. This brigade won glory for its suicidal frontal attacks at Bloody Lane in the Battle of Antietam, Maryland, in September 1862 and again two months later in its assault on Marye's Heights at Fredericksburg, Virginia. The ill-advised and unsuccessful assault from upstate New York against British border outposts in Ontario in 1867 was carried out by IRB Civil War veterans.
12. "Outline of a Report on the Irish Question to the Communist Educational Association of German Workers in London, December 16, 1867," quoted in Karl Marx and Frederick Engels, *Ireland and the Irish Question*, ed. R. Dixon (Moscow: Progress, 1971), 126–39.
13. Andrew Cook, *M: MI5's First Spymaster* (Brimscombe Port, Stroud, Gloucestershire: Tempus, 2004), 30–46.
14. *London Daily News*, April 14, 1914.
15. Beckett, *Making of Modern Ireland*, 436.

Chapter 2. Colonial Security Policy

1. Neligan, *Spy in the Castle*, 172–73.
2. Imperial War Museum, General Hugh Jeudwine Papers, 72/82/2, "A Record of the Rebellion in Ireland 1920–1921 and the Part Played by the Army in Dealing with It," Reproduced in *British Intelligence in Ireland 1920—1921: The Final Reports*, ed. Peter Hart, Irish Narratives, vol. 2 (Cork: Cork University Press, 2002), 45, hereinafter cited as Hart, ed., *Army Record of the Rebellion*.
3. Tom Bowden, "Ireland: Decay of Control," in *Revolt to Revolution: Studies in the 19th and 20th Century European Experience*, eds. Michael Elliott-Bateman, John Ellis, and Tom Bowden (Manchester: Manchester University Press, 1974), 214.
4. Ibid., 215–16.
5. David Stafford, *Churchill & Secret Service* (London: Abacus, 1997), 17–23.
6. Cook, *M: MI5's First Spymaster*, 30–31.
7. Ibid., 35–36.
8. Ibid., 120–28; Richard B. Spence, *Trust No One* (Los Angeles: Feral House, 2003), 268–69.
9. Cook, *M: MI5's First Spymaster*, 149–50.
10. Sir William Robertson, *From Private to Field Marshal* (London: Constable, 1921), 48–52.
11. Churchill's motivation for involvement in intelligence matters grew out of his own experience during the Boer War, during which he personally undertook dangerous "secret service" scouting missions behind enemy lines.
12. Cook, *M: MI5's First Spymaster*, 144–52, 231; Christopher Andrew, *Defence of the Realm* (London: Allen Lane, 2009), 7–8.

13. Andrew, *Defence of the Realm*, 25–26.
14. Bruce Page, David Leitch, and Phillip Knightly, *The Philby Conspiracy* (Garden City, NY: Doubleday, 1968), 109–37. While this book deals with a later episode of British intelligence history, the authors devote an entire chapter to the recruiting and staffing practices and casual attitudes about those practices that prevailed in both MI5 and SIS from their earliest days up to the outbreak of World War II. The authors contend that these traditions contained weaknesses and vulnerabilities that made it relatively easy for Russian spy H. A. R. "Kim" Philby to secure a career appointment in the British Secret Service and flourish there, undetected by MI5, for two decades. This book remains one of the most enlightening essays on the MI5 and SIS personnel practices in the early days of those services.
15. Ibid.; Andrew, *Defence of the Realm*, 23. As Page et al. point out, it was not unusual for MI5 and MI6 officers to rotate assignments even up to the beginning of the Second World War.
16. Andrew, *Defence of the Realm*, 20.
17. Ibid., 58. Surprisingly, the formal relationship between MI5 and Special Branch was not officially codified by the Home Office until 1984.
18. Ibid., 85.
19. Cook, *M: MI5's First Spymaster*, 231; Andrew, *Defence of the Realm*, 64. By 1940, MI9 had morphed into a special operation unit focused on devising escape and evasion routes and tools for British servicemen captured by the Germans. MI9 devised myriad clever technical aids, including maps printed on the inside linings of ties or sewn into the linings of jackets, inks and paper for forging travel documents, and dyes for converting military uniforms into civilian dress. Much of these materials were concealed in Red Cross parcels funneled to British POWs.
20. Andrew, *Defence of the Realm*, 82; Nigel West, *MI5: British Security Service Operations, 1909–1945* (London: Triad/Panther, 1983), 39–48. Until the publication of Andrew's 2009 "authorized history," West's 1983 history of MI5 was the standard. While West portrays a friendly rivalry between Kell and Basil Thomson, Andrew provides evidence of much bitterness between MI5 and Special Branch at that time.
21. Andrew, *Defence of the Realm*, 84–85; Christopher Andrew, *Her Majesty's Secret Service: The Making of the British Intelligence Community* (New York: Viking Penguin, 1986), 191.
22. Sir Basil Thomson, *The Scene Changes* (New York: Doubleday, 1937), 252–397; Andrew, *Defence of the Realm*, 106–9.
23. Andrew, *Her Majesty's Secret Service*, 139–40. See also Ormonde Winter, *Winter's Tale: An Autobiography* (London: Richards, 1955), 184–221. Among the officers who would later reemerge during the Anglo-Irish War was Captain Cecil Aylmer Cameron, an army intelligence officer with a rather checkered past. While serving as an artillery officer in India in 1909, he was introduced to his future wife, Ruby Shawe, by fellow artillery man Ormonde Winter, who would later play a key role in British intelligence operations against Collins. While living in Scotland the following year, both Cameron and his spouse were arrested and charged with insurance fraud involving an alleged missing necklace. Winter took extended leave to come to Cameron's aid, spending several weeks interviewing witnesses who might exonerate Cameron. Despite these efforts, both were convicted and Cameron served two years in prison for his alleged

complicity in the crime. In his autobiography Winter argued that Cameron was wrongly convicted and concluded that Ruby Cameron, a morphine addict, had been living a lifestyle beyond the means of her husband and that she was quite detached from reality if not in fact mentally unbalanced.

Nevertheless, as the son of a distinguished officer, Cameron managed to resume his army career after his release and was accepted into an intelligence billet with the Army Field Intelligence Corps upon the outbreak of war with Germany. Cameron established a collection unit, C1, at Folkstone, U.K., that interviewed and recruited Belgian refugees arriving in Britain via neutral Holland aboard the cross-channel ferry, and C1 reportedly enjoyed considerable success during the first three years of the war. As Christopher Andrew notes, Cameron's activities overlapped with those of MI1c, compelling Mansfield Cumming to demand a geographical delineation of responsibilities. According to Winter, Cameron made a number of espionage forays behind enemy lines in Belgium dressed as a Catholic priest. In 1920, Cameron was posted to Ireland as a case officer with the DMI's Silent Section, MO4x, and soon would assume responsibility for a similar concept on Winter's behalf—the recruitment of Irishmen living in Britain to undertake secret service missions against the IRA. Following the Anglo-Irish War, Cameron's subsequent appointment as military attaché to Riga was overruled by Prime Minister Ramsey McDonald on the basis of Cameron's prior prison record, and the unhappy officer shot himself in his quarters.

24. Eunan O'Halpin, "British Intelligence in Ireland, 1914–1921," in *The Missing Dimension*, eds. Christopher Andrew and David Dilks (Urbana: University of Illinois Press, 1984), 55–70.
25. Ibid.; Bowden, "Ireland: The Impact of Terrorism," in *Revolt to Revolution*, ed. Elliott-Bateman et al., 237.
26. Bowden, "Ireland: Decay of Control," in *Revolt to Revolution*, ed. Elliot-Bateman et al., 215–16.
27. O'Halpin, "British Intelligence in Ireland," 70.
28. Andrew, *Defence of the Realm*, 107–9; David Stafford, *Churchill & Secret Service*, 102. During the period of the Irish Revolution, 1916–1923, Churchill served successively as minister of munitions, secretary of state for war, and secretary of state for the colonies, but throughout most of this period he was also a key member of the government's secret committee on intelligence, and was an ardent supporter of a strong domestic and foreign intelligence capability.
29. Andrew, *Defence of the Realm*, 87–90; James Mackay, *Michael Collins: A Life* (Edinburgh and London: Mainstream, 1996), 49. As director of naval intelligence at the Naval Intelligence Division (DNI/NID), Hall was in charge of the supersecret foreign cable and signals intercept branch ("Room 40") of the Government Codes & Ciphers School. Between August 1914 and April 1916, NID intercepted thirty-two secret cables between the German embassy in Washington, D.C., and Berlin (unbeknownst to President Woodrow Wilson and without the permission of the then-neutral U.S. government), proving collaboration between the German embassy and Irish Nationalists. As noted, when Sir Roger Casement was arrested in April 1916 for his role in organizing British and Irish POWs to fight with the German Army on the Western Front, Casement confessed to the charge during a joint interrogation by Admiral Hall, Basil Thomson, and Major Frank Hall of MI5's Ireland Desk. In addition, the rattled Casement soon revealed the plans for the impending rising. Thus, Blinker Hall

was the only member of the British Intelligence Community who possessed conclusive HUMINT *and* SIGINT information of the rising. Rather than rush this vital intelligence to the cabinet and the prime minister, however, the DNI withheld the intelligence because Hall hoped the Irish Volunteers would be crushed and that repressive measures he personally favored would be introduced in Ireland. In so doing, he was single-handedly responsible for one of the greatest intelligence failures in history. In withholding information about the conspiracy, he unwittingly opened the door to events that would lead to the Anglo-Irish War and eventual independence for the Irish people he despised. It would be the first of many British intelligence failures over the next few years.

30. Andrew, *Defence of the Realm*, 109.
31. Ibid., 116.
32. Sir Basil Thomson, *The Story of Scotland Yard* (Garden City, NJ: Country Life Press, 1935), 322. Scotland House was an annex located across the street from New Scotland Yard—the headquarters of the London Metropolitan Police on the Thames embankment. The foundation of New Scotland Yard was laid in 1875 and by 1890 all divisions of the Metropolitan Police had moved there. After being named Director of Home Intelligence in 1919, Basil Thomson appropriated office space at Scotland House for his expanded intelligence operations.
33. House of Commons (HC) Debate, 23 March 1920, vol. 127, c238.
34. Andrew, *Defence of the Realm*, 117.
35. Ibid.
36. Richard James Aldrich, *Intelligence and the War against Japan* (Cambridge: Cambridge University Press, 2000), 21.
37. Andrew, *Defence of the Realm*, 118; Stafford, *Churchill & Secret Service*, 107. Both Andrew and Stafford state that while Churchill was busy promoting Basil Thomson to the top domestic intelligence post, he was at the same time "appalled" at the reduction of MI5's resources and allegedly argued in vain against it. As Andrew points out, however, Churchill also favored merging NID, Special Branch, MI5, and MI1c into a large single national espionage service but realized that development of such a large central organization could take years. What Churchill sought, but did not get, was a British Central Intelligence Agency.
38. Stafford, *Churchill & Secret Service*, 104–5.
39. HC Debate, 19 August 1919, vol. 119, cc2117–18; Julian Putkowski, "A2 and the Labour Movement," in Lobster, *Journal of Parapolitics* no. 29, 1995, 2–8, and no. 30, 1996, 13–16.

Chapter 3. The Irish Nationalist

1. Mackay, *Michael Collins*, 132. Collins once reportedly told Ned Broy, his double agent inside G Division, "I am a builder, not a destroyer. I get rid of people only when they hinder my work."
2. Many contemporary professional intelligence services rely heavily upon extensive psychological screening and personality indicator tests in the hiring process and in the ongoing professional career development of case officers, analysts, scientists, and administrative specialists. The assumption is that such profiles are key to identifying reliable team players, and to weeding out misfits and those mentally unsuited for the stressful demands of intelligence work. Unfortunately, that assumption is often based upon a preferred personality

profile that is appealing to the psychologists–gate keepers, who themselves are experienced neither in the rigors of field operations nor in meeting high-pressure analytical deadlines day in and day out. Had Michael Collins been screened in this manner, he would never have been selected to lead any Irish government post, much less the sensitive GHQ intelligence staff.

3. Mackay, *Michael Collins*, 147–48; T. Ryle Dwyer, *The Squad and the Intelligence Operations of Michael Collins* (Cork: Mercier, 2005), 206; Tim Pat Coogan, *Michael Collins: The Man Who Made Ireland* (Boulder, CO: Roberts Rinehart, 1996), 133–34. In making the decision to grant Doran's widow and three small children the pension, Collins reportedly remarked, "The poor little devils need the money."

4. Mackay, *Michael Collins*, 15–26.

5. Ibid., 36–42. As Mackay points out, some biographers have suggested that Collins accepted the lower-paying job at Guaranty Trust Company in 1915 on orders from the IRB, which allegedly wanted him to gain further experience in high finance. The notion is not supported by facts nor is it credible, for Collins had already accumulated nearly ten years of expert experience in banking, accounting, stock trading, and finance by the time he joined Guaranty Trust Company.

6. Coogan, *Michael Collins*, 13. Coogan relates that as a youngster Michael Collins wrote a letter of admiration to de Wet and, after the British called for a truce with the IRA in 1921, de Wet answered him with a note of congratulation.

7. Cook, *M: MI5's First Spymaster*, 33–39.

8. John Devoy, *Recollections of an Irish Rebel* (Shannon: Irish University Press, 1969), 382; T. Desmond Williams, "The Irish Republican Brotherhood," in *Secret Societies in Ireland*, ed. T. Desmond Williams (Dublin: Gill and MacMillan, 1973), 138–49. Devoy, an original IRB member, had gained his military expertise in the French Foreign Legion before joining the British Army, where he was successful in recruiting Irish soldiers into the brotherhood during the early 1860s. In 1866, he was arrested and sentenced to fifteen years but served only five. Upon his release in 1871 he emigrated to the United States. There he resumed his secret activities and rose to become the most influential leader of Clan na Gael. Earning his living as a journalist for the *New York Herald*, Devoy made influential contacts in the U.S. Congress and in the Irish American community. He raised funds to support Fenian subversive activity in Britain and Ireland for the rest of his life, including large amounts of money to support the 1916 Easter Rising.

9. Joseph M. Curran, "The Decline and Fall of the IRB," *Eire-Ireland*, Earrach, 1975, 14–23. Curran provides a fine analysis of the IRB in transition between the mid-nineteenth century and the early years of the twentieth century. Among the Young Turks recruited by Clarke was Sean MacDiarmada, who rose to become President of the IRB Supreme Council and who led the organization during the 1916 Easter Rising. MacDiarmada was among the ringleaders executed by the British after the failed rising. Other members of the revitalized IRB after 1906 included the celebrated poet William Butler Yeats and an obscure forty-year-old Protestant railway ditch digger from the north Dublin slums named John Cassidy, who would later become famous to the world as the playwright Sean O'Casey. O'Casey's early plays and his six-volume autobiography provide eyewitness accounts of the turmoil in Ireland during the Troubles.

10. Mackay, *Michael Collins*, 36; Jim Maher, *Harry Boland: A Biography* (Dublin: Mercier, 1998). The IRB's secret oath of allegiance to the president of the Organiza-

tion's supreme council would prove extremely significant for Collins in January 1919, when de Valera appointed him cabinet member (minister of finance) in the revolutionary Dail Eireann government. Although technically de Valera had been elected to the position of "first minister" (*Priombe Aire*) of the Dail, he was popularly referred to as "the president" and did nothing to discourage it, even though the presidential title was only formally approved after the truce with Britain in 1921. Shortly after receiving his ministerial appointment from de Valera, in January 1919, Collins was also secretly elected president of the IRB Supreme Council. Thus, the Irish revolutionary government would have two presidents: de Valera—an openly elected member of Sinn Fein representing the Dail government and seeking recognition for the Irish Republic, and Collins—the militant IRB chief recognized as the de facto president of the same Irish Republic by a significant number of the Irish Volunteers who owed their first allegiance to the Fenian Brotherhood. So it was that Collins became the most powerful man in Ireland during the revolution. Although he worked actively for de Valera's election and publicly deferred to de Valera's political authority, Collins controlled all intelligence and was the architect of the counterintelligence war against the British Secret Service and of the guerrilla military strategy against British armed forces. This situation created considerable tension and jealousy within the revolutionary Dail cabinet and led, ultimately, to a bitter feud with de Valera, Minister of Defence Cathal Brugha (Charles Burgess), and their non-IRB faction. It would also result in tragedy for Ireland during its destructive civil war.

11. Coogan, *Michael Collins*, 40–41; Constantine Fitzgibbon, *The Life and Times of Eamon De Valera* (New York: Macmillan, 1971), 15, 53.

12. Stafford, *Churchill & Secret Service*, 156–57. The German Gymnasium, located at the back of St. Pancras Underground Station and a short distance from King's Cross Station, was the site of the 1908 London Olympic Games and still stands today. In 1914 it not only served as a meeting site for Collins's Irish Volunteer company, but it had long served as a gathering spot and social center for expatriate Germans in London. The premises were undoubtedly high on the MI5–Special Branch watch list as they labored to identify and register German aliens and suspected spies prior to the outbreak of World War I. Whether or not the IRB or the Irish Volunteers conducted secret business with German government agents there in the months leading up to the Easter Rising is a matter of speculation, but it is quite improbable that the Irish Volunteers marching back and forth with wooden rifles at the gymnasium escaped the attention of the Secret Service Bureau, Special Branch, or German intelligence agents, for that matter.

13. Padraig H. Pearse, "From a Hermitage," in *The Collected Works of Padraig H. Pearse: Political Writings and Speeches* (Dublin: Phoenix, 1922), 147.

14. James Connolly, "The Ballot or the Barricades," *Irish Worker*, October 24, 1914.

15. P. O Cathasaigh (Sean O'Casey), *The Story of the Irish Citizen Army* (Dublin: Maunsel, 1919), 1–5, 51–52; C. Desmond Greaves, *The Life and Times of James Connolly* (New York: International, 1971), 377, 401–2. While justifiably a revered national hero, Connolly's alliance with the Irish Volunteers has mystified his most doctrinaire admirers, who are hard-pressed to explain how Ireland's foremost militant Marxist surrendered his own program to a cabal of shop owners, poets, and academics in 1916. Connolly's legacy extended to the post-1923 IRA, which was led for years by communists and socialists with neither the pragma-

tism, nor the strength and influence, to make any progress in reuniting the six counties of Northern Ireland with the Irish Republic. By the time the Catholic student human rights movement erupted in Northern Ireland in 1968, the Official IRA was dominated by aging, overweight, and rather harmless armchair Marxists who were incapable of sustaining any serious opposition to a dangerously neo-fascist Stormont government (Stormont, a suburb of Belfast, was the seat of the Northern Ireland parliament). They were equally ineffectual regarding the extremist Protestant paramilitary gangs that attacked Catholic neighborhoods in Ulster. While this sectarian violence was spinning out of control, a new generation of Young Turks, the Provisional IRA, or "Provos," split off from the Official IRA in 1969 to fill the vacuum. The Provos, while promoting a democratic socialist plan for Ireland, were much less doctrinaire, more pragmatic, and far deadlier than their erstwhile Marxist associates. While the Provos built IEDs and mounted ambushes against the British and Ulster security forces, the "Officials" spent most of their time distributing an endless stream of talking points and turgid propaganda dictated from Moscow. If anything, the Official IRA's Marxist rhetoric served London's goals admirably by allowing the British to point out that the IRA was a communist threat on their doorstep, using this "Red Scare" as a justification for its extended military occupation of Ulster. Meanwhile, naive Americans who sympathized with the Republican cause did not, generally speaking, discern the difference between the Provisional IRA and the Official IRA, contributing huge amounts of money to the coffers of each.

16. Coogan, *Michael Collins*, 39–40.
17. T. Ryle Dwyer, *Michael Collins: The Man Who Won the War* (Dublin: Mercier, 1990), 23; M. R. D. Foot, "The Irish Experience," in *Revolt to Revolution*, Elliot-Bateman et al., 179.
18. Dwyer, *Michael Collins*, 24–25.
19. Ibid.
20. Coogan, *Michael Collins*, 42. De Valera's defiant countenance, captured in a series of photos immediately after his surrender to the British Army, helped him achieve hero status that catapulted his political career. But there were rumors among some veterans of the Third Battalion that de Valera acted panicky and may even have suffered a nervous breakdown during the weeklong fighting. No definitive evidence of this has ever surfaced but if true, de Valera succeeded magnificently in preventing this from becoming public knowledge.
21. Maher, *Harry Boland*, 42–45; Fitzgibbon, *Life and Times of Eamon De Valera*, 55; Coogan, *Michael Collins*, 56.
22. Coogan, *Michael Collins*, 54; Peter Hart, *Mick: The Real Michael Collins* (New York: Viking, 2005), 139–40.
23. Hart, *Mick*, 105.
24. Coogan, *Michael Collins*, 54–57; Mackay, *Michael Collins*, 63–74.
25. O'Halpin, "British Intelligence in Ireland," 61.

Chapter 4. The Phoenix

1. Only the less important internees were paroled at this time. Those considered more dangerous, like de Valera, remained in prison and were not released until mid-June of 1917.
2. Hart, *Mick*, 139–40.
3. Ruth Dudley Edwards, *Patrick Pearse: The Triumph of Failure* (New York: Taplinger 1977), 295; Maher, *Harry Boland*, 51. One of the first acts of the released

prisoners, including Harry Boland, was to sign a proclamation addressed to the president and Congress of the United States declaring the right of the Irish people to defend themselves from external aggression. The proclamation included a quote from President Woodrow Wilson's recent communiqué to Russia that said, "No people must be forced under a sovereignty under which it does not wish to live." The proclamation was hand-carried to the White House and to Capitol Hill by a trusted IRB courier. As events showed, Wilson was a thorough Anglophile and steadfast admirer of British socialism, and he showed no sympathy for the Irish cause. His celebrated public advocacy for self-determination for small, oppressed nations at the end of the First World War did not therefore apply to any colonial possession of the British Empire. Because of his socialist proclivities, Wilson's application of a double standard with regard to Ireland has somehow escaped the attention of most American academics and does not appear in U.S. history textbooks. But it did not go unnoticed by Irish Americans.

4. Ernie O'Malley, *On Another Man's Wound* (Boulder, CO: Roberts Rinehart, 1999), 80–120; Michael Hopkinson, *The Irish War of Independence* (Montreal and Kingston: McGill Queens University, 2002), 116–17. O'Malley also undertook exceedingly dangerous assignments for Collins, including one secret mission to London posing as a British Army officer. When the war began, O'Malley was involved in numerous close-quarters shoot-outs with members of the RIC, the Black and Tans, Auxiliaries, and British regulars.

5. Hart, *Mick*, 141–50.

6. Ibid.; Maher, *Harry Boland*, 58.

7. Sinn Fein made several efforts to get an audience with President Wilson. In December 1918, a delegation that included Collins traveled to London for that purpose; Sinn Fein also sent delegates to the Versailles Peace Conference. Wilson refused to meet with them. Despite this, de Valera never abandoned his faith in the Wilsonian idea that smaller, weaker nations should enjoy self-determination. While serving as prime minister of the Irish Free State in 1932, de Valera was chairman of the League of Nations, and he attended the League's conferences every year until 1940, by which time the League's failure as a peacekeeping body had been amply demonstrated with the outbreak of World War II.

8. Hart, *Mick*, 154–56.

9. Mulcahy as quoted in Ulick O'Connor, *Michael Collins and the Troubles* (New York: W. W. Norton, 1996), 127. Collins was aware of the backroom maneuvering against him. Ever impatient with the bureaucratic process and decision by committee, he reportedly rushed into the meeting room in characteristic fashion and snapped, "Let's get on with it then."

10. Pax O Faolain to Uinseann Mac Eoin, in *Survivors*, ed. Uinseann Mac Eoin (Dublin: Argenta, 1980), 136; Mackay, *Michael Collins*, 87.

11. MacEoin, "The London Associates of Michael Collins," in *Survivors*, 400–10; Paul McMahon, *British Spies & Irish Rebels: British Intelligence and Ireland, 1916-1945* (Woodbridge, UK: Boydell Press, 2008), 23–24. According to evidence uncovered by McMahon, MI5's Major Frank Hall and Special Branch collaborated to install a powerful Dictaphone machine in the conference room to eavesdrop on the backroom negotiations during the Irish Convention.

12. Dwyer, *Michael Collins*, 62. By 1920, Collins relinquished the position of Adjutant General to Geroid O'Sullivan, concentrating his efforts on intelligence,

organization, and finance. Using the shorthand established for senior members of the IRA General Headquarters Staff, Collins signed all of his army correspondence "DI" for Director of Intelligence.

13. Mackay, *Michael Collins*, 87.
14. Coogan, *Michael Collins*, 39. Members of the Fianna had served with the Volunteers in 1916.
15. Cook, *M: MI5's First Spymaster*, 30–31; Stafford, *Churchill & Secret Service*, 36–38.
16. Dwyer, *The Squad*, 13–15; Dwyer, *Michael Collins*, 62–76.
17. Neligan, *Spy in the Castle*, 71–72; Dan Breen, *My Fight for Irish Freedom* (Dublin: Anvil, 1981), 129. Liam Tobin reportedly had a natural talent for organizing files and collating and analyzing information. With a gift for making sense of even the most trivial details, Tobin became adept at developing an overall picture of British movements and intentions. Daniel Breen, one of the IRA's toughest customers, called Tobin and Cullen "daredevils" and "brave to a fault."
18. Neligan, *Spy in the Castle*, 73–74; Dwyer, *Michael Collins*, 76; O'Malley, *On Another Man's Wound*, 94. In his memoirs, originally published in 1936, O'Malley related that Collins frequently used a room in the cellar beneath St. Ita's School in Dublin to carry out secret organizational and intelligence work. The door to this room was reportedly very difficult for any casual visitor to locate. IRA GHQ staff referred to this safe site as the Dug Out.
19. Frank O'Connor, *The Big Fellow* (Dublin: Clonmore Press, 1965), 63; Mackay, *Michael Collins*, 118–19.
20. Mackay, *Michael Collins*, 110, 130.
21. Hopkinson, *Irish War of Independence*, 147–48.
22. Sean MacBride to MacEoin, in *Survivors*, 112–14. MacBride became a constitutional lawyer and defended many IRA prisoners in the 1920s and 1930s. He stepped onto the world stage as Minister of Foreign Affairs for the Irish Republic, and also through his associations with pro-Communist and left-leaning pacifist organizations, including Amnesty International. He was awarded the Nobel Peace Prize in 1974 for his work on human rights, but his leftist sympathies were undoubtedly the defining factor for the Nobel Committee.

Chapter 5. Revolution in Earnest

1. Hart, *Mick*, 159–66.
2. Ibid.
3. Ibid.
4. Dwyer, *Michael Collins*, 47.
5. Maher, *Harry Boland*, 56; Dwyer, *The Squad*, 11–12; Dwyer, *Michael Collins*, 16; Mackay, *Michael Collins*, 90–91. According to Maher's account, a Galway man named Joseph Dowling had been arrested on April 12, 1918, by the RIC acting on an NID tip that Dowling had been landed from a German submarine. The police investigation showed that Dowling had joined Sir Roger Casement's "German Brigade" in 1916 after being captured on the Western Front. While apparently this much was true, there was no evidence of Sinn Fein complicity. Sinn Fein reportedly knew nothing about Dowling and had nothing to do with his strange arrival off the west coast. Dwyer states that it was Blinker Hall, Director of Naval Intelligence, who fabricated the German Plot from this single incident and deliberately blew it out of proportion. Hall misled the cabinet by withholding the details from his superiors.

As mentioned earlier, it was also Hall who, in league with Special Branch's Basil Thomson, fomented an alarmist "Red Menace" campaign in England following Germany's surrender, resulting in Thomson's appointment as Britain's National Intelligence Director at the Home Office in January 1919. The Crown did not need any special justification to arrest the dissidents, but the fabrication of this so-called German Plot provided Downing Street with sufficient window dressing to satisfy Washington and Woodrow Wilson, a hopeless Anglophile who had been similarly manipulated by British Intelligence on previous occasions.

6.   A cutout is someone engaged in passing sensitive information or communications between two parties to protect the identities, affiliations, or locations of both parties. The cutout may be a paid agent of an intelligence service, an unpaid volunteer sympathetic to the government of the intelligence service, or a co-optee who has been compelled through any number of mechanisms to assist the intelligence service. In this case, an openly acknowledged Sinn Fein member was approached by the police officer in hopes that the Sinn Fein member would make contact with leadership of the underground IRA. It was safer for both parties to use a cutout at that early stage of the relationship, before the police officer's loyalties could be vetted, his facts checked, and before Collins could develop the relationship and train the policeman in clandestine tradecraft that would protect his identity and conceal his sub-rosa activities.

Cutouts are also used in false-flag operations, where the objective of the intelligence service is to fool the access agent into believing he/she is sharing information with one party or government, when in fact it is being shared with another party or government whom the agent would ordinarily have nothing to do with. For example, a hotel employee working at a British-owned loyalist hotel in Dublin in 1920 might hold strongly pro-British sympathies and would never consider revealing information to the IRA. That employee might have important access to the hotel registry or to the travel schedules of senior British officers billeted at the hotel. Rather than try to recruit the pro-British employee to aid the IRA—an effort with little chance of success—the IRA might employ a cutout to pose as a British businessman or perhaps as a neutral newspaper reporter. The desired result of such an operation would be that in the course of his daily conversations with the cutout, the hotel employee would become an unwitting IRA agent, passing sensitive information.

7.   Mackay, *Michael Collins*, 123.
8.   Neligan, *Spy in the Castle*, 43.
9.   Ibid., 61. The dramatic reduction in force of the G Division was apparently part of the same government cost-saving campaign that hamstrung the RIC's Crimes Special Branch in the immediate postwar period, as detailed in chapter 2.
10. Coogan, *Michael Collins*, 62, 78. As Coogan observes, the civil service in Ireland was dominated by Protestant sectarianism and freemasonry. Membership in the Freemasons was also considered for many years to be a satisfactory employment vetting tool for admission into the British Secret Service. Since freemasonry requires a secret oath—something Roman Catholics are forbidden to take—the British used it as a mechanism to keep their predominantly Catholic southern Irish subjects from obtaining the most sensitive or important civil service appointments.
11. Mackay, *Michael Collins*, 128. Eamon Broy later claimed that he convinced Collins that the only way to deal with G Division and the RIC would be assassination.

12. Coogan, *Michael Collins*, 78–79.
13. Maher, *Harry Boland*, 56. According to Maher, Kavanagh's note was passed by Gay to Harry Boland, and thence to Collins.
14. Ibid., 57–58.
15. Coogan, *Michael Collins*, 75.
16. Hart, *Mick*, 207.
17. Broy's procedure of passing carbon copies of classified G Division reports to GHQ intelligence staff was expeditious but extremely poor tradecraft, even by the standards of 1918. This would later come back to haunt him and Collins.
18. Neligan, *Spy in the Castle*, 122; Dwyer, *The Squad*, 63, 213; Mackay, *Michael Collins*, 143; and Dwyer, *Michael Collins*, 70. Neligan was the first to name the other police officers that were on the IRA payroll in his 1968 memoirs. In addition to these recruited assets among the police forces, it has been alleged that numerous street constables knew Michael Collins by sight but deliberately turned a blind eye to his frequent comings and goings in the city center. The fact that Collins rode around Dublin on a bicycle with impunity for nearly three years lends credibility to the allegation.
19. Mackay, *Michael Collins*, 123; Neligan, *Spy in the Castle*, 78; Dwyer, *The Squad*, 212; Coogan, *Michael Collins*, 76.
20. Dan Gleeson to MacEoin, in *Survivors*, 262.
21. Beckett, *Making of Modern Ireland*, 445. The old Irish Parliamentary (Home Rule) Party won just six seats, signaling its decline.
22. Mackay, *Michael Collins*, 109–11. At 7:40 p.m. on February 3, 1919, Michael Collins and Harry Boland, assisted by IRB members from Sam Maguire's London Circle, effected the escape of de Valera, IRB leader Sean McGarry, and another Republican prisoner from Lincoln Jail using a duplicate key made from a wax impression. The IRB hid de Valera in Manchester for three weeks, after which they smuggled the prime minister into Ireland. Collins and his intelligence staff became somewhat expert in jail breaking, and successfully freed several Sinn Fein and IRB men from both British and Irish jails over the next two years.
23. Thomson, *The Scene Changes*, 323–24.
24. Maher, *Harry Boland*, 80–82.

Chapter 6. In the Shadow of Gunmen

1. Breen, *My Fight for Irish Freedom*, 31.
2. Hopkinson, *Irish War of Independence*, xiv.
3. Ibid., 51.
4. Peter Hart, *The IRA at War, 1916–1923* (London: Oxford University Press, 2003), 112. Considering that the Irish Volunteers numbered about sixteen thousand men before the Easter Rising and that less than one tenth of that number showed up for muster in April 1916, this was a remarkable achievement by Michael Collins, Ernie O'Malley, and other IRA organizers. It also illustrates the massive shift in popular sentiment from 1916 to 1919.
5. Hopkinson, *Irish War of Independence*, 115–28; Breen, *My Fight for Irish Freedom*. In an interview with Radio-Television Eireann (RTE) near the end of his life, Daniel Breen said of Michael Collins, "I loved him and would gladly have laid down my life for him. It would have been a small price to pay for Irish freedom." But in his memoirs, first published in 1924, Breen strongly criticized IRA GHQ for being lukewarm to the guerrilla warfare strategy, and he accused Dail Eireann politicians of "running away" from it.

6. Desmond Ryan, *Sean Treacy and the Third Tipperary Brigade* (London: Alliance, 1945), 87.
7. Mackay, *Michael Collins*, 94.
8. O'Connor, *Michael Collins*, 141; Coogan, *Michael Collins*, 79.
9. Connie Neenan to MacEoin, in *Survivors*, 238–39.
10. Dorothy Macardle, *The Irish Republic* (New York: Wolfhound, 1999), 279–80, 297; Hopkinson, *Irish War of Independence*, 167.
11. Breen, *My Fight for Irish Freedom*, 54–65; Richard Abbott, *Police Casualties in Ireland, 1919–1923* (Cork: Mercier, 2000), 67.
12. Darrell Figgis, *Recollections of the Irish War* (New York: Doubleday, 1927), 266; Hopkinson, *Irish War of Independence*, 40.
13. *The Times*, October 16, 1954.
14. Coogan, *Michael Collins*, 83. Coogan and Mackay agree that this agent's name was "Merin." Hopkinson seems to agree, but he spells it "Merrin." According to Dwyer, her name was "Merlin." Hart says it was "Mernin," as does McDonagh. All agree on her function as confidential secretary for Lieutenant Colonel Steven S. Hill-Dillon, senior DMI/MO4x officer based at Parkgate Street Barracks, Dublin. Mernin's encoding and decoding work was actually performed in a secure space inside Dublin Castle, however.
15. Mackay, *Michael Collins*, 125–26.
16. John Borgonovo, ed., *Florence and Josephine O'Donoghue's War of Independence* (Dublin and Portland, OR: Irish Academic Press, 2006), 110–24.
17. David Neligan, who was recruited by Collins in May 1920 to spy on G Division, and who later succeeded in penetrating the Secret Service Branch at Dublin Castle, titled his memoirs *The Spy in the Castle*, but he was clearly not the first IRA-controlled agent working there, nor was he necessarily providing the most critical intelligence information.
18. Neligan, *Spy in the Castle*, 98.
19. An access agent is a person with either direct access to information of interest to an intelligence service or with access to an organization, group, network, or business of interest to an intelligence service, or with access to another person/target of interest.
20. Dwyer, *Michael Collins*, 100.
21. Coogan, *Michael Collins*, 81, 382; Mackay, *Michael Collins*, 169. Coogan also alleges that Markham passed a classified intelligence report on Sir Edward Carson prepared by a Special Branch officer named McBrien to Collins on the eve of peace negotiations.
22. Hopkinson, *Irish War of Independence*, 97.
23. Coogan, *Michael Collins*, 107.
24. Mackay, *Michael Collins*, 129.
25. Dwyer, *The Squad*, 40–45.
26. Ibid.
27. Ibid., 46.
28. Mackay, *Michael Collins*, 131–32; IRA officer Oscar Traynor, as quoted in Annie Ryan, *Comrades: Inside the War of Independence* (Dublin: Liberties, 2007), 255.
29. Peter Cottrell, ed., *The War for Ireland* (Oxford: Osprey, 2009), 188–90.
30. Gleeson to MacEoin, in *Survivors*, 262. Stapleton fought in the 1916 Easter Rising and was incarcerated at Frongach. Tipperary IRA veteran Dan Gleeson recalled that Stapleton was not a particularly good shot so he snuck up close behind Hunt before pulling the trigger.

31. Mackay, *Michael Collins*, 131–32; Coogan, *Michael Collins*, 44–45, 117. Collins hoped that Detective Smyth could be persuaded to stop the prosecution of Beaslai and when two strangers discreetly approached the G man one evening and politely requested that he drop the charges, Smyth replied, "I'm not letting young scuts tell me how to do my duty." The "young scuts" were Collins and Harry Boland. As for Detective Hoey, the IRB had a long-standing grudge against him for his role in helping the British identify the leaders of the 1916 Easter Rising. Hoey moved among the Volunteer prisoners, specifically fingering Sean MacDiarmada, chairman of the IRB Supreme Council. MacDiarmada, who had escaped the initial screening of prisoners, was about to board a transport to an English internment camp when the alert Hoey picked him out and handed him over to the British. The popular young IRB chief was subsequently tried by court-martial and executed by a British firing squad at Kilmainham Jail. Collins also had ex–British Army Captain Lee-Wilson executed for his cruel treatment of prisoners following the Rising. Lee-Wilson had ordered Thomas Clarke to strip naked in front of a crowd of onlookers, and when Clarke moved too slowly, Wilson ripped the clothes from Clarke's body, opening an old wound in the process. Witnessing this, Collins was enraged. By 1919, Lee-Wilson had left the army and was serving as an RIC constable in County Wexford where Collins sent the Squad expressly to settle accounts with him. Lee-Wilson's bullet-ridden body was dumped along a roadside.

32. Dwyer, *Big Fellow, Long Fellow: A Joint Biography of Collins & de Valera* (New York: St. Martin's Press, 1998), 99–100.

33. Coogan, *Michael Collins*, 116.

34. Neligan, *Spy in the Castle*, 156–57.

35. O'Connor, *Michael Collins and the Troubles*, 142.

36. Dwyer, *The Squad*, 80.

37. Neligan, *Spy in the Castle*, 61.

38. Dwyer, *Michael Collins*, 68.

39. Macardle, *Irish Republic*, 300.

40. John Ainsworth, *British Security Policy in Ireland, 1920–1921: A Desperate Attempt by the Crown to Maintain Anglo-Irish Unity by Force*, manuscript, Queensland University of Technology, Brisbane, 2000.

41. Mackay, *Michael Collins*, 99.

42. Charles Townsend, *The British Campaign in Ireland, 1919–1920* (London: Oxford University Press, 1975), 29.

43. Coogan, *Michael Collins*, 117.

44. Townsend, *British Campaign in Ireland*, 30.

45. Macardle, *Irish Repulic*, 316; Ainsworth, *British Security Policy*, 1.

46. Liam Deasy, *Towards Ireland Free* (Cork: Royal Carbery Books, 1973), 81.

47. Townsend, *British Campaign in Ireland*, 34–37.

48. Dwyer, *The Squad*, 74–75.

49. Dwyer, *Big Fellow, Long Fellow*, 101.

50. Dwyer, *The Squad*, 73. The IRA made no fewer than twenty attempts to assassinate Lord Lieutenant French who, as Viceroy, was the symbolic embodiment of the English colonial system. Despite some close calls, the Viceroy escaped each attack unscathed.

Chapter 7. Spies at the Window

1. Hopkinson, *Irish War of Independence*, 31.

2. Townsend, *British Campaign in Ireland*, 44, 217–20.

3. Hart, ed., *Army Record of the Rebellion*, 19.
4. Neligan, *Spy in the Castle*, 135. Neligan, Collins's police mole who later joined the secret service, reported that he had to come up with his own cover, further illustrating the amateurish nature of British intelligence operations in Ireland.
5. Ibid.; McMahon, *British Spies and Irish Rebels*, 32, 178; Major General T. O. Marden, ed., *A Short History of the 6th Division* (London: Hugh Rees, 1920), 76; Tilar J. Mazzeo, *The Secret of Chanel No.5: The Intimate History of the World's Most Famous Perfume* (New York: HarperCollins, 2010), 252n; and anonymous, *Roll of Honour, 1st and 7th Battalions of the Royal Irish Rifles*, http://royalirishrifles. webs.com/. Lieutenant Colonel Steven Searl Hill-Dillon, who established the MO4x unit in Ireland, had served for some unknown period with MI5 during or shortly after the First World War and undoubtedly recognized the value of maintaining a central registry of suspects and targets. Hill-Dillon entered war service with the Royal Irish Rifles in 1914 and distinguished himself as a junior officer, earning the Distinguished Service Order (DSO) in February 1915. Hill-Dillon was also mentioned in dispatches in 1914, 1915, and 1917. Promoted to major, he served as General Staff Officer 2 (Intelligence) for the Sixth Division from April to June 1918. He was brevetted to lieutenant colonel and apparently was assigned to MI5 after that. In 1923, Hill-Dillon was appointed chief of the DMI's southern Ireland section. He retired from the army in 1927, but in 1940 he was brought out of retirement to become intelligence advisor to the commander of the Ulster Military District. He subsequently held an intelligence post in General Eisenhower's Allied Force Headquarters during World War Two.
6. Hart, ed., *Army Record of the Rebellion*, 44.
7. HC Debate, 12 February 1920, vol. 125, cc197–98; Hart, ed., *Army Record of the Rebellion*, 21.
8. Hart, ed., *Army Record of the Rebellion*, 45.
9. Ibid, 20; Dwyer, *Michael Collins*, 79.
10. Mackay, *Michael Collins*, 142–43.
11. Ibid., 136–37.
12. Coogan, *Michael Collins*, 131.
13. Dwyer, *Michael Collins*, 75.
14. Ibid.; Mackay, *Michael Collins*, 136–38.
15. John Borgonovo, *Spies, Informers and the "Anti-Sinn Féin Society": The Intelligence War in Cork City, 1920–1921* (Dublin and Portland: Irish Academic Press, 2007), 76–83.
16. Borgonovo, *Spies, Informers*, 167–77; Peter Hart: *The IRA and Its Enemies: Violence and Community in Cork, 1916–1923* (Oxford: Clarendon Press, 1998), 99; Hart, *The IRA at War*, 79; Brian P. Murphy, OSB, and Niall Meehan, "Troubled History" (Millstreet, Ireland: The Aubane Historical Society, 2008), 12–15.
17. Neenan to MacEoin, in *Survivors*, 239.
18. Borgonovo, *Spies, Informers*, 179.
19. Tom Barry, *Guerilla Days in Ireland* (Dublin: Anvil, 1981), 105–14.
20. Borgonovo, *Spies, Informers*, 136–37.
21. Neligan, *Spy in the Castle*, 72–73; Mackay, *Michael Collins*, 146–47; Dwyer, *Big Fellow, Long Fellow*, 107. As is the case with some other principal figures of the Anglo-Irish War, Collins's biographers disagree about the spelling of this agent's name. Most accounts cite his name as Brian Fergus Mulloy, or Molloy. David Neligan wrote in the introduction to his memoir that he altered some of

the names of personalities mentioned in his narrative to protect their true identities. Neligan referred to this spy as "Bernard Hugh Mulloy" and stated that Mulloy reported to someone in the Castle. All other accounts state that he was run by army intelligence (MO4x) from Parkgate Street. Some of MO4x staff, including its confidential code clerk Lily Mernin, did work in the Castle, rather than at Parkgate. Neligan also states that Mulloy enclosed a will with his letter that was examined by British intelligence officers at the Castle and that it was through this that they identified Liam Tobin as Collins's senior deputy. Neligan further stated that Collins obtained the will from sources in the United States some time after Mulloy was executed.

22. Coogan, *Michael Collins*, 133.
23. Andrew, *Defence of the Realm*, 108–9. A dangle operation is an active measure by an intelligence service to penetrate an organization, group, or opposition service (the target) by baiting it with an agent or agents who ostensibly offer attractive services, access, or information to the target. The intelligence service is thus said to be "dangling" their bait in front of the target. It must take care in crafting the operational scenario for introducing the bait to the target in order to avoid the approach appearing too provocative. Dangle operations therefore tend to be long term in nature, usually requiring that the bait be exposed to the target indirectly and gradually. If the target is convinced that the agent is genuine and "takes the bait," the agent will succeed in penetrating the target organization, gaining invaluable access to the target's plans, intentions, information, and organization. In this famous case, John Jameson was the "bait" that was "dangled" by Special Branch to the IRA indirectly through Art O'Brien in London. Once Jameson succeeded in winning O'Brien's full confidence, O'Brien himself ensured entrée for Jameson to Collins and his inner circle. The assurances made to Collins by his own agent, the former RIC man McElligott, who had met Jameson a year earlier, were undoubtedly a key factor in Collins's decision to take the bait. Thus, Collins accepted their recommendation of Jameson at face value, without properly vetting Jameson's bona fides.
24. Dwyer, *Michael Collins*, 78; Mackay, *Michael Collins*, 138; Hart, *Mick*, 224–37.
25. Stafford, *Churchill & Secret Service*, 105; Andrew, *Defence of the Realm*, 96–97; Hart, *Mick*, 225–26; Julien Putkowski, "A2 and the Labour Movement," in Lobster, *Journal of Parapolitics*, no. 29 (1995): 2–8, and no. 30 (1996): 13–16.
26. Thomson, *The Scene Changes*, 426.
27. Ibid.
28. Hart, *Mick*, 228; Neligan, *Spy in the Castle*, 54–56; Dwyer, *Big Fellow, Long Fellow*, 97–98. Neligan, who changed some names to protect true identities, gives this agent's name as "J. J. McElligott," while Dwyer says "Thomas J. McElligott." Hart suggests that Collins first met Jameson in London following a visit to Manchester to meet with some recently released IRA operatives.
29. Coogan, *Michael Collins*, 128; Thomson, *The Scene Changes*, 426.
30. Thomson, *The Scene Changes*.
31. Coogan, *Michael Collins*, 128. For security reasons, Special Branch further encoded agent Jameson as "Number 8" in its operational reports.
32. Mackay, *Michael Collins*, 141–46.
33. Ibid.; Dwyer, *Michael Collins*, 79.
34. Neligan, *Spy in the Castle*, 180.
35. Ibid., 77. Bell apparently assembled a team of experts to sift through bank accounts in order to identify those held by or on behalf of Sinn Fein. The term

"Star Chamber" dates to the fifteenth century, when a royal tribunal was established at the court of Henry VII to guarantee that the most wealthy, powerful, and influential Britons could not be convicted of crimes by common court proceedings. Over the next two hundred years, the Star Chamber evolved into an Inquisition-like body that operated in secret, with no indictments, no right of appeal, no juries, and no witnesses until it inevitably came to symbolize the monarchy's abuse of power. It was abolished in 1641. Neligan's use of the terminology underscored that Bell's secret investigations were compartmented—and untouchable by other Crown agencies.

36. Ibid.
37. O'Halpin, *British Intelligence in Ireland*, 73–74; Macardle, *Irish Republic*, 332. In January 1920, Bell sent a memo to Lord French stating, "In the course of their moving about, my men have picked up a good deal of useful information that leads to raids."
38. Dwyer, *Big Fellow, Long Fellow*, 107–8.
39. Mackay, *Michael Collins*, 145–46.
40. Hopkinson, *Irish War of Independence*, 56.
41. Dwyer, *Michael Collins*, 81; Hart, *Mick*, 225.
42. Dwyer, *The Squad*, 82.
43. Hart, *Mick*, 243 and 225. British researcher Julien Putkowski also discovered the A2 files at Yale University in the early 1990s and subsequently published the most detailed account of Jack Byrnes's fascinating early career spying on British labor radicals. See footnote 25 of this chapter.
44. Paul Bew, *Ireland: The Politics of Enmity, 1789–2006* (Oxford: Oxford University Press, 2007), 400–2. Ackerman had made his reputation as a correspondent during the Great War working for United Press International. After newspaper jobs, including the *Ledger*, Ackerman became dean of the Columbia University School of Journalism.
45. Paul Bew, "Collins and Adams, LG and Blair," *Spectator*, May 31, 1997.
46. Maire Comerford to MacEoin, in *Survivors*, 42.

Chapter 8. Unification by Force

1. Macardle, *Irish Republic*, 330.
2. O'Malley, *Another Man's Wound*, 179–80; Breen, *My Fight for Irish Freedom*, 103; Dwyer, *Big Fellow, Long Fellow*, 122.
3. Dwyer, *Big Fellow, Long Fellow*, 122.
4. Hopkinson, *Irish War of Independence*, 50.
5. Mackay, *Michael Collins*, 161.
6. Anonymous, "The Auxiliary's Story," in James Gleeson, *Bloody Sunday* (London: Peter Davies, 1962), 59.
7. Dwyer, *Michael Collins*, 90; Neligan, *Spy in the Castle*, 87.
8. For details of the organization, role, and actions of the German Order Police in World War II, see Christopher Browning, *Ordinary Men: Reserve Police Battalion 101 and the Final Solution* (New York: HarperCollins, 1992); Richard Rhodes, *Masters of Death: The SS Einsatzgrupen and the Invention of the Holocaust* (New York: Alfred A. Knopf, 2002); and Daniel Jonah Goldhagen's more controversial study, *Hitler's Willing Executioners* (New York: Alfred A. Knopf, 1996).
9. *Report of the American Commission on Conditions in Ireland, Interim Report* (London, Hardin & Moore, 1921); Ainsworth, *British Security Policy In Ireland*, 3; Dwyer, *The Squad*, 195, 217, 226.

10. Hart, ed., *Army Record of the Rebellion*, 20.
11. Ibid., 21.
12. Townsend, *British Campaign in Ireland*, 78; Eunan O'Halpin, "Sir Warren Fisher and the Coalition, 1919–1922," in *Historical Journal* 24, no. 4 (December 1981): 907–27.
13. Hopkinson, *Irish War of Independence*, 120.
14. Frank Gallagher, *Four Glorious Years* (Dublin: Irish Press, 1953), 90.
15. Hopkinson, *Irish War of Independence*, 42–43; *The Times*, September 21, 1920.
16. "History of the 5th Division, 1920 to 1922," from "Record of the Rebellion in Ireland in 1920-21 and the Part Played by the Army in Dealing With It," in *Hearts and Mines*, ed. William Sheehan (Cork: Collins Press, 2009), 12, 63.
17. Hart, ed., *Army Record of the Rebellion*, 21; Caroline Woodcock, *Experiences of an Officer's Wife in Ireland*, (Edinburgh and London: William Blackwood, 1921), 11, 69; Gleeson, "Auxiliary's Story," in *Bloody Sunday*, 134; McMahon, *British Spies and Irish Rebels*, 33.
18. Townsend, *British Campaign in Ireland*, 91.
19. Bowden, "Ireland: The Impact of Terror," in *Revolt to Revolution*, ed. Elliott-Bateman et al., 258–59.
20. "Memoir of Captain R. D. Jeune," in *British Voices from the Irish War of Independence 1918–1921: The Words of British Servicemen Who Were There*, ed. William Sheehan (Cork: Collins Press, 2005), 83–85; Woodcock, *Experiences*, 84–85; Dwyer, *The Squad*, 182. During the combined assaults by the IRA on November 21, 1920, some of the doomed officers tried to pull their weapons to defend themselves. According to Squad member Vinny Byrne's account of the killing of MO4x case officer George Bennett, a fully loaded Colt .45 semiautomatic pistol and fifty rounds of ammunition were discovered under a pillow in his room.
21. Sheehan, ed., *British Voices*, 83–85; Gleeson, "Auxiliary's Story," in *Bloody Sunday*, 134.
22. Bew, "Collins and Adams, LG and Blair," *Spectator*, May 31, 1997, 409; Neligan, *Spy in the Castle*, 137. Bew bases his figures on a 1921 story published in an obscure newspaper, *The Northern Whig*. Thus, while the numbers are plausible, the accuracy of the source is open to question.
23. Hart ed., *Army Record of the Rebellion*, 38.
24. Ibid., 55.
25. Ibid., 22.
26. Borgonovo, *Spies, Informers*, 123; West, *MI5*, 173.
27. Andrew, *Defence of the Realm*, 321, 324.
28. Stafford, *Churchill & Secret Service*, 162.
29. Mackay, *Michael Collins*, 165–66; Barry, *Guerilla Days*, 27. Barry reported that he and his men also made an unsuccessful attempt on Percival's life in the town of Bandon, West Cork, in the fall of 1920 At the time, the West Cork Brigade mistakenly believed that Percival was commanding officer of the Essex Regiment, when in fact Percival was the regimental IO.
30. Stafford, *Churchill & Secret Service*, 162–63.
31. Hart, *The IRA at War*, 73–86; Murphey and Meehan, "Troubled History," 12–28. In their examination of Peter Hart's conclusions, methodology, and evidence regarding alleged IRA atrocities in Cork, Murphey and Meehan describe Hart's methodology as "journalism applied to history" and "entwining his tale of dark forces with an essentially contemporary tabloid tale of their motivation."
32. Borgonovo, *Spies, Informers*, 30.
33. Ibid., 120–24 and 158.

34. Barry, *Guerrilla Days in Ireland*, 106–7. In April 1921, GHQ issued a general order directing that sentences of execution be reviewed by the local brigade commander.

35. Ormonde Winter, *A Report on the Intelligence Branch of the Chief of Police, Dublin Castle, from May 1920 to July 1921*, PRO, WO/35/214, in *British Intelligence in Ireland 1920–1921: The Final Reports*, ed. Peter Hart (Cork: Cork University Press, 2002), 91, hereinafter cited as Winter, *Report on the Intelligence Branch*.

36. John Joe Sheehy to MacEoin in *Survivors*, 357.

37. Con Casey to MacEoin, ibid., 372–73.

38. "Memoir of Lieutenant Colonel Evelyn Lindsay Young," in *British Voices*, ed. Sheehan, 161–64.

39. Hart, *The IRA and its Enemies*, 307. Lieutenant Grazebrook, an IO working in the area of Kanturk, arrested IRA officer Sean Moylan in May 1921. Moylan was reportedly dumbfounded to learn during interrogation that Grazebrook "seemed to have the names of every member of the Active Service Unit and also had the names of some of the most prominent under-cover men." Grazebrook's diary indicates that three of his sources were members of the IRA and a fourth was the brother of an IRA captain.

40. Macardle, *Irish Republic*, 341.

41. Hopkinson, *Irish War of Independence*, 61–64; Townsend, *British Campaign in Ireland*, 80. The dynamic Anderson later served in Churchill's War Cabinet during the Second World War.

42. Coogan, *Michael Collins*, 143–44.

43. John Bourne, *A Biography of Ormonde de l'Épée Winter, Brigadier General, CB CMG DSO, CRA, Cheltenham College, RMA Woolwich, Royal Horse Artillery*. Monograph. The Centre for First World War Studies, University of Birmingham, June 2003.

44. Ibid.; Winter, *Winter's Tale*, 96–98. Winter wrote in his autobiography that he considered the removal of this prejudicial remark from his service record "the one and really great achievement of my career, for never in my thirty years of service have I heard of even one other successful appeal by a Junior Officer against an adverse confidential report by a General Officer." Winter was knighted in 1922 and retired from the army with the honorary rank of brigadier general in February 1924. In 1927, at the age of fifty-two, Winter married a cousin of the Royal Family and they lived a very comfortable cosmopolitan life in London. In 1938–1939, Winter was director of communications for the International Board for Non-Intervention in Spain; in 1940, at the age of sixty-five, he went to fight in Finland as part of the International Volunteer Force but contracted a life-threatening fever and had to be evacuated. His colorful and highly entertaining memoir is marred by a disingenuous and self-serving chapter covering his period in Dublin Castle, in which he defended his own performance and whitewashed the interrogations and murders of Dick McKee and Peadar Clancy, two key IRA leaders arrested the night before Bloody Sunday. He defended British use of force by highlighting several alleged IRA atrocities and condemned Republicans, including some members of the Catholic clergy, as terrorists. He died peaceably in London in February 1962 at age eighty-seven.

45. Bourne, *A Biography*.

46. Ibid., from a eulogy to Winter.

47. Ibid.

48. Neligan, *Spy in the Castle*, 101.

49. Winter, *Winter's Tale*, 333–34. As Winter noted, had his chauffer-driven car been traveling a split second faster, he would have suffered a fatal shot to the head.
50. Coogan, *Michael Collins*, 172; *Who's Who in English Literature*, 1951. Certainly one of the most interesting figures of the Anglo-Irish War, J. L. Hardy had led an adventurous life before he ever set foot in Ireland. Born in 1894, he passed through Sandhurst and served on the Western Front. Captured in 1914, Hardy made several unsuccessful escape attempts and twice was re-arrested just as he was about to cross into neutral Holland. He finally succeeded in early 1918 and was returned to his regiment at the front. There he sustained a number of wounds in combat, including the loss of a leg. Fitted with a prosthesis, he walked with a limp the rest of his days and earned the moniker "Hoppy Hardy." Neverthless, Hardy was awarded a Distinguished Service Order medal—and a second bar—for his wartime escapades. Details of Hardy's intelligence affiliation are fuzzy; he appears to have been seconded to MI5 shortly before the end of the war or immediately thereafter. Hardy appears to have shifted over to Special Branch for intelligence service in Ireland. But because of his close association with the Auxiliaries, and in particular with the Auxiliary IO "Tiny" King, it is plausible that he may have been discharged from the army in the middle of his Irish tour and transferred to the Auxiliaries as an IO. Following the Anglo-Irish War, Hardy became a rather famous novelist, writing a dozen or more thrillers focused on espionage and wartime prison breaks. Sir Arthur Conan Doyle, the creator of Sherlock Holmes, wrote the introduction for Hardy's novel *I Escape*, and at least two of Hardy's novels were later turned into films.
51. Neligan, *Spy in the Castle*, 74–75.
52. Hopkinson, *Irish War of Independence*, 79–83.
53. Dwyer, *Michael Collins*, 129.
54. M. R. D. Foot, "The Irish Experience," in *Revolt to Revolution*, ed. Elliott-Bateman et al., 181.
55. Dwyer, *The Squad*, 102–3.
56. Neligan, *Spy in the Castle*, 93.
57. Ibid., 92.
58. Ainsworth, *British Security Policy in Ireland*, 4–5; Bew, "Collins and Adams, LG and Blair," *Spectator*, May 31, 1997, 400.
59. Hopkinson, *Irish War of Independence*, 63–65.
60. Ainsworth, *British Security Policy in Ireland*, 5.

Chapter 9. Within the Gates

1. Winter, *Report on the Intelligence Branch*, 97; Andrew, *Defence of the Realm*, 73, 128; Cook, *M: MI5's First Spymaster,"* 77–82; Neligan, *Spy in the Castle*, 91, 135, 150, 153, 163. In addition to core collection responsibilities, Special Branch helped to fill the vacuum left by the decimated G Division in investigating political murders; its officers also carried out VIP protection duty, providing armed escort of senior military officers and Castle officials and their families both in Dublin and while on official visits to London. Executive protection had been a specialty of Scotland Yard dating back to the 1880s. While Special Branch obviously could not prevent every assassination attempt, the mere sight of these big burly detectives surrounding key army and Castle officials was enough to make Collins's gunmen think twice before proceeding with a holdup, kidnapping, or attack. They surely prevented some IRA assassination attempts,

including several attempts on Lord French. By mid-1920, gun-toting Special Branch detectives were seemingly ubiquitous throughout Dublin and at all of the cross-channel points of embarkation. Caroline Woodcock, wife of one of the regimental officers shot by mistake by the IRA on Bloody Sunday, provided a graphic description of security conditions in Dublin at this time. Not only had she come close to becoming a victim herself on Bloody Sunday, but after she was hastily evacuated to Britain, Special Branch subsequently requested her assistance in the murder investigation. This required her to return to Dublin and to be escorted to prisons under heavy guard by Special Branch detectives where she was asked to try to identify some of the IRA suspects in custody. See Woodcock, *Experiences*, 98–128.

2. Winter, *Report on the Intelligence Branch*, 84.
3. McMahon, *British Spies and Irish Rebels*, 38–39; Winter, *Winter's Tale*, 288–347. Cosmopolitan that he was, the irrepressible Winter appears to have been extremely fond of modern technical innovation; in his autobiography he wrote that he often secured the services of an airplane to get from Dublin to various points up-country.
4. Winter, *Report on the Intelligence Branch*, 78–79.
5. McMahon, *British Spies and Irish Rebels*, 38.
6. Neligan, *Spy in the Castle*, 73.
7. Ibid., 84, 147; Winter, *Report on the Intelligence Branch*, 79; Charles Silvestri, "An Irishman Is Specially Suited to be a Policeman: Sir Charles Tegart and Revolutionary Terrorism in Bengal, *History Ireland* 8, no. 4 (winter 2000).
8. Neligan, *Spy in the Castle*, 91; *The Times*, January 1, 1931, and August 24, 1924. The "Count Sevigne" that Neligan referred to in this passage was in fact Captain Victor Marcel Childs de Sarigny, who was entitled to the title of count by virtue of his blood lines and who preferred to use the more stylish "Count M. C. Barrois de Sarigny." This appears to be one of the names that Neligan deliberately changed in his memoir. Sarigny was not the head of the British Secret Service in Dublin as Neligan supposed, but rather a section leader or branch chief. He was married in 1922 to Ethel Russell, whose family owned property in Ireland, including the Russell Hotel near St. Stephen's Green, Dublin. After leaving D Branch, Sarigny managed the hotel for many years, and was a popular member of the fashionable British Empire Club. Inexplicably, Sarigny shot himself in the head on New Year's Eve, 1930, in his room at the Royal Palace Hotel in Kensington, London. He was the last of seven intelligence officers who served under Ormonde Winter to commit suicide. Five killed themselves while on active service in Winter's department. The sixth was Major Cecil Aylmer Cameron, the former Intelligence Corps officer who had taken over as deputy chief of Winter's London Bureau after the departure of Tegart and Denham in late 1920. In August 1924, Cameron shot himself in his quarters at Hillsborough Barracks, U.K. Letters found in Cameron's pocket indicate he was despondent over financial problems and his failure to secure an army attaché posting.
9. Neligan, *Spy in the Castle*, 91; Coogan, *Michael Collins*, 134, 57–58. Coogan insists that the name came from their past service in the Middle East, and had nothing to do with their frequent patronage of the Café Cairo.
10. Neligan, *Spy in the Castle*, 100.
11. Winter, *Report on the Intelligence Branch*, 68; Dwyer, *The Squad*, 164.
12. Neligan, *Spy in the Castle*, 139–40.
13. "The History of the 5th Division," from "A Record of the Rebellion in Ireland

1920–1922 and the Part Played by the Army in Dealing With It," Sir Hugh Jeud-wine Papers, in *Hearts and Mines*, ed. William Sheehan, 62, 116.

14. Bowden, "Ireland: The Impact of Terror," in *Revolt to Revolution*, Elliott-Bate-man et al., 259–60; Gleeson, *Bloody Sunday*, 119; Joe Ambrose, *Sean Treacy and the Tan War* (Cork: Mercier, 2007), 210. Bowden was among the first to assemble a detailed background on some of the key members of the Cairo Gang, but he mistakenly concluded that some of these victims were MI1c officers, or for-mer MI1c officers, based solely on their prior assignments in foreign countries, where Cumming's department supposedly had exclusive responsibility. While some of the Cairo Gang may have worked closely with MI1c stations abroad from mid-1919 onward, in Ireland they were employed by MO4x, the DMI's so-called Silent Section. A well-known account cited by Ambrose and others is that one of the slain officers, Wilde, was a secret service officer who had served in Spain during the First World War. This assertion is allegedly based on a statement by the then-manager of the Gresham Hotel. It is not implausible, as MI1c was quite active in Spain during the war. If correct, Wilde was almost certainly an MI1c officer, not a member of M04X, MI5, or Special Branch.

15. Coogan, *Michael Collins*, 132; Dwyer, *The Squad*, 127–28.

16. Bowden, "Ireland: The Impact of Terror," in *Revolt to Revolution*, Elliott-Bate-man et al. 252; *The Irish Bulletin*, September 20, 1920. In addition to the inter-cepted letter referring to "the little stunt," Collins's staff had also purloined some classified dispatches authored by Harper-Shove of "General Staff Intel-ligence (GS (I)) Dublin District" addressed to the chief commissioner of the Dublin Metropolitan Police. The IRA turned these over to the Dail Propaganda Department, which published them on September 20, 1920.

17. Coogan, *Michael Collins*, 132; Dwyer, *The Squad*, 163.

18. Neligan, *Spy in the Castle*, 100–1.

19. Dwyer, *The Squad*, 137–39.

20. Ibid.

21. Ibid.

22. Winter, *Report on the Intelligence Branch*, 79.

23. Dwyer, *Big Fellow, Long Fellow*, 127.

24. HC Debate, 19 October 1920, vol. 133, cc 768–69.

25. Breen, *My Fight for Irish Freedom* (Dublin: Anvil, 1981) 131–50, 26; Dwyer, *Big Fellow, Long Fellow*, 150.

26. Dwyer, *The Squad*, 150.

27. Coogan, *Michael Collins*, 151–52; Breen, *My Fight for Irish Freedom*, 153–54. Breen's account differs from that of later historians, although Breen was not himself an eyewitness to Treacy's death. In his memoirs Breen says that Treacy had come to meet Squad members at Peadar Clancy's shop in Talbot Street for the purpose of organizing a rescue party after the military had surrounded Mater Hospital looking for Breen.

28. Neligan, *Spy in the Castle*, 130–32; Coogan, *Michael Collins*, 152. Neligan does not mention killing his stalker in his memoirs. Coogan interviewed Neligan fifty years later and this incident appeared for the first time in Coogan's biog-raphy of Collins. Some contemporary students of the Anglo-Irish War question whether this incident ever happened. Neligan's reputation suffered greatly because of his role as a senior intelligence officer with the Free State Army's Dublin Guard during the Civil War. In that capacity Neligan was in Tralee, County Kerry, in March 1923 when Free State troops tortured and executed eight Republican prisoners as a reprisal by chaining them to a large land mine

and detonating it—an incident known thereafter as the Ballyseedy Massacre. Controversy has raged over Neligan's role in the episode, but there is no doubt he was present and conducted the interrogations of the victims. Neligan subsequently became Director of National Army Intelligence for the Free State and even later was appointed a Chief Superintendent of the Garda Síochána (national police). With the ascendancy of de Valera's Fianna Fáil Party after 1932, however, Neligan was dismissed from the Garda and handed a minor civil service posting outside of the security services. The IRA has reviled Neligan since the end of the civil war; thus some observers believe he may have invented the account of killing the British detective during his interview with Coogan in order to bolster his bona fides as an Irish Nationalist. While frustrating to students of the Anglo-Irish War, the uncertainty over the accuracy of his account may reveal something about how Neligan viewed his own long career as he neared the end of his life.

29. Coogan, *Michael Collins*, 154–55; Dwyer, *The Squad*, 155–65; Con Casey to MacEoin, in *Survivors*, 372.

30. A widely published photo alleging to depict members of the Cairo Gang posing together in a Dublin alley probably depicts a different group of British operatives. None of the men in the group photo closely resembles any of the DDSB officers assassinated on Bloody Sunday and whose pictures appeared in the December 4, 1920, pages of the *Illustrated London News*. This said, the photograph was reportedly found among the papers of Collins's close associate Piaras Beaslai, whose cousin, Lily Mernin, was the IRA mole working for MO4x's Lieutenant Colonel S. S. Hill-Dillon in the Castle code room, and that would seem to suggest that the subjects in the photo were military case officers. Each of the men in the photo is identified by a number, clearly indicating the image was analyzed for intelligence purposes. Although the precise identity of the men in this photograph remains a mystery, it is very possible they were either member's of Ormonde Winter's notorious Identification Branch—the so-called Igoe Gang—a group of Auxiliary officers in civilian clothes, or perhaps the band of freelance British operatives who David Neligan claimed were unofficially on the Castle payroll to track down Collins and other high-ranking IRA leaders.

31. Coogan, *Michael Collins*, 158.

32. Woodcock, *Experiences*, 80–81.

33. Dwyer, *The Squad*, 165, 168.

34. Bowden, "Ireland: The Impact of Terror," in *Revolt to Revolution*, ed. Elliott-Bateman et al., 258–59; Gleeson, *Bloody Sunday*, 101–42; Coogan, *Michael Collins*, 157–64.

35. Dwyer, *The Squad*, 168.

36. Woodcock, *Experiences*, 86.

37. Ibid.; Bowden, "Ireland: The Impact of Terror," in *Revolt to Revolution*, ed. Elliott-Bateman et al., 265. Bowden believed that Colonel Woodcock was also an intelligence officer, but provides no compelling argument for this, relying only on his belief that such a "swashbuckling" military hero as Woodcock fit the pattern of a secret service officer.

38. Jeune, in *British Voices*, ed. Sheehan, 88–89.

39. Dwyer, *The Squad*, 177–85.

40. Ibid.

41. Ibid.

42. *The Times*, November 22, 1920.

43. Gleeson, *Bloody Sunday*, 135; HC Debate, 22 November 1920, vol. 135, cc34–38; Ambrose, *Sean Treacy*, 176. Ambrose attributes Patrick Doyle's testimony about Wilde to a "private source." Readers are advised to treat the information with caution.
44. Bowden, "Ireland: The Impact of Terror," in *Revolt to Revolution*, Elliott-Bateman et al., 260–64; Breen, *My Fight for Irish Freedom*, 156; HC Debate, 18 November 1920, vol. 134, cc2066–68.
45. Dwyer, *The Squad*, 174.
46. Ibid., 192–93; Neligan, *Spy in the Castle*, 124–25.
47. Jeune, in *British Voices*, ed. Sheehan, 90; "Memoirs of Private J. D. Swindlehurst," in *British Voices*, ed. Sheehan, 19.
48. Jeune, ibid.; Dwyer, *The Squad*, 166; HC Debate, 24 November 1920, vol. 135, cc 487–601. Captain Jeune describes clandestine surveillance operations and his part in masterminding a surreptitious entry operation against Arthur Griffith's office. He also led raids, and it appears that Jeune and his MO4x colleagues wore civilian attire to conduct surveillance but sometimes switched into uniform to lead raids and interrogate prisoners. Regarding the carrying of firearms, during a subsequent inquiry into the events of November 21, the government revealed that the secret service officers had been prohibited from carrying arms of any kind on their assignment to Ireland, a fact that created an uproar in the House of Commons. If correct, the men of the MO4x clearly ignored that order, or more likely were exempted from it, given their acknowledged "executive" (lethal) responsibilities. Several attempted to pull Model 1911 Colt .45 semiautomatic pistols on their attackers on November 21. Moreover, when IRA teams searched the rooms of the slain officers for classified documents, they discovered some Model 1911s concealed under pillows and stuffed between mattresses. Carolyn Woodcock recounted that regimental officers were warned about having weapons at their residences, in the mistaken belief that, if they did not carry weapons, they would not be considered a threat and would be left alone by the IRA. Assuming most regimental officers complied with orders, the presence of such high-powered semiautomatic pistols—particularly non–British issue weapons—appears to be a telltale identifier that helps sort out which of the Bloody Sunday victims were intelligence officers, and which were not. None of this was apparently conveyed to members of the House of Commons. As a direct result of Bloody Sunday, the army changed its policy in February 1921, ordering all officers to carry weapons for self-defense when off duty; .32-caliber semiautomatics were issued because they could be better concealed than the standard army .45-caliber Webley service revolver.
49. Coogan, *Michael Collins*, 164.
50. Neligan, *Spy in the Castle*, 125.
51. Tim Carey and Marcus de Burca, "Bloody Sunday 1920: New Evidence," *History Ireland* 11, no. 2 (summer 2003): 1–5.
52. *The Times*, November 24, 1920.
53. Hart, ed., *Army Record of the Rebellion*, 27; Winter, *Report on the Intelligence Branch*, 67.
54. Barry, *Guerrilla Days*, 36–51; Hart, *The IRA and Its Enemies*, 21–38; Brian P. Murphy and Niall Meehan, "Troubled History," 20–28; *Affidavit of John Young*. The British usually referred to this action as the "Macroom ambush" because the Auxiliary company was based at Macroom Castle, a few miles distant from the actual battle site. Journalist Gleeson offers a dramatic account of the action

by an officer of the Auxiliary company who was not with the patrol but who investigated the scene hours after the fight.

Much controversy has surrounded the Kilmichael ambush over the years, because of inconsistent reports of various surviving IRA participants. Critics, led by Peter Hart, allege that Barry's various accounts of the ambush contain inconsistencies. In his memoirs, Barry stated that after most of the Auxiliaries had been killed, a few survivors threw up their hands to surrender. When some of Barry's men came forward to disarm them, the Auxiliaries allegedly drew their pistols, shot, and killed the IRA men, after which Barry reportedly gave the order to kill them. Peter Hart disputed the "false surrender" account, claiming that it never happened and that a bloodthirsty Barry simply ordered all of the Auxiliaries executed. This latter claim gained momentum after violence erupted in Ulster in the 1970s, shocking human rights activists and embarrassing Irish and Euro-Left pacifists. Judging Barry's actions by late-twentieth/early-twenty-first-century standards, these critics condemned Barry's actions at Kilmichael. Hart based his assertion on alleged "anonymous" interviews in the early 1990s with two surviving members of Barry's column, whom Hart would identify only by two letter initials. But critics of Hart have now successfully deciphered the initials to unmask the names of the IRA veterans of Kilmichael whom Hart cited as his sources. One of these was deceased by the time Hart claims to have interviewed him. As for the other veteran, he was in his mid-nineties when Hart claims to have interviewed him and in 2007 the man's son produced a sworn affidavit stating that he was the prime care giver of his father in his last years, was with his father daily, and that no one ever interviewed his father about the events at Kilmichael. For students of insurgency warfare, however, the question of a false surrender is a moot point. Small guerrilla units living off the countryside and facing daily—indeed hourly—threats from a numerically superior and vastly better armed force are not likely to have the capability to deal with prisoners, nor the inclination to spare their lives. As disturbing as this may seem to some critics, the battleground in West Cork in 1920 had much in common with later battlegrounds in Vietnam, Laos, Cambodia, El Salvador, Angola, Iraq, and Afghanistan. Like so many IRA officers, Barry did what he had to do to neutralize a dangerous enemy and protect his men from further exposure to danger. In war, and especially a guerilla war, this is certainly considered the measure of a wise and effective combat leader.

55. Barry, *Guerrilla Days*, 61.
56. Hopkinson, *Irish War of Independence*, 83.
57. Coogan, *Michael Collins*, 164–65.
58. Gleeson, *Bloody Sunday*, 94–95.
59. Ibid.
60. Hopkinson, *Irish War of Independence*, 148.
61. "Volunteer M" to MacEoin, in *Survivors*, 424–25.
62. Hopkinson, *Irish War of Independence*, 148.
63. Coogan, *Michael Collins*, 185–86; Dwyer, *Michael Collins*, 91–107.
64. Dwyer, *Michael Collins*, 91.
65. Ibid., 93.
66. Ibid., 107.
67. Ibid.
68. Coogan, *Michael Collins*, 166–67; Neligan, *Spy in the Castle*, 107. Neligan says the McGrane raid occurred on December 3. Coogan, who interviewed Neligan years later, apparently has the correct date.

Chapter 10. Endgame

1. Hopkinson, *Irish War of Independence*, 92.
2. W. W. Hicks, *Memorandum on British Secret Service Activities in This Country, November 2, 1920*, National Archives and Record Service (NARS) Doc. 9771-745-45; Richard James Popplewell, *Intelligence and Imperial Defence: British Intelligence and the Defence of the Indian Empire 1904–1924* (London: Frank Cass, 1995), 241; McMahon, *British Spies and Irish Rebels*, 42; Stafford, *Churchill & Secret Service*, 140; Andrew, *Her Majesty's Secret Service*, 214; Spence, *Trust No One*, 184–85.

Sidney Reilly lived in the United States from 1915 to 1918, where he either directly co-owned or was a major investor in an ordnance factory that manufactured artillery shells for the Russians, earning him a fortune. During this period Reilly was, inter alia, a cooperative contact of the British MI1c (SIS) station in New York, providing information elicited from his Russian contacts to Colonel Norman Thwaites, MI1c's acting Head of Station. The entry of the United States into the war in April 1917, followed by Russia's withdrawal from the conflict six months later, burst this lucrative bubble when the Russian market collapsed.

With the Bolshevik seizure of power in Russia, Reilly anticipated that the British Secret Service would need experienced men to target Lenin's regime. In 1917 Reilly sought Thwaites's advice and assistance in securing a military commission and an appointment at MI1c. Hoping to derail Reilly's ambition, Thwaites wrote a letter to Cumming describing Reilly in most derogatory terms. Thwaites characterized Reilly as having a "complexion swarthy, a long straight nose, piercing eyes, black hair brushed back from the forehead suggesting keen intelligence, a large mouth, figure slight, of medium height, always clothed immaculately." But Thwaites also forwarded an assessment from one of his American sources that described Reilly as "a shrewd businessman of undoubted ability but without patriotism or principles and therefore not recommended for any position which requires loyalty as he would not hesitate to further his own commercial interests." To underscore this, Thwaites pointed to Reilly's past espionage work on behalf of Japan and stated that the New York station had kept Reilly under "observation" since 1916. Thwaites concluded his letter saying, "We consider him untrustworthy and unsuitable to the work suggested."

Nevertheless, Reilly went to Toronto, obtained an officer's commission in the Royal Canadian Flying Corps, and was subsequently met in London by Cumming himself on March 15, 1918. Cumming ignored Thwaites's assessment, and Reilly was duly sworn in as an SIS staff officer. From there he engaged in various efforts to topple the Bolshevik government, to assassinate Lenin, and to penetrate the Comintern until he was finally withdrawn by MI1c for his own safety when he was tried in absentia and sentenced to death by the Soviets. MI1c could no longer risk using Reilly against the Russian target. By 1925 Reilly had left SIS and, acting on his own initiative, was lured back to Russia by a clever Soviet secret police dangle operation. He was incarcerated and eventually his prior death sentence was carried out.
3. Jeune, in *British Voices*, ed. Sheehan, 90; McMahon, *British Spies and Irish Rebels*, 38.
4. Hart, ed., *Army Record of the Rebellion*, 16, 29.
5. Jeune, in *British Voices*, ed. Sheehan, 90. Jeune relates that after his departure from DDSB, he later ran into Jeffries, who reported that the reorganization of the unit had been "very successfully accomplished."

6. Dwyer, *The Squad*, 224–25; McMahon, *British Spies and Irish Rebels*, 149; Andrew, *Defence of the Realm*, 59, 60, 63; Cook, *M: MI5's First Spymaster*, 259. A December 1919 seniority list of MI5 officers showed that while Haldane held the title of assistant director in MI5, he had the lowest seniority. The handwritten annotation next to Haldane's name reads "left."

7. Swindlehurst, in *British Voices*, ed. Sheehan, 19–20.

8. Townsend, *British Campaign in Ireland*, 161.

9. Dwyer, *The Squad*, 224–25; McMahon, *British Spies and Irish Rebels*, 44; Reuters, March 29, 1921; *Singapore Straits Times*, March 31, 1921.

10. Hart, ed., *Army Record of the Rebellion*, 31.

11. Ibid., 27.

12. Hopkinson, *Irish War of Independence*, 94–95.

13. Coogan, *Michael Collins*, 182–83.

14. Mackay, *Michael Collins*, 194.

15. Breen, *My Fight for Irish Freedom*, 183, 130–50; Sergeant Igoe later applied for a British pension in recognition of the dangerous undercover work he had carried out on behalf of the British during the war. By 1922, Colonel Ormonde Winter had taken on the duties of organizing pensions for British civil servants and he appealed on behalf of Igoe's claim. The pension committee gave
  considerable attention to Head Constable Igoe's case. Winter gave evidence on Igoe's behalf and emphasized the Head Constable's loyalty and devotion to duty and his quite exceptional danger, which may involve him in frequent removals from one part of the globe to another. The tribunal also saw Igoe himself; he created a favourable impression. One feature of hardship is that Igoe will never be able to return to a 43-acre farm in Ireland to which he had hoped to return when he left the RIC. Col. Winter considers See also Coogan, *Michael Collins*, 183£1,500 the least that Igoe deserves. He suggests annuity and lump sum.

16. Townshend, *British Campaign in Ireland*, 163–64.

17. Borgonovo, *Spies, Informers*, 135–36.

18. Ibid.

19. Ibid., 139.

20. Hopkinson, *Irish War of Independence*, 75; Barry, *Guerilla Days*. Barry's account of his service remains one of the best narratives of IRA small-unit operations in the Anglo-Irish War. IRA flying columns moved as much as thirty miles in a single day to set up ambushes and then withdraw to a distant district for rest and resupply or disbursement. Volunteers often moved for days in freezing weather, in wet boots and clothes and with little food or sleep, in order to launch a surprise attack and then retreat into the countryside to avoid being enveloped and wiped out by reinforcing British troops.

21. Kelleher to MacEoin, in *Survivors*, 220–23.

22. Dwyer, *Michael Collins*, 121–22.

23. Ibid.

24. Ibid.; Mackay, *Michael Collins*, 198–99; Hopkinson, *Irish War of Independence*, 103.

25. Dwyer, *The Squad*, 250.

26. Coogan, *Michael Collins*, 147; Neligan, *Spy in the Castle*, 129–30; Hart, *The IRA at War*, 156–57. Hart claimed that Fourvargue was a British double agent from the outset, "probably on the orders of Basil Thomson," but he does not explain why he believed this.

27. Dwyer, *Michael Collins*, 99.
28. Tomas' O'Maoileoin to MacEoin, in *Survivors*, 93–94.
29. Neligan, *Spy in the Castle*, 130–32; Dwyer, *The Squad*, 215.
30. Neligan, *Spy in the Castle*, 146; Dwyer, *Michael Collins*, 133, 136.
31. Dwyer, *Michael Collins*, 137.
32. Mackay, *Michael Collins*, 198.
33. Neligan, *Spy in the Castle*, 107–10.
34. Ibid.
35. Ibid.
36. Ibid., 135.
37. Ibid., 136–38. Many British intelligence officers and Special Branch detectives were Freemasons. It appears that this was a vetting standard for reliability because the British knew that Catholicism forbids the taking of secret oaths. If they assumed this would prevent predominantly Catholic IRA agents from penetrating the secret service, then they overlooked the fact that membership in the IRB required an equally secret oath.
38. Ian Keneally, *The Paper Wall* (Cork: Collins Press, 2008), 46–75. Keneally's brilliant volume is the first comprehensive study of the propaganda war.
39. Ibid., 19–42; Bowden, "The Impact of Terror," in *Revolt to Revolution*, ed. Elliott-Bateman et al., 245.
40. Neligan, *Spy in the Castle*, 138; O'Malley, *On Another Man's Wound*, 195–96.
41. Neligan, *Spy in the Castle*, 142–43.
42. Tim Pat Coogan, *The IRA* (New York: Palgrave, 2000), 26; Macardle, *Irish Republic*, 449.
43. Coogan, *Michael Collins*, 276, 451–55.
44. Sean MacBride to MacEoin, in *Survivors*, 117.
45. Coogan, *Michael Collins*, 387
46. Maher, *Harry Boland*, 241–44.
47. Meda Ryan, *The Day Michael Collins Was Shot* (Dublin: Poolbeg, 1991), 94–105.

Chapter 11. Conclusion

1. Neligan, *Spy in the Castle*, 155.
2. MacMahon, *British Spies and Irish Rebels*, 56–82.
3. For American intelligence professionals, the politicized 9-11 Commission Report comes to mind.
4. U.S. Interagency Counterinsurgency Initiative, *U.S. Government Counterinsurgency Guide* (Washington, DC: U.S. Department of State Bureau of Political-Military Affairs, 2009), 3, 14.
5. See for example, "The History of the 5th Division, 1920–1922," in *Hearts and Mines*, ed. Sheehan.
6. Sheehan, ed., *British Voices*, for example.
7. Sheehan, ed., *Hearts and Mines*, 63, 85.
8. Hart, ed., *Army Record of the Rebellion*, 45.
9. Sheehan, ed., *Hearts and Mines*, 138–39.
10. Andrew, *Defence of the Realm*, 119–20. Unfortunately, Americans are still searching for that stability. The U.S. intelligence community is suffering its fourth director of national intelligence (DNI) since 2004, when the position was created in a highly politicized atmosphere. It has been neither a successful nor happy arrangement. The DNI's ill-defined authorities and absence of any apparent meaningful purpose has resulted in a U.S. intelligence community that—already

weakened by years of politically motivated staff and budget cuts—is further encumbered by turf battles, confusion over lines of authority, and separate and competing lines of communication to policymakers. This is precisely the same set of problems that plagued Britain's intelligence community during Basil Thomson's tenure as director of Home Intelligence. Worse still, the DNI infrastructure has sent mixed signals to America's foreign liaison partners, wreaking havoc on a successful system of international cooperation painstakingly forged over six decades.

11. Hart, ed., *Army Record of the Rebellion*, introduction, 1.
12. Barry, *Guerrilla Days*, 207–8.
13. Winter, *Report on the Intelligence Branch*, 74–75.
14. Roy Jenkins, *Churchill: A Biography* (London: Macmillan, 2001), 366.

Appendix A. Sinn Fein's Suspicious Cousins

1. Uinseann MacEoin, "The London Associates of Michael Collins," in *Survivors*, 400–9.
2. Ibid.
3. Ibid.
4. Maire Comerford, to MacEoin, in *Survivors*, 35–55.
5. Stafford, *Churchill & Secret Service*, 102.

Appendix B. On His Majesty's Secret Service

1. Charles Silvestri, "An Irishman Is Specially Suited to Be a Policeman: Sir Charles Tegart and Revolutionary Terrorism in Bengal," *History Ireland* 8, no. 4 (winter 2000).
2. Ibid.
3. Ibid.
4. "Deportation in Cellular Jail," *History of India*, Indianetzone.com, March 31, 2009.
5. McMahon, *British Spies and Irish Rebels*, 38–39.
6. Silvestri, "An Irishman Is Specially Suited."
7. Ibid.
8. Ibid.
9. David Hacohen, *Time to Tell: an Israeli Life, 1898–1984* (New York: Cornwall Books, 1985), 103–112.
10. David Stafford, *Churchill & Secret Service*, 205; McMahon, *British Spies and Irish Rebels*, 315–18; *The Times*, April 8, 1946. Stafford writes that Tegart was employed by MI5 during his 1940 Irish mission, but McMahon makes a convincing argument that SIS was the lead agency on Ireland during the war and that Tegart was reporting directly to SIS's Vivian.
11. Peer M. Akbur, "Policing Singapore in the 19th & 20th Centuries," Singapore Police Force, 2002.
12. National Archives (U.K.), "The American Mission of G. C. Denham." KV–2/206–207; Nigel West, *MI5* (London: Triad/Panther, 1981), 364; *The Times*, October 13, 1956.

BIBLIOGRAPHY

Memoirs

Barry, Tom. *Guerilla Days in Ireland*. Originally published 1949. Rev. ed. by Anvil, 1981.

Breen, Dan. *My Fight for Irish Freedom*. Originally published 1926. Rev. ed. by Anvil, 1981.

de Montmorency, Hervey. *Sword and Stirrup: Memories of an Adventurous Life*. London: G. Bell, 1936.

Devoy, John. *Recollections of an Irish Rebel*. Shannon, Ireland: Irish University Press, 1969.

Figgis, Darrell. *Recollections of the Irish War*. New York: Doubleday, 1927.

French, Lord John. *The Despatches of Lord John French*, vol. 1. London: Chapman & Hall, 1917.

MacEoin, Uinseann, ed. *Survivors*. Dublin: Argenta, 1980. Interviews: Con Casey, Maire Comerford, Dan Gleeson, Tom Kelleher, Sean MacBride, Connie Neenan, Pax O Faolain, Tomas' O'Maoileoin, John Joe Sheehy, Volunteer "M."

Neligan, David. *The Spy in the Castle*. Originally published 1968 by HarperCollins. Reprinted 1999 in London by Prendeville.

O Cathasaigh (Cassidy), P. *The Story of the Irish Citizen Army*. Dublin: Maunsel, 1919.

O'Malley, Ernie. *On Another Man's Wound*. Originally published 1936. Reprinted 1999 by Roberts Rinehart.

Robertson, Sir William. *From Private to Field Marshal*. London: Constable, 1921.

Sheehan, William, ed. *British Voices from the Irish War of Independence 1918–1921: The Words of British Servicemen Who Were There*. Cork: Collins Press, 2005. Captain Robert D. Jeune, J. P. Swindlehurst

Thomson, Sir Basil. *The Scene Changes*. New York: Doubleday, 1937.

Winter, Ormonde. *Winter's Tale: An Autobiography*. London: Richards, 1955.

Woodcock, Caroline. *Experiences of an Officer's Wife in Ireland*. Edinburgh and London: William Blackwood, 1921.

British After-Action Reports

Imperial War Museum, General Hugh Jeudwine Papers, 72/82/2. "The Development and Organisation of Intelligence in Ireland," from "A Record of the Rebellion in Ireland in 1920–21 and the Part Played by the Army in Dealing With It." Reproduced in *British Intelligence in Ireland 1920–1921: The Final Reports*, edited

by Peter Hart. Irish Narratives series, vol. 2. Cork: Cork University Press, 2002.
———. "The History of the 5th Division 1920 to 1922," from "A Record of the Rebellion in Ireland in 1920–21 and the Part Played by the Army in Dealing With It." Reproduced in *Hearts and Mines: The British 5th Division, Ireland,* edited by William Sheehan. Cork: Collins Press, 2009.
Colonel Ormonde Winter, Deputy Police Commissioner. *A Report on the Intelligence Branch of the Chief of Police, Dublin Castle, from May 1920 to July 1921,* Public Record Office (PRO WO.35/214). Reproduced in *British Intelligence in Ireland 1920–1921: The Final Reports,* edited by Peter Hart. Irish Narratives series, vol. 2. Cork: Cork University Press, 2002.

Government Documents
National Archives (U.K.): *American Mission of G. C. Denham.* Doc. KV 2/206–7.
National Archives and Record Service (NARS): W. W. Hicks, *Memorandum on British Secret Service Activities in This Country, November 2, 1920.* Doc. 9771-745-45, declassification no. 740058, April 15, 1987.
U.S. Interagency Counterinsurgency Initiative. *U.S. Government Counterinsurgency Guide.* Washington, DC: U.S. Department of State Bureau of Political-Military Affairs, 2009.
Parliament Debates—House of Commons (HC):
    HC, 19 August 1919, vol. 119, cc2117–8.
    HC, 12 February 1920, vol. 125, cc196–97.
    HC, 23 March 1920, vol. 127, c238.
    HC, 19 October 1920, vol. 133, cc 768–69.
    HC, 18 November 1920, vol. 134, cc2066–68.
    HC, 22 November 1920, vol. 135, cc34–38.
    HC, 24 November 1920, vol. 135, cc 487–601 487.

Nongovernment Organization Report
The American Commission on Conditions in Ireland Interim Report. London: Hardin & Moore, 1921.

Reference Sources
Who's Who in English Literature, 1951.
Oxford Dictionary of National Biography

Monographs
Akbur, Peer M. *Policing Singapore in the 19th & 20th Centuries.* Singapore: Singapore Police Force, 2002.
Anonymous. *Roll of Honour of the 1st and 7th Battalions, The Royal Irish Rifles 1914–1918.* http://royalirishrifles.webs.com/.
Bourne, John. *A Biography of Ormonde de l'Épée Winter, Brigadier General, CB CMG DSO, CRA. Cheltenham College, RMA Woolwich, Royal Horse Artillery.* Centre for First World War Studies, University of Birmingham, no date. www.firstworldwar.bham.ac.uk/donkey/winter.htm.
Kostal, Captain Devlin, USAF. *"Can't We All Just Get Along?": British Military Intelligence-Law Enforcement Integration in the Irish War of Independence, 1919–1921.* Washington, DC: The Center for Strategic Intelligence Research, National Defense Intelligence College, June 2007.

Manuscripts
Ainsworth, John. "British Security Policy in Ireland: A Desperate Attempt by the Crown to Maintain Anglo-Irish Unity by Force." Unpublished manuscript. Queensland University of Technology, Brisbane, 2000.
Brosnan, Matthew. "The Tactical Development of the 56th (London) Division on the Western Front, 1916–1918." PhD diss., Center for First World War Studies, University of Birmingham, September 2005.

Journals
Bew, Paul. "Collins and Adams, LG and Blair." *Spectator,* May 31, 1997.
Carey, Tim, and Marcus de Burca. "Bloody Sunday 1920: New Evidence," *History Ireland* 11, no. 2 (summer 2003).
Curran, Joseph M. "The Decline and Fall of the IRB." *Eire-Ireland,* Earrach, 1975, 14–23.
Lane, Jack. "Peter Hart Digs a Bigger Hole" Indymedia Ireland, August 5, 2005.
Murphy, Brian P., OSB, and Niall Meehan. "Troubled History." Millstreet, Ireland: The Aubane Historical Society, 2008.
O'Halpin, Eunan. "Sir Warren Fisher and the Coalition, 1919–1922." In *Historical Journal* 24, no. 4 (December 1981): 907–27.
Putkowski, Julien. "A2 and the Labour Movement" Lobster: Journal of Parapolitics, nos. 28, 29, 30, 1995–1996.
Silvestri, Charles. "An Irishman Is Specially Suited to Be a Policeman: Sir Charles Tegart and Revolutionary Terrorism in Bengal," *History Ireland* 8, no. 4 (winter 2000).

Newspapers
Illustrated London News, December 4, 1920.
The Irish Bulletin, September 20, 1920.
Irish Examiner, December 1, 1999.
Irish Worker, October 24, 1914.
London Daily News. April 14, 1914.
An Phoblacht ("The Republic"), November 20, 1997; December 16, 1999.
Reuters, March 29, 1921.
Singapore Straits-Times, March 31, 1921.
The Times:
> September 21, 1920
> November 22, 1920
> November 24, 1920
> November 27, 1920
> August 21, 1924
> July 11, 1928
> January 1, 1931
> September 5, 1942
> April 8, 1946
> August 8, 1946
> October 16, 1954
> January 26, 1956
> October 13, 1956

Books
Abbott, Richard. *Police Casualties in Ireland, 1919–1923.* Cork: Mercier, 2000.
Aldrich, Richard. *Intelligence and the War against Japan.* Cambridge: Cambridge University Press, 2000.

Ambrose, Joe. *Dan Breen and the IRA*. Cork: Mercier, 2007.

———. *Sean Treacy and the Tan War*. Cork: Mercier, 2005.

Andrew, Christopher, *The Defence of the Realm*. London: Allen Lane, 2009.

———. *Her Majesty's Secret Service: The Making of the British Intelligence Community*. New York: Viking Penguin, 1986.

Andrew, Christopher, and David Dilks, eds. *The Missing Dimension*. Urbana and Chicago: University of Illinois Press, 1984.

Becket, J. C. *The Making of Modern Ireland*. London: Faber & Faber, 1966.

Bew, Paul. *Ireland: The Politics of Enmity, 1789–2006*. Oxford: Oxford University Press, 2007.

Borgonovo, John. *Florence and Josephine O'Donoghue's War of Independence*. Dublin and Portland, OR: Irish Academic Press, 2006.

———. *Spies, Informers and the "Anti-Sinn Féin Society": The Intelligence War in Cork City, 1920–1921*. Dublin and Portland, OR: Irish Academic Press, 2007.

Browning, Christopher. *Ordinary Men: Reserve Police Battalion 101 and the Final Solution*. New York: HarperCollins, 1992.

Clarkson, J. Dunsmore. *Labour and Nationalism in Ireland*. New York: Columbia University, 1925.

Coffey, Thomas M. *Agony at Easter*. London: George G. Harrap, 1970.

Coogan, Tim Pat. *The IRA*. New York: Palgrave, 2000.

———. *Michael Collins: The Man Who Made Ireland*. Boulder, CO: Roberts Rinehart, 1996.

Cook, Andrew. *M: MI5's First Spymaster*. Brimscombe Port, Stroud, Gloucestershire: Tempus, 2004.

Cottrell, Peter, ed. *The War for Ireland*. Oxford: Osprey, 2009.

Cullen, L. M. *An Economic History of Ireland Since 1660*. New York: Harper & Row, 1972.

Curtis, Edmund, and R. B. McDowell. *Irish Historical Documents 1172–1922*. London: Methuen, 1968.

Davies, Philip H. J. *MI6 and the Machinery of Spying*. London: Frank Cass, 2004.

Deasy, Liam. *Towards Ireland Free*. Cork: Royal Carbery Books, 1973.

Dwyer, T. Ryle. *Big Fellow, Long Fellow: A Joint Biography of Collins & de Valera*. New York: St. Martin's Press, 1998.

———. *Michael Collins: The Man Who Won the War*. Dublin: Mercier, 1990.

———. *The Squad and the Intelligence Operations of Michael Collins*. Cork: Mercier, 2005.

Edwards, Owen Dudley, and Fergus Pyle. *1916: The Easter Rising*. London: MacGibbon and Kee, 1968.

Edwards, Ruth Dudley. *Patrick Pearse: The Triumph of Failure*. New York: Taplinger, 1978.

Elliott-Bateman, Michael, John Ellis, and Tom Bowden, eds. *Revolt to Revolution: Studies in the 19th and 20th Century European Experience*. Manchester: Manchester University Press, 1974.

Ellis, P. Beresford. *A History of the Irish Working Class*. New York: George Brazziler, 1973.

Farry, Michael. *The Aftermath of Revolution: Sligo—1921–1923*. Dublin: University College Press, 2000; Trim: Irish Books and Media, 2005.

———. *Sligo, 1914–1921: A Chronicle of Conflict*. Trim: Irish Books and Media, 1993.

Fitzgibbon, Constantine. *The Life and Times of Eamon De Valera*. New York: Macmillan, 1971.

Foster, R. F. *The Oxford History of Ireland*. Oxford: Oxford University Press, 1989.

Fox, R. M. *Green Banners*. London: Seckler and Warburg, 1938.

Freeman, T. W. *Ireland*. London: Methuen, 1972.

Gallagher, Frank. *Four Glorious Years*. Dublin: Irish Press, 1953.

Gash, Norman, ed. *The Age of Peel*. London: Edward Arnold, 1968.

Gleeson, James. *Bloody Sunday*. London: Peter Davies, 1962.

Goldhagen, Daniel Jonah. *Hitler's Willing Executioners*. New York: Alfred A. Knopf, 1996.

Greaves, C. Desmond. *The Life and Times of James Connolly*. New York: International, 1971.

Hacohen, David. *Time to Tell: An Israeli Life, 1898–1984*. New York: Cornwall Books, 1985.

Hart, Peter. *The IRA and Its Enemies: Violence and Community in Cork, 1916–1923*. London: Oxford University Press, 1998.

———. *The IRA at War, 1916–1923*. London: Oxford University Press, 2003.

———. *Mick: The Real Michael Collins*. New York: Viking, 2006.

Havens, M. C., Carl Leiden, and Karl M. Schmit. *The Politics of Assassination*. Englewood Cliffs, NJ: Prentice Hall, 1970.

Hopkinson, Michael. *The Irish War of Independence*. Montreal & Kingston: McGill-Queen's University Press, 2002.

Inglis, Brian. *Roger Casement*. New York: Harcourt Brace, 1973.

Jenkins, Roy. *Churchill*. London: Macmillan, 2001.

Kenneally, Ian. *The Paper Wall*. Cork: Collins Press, 2008.

Larkin, Emmet. *James Larkin*. Cambridge, MA: M.I.T. Press, 1965.

Levenson, Samuel. *James Connolly*. London: Martin, Brian & O'Keefe, 1973.

Longford, Lord, and Thomas P. O'Neil. *Eamon De Valera*. Boston: Houghton Mifflin, 1971.

Lyons, F. S. L. *Ireland Since the Famine*. New York: Charles Scribner's Sons, 1971.

Macardle, Dorothy. *The Irish Republic*. First published 1937. Rev ed., New York: Wolfhound, 1999.

MacDonagh, Oliver. *Ireland*. Englewood Cliffs, NJ: Prentice-Hall, 1968.

Mackay, James. *Michael Collins: A Life*. Edinburgh and London: Mainstream, 1996.

Maher, Jim. *Harry Boland*. Dublin: Mercier, 1998.

Marden, Major-Gen. T. O., ed. *A Short History of the 6th Division*. London: Hugh Kees, 1920.

Martin, F. X., ed. *Leaders and Men of the Easter Rising: Dublin, 1916*. Ithaca, NY: Cornell University Press, 1967.

Martin, F. X., and F. J. Byrne. *The Scholar Revolutionary: Eoin Macneil*. New York: Barnes & Noble, 1973.

Marx, Karl, and Frederick Engels. *Ireland and the Irish Question*. Edited by R. Dixon. Moscow: Progress, 1971.

Mazzeo, Tila J. *The Secret of Chanel No.5: The Intimate History of the World's Most Famous Perfume*. New York: HarperCollins, 2010.

McMahon, Paul. *British Spies and Irish Rebels: British Intelligence and Ireland, 1916–1945*. Woodbridge, UK: Boydell Press, 2008.

O'Brien, Nora Connolly. *James Connolly: Portrait of a Rebel Father*. Dublin: Four Masters, 1975.

O Cathasaigh, P. (Sean O'Casey). *The Story of the Irish Citizen Army*. Dublin: Maunsel, 1919.

O'Connor, Frank. *The Big Fellow*. Originally published 1937. Rev. ed. by Clonmore, 1965.

————. *Guests of the Nation*. Chester Springs, PA: Dufour, 1999.

O'Connor, Ulick. *Michael Collins & the Troubles*. New York: W. W. Norton, 1996.

O'Halpin, Eunan. "British Intelligence in Ireland, 1914–1921." In *The Missing Dimension*, edited by Christopher Andrew and David Dilks. Urbana: University of Illinois Press, 1984, 55–70.

Page, Bruce, David Leitch, and Phillip Knightly. *The Philby Conspiracy*. Garden City, NY: Doubleday, 1968.

Pearse, Padraig H. "From a Hermitage." In *The Collected Works of Padraic H. Pearse: Political Writings and Speeches*. Dublin: Phoenix, 1929.

Popplewell, Richard James. *Intelligence and Imperial Defence: British Intelligence and the Defence of the Indian Empire, 1904–1924*. London: Frank Cass, 1995.

Rhodes, Richard. *Masters of Death: The SS Einsatzgrupen and the Invention of the Holocaust*. New York: Alfred A. Knopf, 2002.

Ryan, Annie. *Comrades: Inside the War of Independence*. Dublin: Liberties, 2007.

Ryan, Desmond. *Sean Treacy and the Third Tipperary Brigade*. London: Alliance, 1945.

————. *James Connolly*. Dublin: Talbot, 1924.

Ryan, Meda. *The Day Michael Collins Was Shot*. Dublin: Poolbeg, 1991.

Shelly, John R. *A Short History of the Third Tipperary Brigade*. Cashel, Ireland: John Shelly, 1996.

Spence, Richard B. *Trust No One*. Los Angeles: Feral House, 2003.

Stafford, David. *Churchill & Secret Service*. London: Abacus, 1997.

Stephens, James. *Arthur Griffith, Journalist and Statesman*. Dublin: Wilson, Hartnett, 1922.

Thomas, Gordon. *Secret Wars*. New York: St. Martin's Press, 2009.

Thomson, Sir Basil. *The Story of Scotland Yard*. Garden City, NY: Country Life Press, 1935.

Thompson, William Irwin. *The Imagination of an Insurrection*. New York: Harper Colophon, 1967.

Townsend, Charles. *The British Campaign in Ireland 1919–1920*. London: Oxford University Press, 1975.

West, Nigel. *MI5: British Security Service Operations 1909–1945*. London: Triad/Panther Edition, 1983.

Williams, T. Desmond. "The Irish Republican Brotherhood." In *Secret Societies in Ireland*. Dublin: Gill & Macmillan, 1973.

INDEX

ABOUT THE AUTHOR

J. B. E. Hittle received his MA in Modern European History from Louisi-
ana State University where his research focused on the polemics of Irish
Marxist James Connolly. He served as a U.S. intelligence officer for more
than thirty years.